Contemporary Studies on the North

Series editor: Chris Trott

Settlement, Subsistence, and Change Among the

Labrador Inuit

THE NUNATSIAVUMMIUT EXPERIENCE

EDITED BY DAVID C. NATCHER,
LAWRENCE FELT, AND ANDREA PROCTER

University of Manitoba Press

University of Manitoba Press
Winnipeg, Manitoba
Canada R3T 2M5
uofmpress.ca

16 15 14 13 12   1 2 3 4 5

Printed in Canada
Text printed on chlorine-free, 100% post-consumer recycled paper

Cover design: Frank Reimer
Cover image: Peter Whitridge
Interior design: Karen Armstrong Graphic Design

Library and Archives Canada Cataloguing in Publication

Settlement, subsistence and change among the Labrador
Inuit : the Nunatsiavummiut experience / edited by David
C. Natcher, Lawrence Felt and Andrea Procter.

(Contemporary studies on the north, 1928–1722 ; 2)
Includes bibliographical references and index.
ISBN 978-0-88755-731-6 (pbk.)
ISBN 978-0-88755-419-3 (PDF e-book)
ISBN 978-0-88755-425-4 (epub e-book)

1. Inuit—Newfoundland and Labrador—Labrador—Claims.
2. Inuit—Newfoundland and Labrador—Labrador—Ethnic identity.
3. Inuit—Newfoundland and Labrador—Labrador—Social life and
customs. 4. Inuit—Newfoundland and Labrador—Labrador—History.
I. Natcher, David C., 1967– II. Felt, Larry, 1943– III. Procter, Andrea H., 1974–
IV. Series: Contemporary studies on the north ; 2.

E99.E7S48 2012   971.8'200497124   C2011-908243-8

The University of Manitoba Press gratefully acknowledges the financial
support for its publication program provided by the Government of Canada
through the Canada Book Fund, the Canada Council for the Arts, the Manitoba
Department of Culture, Heritage, Tourism, the Manitoba Arts Council,
and the Manitoba Book Publishing Tax Credit.

FSC
www.fsc.org
MIX
Paper from
responsible sources
FSC® C016245

CONTENTS

ACKNOWLEDGEMENTS

This book, like the history of the Nunatsiavummiut, has been a long and unfolding process. First proposed in 2008, our intention was to compile a collection of original chapters that would trace the settlement and subsistence patterns of the Labrador Inuit since first arriving on the shores of Labrador, through nearly thirty years of land claims negotiation, and finally through the formation of the present Inuit regional government of Nunatsiavut. The chapters in this volume were to explore how during this time Inuit of Nunatsiavut adapted to a multitude of changes brought about by colonialism, resettlement, globalization, and environmental and climatic change. In setting out such ambitious objectives, we soon accepted that the complexity of Inuit history could not be captured in any single volume. As such this book has compiled only a small, albeit critical collection of papers that have all been informed by a wealth of scholarship that predates them, most notably through the work of Carol Brice-Bennett, Stephen Loring, Bill Fitzhugh, John Kennedy, Tony Williamson, Garth Taylor, and others. Without the foundational work of these scholars we would never have reached a point to even consider a compilation of this kind. Benefitting from the work of these and other scholars we are pleased with the story this volume tells, albeit incomplete.

The chapters in this book represent a multidisciplinary exposition of Inuit history, culture, and economy with contributors coming from the fields of anthropology, archaeology, sociology, biology, environmental studies, and geography. Together the chapters offer a unique and critical examination of Inuit social, economic, and political adaptation. Not only are Inuit settlement and subsistence patterns examined, but so too are the underlying values that have long informed Inuit social, economic, and political organization. Given that the Nunatsiavut Government is in the process of re-establishing control over their own cultural, economic, and political destiny through the settlement of comprehensive land claims and the implementation of self-government measures, we sincerely hope this volume will be of assistance to their efforts. We also hope that this book will enlighten those unfamiliar with Nunatsiavut and to appreciate the historical and political journey of the Labrador Inuit.

This volume benefitted from the generous support and collaboration of a number of organizations, including the Nunatsiavut Government, the Canadian Wildlife Service, the Social Sciences and Humanities Research Council, and the Social Economy Research Network of Northern Canada. We gratefully acknowledge their support during the research and subsequent development of this book. Many individuals deserve thanks for their work and devotion in bringing this book to publication as well. Special acknowledgement goes to the authors for their contributions and for their patience as this book was brought to print. We would also like to thank the University of Manitoba Press and particularly David Carr, Glenn Bergen, and Christopher Trott for their unwavering commitment. Three anonymous reviewers offered insightful and informed comments that led to substantive improvements to the final manuscript.

On a personal note we would like to thank a number of individuals who made this book possible. They include Tim McNeil, Doug Blake, John Lampe, Ian Winters, Darren Winters, Jimmie Goudie, Rebecca Willcott, and Tanya Schlossek of the Government of Nunatsiavut, and Keith Chaulk, Martha Macdonald, and Ron Sparkes of the Labrador Institute. We would be remiss not to acknowledge the significant contribution of Stanley Oliver. Stanley's commitment to improving the lives of all who call Labrador home is nothing short of inspiring—it has been a privilege knowing and working with you.

Finally, and most of all, we join the chapter contributors in thanking the people of Nunatsiavut for putting their trust in us to share a glimpse of their proud and unique history. We hope this book does that history justice.

David Natcher, Lawrence Felt, and Andrea Procter

Settlement, Subsistence, and Change Among the

Labrador Inuit

THE NUNATSIAVUMMIUT EXPERIENCE

INTRODUCTION

Andrea Procter, Lawrence Felt, and David C. Natcher

The signing of the Labrador Inuit Land Claims Agreement was an extraordinary event for Labrador and is arguably the most important event in recent history in the region for Inuit and non-Inuit alike. The agreement and the resulting creation of the Inuit government of Nunatsiavut represent the culmination of a long, complex negotiating process. The agreement's realization provides a powerful integrating foundation for understanding Inuit history as well as a perspective and context through which to explore and understand future challenges that await not only Inuit but other Labradorians as well. It is for this reason that we start this volume with a discussion of the land claims agreement and the creation of the Inuit self-government of Nunatsiavut.

The sense of anticipation and hope were evident on 22 January 2005 when Inuit from communities throughout northern and central Labrador gathered in Nain's school gymnasium to witness the signing of the Labrador Inuit Land Claims Agreement and to celebrate the long-awaited creation of their own regional government of Nunatsiavut. It had been almost thirty years since the first leaders of the Labrador Inuit Association filed a Statement of Claim on behalf of the Inuit and Kablunângajuit[1] of Labrador

---

1 *Kablunângajuit* is an Inuttitut word meaning "resembling a white person" and is used for the people of northern Labrador who formerly called themselves "settlers," most of whom are of mixed Inuit-white ancestry (see Brody 1977, 311).

to the lands and resources of the north coast. The president of the Labrador Inuit Association at the time, William Andersen III, described his optimism about the agreement: "The Labrador Inuit Land Claims Agreement will bring real and meaningful benefits to all of us—Labrador Inuit, Newfoundlanders and Labradorians and all Canadians. It provides for certainty and rights and creates clarity for the future. It will allow us to build on the partnerships we have begun to work toward sustainable development, economic growth and social justice" (INAC 2005b).

The negotiated consensus between the Labrador Inuit Association, the government of Canada, and the provincial government to create Nunatsiavut is remarkable in and of itself. In 1949, when Newfoundland joined the Canadian Confederation as its tenth province, the idea, let alone the reality, of a self-governing Inuit homeland in northern Labrador would have seemed unimaginable. During negotiations in 1948 on the Terms of Union for joining Canada, politicians from both Newfoundland and Ottawa discussed responsibility for Aboriginal peoples within the province, but in the end they removed all mention of them from the final agreement. The omission of the Inuit, Innu, Mi'kmaq, and Métis of Labrador and Newfoundland from the Terms of Union implied that they deserved no special status or recognition, unlike Aboriginal peoples in the rest of Canada, and that they should instead be considered as provincial citizens like everyone else in the province (Tanner et al. 1994). Even when the federal and, much later, the provincial government acknowledged their responsibilities towards the Aboriginal peoples of the province, the fight for the recognition of Aboriginal rights was painstakingly slow. While both the Labrador Inuit and the Innu initiated statements of claim over land and other resources at approximately the same time, in the mid 1970s, actual negotiations involved only the Labrador Inuit at that time as a result of a federal policy that restricted the number of Aboriginal groups the Canadian government would officially recognize and negotiate with. The Innu were not on that list. The tripartite nature of the land claim negotiations between the Labrador Inuit Association, the province, and the federal government created numerous stumbling blocks. In the ensuing twenty-eight years, the Inuit had to contend with reluctant governments, unclear jurisdictions, inflexible positions, and unrelenting mineral exploration and other developments on claimed lands (Haysom 1992; Andersen and Rowell 1993). In fact, it was only when the lucrative Voisey's Bay nickel mine development was proposed in the late 1990s that the three parties accelerated their negotiations (Alcantara 2007). The final version of the Labrador Inuit Land Claims Agreement was therefore hammered out in the shadow of the multi-billion-dollar mining project, but it solidified the rights of Labrador Inuit to govern their own homeland.

The Labrador Inuit Land Claims Agreement

The land claims agreement represents the final settlement concerning the extent of the Aboriginal rights for the Labrador Inuit, in terms of both governance and land ownership rights (INAC 2005a). The agreement established the Nunatsiavut government and the Labrador Inuit Settlement Area, a region consisting of 72,520 square kilometres of land and a three-kilometre coastal extension totalling 48,690 square kilometres (see Map 1). The region encompasses the five contemporary, predominantly Inuit communities of Rigolet, Makkovik, Postville, Hopedale, and Nain, as well as the Torngat Mountains National Park and portions of the proposed Mealy Mountains National Park Reserve. It excludes the Voisey's Bay area (which the provincial government took off the negotiating table once the huge value of the development was recognized), as well as a swath of land between Nain and Hopedale, which contains the Innu community of Natuashish and the former site of the Davis Inlet community, and where the Innu Nation has outstanding land claims.

The settlement area consists of two main categories of land: Labrador Inuit lands (15,800 square kilometres), which are owned by Inuit (although the subsurface resources are not), and the remaining settlement lands, which are owned by either the provincial or the federal government. The Nunatsiavut government has jurisdiction over Labrador Inuit lands and shares jurisdiction over the remaining settlement lands with either the provincial or federal government (within national parks and in the coastal zone). Nunatsiavut also signed overlap agreements with Nunavik Inuit in 2005 concerning regions in northern Labrador and offshore areas where the two groups had overlapping claims, and it will likely negotiate overlap agreements with the Innu Nation in the future.

While Nunavut and Nunavik are both northern public governments that represent a high percentage of Inuit residents, the Nunatsiavut government is currently the only ethnic Inuit government in Canada (Rodon and Grey 2009). Eligibility criteria for enrolment as an Inuit beneficiary of Nunatsiavut are identified in the land claim agreement. In terms of resource use, such beneficiaries have the right to fish and to harvest wildlife and plants, both for food and for social and ceremonial uses within Nunatsiavut. A number of co-management boards consisting of Inuit, provincial, and/or federal representatives make recommendations to governments on issues of resource management and land use planning. Companies must negotiate Inuit Impact and Benefit Agreements before any development occurs on Labrador Inuit lands and before any major development proceeds in the Labrador Inuit Settlement Area outside Labrador Inuit lands. The Nunatsiavut government is entitled to 25 percent of provincial revenues from any mining development on Labrador Inuit lands and 5 percent of provincial revenues (plus half of the first $2 million) from developments elsewhere in the settlement area. The Nunatsiavut government also receives 5 percent of provincial revenues from the Voisey's Bay nickel mine and has an Impact and Benefit Agreement in place for the project. The federal government will transfer $140 million to the Nunatsiavut government over fifteen years, as well as $156 million for implementation (INAC 2005a).

The structure of self-government is outlined in the Labrador Inuit Constitution. The Nunatsiavut Assembly is the regional body that represents all Inuit beneficiaries, while each of the five communities has its own elected Inuit Community Government, or ICG (the equivalent of municipal government). Nunatsiavut can also establish Inuit Community Corporations to provide a means for Inuit who live outside the settlement area to be involved in self-government. Currently, there are two Inuit Community Corporations: Sivunivut, serving beneficiaries in North West River and Sheshatshiu, and NunaKatiget, serving beneficiaries in Happy Valley–Goose Bay and Mud Lake. Under the land claims agreement, the Nunatsiavut Assembly has the ability to pass legislation on a number of issues, including education, health, Inuit culture and Inuktitut, environmental protection, child and family services, and income support. It may also establish a justice system concerning Inuit laws and may formally recognize Inuit customary law. Most self-government jurisdictions rest with the Nunatsiavut Assembly, but the ICGs can also pass by-laws (INAC 2005a).

The Nunatsiavut Assembly currently consists of eighteen elected representatives: one regionally elected president; ten members from the seven constituencies (one member each from Rigolet, Postville, Makkovik, and Hopedale, and two members each from Nain, Upper Lake Melville, and the Canadian constituency, which encompasses Labrador Inuit who do not live in the other constituencies); the AngajukKâk, or mayor, from each of the five ICGs; and the two Chairs of the Inuit Community Corporations in North West River and Happy Valley–Goose Bay (Nunatsiavut Government 2010). The administrative centre of Nunatsiavut is in Nain, and the assembly building is in the legislative capital, Hopedale. Each Nunatsiavut community contains some government agencies, although a number of offices are based in Happy Valley–Goose Bay.

Negotiated Boundaries and Land Claims Implications

The Labrador Inuit Land Claim Agreement is a negotiated treaty that defines Inuit Aboriginal rights in order to establish "certainty" (INAC 2005a, 2.11). In doing so, it delineates the settlement area, beneficiary enrolment criteria, and specifically Inuit governance and ownership rights. These boundaries—around land, around people, and around the right to self-govern—may appear to be natural or obvious. Yet, as with any negotiated agreement, the treaty is the result of both historical processes and negotiated compromises between the Labrador Inuit Association and the provincial and federal governments. From this premise, this book explores how the structures and requirements of the agreement reflect the complex history of Labrador, and how the agreement may work to influence both future governance and daily life in Nunatsiavut.

A fundamental aspect of the land claim agreement is the close connection between the geographical boundaries of Nunatsiavut and the criteria for beneficiary status. During land claims negotiations, the Labrador Inuit Association decided to create a regional government based on ethnicity in order to ensure that the new government would focus on supporting Inuit goals, as well as to provide a form of self-government for those Inuit living outside of Nunatsiavut (Rodon and Grey 2009). This decision was deemed necessary by Inuit negotiators, but the resulting focus on beneficiary status creates tensions among some Inuit. Some of the criteria used by the Nunatsiavut government to determine beneficiary eligibility relate to historical or current residency in the land claims area. Beneficiaries must either live in the settlement area or have a connection to it. As chapters in this book illustrate (Whitridge; Kaplan; Rankin et al.; Hanrahan; Evans; Procter and Chaulk), however, Inuit have had a long history of migrating and living throughout Labrador and of interacting with other cultural groups. Although Nunatsiavut is now called the Labrador Inuit homeland, all Inuit have not lived and do not live within its borders.

Chapter 1 (Kaplan) and Chapter 2 (Whitridge) of this volume describe paleo-Eskimo and Inuit migrations into and within the Labrador region since approximately the 1500s. Groups that settled in central and southern Labrador interacted and traded with Europeans, and they likely acted as trade middlemen for Inuit who lived farther north (Kaplan 1983; Kennedy 2009). In the late 1700s, intent on isolating Inuit to Labrador's north coast, Moravian missionaries were the first outsiders to make a concerted effort to define and foster ethnic and geographical distinctions between Inuit, Inuit of mixed ancestry (Kablunângajuit), and non-Inuit (Hiller 1971). With the support of the British and colonial governments, the Moravians began to establish mission stations on 100-acre land grants near Nain, Okak, and Hopedale, and, over the next century, at Hebron, Ramah, Zoar, Makkovik, and Killinek (Brice-Bennett 1977). However, as Lisa Rankin et al. (Chapter 3) demonstrate, despite the Moravian "containment policy" of encouraging

Inuit to live at their mission stations, Inuit continued to live on Labrador's south coast (and elsewhere), beyond the current boundaries of Nunatsiavut. Inuit on the north and south coasts today still maintain strong family and social connections, as well as connections with Inuit throughout many regions of Labrador and Nunavik (see Hanrahan in this volume).

Despite their inability to contain all Inuit within their mission stations, the Moravians eventually succeeded to some extent in creating an Inuit enclave in a portion of coastal Labrador in the early nineteenth century, as the Mission controlled both trade and migration into its communities (Brice-Bennett 1990). However, in the mid-1800s, with more families moving into the region, the missionaries agreed to accept Kablunângajuit and non-Inuit into community and religious life. The Mission attempted to keep the ethnic groups separate, but formal distinctions concerning Inuit identity were not a matter of administrative interest until after Confederation, when the federal and provincial governments began to take more of an interest in Labrador.

In 1953 the federal government finally acknowledged that it did have some fiduciary responsibility for Aboriginal peoples in the province, and it negotiated a cost-sharing agreement with the province to fund health services and community infrastructure (Hanrahan 2003; Tanner et al. 1994). This was the first time that Inuit had been recognized as a distinct population in Labrador, and the long history of intermarriage and lack of census data on ethnicity made it difficult for the provincial and the federal governments to determine who exactly was Inuit (especially as they failed to consult Inuit themselves) (Jenness 1965). The governments ultimately decided to designate communities (instead of individuals) as Inuit, and so the first cost-sharing agreements created funding for health services and infrastructure for Hebron, Nutak, Nain, Hopedale, Makkovik, and Postville (Tanner et al. 1994). This decision caused much controversy, however, because the many Inuit who did not live in these communities were prevented from accessing these services. As Peter Evans argues in Chapter 4, Labrador Inuit experienced increasingly more government involvement in their lives after 1949 through a welfare administration that weakened both the authority of the Moravian missionaries and the autonomy of Inuit themselves. A number of influences caused Inuit to move within both the Nunatsiavut region and Labrador in the 1950s and 1960s, moves that have resulted in long-term social, political, and economic consequences. The federal welfare state and mandatory schooling introduced after Confederation encouraged more families to live in the communities, as did the increased wage labour opportunities from U.S. military developments in Goose Bay, Hopedale, and Makkovik (Brice-Bennett 1986; Flanagan 1984; Zimmerly 1975; Richling

1978). The relocations of Nutak and Hebron in 1956 and 1959, respectively, as discussed in detail by Evans in Chapter 4, brought almost 500 Inuit from northern Labrador—"the historical stronghold of independent Inuit," as Evans calls it—to Nain, Hopedale, Makkovik, and North West River, and caused massive social hardships that are still felt today. The politics of identity in the area, first fostered by the Moravians and then accentuated by forced relocations and by government policy, have been explored by a number of researchers (Brantenberg 1977; Kennedy 1995; Richling 1978; Brice-Bennett 1986). Evans (Chapter 4) and Andrea Procter and Keith Chaulk (Chapter 10) contribute to this body of research as they examine how relocation, welfare administration, and industrialization caused extensive changes to the demographic and cultural landscape of Labrador in the mid-twentieth century. Inuit have since based their decisions on where to live within Labrador and beyond on various other criteria, such as education, employment, social networks, and wildfood production. The current configuration of Inuit settlement in Labrador is therefore the result of both historical and more recent social, political, and economic factors, and settlement continues to be a fluid process.

Despite the complexity of both historical and current population patterns and their influence on the politics of identity in the region, official recognition of Inuit status was often heavily based on geographical location. The federal-provincial funding agreements centred on designated Inuit communities. The health provider for much of Labrador in the mid-twentieth century, the International Grenfell Association, used a definition that stipulated that an Inuk would lose Inuit status "if relocated to wage-earning communities and independent means of employment" (Brantenberg 1977, 402). In similar fashion, the structure of land claims agreements requires that the settlement area be connected to beneficiary enrolment and Aboriginal rights. In simplified terms, one of the enrolment criteria in the agreement specifies that the beneficiary or the beneficiary's ancestors must have been permanent residents of Nunatsiavut before 1940, which is when the Goose Bay air base was built and when many people from the coast moved to Upper Lake Melville for work.

The need to demarcate the territorial boundaries of Nunatsiavut and to connect them with beneficiary status is driven by the legal and administrative requirements of the land claims process. The "certainty" that is so fundamental to the land claims process, like other administrative practices, dictates that these definitions be precise and final. Nonetheless, the fluidity of people's lived experiences has not and does not always match the rigid constraints of the agreement. As an example, the formal territorial boundaries of Nunatsiavut do not reflect current configurations of Inuit residence, as almost half of all Inuit beneficiaries live outside the land claims settlement area. In 2009 about 2,609 (or 37 percent) of the approximately 7,027 Inuit beneficiaries lived in one of the five communities within Nunatsiavut. Another 2,323 (or 33 percent) lived in the Upper Lake Melville area of Labrador in the communities of Happy Valley–Goose Bay, Mud Lake, and North West River. The remaining 2,095 Inuit beneficiaries (or 30 percent) lived elsewhere in Canada or beyond (Nunatsiavut Government 2009).

Many of the other characteristics of the agreement have similarly complex relationships with historical and current reality. As Procter explores in Chapter 8, one of the fundamental aspects of the historical development of official Inuit status is subsistence harvesting, despite the long-standing Inuit involvement in the global economy. Although every outside organization to impact Inuit society in Labrador since the 1700s has made some effort to either support or undermine Inuit subsistence practices, the connection between Inuit identity and wildlife harvesting has remained strong. At various points in time, and for various reasons, the Moravian Mission encouraged both subsistence and commercial wildlife harvesting. Traders such as the Hudson's Bay Company employed policies that hampered subsistence harvesting. The provincial government, at different times, both encouraged and impeded wildfood production (Brice-Bennett 1986). By the mid-twentieth century, as Evans also examines in Chapter 4, a belief among officials in the benefits of modernization resulted in pervasive policies for transforming Inuit into wage-earning citizens. Despite all efforts to discourage or disparage Inuit subsistence practices, however, governmental policy and Inuit themselves have both maintained that there is a fundamental connection between Inuit identity and subsistence. As Procter discusses in Chapter 8, official recognition of Inuit status has often involved some reference to non-commercial activities, and the increasing body of legal opinion about Aboriginal rights centres on subsistence practices. Labrador Inuit have also proven to be resilient to all attempts to challenge subsistence harvesting practices, as Maura Hanrahan (Chapter 5), Lawrence Felt et al. (Chapter 6), David Natcher et al. (Chapter 7), and Laura Fleming et al. (Chapter 9) discuss in detail. As these chapters relate, Inuit have continued to uphold the cultural importance of harvesting and sharing, and have continued to adapt these practices to the global economy and to environmental and social change, despite all the social upheaval caused by governmental attempts to control their lives over the past 250 years.

The land claim agreement further supports the continuity of harvesting activities and wildfood sharing by recognizing the Inuit right to harvest within the settlement area for their food, social, and ceremonial needs (INAC 2005a). But with the recognition of rights come also the responsibilities and incursions of governance. In granting these harvesting rights, the agreement requires that specific governance tools be used to control and monitor this harvesting. Felt et al. (Chapter 6) discuss the stipulations in the agreement that the Nunatsiavut government must control subsistence harvesting by using Inuit domestic harvest levels. These requirements in turn produce new research needs, and both Chapters 6 and 7 discuss the ways in which the Nunatsiavut government approaches Inuit governance through an integration of scientific and Inuit knowledge. Once almost invisible to government administration, subsistence harvesting is becoming increasingly scrutinized, but this time by an Inuit government. In similar fashion, the agreement requires that the Nunatsiavut government engage in a land use planning process. As Procter and Chaulk discuss in Chapter 10, the governance tools of land use planning can be seen as insidious methods of facilitating development and appropriating Inuit resources. However, as they argue, in the hands of Inuit the tools of land use planning can also offer "the opportunity to employ techniques of state control to pursue their own goals and to control their own social and economic development."

The decision by Labrador Inuit to engage in the land claims process in order to further their goals of self-governance has therefore had many different consequences. As the chapters of this book discuss, the complex history of Nunatsiavut has resulted in the current social and demographic diversity. The legal and administrative requirements of the agreement can generate tension between its definitive social and geographic boundaries and the complexity of multiple lived realities. The governance requirements of the agreement also often intensify governmental presence in people's lives and on their lands. Nonetheless, as Procter and Chaulk argue, many Inuit see the land claims process and the Nunatsiavut government that it has created as the Inuit's best chance to withstand the pressure by outside governments and powerful industrial interests to control their lives and appropriate their resources. By taking things into their own hands, Inuit will be better able to deal with the complexities and incongruities of governing Nunatsiavut.

The book concludes with a discussion of government and governance in Nunatsiavut within a broader political and analytical context, while at the same time drawing from the themes developed in other chapters. By widening the analytical focus, we can better understand "end of line" government decisions among a much wider array of players and reinforce the perspective that government decision making is the final step in a complex and increasingly inclusive process of interaction, lobbying, and negotiation. With this context in mind, three areas of challenge and opportunity facing the new government and its people seem particularly relevant: 1) maintenance of traditional institutions of government and governance; 2) the ethnic basis of membership; and 3) effective participation and relationships in wider levels of governance at regional, provincial, national, and pan-ethnic levels. Each contains both challenges and opportunities for the new government and its people. Past political and socio-economic experiences, as explored in the chapters of this book, bode well for the future of Nunatsiavut. Given the history of cultural continuity in the face of political, social, economic, and environmental change and intervention, Labrador Inuit will no doubt be able to adapt the new governance structures to their own purposes and to the way toward a bright future.

References

Alcantara, C. 2007. "Explaining Aboriginal Treaty Negotiation Outcomes in Canada: The Cases of the Inuit and Innu in Labrador." *Canadian Journal of Political Science* 40, 1: 185–207.

Andersen, Toby, and Judy Rowell. 1993. "Environmental Implications for the Labrador Inuit of Canada's and Newfoundland's Land Claims Policies." In *Common Ground: Northern People and the Environment*, edited by John Jacobs and William Montevecchi. St. John's: ISER Books.

Brantenberg, Terje. 1977. "Ethnic Values and Ethnic Recruitment in Nain." In *The White Arctic: Anthropological Essays on Tutelage and Ethnicity*, edited by R. Paine, 326–343. Newfoundland Social and Economic Papers No. 7. St. John's: ISER Books.

Brice-Bennett, Carol. 1977. "Land Use in the Nain and Hopedale Regions." In *Our Footprints Are Everywhere: Inuit Land Use and Occupancy in Labrador*, edited by Carol Brice-Bennett, 97–203. Nain: Labrador Inuit Association.

_____. 1986. *Renewable Resource Use and Wage Employment in the Economy of Northern Labrador*. St. John's: Royal Commission on Employment and Unemployment, Newfoundland and Labrador.

Brody, Hugh. 1977. "Permanence and Change among the Inuit and Settlers of Labrador." In *Our Footprints Are Everywhere: Inuit Land Use and Occupancy in Labrador*, edited by Carol Brice-Bennett, 311–347. Nain: Labrador Inuit Association.

Hanrahan, Maura. 2003. *The Lasting Breach: The Omission of Aboriginal People from the Terms of Union between Newfoundland and Canada and its Ongoing Impacts*. Report for the Royal Commission on Renewing and Strengthening our Place in Canada. Ottawa: Indian and Northern Affairs Canada.

Haysom, Veryan. 1992. "The Struggle for Recognition: Labrador Inuit Negotiations for Land Rights and Self-government." *Études/Inuit/Studies* 16, 1–2: 179–97.

Hiller, James. 1971. "Early Patrons of the Labrador Eskimos: The Moravian Mission in Labrador, 1764–1805." In *Patrons and Brokers in the East Arctic*, edited by R. Paine, 89–93. St. John's: ISER Books.

INAC (Indian and Northern Affairs Canada). 2005a. *Labrador Inuit Land Claims Agreement*. Ottawa: INAC.

———. 2005b. Labrador Inuit Land Claims Agreement Signed. http://www.ainc-inac.gc.ca/aiarch/mr/nr/j-a2005/2-02574-eng.asp (accessed 22 September 2011).

Jenness, D. 1965. *Eskimo Administration, Vol. III: Labrador*. Technical Paper No. 16. Calgary: Arctic Institute of North America.

Kaplan, Susan. 1983. "Economic and Social Change in Labrador Neo-Eskimo Culture." PhD diss., Bryn Mawr College.

Kennedy, John C. 1995. *People of the Bays and Headlands: Anthropological History and the Fate of Communities in the Unknown Labrador*. Toronto: University of Toronto Press.

Kennedy, J. 2009. "Two Worlds of Eighteenth-Century Labrador Inuit." In *Moravian Beginnings in Labrador: Papers from a Symposium Held in Makkovik and Hopedale,* edited by H. Rollman, 23–36. St. John's: Newfoundland and Labrador Studies.

Nunatsiavut Government. 2009. Beneficiary data, Membership Office. Nain: NG.

Nunatsiavut Government. 2010. Nunatsiavut Assembly Structure. http://www.nunatsiavut.com/index.php?option=com_content&view=article&id=93&Itemid=90&lang=en.

Richling, B. 1978. "Hard Times, Them Times: An Interpretative Ethnohistory of Inuit and Settlers in the Hopedale District of Northern Labrador." PhD diss., McGill University.

Rodon, Thierry, and Minnie Grey. 2009. "The Long and Winding Road to Self-government: The Nunavik and Nunatsiavut Experiences." In *Northern Exposure: Peoples, Powers and Prospects in Canada's North*, edited by Frances Abele, Thomas Courchene, Leslie Seidle, and France St-Hilaire, 317–43. Montreal: Institute for Research on Public Policy.

Tanner, Adrian, John C. Kennedy, Susan McCorquodale, and Gordon Inglis. 1994. "Aboriginal Peoples and Governance in Newfoundland and Labrador." St. John's: Royal Commission on Aboriginal Peoples.

Zimmerly, David William. 1975. *Cain's Land Revisited: Culture Change in Central Labrador, 1775–1972*. St. John's: ISER Books.

CHAPTER 1

Labrador Inuit Ingenuity and Resourcefulness: Adapting to a Complex Environmental, Social, and Spiritual Environment

Susan A. Kaplan

This chapter discusses how, over the course of 500 years, the Thule ancestors of today's Labrador Inuit effectively responded to the geography of the region, as well as to environmental and social changes that presented them with both challenges and opportunities. The chapter also explores ways in which Inuit might have dealt with spiritual dangers presented by Labrador's forested landscapes, which were unfamiliar to them and possibly harboured powerful beings.

The first part of this chapter reviews the major settlement pattern shifts undertaken by Labrador Inuit groups and provides an economic view of the flexibility Inuit exhibited from the time they first occupied coastal Labrador to the nineteenth century. The chapter then looks closely at the life of one eighteenth-century household, examining its use of the region's marine and terrestrial resources, including plants. The chapter concludes by discussing some of the spiritual concerns Inuit might have faced as they encountered forested land and how they might have dealt with those challenges. The chapter suggests that Inuit might have spiritually adapted to Labrador by deforesting tracks of land around their sod house settlements, thus domesticating the landscapes around their homes and moving a potentially dangerous environment away from their families.

Inuit Adaptations to Labrador, the Broad Picture

Moving into the Region

Thule people began settling northern Labrador around the end of the thirteenth century CE (Fitzhugh 1994, 253). Whether the newcomers travelled from Baffin Island via the Button Islands or from areas further west is not yet known (see Figure 1). Northern Labrador had been inhabited previously by Maritime Archaic and various Paleoeskimo groups, including, most recently, groups known archaeologically as the Late Dorset people. Archaeologists do not yet know whether Late Dorset groups were living in Labrador when Thule people arrived, for clear material evidence of contact remains archaeologically elusive (Fitzhugh 1994).

Labrador's Thule migrants arrived with sophisticated strategies, techniques, and technologies with which to hunt, gather, and process foods, as well as make the clothes, boats, shelters, implements, and weapons they needed. Very small pieces of ground and drilled fine-grained slates (fragments of harpoon endblades, and knife and ulu blades) found in early north coast sites, and the absence of fine-grained debitage (debris left after making an implement) suggest that Thule families brought their equipment with them to Labrador hoping to replace it once they knew where to find certain resources (Kaplan 1985, 50). In some northern sites the fine-grained slate tool fragments appear along with coarse-grained slate objects and debitage. The presence of coarse-grained slates that are local to the area suggests that relatively soon after settling in Labrador people found and began using local lithic resources.

If archaeologists can pinpoint the sources of these and other raw materials the newcomers used to make their slate tools, soapstone pots and lamps, sandstone whetstones (grinding and sharpening stones), and ground nephrite endblades and drill bits, they might be able to discuss where the groups migrated from and the speed with which the newcomers found and began to use local resources. There is the possibility that Thule people learned the locations of local lithic sources and figured out where productive living and hunting sites were situated by finding remains of previous occupants' quarrying activities, structures, and hunting and butchering sites.

Many of northern Labrador's general features—tundra-covered hills with bedrock outcrops, bold headlands and gently sloping beach passes, fast-running rivers cutting through complex mountain valleys, deep fjords and bays, and near-shore and offshore islands—would have been familiar to the newcomers, though they would have had to learn the particular geography

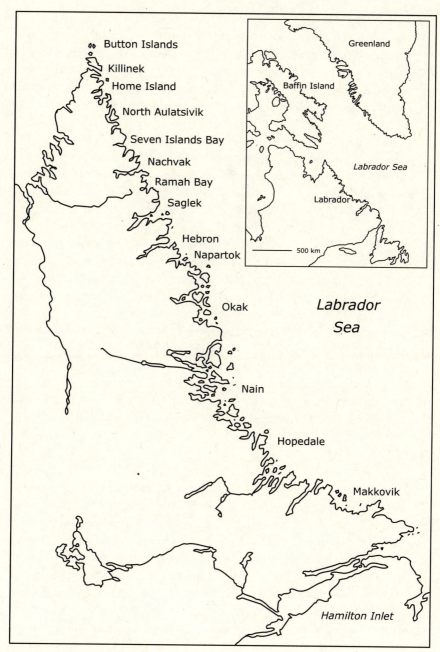

Figure 1. *Map of Labrador.*

of the region. They would also have known about the ice foot, the *sina* (ice edge where fast ice and open water meet), rattles (areas with swift currents that make a rattling noise and that remain open much of the year), polynyas (large areas of perennially open water formed by swift currents and wind action), and pack ice. However, the boreal forests growing as far north as Napaktok Bay would have presented Thule people with a new and unfamiliar environment.

The Inuit would have had much to learn about Labrador, including what animals were attracted to specific sections of the coast, because game is not uniformly distributed throughout the peninsula. Also, they had to observe the seasonal movements of their prey. For instance, bearded seals (*Erignathus barbatus*), the largest of Labrador's seals, spend the winter months along the floe-edge and in pack ice, and enter fjords and bays in the spring to feed on cod. They are generally unavailable to Labrador hunters in the summer, when the seals swim to cool waters north of Labrador (Boles 1980, 56, 66; Schwartz 1977, map 87). Harp seals (*Phoca groenlandica*) are around Labrador twice a year. They swim up the coast in late April and early May en route to Baffin Bay and the Davis Strait region, where they spend the summer. They return to Labrador in the fall, entering the region's bays and fjords in pursuit of cod and capelin (Banfield 1974; Boles 1980; Pinhorn 1976). In contrast to the gregarious migratory harp seal, the solitary ringed seal (*Phoca hispida*) remains in Labrador waters year round. It builds birthing lairs or dens in the fast ice. In the winter and spring, mature animals tend to maintain breathing holes in the fast ice, while the immature animals frequent polynyas and the ice edge (Boles 1980, 29; McLaren 1958, 60).

Settling In

The Thule people built small, four-metre by six-metre, oval-to-rectangular (or bi-lobed) semi-subterranean sod houses, with long entrance tunnels equipped with cold traps. Initially, they chose to construct these on far outer islands and outer sections of fjords and bays. These locations placed the sod-house settlements close to the *sina* or near rattles and polynyas , all places where hunting marine mammals was very productive in the winter and spring. For instance, they built sod houses along the southern shore of McLellan Strait, a constricted waterway between the tip of Labrador and Killinek Island and the location of a major polynya. They also built sod houses on the north shore of Nachvak Fjord, where it joins Tallek Arm, an area where a small polynya appears most years. Sod house clusters from this early period have been located on outer islands, such as Staffe Island in northern Labrador (Kaplan 1983; Fitzhugh 1994), Green Island and Okak Island in the Okak

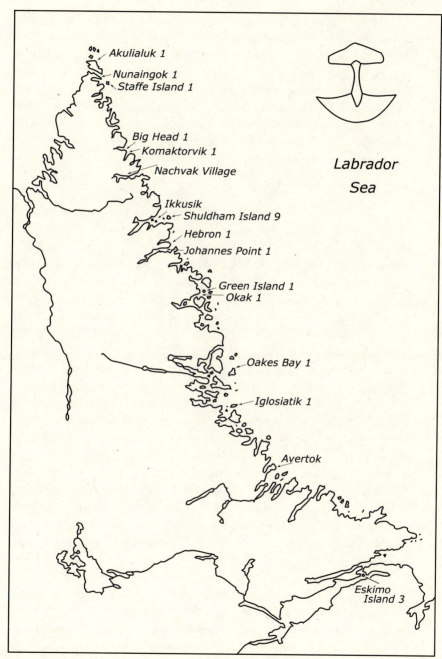

Figure 2. *Thule sod house sites along the northern and central coast of Labrador.*

region (Cox 1977; Kaplan 1983 and 2009; Kaplan and Woollett 2000; Woollett 2003), and Iglosiatik Island in the outer portion of Voisey's Bay (Kaplan 1983). Early period sod house sites have been found in the Hebron (Kaplan 1983) and Hopedale (Bird 1945) areas as well (Figure 2). People hunted bowhead whales, walrus, seals, polar bears, and birds from these locations. The Inuit probably felt quite comfortable in these places; the tundra-covered landscapes and the open seascapes and icescapes resembled more northerly regions from which they had migrated, and they would have been familiar with the game available to them in these exposed coastal locations.

New, Exotic, and Useful Things

Inuit continued their exploration of the coast throughout the 1500s and 1600s, venturing into southern Labrador—as is evident from sod house sites on Eskimo Island in Hamilton Inlet (Jordan 1978; Jordan and Kaplan 1980) and in Snack Cove in the Sandwich Bay region (Brewster 2008), as well as from structures further south (see Rankin et al. in this volume as well as Stopp 2002 for an extended discussion of southern Labrador archaeological and ethnohistorical evidence). Some of these forays were probably staged from Avertok, the major whaling settlement in the Hopedale area. In the process of establishing themselves along the coast, the Inuit encountered another ethnic group, known archaeologically as the Point Revenge Indians (Fitzhugh 1978; Loring 1992). How these two groups reacted when encountering one another is not known. The Point Revenge presence clearly did not dissuade the Inuit, however. They appear to have been drawn south by hunting opportunities (Trudel 1980) and by growing knowledge of the existence of exotic objects brought to the New World by Basque whalers, who began to frequent southern Labrador around the time the Inuit were moving down the coast (Barkham 1977, 1978, 1980; Kaplan 1985; Logan and Tuck 1990).

We do not know when Inuit and Basque first met. Initially, the Inuit may have happened upon discarded or stored Basque materials (metals, hardwoods, roofing tiles, glass and ceramic sherds, etc.) before coming face to face with the strangers. As is evident in historic records (Barkham 1980) and on Eskimo Island, where Basque materials were recovered from inside a sod house (Kaplan 1983), the Inuit realized how useful these new materials could be and quickly made use of them. Inuit adopted Western-made metal fishhooks and lead sinkers, leaving them unmodified, while reworking other materials. For instance, they cold hammered large spikes into harpoon heads, fashioned fragments of roofing tiles into whetstones, and cut and sharpened thin pieces of iron that they made into end blades, knife blades, and scrapers. Sherds of glass and ceramics, clothing fasteners, coins, cuff links, beads, and other such objects were collected as curiosities and would eventually become prestige items to be prominently displayed on clothing or incorporated into jewellery. Inuit all along the Labrador coast soon desired these exotic materials, particularly the iron, which quickly replaced slate.

Within 200 years of their arrival in Labrador, the Thule people had explored the coast and figured out where best to live, how to make a living, and where to find the raw materials they needed. Along the way they encountered at least three different ethnic groups on land: the Late Dorset, Point Revenge, and Basque. Dutch traders were plying Labrador waters as well, and while they have not been identified archaeologically in Labrador, they would have added to the number of exotic goods entering Inuit exchange systems (Kaplan 1985, 55). The nature of the relationships between Inuit and these groups remains unclear. It is evident, however, that Inuit came to dominate most of coastal Labrador and quickly and creatively incorporated Western goods into their toolkits.

New Approaches to the Land and Resources

The successful settlement of Labrador resulted in a growth in the size of the resident Inuit population, and in all likelihood certain families preferred and became associated with specific sections of the coast. Some time in the late 1600s or early 1700s, northern and central Labrador Inuit shifted the locations of their sod house settlements from far outer islands to more protected and centrally located inner islands and mainland locations, places such as Ikkusik Island in Saglek Fjord, Nuasornak Island in Okak, Nukasusutok Island and Dog Island in the Nain region, and Uivak Point on the mainland in Okak. Resource-rich areas such as McLellan Strait, Hebron, Okak, and Hopedale continued to be occupied more intensively while the landscape filled up, with sections of the coast such as Nain and Makkovik becoming home to eighteenth-century groups (Kaplan 1985; Loring and Rosenmeier 2005; Taylor and Taylor 1977) (Figure 3). A variety of factors contributed to this settlement shift, which also involved changes in house form and an increase in the size of households and communities.

Possible triggers for changes in settlement location might have been access to food supplies and a population increase. Outer islands would have been wonderful places to live in the winter and spring under favourable circumstances, but if animals were scarce or stormy weather destroyed the fast ice, preventing people from hunting and travelling, families could have been trapped on those outer islands. If they had not stored adequate supplies of food and blubber (used as fuel for cooking and lighting), hardship would have resulted. If populations were growing, it would have become increasingly difficult to store enough reserve food.

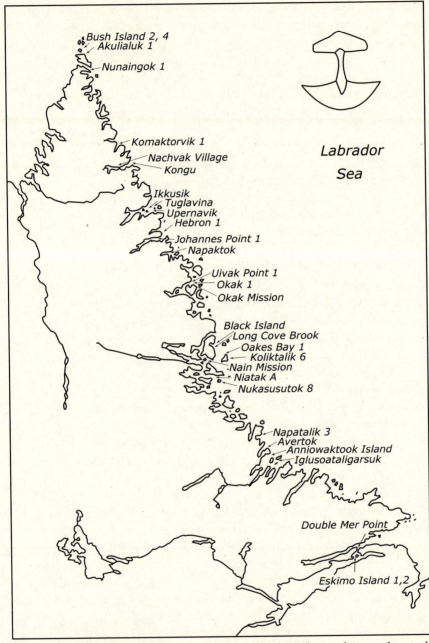

Figure 3. *Eighteenth-century Inuit sod house sites along the northern and central coast of Labrador.*

In addition, first the Basque, then the Dutch, and finally a variety of other groups carried out intensive commercial whaling, such that the North Atlantic was depleted of large numbers of whales (Romero and Kannada 2006). Inuit probably noted a drop in availability of these large marine mammals and intensified their hunting of seals. By shifting their winter houses from extreme locations to more central places, hunters had a broader range of hunting options. They could travel to the ice edge to hunt bearded seals and young ringed seals, exploit basking ringed seals and—later in the spring—their pups in inner waterways, and reach the mainland to go caribou hunting or ice fishing at interior lakes. They could also more easily visit one another from these central places, using protected routes when necessary. The ability of communities to reach one another created a social safety net essential when a household or an entire community experienced food short-ages. Thus it would have been possible to support larger numbers of people in these central places than on outer islands.

The sod house sizes changed as well. The earliest houses were built with one raised sleeping and sitting platform, usually fashioned out of sands and edged in stone. A variety of household activities would have taken place on this platform (see Briggs 1970 for an ethnographic description of household activities that took place around sleeping and sitting platforms). A stand for a soapstone lamp, a kitchen area near the house entrance, and storage com-partments completed the house (Figure 4). Each house containing a single platform was probably home to between four and eight related people. Early sites usually contain a handful of sod house remains, so an outer island settle-ment might have supported twenty to thirty people.

By the mid 1700s the Labrador Inuit were building largely rectangular semi-subterranean sod houses, referred to in the literature as "communal houses," ranging in size from 7 metres by 6 metres to 16 metres by 8 metres. The sod houses were still equipped with entrance passages and cold traps and, like earlier houses, exhibited tightly paved stone slab floors. Typically the houses were furnished with two or three sleeping platforms and multiple lamp stands (Figure 4). The Moravian missionaries travelling through the re-gion in the eighteenth century reported that each house was occupied by an average of twenty people, though some were home to up to thirty-five people (Taylor 1974), and a number of sod houses in a community were occupied at the same time. The Moravians observed that a household typically consisted of a father, his married sons, and their wives and children. A number of men had two and sometimes even three wives. People in a house were involved in cooperative hunting and trading ventures, with the father being the key figure in the house. This concentration of people probably provided needed

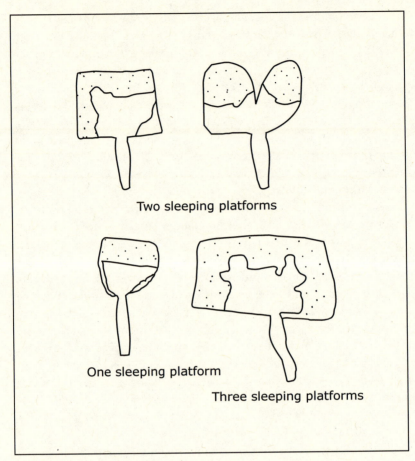

Figure 4. *Sod house forms.*

labour for whale hunting, which continued even though fewer whales were being caught than previously, and for long-distance trading enterprises (see Kaplan 1983; Kaplan and Woollett 2000; Taylor 1974 and 1988).

Stresses and New Opportunities

During the period of communal or multi-family-house living, a growing number of French and British traders and cod fishermen, attracted by the region's natural resources, visited Labrador's southern shore. Inuit continued to make journeys to southern Labrador, and indeed a long-distance trade developed in which baleen, furs, and feathers were traded south by Inuit in exchange for metals (on which Inuit were now totally dependent), fire-arms (highly desired by hunters), hardwoods, and items such as glass beads (symbols of prestige). Some face-to-face interactions were straightforward trading ventures, while others resulted in altercations between Inuit and Westerners as Inuit grew bolder in their pursuit of goods (Kaplan 1985, 64). The result was violence that depressed the Western fishery. In addition, Inuit men, in particular, were losing their lives in boating accidents on these long-distance voyages, in altercations, and probably as a result of communicable diseases introduced by the Westerners. A shortage of men might have been one reason men on the north and central coast had multiple wives. Aside from the economic benefits mentioned above, polygamy could have been a means of caring for relatives left without a hunter in the house.

More Newcomers

Members of the Unitas Fratrum first visited Labrador in 1752 and established a mission station in the Nain region in 1771. Referred to as Moravians, they had already worked amongst Inuit in Greenland, and they arrived in Labrador able to converse in Inuktitut. The Moravians were the first Westerners to take up residence among Inuit of the central coast. They established additional mission stations in Okak and Hopedale in the late 1700s as they sought to bring Christian beliefs to the population. They incorporated trading stores into their mission stations, hoping these would both attract Inuit to the mission and curtail the southern voyages (Whiteley 1964). Initially this strategy did not work because the missionaries refused to provide firearms to Inuit, and people thus continued their forays south. Over time, however, Inuit traded with the Moravians, worked for them, and came to rely on them as another safety net in times of food shortages (see Evans in this volume).

The Hudson's Bay Company (HBC), a major British-based trading empire, established a presence in Labrador in the 1830s and tried to muscle out other traders already established in the Hamilton Inlet area. In 1852, when Donald Smith (later Lord Strathcona) took charge of the Labrador HBC posts, he turned his gaze to the north Labrador coast and began to compete openly with the Moravians, whose trading enterprises had continued to expand. Smith aggressively established posts along the northern coast one decade later (Kaplan 1983, 180–83). The HBC encouraged Inuit to trap fox, exchanging the fox furs for ammunition, metal traps, and dry goods. The Moravians responded to the HBC advance by building more mission stations, and the two organizations leapfrogged their way up the north coast (Figure 5). Each tried to demand Inuit loyalty to their organization, to the exclusion of the other, through a process of inducements and threats (Brice-Bennett 1981; Kaplan 1983).

By the late 1800s Inuit had changed their settlement locations and house forms for a second time. Many nuclear families built small sod and above-

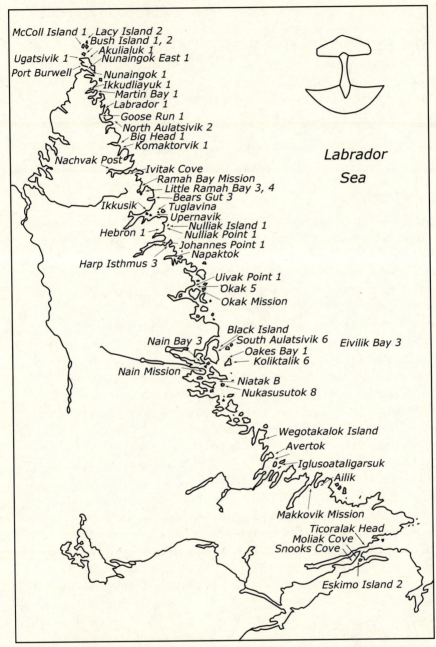

Figure 5. *Nineteenth-century sod house sites along the northern and central coast of Labrador.*

ground houses in close proximity to Moravian mission stations or HBC posts. (The Moravians had been encouraging use of above-ground houses, considering the semi-subterranean sod houses unsanitary, and had been discouraging polygamy.) The non-Aboriginal settler population had moved into sections of the north coast that Inuit had never occupied because of poor living and hunting conditions, most notably Ramah Bay, and the Inuit followed (Kaplan 1983). A new settlement pattern emerged, based not on natural resource access alone, but on access to mission stations and trading posts. As a result, three populations of Inuit emerged along the north coast: those who expressed loyalty to the missionaries and lived in proximity to the stations, those who traded regularly with the HBC and lived near them, and those who wanted to maintain their distance from all settlers. This last group lived in the Komaktorvik area and further north and were of concern to the missionaries and Nachvak HBC factor (Kaplan 1983). The unified, long-distance trade networks that characterized the eighteenth century were no longer tenable, large sea mammal hunting opportunities had disappeared, and traditional social safety nets had been disrupted, particularly between converts and the rest of the population (Brice-Bennett 1981).

Inuit material culture continued to be used; though, as noted earlier, slates were entirely replaced by metals. By this time firearms had replaced the bow and arrow, and metal fox traps had been introduced, as had sealing nets. Ceramic cups and bowls had become household items, and in some cases were used instead of soapstone vessels (Loring and Arendt 2009; Loring and Cabak 2000).

Flexibility and Resourcefulness

As is evident from the above discussion, the Thule Inuit who moved into coastal Labrador quickly adapted to the region. Over the course of the next 500 years they repeatedly responded to environmental and social changes. Local exchange and sharing networks were augmented in the eighteenth century by a unifying long-distance trade network. That network was abandoned when groups developed relationships with local traders and missionaries. Inuit assessed the utility of European goods and quickly adapted new technologies to meet their needs. While Inuit had to change the focus of some of their hunting due to the overhunting of large marine mammals by commercial whalers, individuals did not specialize. They maintained a generalized adaptation that involved making use of the range of resources available to them to feed their families. These resources included animals they hunted and trapped, traditional sharing networks, and reliance on European establishments.

This ability to adapt to changes, environmental and social, by maintaining a diversity of skills, as well as mental and social flexibility to adjust lifestyles, are the defining characteristics of the Labrador Inuit. Today, people are concerned about the warming of the Arctic and the impact of rapid cultural change resulting from increased influences from the outside. It is in this contemporary context that the Thule/Labrador Inuit history of flexibility and ingenuity might be most instructive.

An Eighteenth-century Home

This broad view of Labrador Inuit settlement history is useful, but it is limited as well. It is a picture pieced together using data derived from archaeological surveys, some excavations, and interpretations of historic records. The above sketch is lacking in a few key ingredients because it centres mostly on economic considerations and is largely maritime focused. This section of the chapter will take a close look at an eighteenth-century household based on examination of a sod house at Uivak Point, in the Okak region, where eighteenth-century communal houses were built. The discussion will reveal the extent to which Inuit learned to use not only marine but also terrestrial resources of the region and, in doing so, learned to make a house a home and live a bountiful life.

Examining an Eighteenth-century House

In order to develop a detailed picture of what life would have been like for one group of Inuit living in a large communal house in the late 1700s, a semi-subterranean sod house in the Okak region was excavated (Figure 3). The sod house site, located on the mainland directly across from Okak Island, is known in the Provincial Archaeology Office records as *Uivak Point 1* (HjCl-09). The archaeology site's name is redundant, since *uivak* means "point" in Inuktitut, and is probably a reference to the point of land on which the sod houses were built. Moravians who visited the community recorded its name as *Uibvak* or *Uivakh* (Taylor and Taylor 1977). Uivak was one of three eighteenth-century Inuit whaling settlements in Okak. Uivak Point 1 includes the remains of nine semi-subterranean sod houses built into a raised beach on the protected southwestern shore. The sod houses, as well as tent rings, hunting blinds, graves, route markers, caches, extensive middens, and outdoor hearths, testify to the intense use of this area.

The hills above the sod houses offer a panoramic view of the open North Atlantic as well as expansive views of the protected waterways of inner Okak Bay. From these hills people probably watched for and intercepted migrating bowhead whales and harp seals, could spot sunning and denning ringed seals found in the stable ice in inner Okak Bay, and looked for a variety of sea mammals at the *sina*, which was close by.

Three-fourths of House 7 and a large portion of its midden were excavated. The work revealed that House 7 was an eighteen-metre by twelve-metre structure, truly a large house (Kaplan 2009; Kaplan and Woollett 2000; Woollett 2003 and 2007). The thirty-two one-square-metre excavation units exposed House 7's entrance passage, cold trap, and house floor, which were nicely paved with large flat stones chinked with smaller paving stones, revealing the care that went into the structure's construction. A raised sleeping platform ran the entire length of the back wall of the house, and a second platform ran along portions of a side wall. Lamp stands fashioned out of stone and whale vertebrae were identified as well. The interior features suggest at least two related families lived together in the house.

Collapsed house posts and beams, some made out of whale ribs, one out of a whale scapula, and others out of wood, were uncovered in the house and entrance passage. Cast-off wooden structural supports were also recovered in the midden. The use of whale bones as supports was pragmatic but also probably had a spiritual significance, given the close association of whales, women, and houses, as found in north Alaska and the Canadian high Arctic (see, for instance, Bodenhorn 1990; Savelle and Habu 2004).

Inuit-made artifacts fashioned out of bone, antler, walrus ivory, baleen, hide, and wood were recovered from the house and midden. The artifacts include hunting implements such as toggling harpoon heads, harpoon socket pieces and finger rests, float inflation nozzles and wound plugs, bow fragments, and knife handles. Dog harness traces and toggles, pieces of sled runners, kayak and umiak parts, and bone paddle tips were among the types of objects recovered. These are remains of implements that the occupants of House 7 used when they hunted and travelled on land, in open water, along the ice edge, over snow-covered terrain, and on the sea ice.

Bucket and bowl bottoms, a wooden bowl carved out of a burl, fragments of stitched hide, ulu handles, decorative pendants, soapstone pot and lamp fragments, a wooden doll, a toy wooden bear, a comb, and mattock blades hint at the many domestic activities taking place in and around the house.

European-manufactured materials were used along with traditional materials in the subsistence and domestic spheres. Found items include glass beads, a mouth harp, a metal thimble, fine-toothed ivory combs, glass buttons, a coin, sherds of decorated earthenware, kaolin pipe fragments, pieces of bottle and window glass, a glass door knob, iron nails and spikes, metal knife blades, gun flints, lead shot, firearm parts, and iron bowl fragments. Pieces of metal were inserted into harpoon heads and fashioned into knife and ulu blades; pipes were used for smoking tobacco. Metal thimbles were used in addition to the traditional leather variety; fine-toothed manufactured combs were used along with hand-made combs. Beads adorned clothes and earrings. This inventory reveals the extent to which exotic goods had been incorporated into many facets of Inuit life. The European-made objects suggest that the house dates to the late eighteenth century. This date is in keeping with Moravian accounts that document people living at Uivak between the 1770s and 1790s (Kaplan and Woollett 2000; Taylor and Taylor 1977, 60; Woollett 2003).

Jim Woollett, a zooarchaeologist, analyzed the 52,543 animal bones recovered from the House 7 midden. His analysis supports the subsistence picture suggested by the artifacts. Over 70 percent of the 26,769 identified bones belonged to sea mammals. Ringed and harp seals, the one ice dependent and the other open-water dependent, were the most frequently hunted animals, with harbour and bearded seals appearing in fewer numbers (Woollett 2003 and 2007). Fish, mussels, birds, caribou, and fur-bearing animals were additional food resources. Bones from large whales were found at the site as well. Moravian missionaries reported that people in the Okak region caught a whale every few years. This suggests that these large marine mammals were valuable but not dependable sources of food. When one was caught there was cause for great celebration, and communities from surrounding areas shared in the catch. The procurement of a whale reinforced the whalers'/hunters' sense of identity, while the celebration and distribution of meat brought to light the kinship ties and networks of mutual aid between communities.

The faunal remains and artifacts indicate that Uivak House 7 inhabitants hunted in a variety of environments and practised an economy generalized in scope; they procured a diversity of animals, most harvested from the sea. Woollett extracted well-preserved teeth from recovered seal jaws and examined tooth-thin sections in order to determine the age of the seals, when they died, and during what season they were killed. His season-of-death estimates indicate that the people living in House 7 hunted the various seals when the animals were most accessible. For instance, harp seals were intensively hunted in the fall, when they lingered close to shore, adult ringed seals were hunted at breathing holes throughout the winter, and young ringed seals were a focus in the spring, when they emerged from their dens in the fast ice (Kaplan and Woollett 2000; Woollett 2003 and 2007).

In all likelihood, Uivak was not occupied in late summer, or if it was, people lived in tents, given that the sod houses would have been unpleasant places at that time of year. Fall is the time when caribou are in their prime, and families probably moved to places where they could reliably intercept large numbers of these animals. They would dry and cache the meat and process the skins, which would be made into warm fur clothes and bedding. This would account for the few caribou bones found in the sod house midden.

Archaeological Puzzles

House 7 contained well-preserved wooden support beams. Analysis of the growth rings in the beams was undertaken to learn more about how the local climate changed over time. This helped researchers understand how Labrador Inuit had responded to the North Atlantic's dynamic climate conditions, particularly the Little Ice Age. Also, two distinct occupation periods of House 7 were identified using a combination of tree ring data and the historic artifacts; one occupation dated from 1772 to 1780, the other from 1792 to 1806 (Woollett 2003).

Existing climate records from the late 1700s revealed that Inuit had inhabited House 7 during a cold, but environmentally stable, period that was followed by a period of severe cold. These findings and the results of archaeological and faunal analyses, as well as Moravian accounts that Inuit maintained large dog teams (which would have required a great deal of meat to support), indicate that the inhabitants of Uivak enjoyed a bountiful life. Why was the site abandoned? Was it because of the 1800 cold snap or the dwindling number of whales? Did the collapse of the long-distance trade network or the proximity of the Okak Moravian mission station, established in 1776, have anything to do with the site's abandonment? Hopefully, future research will produce answers to these questions.

Twisted Wood, Twigs, Seeds, and Beetles

Archaeologists working in Labrador have generally been most interested in questions of economy of maritime hunters. Until the excavation of House 7, Inuit relationships to Labrador's terrestrial environment had not been considered. As a result, the archaeological reconstructions of Inuit economy are probably under-representing the terrestrial component of the Inuit diet. Also, the reconstructions are overlooking contributions of important segments of the Inuit population, namely the women, children, and elders who would have been harvesting many of the land-based resources.

House 7 yielded a great deal of spruce wood that was twisted and gnarly. The wood was from white spruce (*Picea glauca*) krummholtz. Krummholtz are highly stunted, slow-growing trees (Figure 6). Their growth rings are very dense, and as a result the wood is very strong. The occupants of House 7 at Uivak harvested krummholtz and used them, as well as whale bone, to

Figure 6. *Photographs of a krummholtz and twisted wood.*

support their large dwelling. Whether this was the only wood available, or whether Inuit selected it for its strength, we do not know (see Payette et al. 1985 for discussions of krummholtz in Labrador and Quebec).

Bulk soil samples from the sleeping platform, interior house floor, entrance passage, and midden were collected for further analysis in a laboratory setting. Cynthia Zutter (2000 and 2009) examined the plant remains (called macrobotanical remains) in these samples and those from an off-site location. Analysis of the turf collected from the sleeping platform revealed that this wooden platform had been covered with a variety of spruce, crowberry, willow, and birch boughs (Zutter 2009). In all likelihood the boughs provided insulation and padding for the families that slept on the platform under fur blankets. The soils collected from the house floor and entrance passage included crowberry and birch twigs in addition to spruce needles (Zutter 2000 and 2009). The house occupants might have spread the twigs and needles on the floor to collect grease and food particles, and perhaps to freshen the house. The twigs and needles also would have prevented objects left on the paved floor from freezing to the stone. Discrete piles of household debris, including twigs and spruce needles, were found in the midden and probably represent house floor sweepings tossed out the door after a cleaning.

Zutter also identified high concentrations of crowberry, bearberry, and blueberry seeds throughout the house and the midden. The presence of these thousands of seeds in the midden in particular suggests that the berries had been eaten and the seeds deposited into the midden in human feces, also identified at the site (Zutter 2009).

Allison Bain (2000) recovered fly and beetle remains in the soil samples from House 7. Her study of insect remains (paleoentomology) focused on the beetles. Within the house she identified varieties of beetles that were unknowingly brought into the house when people carried in freshly cut wood for use as posts and beams, and boughs and mosses for use on the floor and sleeping platforms. These included ground beetles typically found in conifers and mosses, bark beetles usually attracted to recently cut wood, and rove beetles found in willow and alder-leaf litter.

The plant and insect remains found in the soils in the house and midden suggest that the inhabitants of House 7 harvested berries intensively in the late summer and fall, possibly prior to moving into the house. They probably stored large quantities of the fruits, which they consumed later in the winter. They also cut down trees and gathered tree branches, bush, and mosses from areas surrounding Uivak on an ongoing basis. Due to preservation issues and the season when the house would have been occupied, soft tissue plants that might have been harvested by Uivak residents in the early fall for use as food or medicine have not been recovered. E.W. Hawkes (1970, 35–37) discusses a variety of leafy plants collected for those purposes. Despite the lack of archaeological evidence of most soft tissue plants, it is clear that the inhabitants of House 7 used plants regularly to make their home comfortable and to supplement their diet. In all likelihood, women, children, and elders did the vital, hard work of collecting the plants. In addition, wood was used in house construction, and probably also to build drying racks and kayak and umiak stands, although these structures have not been identified archaeologically at Uivak.

Adapting to Forested Areas

The site of *Oakes Bay 1* (HeCg-08) on Dog Island in the Nain region is also an eighteenth-century communal house site. Known as *Parngnertokh* (Taylor and Taylor 1977), the site consists of seven discrete semi-subterranean houses. The Oakes Bay 1 middens are shallow, suggesting that the site was not occupied intensively or for a long period of time. The sod houses are on a tundra-covered expanse with a thin scattering of krummholtz spruce on the hillside behind the site. Across the bay from Oakes Bay 1 are dense stands of spruce. Upon consideration, archaeologists realized that the land

Figure 7. *Tundra-covered pass and Uivak Point 1.*

on which Oakes Bay 1 is located was probably once heavily forested as well. Areas would have been cleared of trees to make room for the sod structures and the wood used to build and furnish the homes, and for numerous other uses such as making drying racks.

Analyses of tree stumps found amongst the krummholtz behind the site reveal that a number of trees were cut in the early twentieth century (Rosanne D'Arrigo 2001, pers. comm.). Today trees around Oakes Bay are being cut for firewood by Nain residents. Here, then, is an example of a landscape gradually being transformed from forest to tundra by human deforestation.

The Uivak site has no trees in its vicinity at present (Figure 7), but like the Oakes Bay site, forested areas exist nearby, such as across the bay from the Uivak site, as well as further west. Extensive middens suggest that Uivak was more intensively occupied than Oakes Bay. Did the occupants of Uivak deforest the area around their settlement? S. Payette et al. (1985) discuss a massive mortality of old spruce in the late 1800s as a result of climate changes. The lack of trees in the Uivak area itself and thinning at the Oakes Bay site do not appear to be related to climate-caused die-off, but rather to human activities. The tree harvesting raises additional questions about Inuit adaptations to forested regions of Labrador.

A Land of Plenty Harbouring Dangers

The earlier discussion of Thule and Inuit people presents a picture of extraordinarily competent people moving into the region with confidence and swiftly becoming a dominant force. Inuit were not simply concerned with the physical environment around them, however. Spiritual matters were ever present in their minds (see, for instance Burch 1971; Laugrand, Ooosten, and Trudel 2002; Taylor 1997). Given the importance of spiritual matters, an admittedly speculative discussion of what might have been the Inuit's spiritual response to Labrador forests follows in hopes of broadening and advancing our understanding of Inuit adaptations to the region.

Among the characteristics of Labrador mentioned only briefly at the beginning of the chapter is its boreal forest. The treeline is currently at Napaktok, where dense stands of spruce abound and stands of larch trees can also be found. There are areas of alder, sedge, and willow brush here and in protected areas further north as well. The presence of dense forests must have both excited the Inuit and given them pause. The excitement would have stemmed from the realization that they now had access to growing trees; they would no longer have to rely solely on driftwood as did Inuit in Baffin Island and other northern regions (Laeyendecker 1993; also see Alix 2005 for discussion of reliance on driftwood in other parts of the Arctic). People could now carefully select specific trees or branches to harvest in order to build boats, sleds, dwellings, and other structures, and to make weapons and implements. For instance, they could cut down a larch tree, whose timber was relatively free of knots, and make robust sled runners; they could select strong and resilient wood to make into sinew-backed bows (Turner 2001, 241, and 246) or cut individual branches that would yield straight grained wood from which to fashion arrow shafts.

Where did trees fit into Inuit ideology? Lucien Turner collected two different accounts concerning the place of trees in the chain of beings in Ungava Bay Inuit origin myths. In one case trees are the source of all animals. According to the account, "a man who was cutting down a tree observed that the chips continued in motion as they fell from the blows. Those that fell into the water became the inhabitants of the water. Those that fell on the land became the various animals and in time were made the food of mankind" (Turner 2001, 261). In the other account, trees and other vegetation have a maritime origin, as they are associated with seaweed (261). In these accounts, trees have a beneficial and benign association. It would be worth reviewing accounts collected by Moravian missionaries and other travellers to help understand the place of trees in the ideology of Labrador Inuit.

The excitement generated by standing trees might have been tempered by some trepidation about forests. The terrain of densely packed trees and brush that Inuit would have encountered as they proceeded south of Napaktok would have been difficult to walk through. In addition, the expansive vistas and unhampered views, so typical of the tundra and so familiar to Inuit, would have been replaced by a landscape that must have seemed rather claustrophobic. The forests were also home to many forms of life with which the Inuit would not have been familiar and about which they would have had no oral history or mythology to guide them. Small creatures, including spiders, beetles, flies, bees, moths, and worms, might have been of particular concern, judging from ethnographic studies of Inuit from other parts of the Arctic. For instance, among Baffin Inuit, these small creatures were known as *qupirriut* (Laugrand and Oosten 2010). Among many Inuit across the Arctic, *qupirriut* were seen as spiritually powerful, their larvae and adult phases evoking transformation imagery. While some could be helping spirits, many were deemed dangerous (Burch 1971; Laugrand and Oosten 2010). The diversity and quantity of such creatures in the boreal forest must have been quite unsettling. According to Frédéric Laugrand (2009, pers. comm.), Inuit in Baffin often associated large numbers of creatures, such as swarms of mosquitoes or herds of caribou, with the concept *qupirriuk*. Did the Labrador Inuit associate the sheer number of trees in large stands of forest with that concept as well?

There is another reason to think that the forested areas, if not the trees themselves, were associated with spiritual dangers. Bjarne Grønnow (Grønnow 2009) explains that eighteenth- and nineteenth-century West Greenland Inuit who were living in coastal areas ventured into interior regions near the Ice Cap with extreme caution. They believed this unfamiliar interior region was populated by dangerous supernatural beings in the forms of human outcasts, ghosts, giants, and monstrous animals and insects. Inuit travelled to the interior and camped there when pursuing caribou, but they were always mindful of the dangers that lurked on that landscape. Like the interior of Greenland, the forested areas of Labrador might have been places to go to in search of resources, but not to linger in for prolonged periods of time. Further south, the association of forested regions with Point Revenge and later Innu might have only increased Inuit's unease about forested regions and the dangers lurking in them.

If these suggestions have merit, it is possible to begin to consider some of the settlement choices pioneering Inuit and subsequent populations made in a new light. The original settlement of far outer islands and other extreme coastal locations would have made spiritual as well as economic sense. Inuit would have moved onto landscapes in which they were spiritually comfortable, keeping forested areas at a distance. The move to central places in the eighteenth century would have made economic and ecological sense, but probably would have caused the Inuit some spiritual distress because the move would have placed them in close proximity to, if not within, forested areas.

In this context, the harvesting of large numbers of trees around Uivak, Oakes Bay, and other eighteenth-century sites south of the treeline might have made practical as well as spiritual sense. As noted earlier, the trees would have been cut down to make way for sod houses and the timber utilized in house construction, while the boughs of downed trees would have been used to appoint the homes. Additionally, Inuit might have been motivated to harvest large numbers of trees because of a need to push the forests away from habitations, thereby eliminating the claustrophobic sense generated by the forested landscape, as well as creating distance between Inuit families and the spiritual dangers associated with the forest. Labrador Inuit might have been actively domesticating the landscape around their homes, transforming the unfamiliar and therefore dangerous forested lands into familiar, open tundra expanses. The spiritual beings associated with the tundra would have been well known, the systems of coping with or mediating its hazards well understood. The Labrador Inuit newcomers might have been reacting to Labrador's forest cover in much the way that pioneering families in western United States and Canada reacted to dense growth there. The western pioneers cleared and fenced land for ranching and farming, but also to keep the wilderness, with all its real and perceived dangerous associations, away from their homesteads.

Summary

Surveys and excavations of northern and central Labrador Inuit sites have provided a broad picture of how Inuit economically adapted to those sections of the coast and responded to changes in their natural and social environment. An in-depth examination of an eighteenth-century sod house has provided a more detailed picture of an Inuit household's extensive use of both marine and terrestrial resources. In particular, Inuit use of plants to build and furnish their homes, as well as to provide additional sources of food, became evident in the analysis. These examinations of Inuit life on two different scales reveal that Inuit maintained flexibility and used considerable ingenuity when dealing with changes to their world.

A consideration of how the Inuit responded to a new resource—living trees—and an unfamiliar environment—the forest—indicates yet another way Labrador Inuit adjusted to life in a land that proved challenging in both the physical and spiritual sense. The chapter suggests that initially Labrador Inuit appear to have taken care to avoid spiritual dangers associated with the forest by settling on familiar landscapes at some distance from that claustrophobic, unfamiliar environment. When economic circumstances led the eighteenth-century Inuit to relocate sod house settlements close to or within forested areas, people appear to have continued to adapt. They cut down forests around their sod house settlements, creating landscapes that exhibited familiar physical and spiritual characteristics. In dealing with spiritual concerns, as well as environmental and social challenges, the Labrador Inuit exhibited much resourcefulness and ingenuity.

Acknowledgements

The research discussed here could not have been accomplished without the collaboration of Jim Woollett. I also want to thank Brendan Buckley, Rosanne D'Arrigo, Allison Bain, and Cynthia Zutter for their efforts on behalf of this project, and the many crews of students for their careful work in the field. I am also grateful to Henry Webb and The Torngâsok Cultural Centre for logistical assistance over many years. I also want to thank Claire Alix for her comments on the character of the Uivak wood, and Frédéric Laugrand for his thoughtful observations about trees. Grants from the Office of Polar Program, National Science Foundation, awarded to Susan A. Kaplan (OPP-9307845 and OPP-9615812) and Jim Woollett (OPP-9616802), supported the bulk of the fieldwork reported here. Bowdoin College and Kane Lodge Foundation, Inc. provided additional support. Permission to conduct the research was provided by The Torngâsuk Cultural Centre and the Provincial Archaeology Office, Department of Tourism, Culture and Recreation, Newfoundland-Labrador. All figures and photos by Susan A. Kaplan.

References

Alix, Claire. 2005. "Deciphering the Impact of Change on the Driftwood Cycle. Contribution to the Study of Human Use of Wood in the Arctic." *Global and Planetary Change* 47: 83–98.

Bain, Allison. 2000. "Uivak Archaeoentomological Analysis 2." Report on file in the office of Susan A. Kaplan, Bowdoin College.

Banfield, A.W.F. 1974. *The Mammals of Canada*. Toronto: University of Toronto Press.

Barkham, Selma.,1977. "Guipuzcoan Shipping in 1571 with Particular Reference to the Decline of the Transatlantic Fishing Industry." In *Anglo-American Contributions to Basque Studies: Essays in Honor of Jon Bilbao,* edited by William A. Douglass, Richard W. Etulain, and William H. Jacobsen, Jr., 73–81. Publications on the Social Sciences No. 13. Reno: Desert Research Institute.

_____. 1978. "The Basques: Filling a Gap in our History between Jacques Cartier and Champlain." *Canadian Geographical Journal* 49, 1: 8–19.

_____. 1980. "A Note on the Strait of Belle Isle during the Period of Basque Contact with Indians and Inuit." *Études/Inuit/Studies* 4, 1–2: 51–58.

Bird, Junius B. 1945. *Archaeology of the Hopedale Area, Labrador.* Anthropological Papers of the American Museum of Natural History 39, 2. New York: American Museum of Natural History.

Bodenhorn, Barbara. 1990. "I'm Not a Great Hunter, My Wife Is: Iñupiat and Anthropological Models of Gender." *Études/Inuit/Studies* 14, 1–2: 55–74.

Boles, Bruce. 1980. *Offshore Labrador Biological Studies, 1979: Seals.* St John's: Atlantic Biological Services.

Brewster, Natalie. 2008. "The Archaeology of Snack Cove 1 and Snack Cove 3." *North Atlantic Archaeology* 1: 25–42.

Brice-Bennett, Carol. 1981. "Two Opinions: Inuit and Moravian Missionaries in Labrador 1804–1860." MA thesis, Memorial University of Newfoundland.

Briggs, Jean. 1970. *Never in Anger: Portrait of an Eskimo Family.* Cambridge: Harvard University Press.

Burch, Ernest S. 1971. "The Nonempirical Environment of the Arctic Alaskan Eskimos." *Southwestern Journal of Anthropology* 27, 2: 148–65.

Cox, Steven. 1977. "Prehistoric Settlement and Culture Change at Okak, Labrador." PhD diss., Harvard University.

Dahl, Jens. 2000. *Saqqaq: An Inuit Hunting Community in the Modern World.* Toronto: University of Toronto Press.

D'Arrigo, Rosanne, Brendan Buckley, Susan A. Kaplan, and Jim Woollett. 2003. "Interannual to Multidecadal Modes of Labrador Climate Variability Inferred from Tree Rings." *Climate Dynamics* 20: 219–28.

Fitzhugh, William. 1978. "Winter Cove 4 and the Point Revenge Occupation of the Central Labrador Coast." *Arctic Anthropology* 15, 2: 146–74.

_____. 1994. "Staffe Island 1 and the Northern Labrador Dorset-Thule Succession." In *Threads of Arctic Prehistory: Papers in Honour of William E. Taylor, Jr.,* edited by David Morrison and Jean-Luc Pilon, 239–69. Hull: Canadian Museum of Civilization.

Grønnow, Bjarne. 2009. "Blessings and Horrors of the Interior: Ethno-historical Studies of Inuit Perceptions Concerning the Inland Region of West Greenland." *Arctic Anthropology* 46, 1–2: 191–201.

Hawkes, E.W. 1970 [1916]. *The Labrador Eskimo*. Canadian Department of Mines, Geological Survey Memoir 91, Anthropological Series No. 14. Ottawa: Government Printing Bureau.

Jordan, Richard H. 1978. "Archaeological Investigations of the Hamilton Inlet Labrador Eskimo: Social and Economic Responses to European Contact." *Arctic Anthropology* 15, 2: 175–85.

Jordan, Richard H. and Susan A. Kaplan. 1980. "An Archaeological View of the Inuit/European Contact Period in Central Labrador." *Études/Inuit/Studies* 4, 1–2: 35–45.

Kaplan, Susan A. 1983. "Economic and Social Change in Labrador Neo-Eskimo Culture." PhD diss., Bryn Mawr College.

_____. 1985. "European Goods and Socio-economic Change in Early Labrador Inuit Society." In *Cultures in Contact: The European Impact on Native Cultural Institutions in Eastern North America, A.D. 1000–1800*, edited by W.W. Fitzhugh, 45–70. Washington, DC: Smithsonian Institution Press.

_____. 2009. "From Forested Bays to Tundra Covered Passes: Transformation of the Labrador Landscape." In *On Track of the Thule Culture from Bering Strait to East Greenland*, edited by Bjarne Grønnow, 119–28. Studies in Archaeology and History, Vol. 15. Copenhagen: National Museum.

Kaplan, Susan A., and James M. Woollett. 2000. "Challenges and Choices: Exploring the Interplay between Climate, History, and Culture on Canada's Labrador Coast." *Arctic, Antarctic, and Alpine Research* 32, 3: 351–59.

Laeyendecker, Dosia. 1993. "Analysis of Wood and Charcoal Samples from Inuit Sites in Frobisher Bay." In *The Meta Incognita Project,* edited by S. Alsford, 199–210. Contributions to Field Studies, Vol. 6. Gatineau, QC: Canadian Museum of Civilization.

Laugrand, Frédéric, and Jarich Oosten. 2010. "*Qupirruit*: Insects and Worms in Inuit Traditions." *Arctic Anthropology* 47, 1: 1–21.

Laugrand, Frédéric, Jarich Oosten, and François Trudel. 2002. "Hunters, Owners, and Givers of Light: The Tuurngait of South Baffin Island." *Arctic Anthropology* 39, 1–2: 27–50.

Logan, Judith A., and James A. Tuck. 1990. "A Sixteenth Century Basque Whaling Port in Southern Labrador." *Association for Preservation Technology International*, Bulletin 22, 3: 65–72.

Loring, Stephen. 1992. "Princes and Princesses of Ragged Fame: Innu (Naskapi) Archaeology and Ethnohistory in Labrador." PhD diss., University of Massachusetts.

Loring, Stephen, and Beatrix Arendt. 2009. "'…they gave Hebron, the city of refuge…' (Joshua 21:13): An Archaeological Reconnaissance at Hebron, Labrador." *Journal of the North Atlantic* Special Volume 1: 33–56.

Loring, Stephen, and Melanie Cabak. 2000. "A Set of Very Fair Cups and Saucers: Stamped Ceramics as an Example of Inuit Incorporation." *International Journal of Historical Archaeology* 4, 1: 34–52.

Loring, Stephen, and Leah Rosenmeier, eds. 2005. *Angutiup Ânguanga/Anguti's Amulet. Central Coast of Labrador Archaeology Partnership*. Truro, NS: Eastern Woodland Publishing, Millbrook First Nation.

McLaren, Ian A. 1958. *The Biology of the Ringed Seal* (Phoca hispida schreber) *in the Eastern Canadian Arctic*. Bulletin 118. Ottawa: Fisheries Research Board of Canada.

Payette, S., L. Filon, L. Gauthier, and Y. Boutin. 1985. "Secular Climate Change in Old-growth Tree-line Vegetation of Northern Quebec." *Nature* 315: 135–38.

Pinhorn, A.T. 1976. *Living Marine Resources of Newfoundland-Labrador: Status and Potential*. Fisheries Research Board of Canada Bulletin 194. Ottawa: Department of the Environment, Fisheries and Marine Service.

Romero, Aldemaro, and Shelly Kannada. 2006. "Comment on 'genetic analysis of 16th-century whale bones prompts a revision of the impact of Basque whaling on right and bowhead whales in the western north Atlantic.'" *Canadian Journal of Zoology* 84: 1059–65.

Savelle, James M., and Junko Habu. 2004. "A Processual Investigation of a Thule Whale Bone House: Somerset Island, Arctic Canada." *Arctic Anthropology* 41, 2: 204–21.

Schwartz, Fred. 1977. "Land Use in the Makkovik Region." In *Our Footprints Are Everywhere: Inuit Land Use and Occupancy in Labrador*, edited by Carol Brice-Bennett, 239–78. Nain: Labrador Inuit Association.

Stopp, Marianne P. 2002. "Reconsidering Inuit Presence in Southern Labrador." *Études/Inuit/Studies* 26, 2: 71–108.

Taylor, J. Garth. 1974. *Labrador Eskimo Settlements of the Early Contact Period*. National Museums of Canada Publications in Ethnology, 9. Ottawa: National Museums of Canada.

_____. 1988. "Labrador Inuit Whale Use during the Early Contact Period." *Arctic Anthropology* 25, 1: 120–30.

_____. 1997. "Deconstructing Deities: *Tuurngatsuak* and *Tuurngaatsuk* in Labrador Inuit Religion." *Études/Inuit/Studies* 21, 1–2: 141–53.

Taylor, J. Garth, and Helge Taylor. 1977. "Inuit Land Use and Occupancy in the Okak Region, 1776–1830." In *Our Footprints Are Everywhere: Inuit Land Use and Occupancy in Labrador*, edited by Carol Brice-Bennett, 59–82. Nain: Labrador Inuit Association.

Trudel, François. 1980. "Les relations entre les Français et les Inuit au Labrador Méridional, 1660–1760." *Études/Inuit/Studies* 4, 1–2: 135–45.

Turner, Lucien M. 2001. [1894] *Ethnology of the Ungava District, Hudson Bay Territory*. Eleventh Annual Report of the Bureau of Ethnology. Reissued as part of Classics of Smithsonian Anthropology Series. Washington, DC: Smithsonian Institution.

Whiteley, W.H. 1964. "The Establishment of the Moravian Mission in Labrador and British Policy 1763–83." *Canadian Historical Review* 45, 1: 29–50.

Woollett, James M. 2003. "An Historical Ecology of Labrador Inuit Culture Change." PhD diss., City University of New York.

_____. 2007. "Labrador Inuit Subsistence in the Context of Environmental Change: An Initial Landscape History Perspective." *American Anthropologist* 109, 1: 69–84.

Zutter, Cynthia. 2000. "Archaeobotanical Investigations of the Uivak Archaeological Site, Labrador, Canada." Report on file in the office of Susan A. Kaplan, Bowdoin College.

_____. 2009. "Paleoethnobotanical Contributions to 18th-century Inuit Economy: An Example from Uivak, Labrador." *Journal of the North Atlantic* Special Volume 1: 23–32.

CHAPTER 2

Invented Places: Environmental Imaginaries and the Inuit Colonization of Labrador

Peter Whitridge

> The great sea moves me!
> The great sea sets me adrift!
> It moves me like algae on stones
> In running brook water.
> The vault of heaven moves me!
> The mighty weather storms through my soul.
> It tears me with it and I tremble with joy.
> (Petrone 1988, 21)

The above epigraph is a transliteration of a song that used to send the Iglulingmiut shaman Uvuvnak into a trance. It embodies a particular engagement with place and landscape that distinguishes this woman's personal lifeworld from those of people around her, and from our own. While it is not opaque, it does suggest how distinctive an individual's relation to his or her own place and time and history can be. The distance between an archaeologist's experience of the world and that of a particular Inuk's in the past is vast. Nevertheless, archaeologists owe it to themselves and their audience to attempt to grasp and illuminate the particularity of past events and settings. The new phenomenological (Tilley 1994; Hamilton and Whitehouse 2006; Witmore 2004) and sensory (Hamilakis et al. 2002; Loren 2008; Skeates 2008) archaeologies, together with parallel trends in archaeological science (e.g., Jahn et al. 1996; Scarre and Lawson 2006), have increasingly encouraged archaeologists to project themselves into the perceptual and sensory worlds of past actors. Any attempt to unfold Inuit understandings of Labrador during the period of first settlement illustrates the difficulty of this task.

Labrador (together with Nunavik) appears to have been colonized by the Thule from Baffin Island in the mid- to late-fifteenth century CE (Kaplan 1983; Schledermann 1971; Whitridge 2008); other researchers assign this event to about 1300 (Fitzhugh 1997, 407), or to the late thirteenth to early fifteenth century (Woollett 2007, 71). This represented the last major Inuit territorial expansion before the inception of contact with post-Norse Europeans in the sixteenth century (Sturtevant 1980). In the course of rapidly settling the Eastern Arctic, Classic Thule–phase Inuit encountered a succession of radically different land-, sea- and icescapes, to which they had to adjust their habits of making a living (Whitridge 2004). Such an adjustment involved not merely learning the biotic schedules and spatial layouts of new territories, but also assimilating profoundly new sorts of organisms, people, and places to a foreign worldview. The archaeological record of Inuit colonization of the southeastern Canadian Arctic reflects this interplay between a resilient cognitive style and novel ecological situations. As Inuit expanded south from Baffin Island into northern Labrador and Quebec they encountered the transition from arctic tundra to subarctic forest for perhaps the first time since their ancestors had left the Western Arctic. The novel patterns of residence and land use, and representations of the world that emerged here, represent an interesting instance of cultural accommodation to a novel environment—the forging of a distinctive "ecoreality."

The notion explored in this chapter is that colonization often involves an imaginative engagement with profoundly new sorts of places, resulting in a creative reworking of the mental, social, and material frames through which people grasp the world. Flexible cognitive templates—ecological taxonomies, landscape models, architectural strategies, technological repertoires, economic tactics, and the social constellations appropriate to each—seem to have effectively equipped Inuit groups as they progressively covered an enormous region during their eastward push through the Arctic Archipelago. However, people did not simply "discover" and unproblematically "colonize" these new place, as some models of the colonization process seem to suggest (Rockman 2003); they had to actively create a home for themselves, naming places on the land, sea, and ice, and gradually (and in locally distinctive ways) learning their respective animals, plants, geology/hydrology, climate, and seasonal schedules. The imaginative quality of the landscapes that ensued is reflected in the surprising mix of generic and novel place names they acquired (Stewart et al. 2004; Whitridge 2004). Regions had their Nuvuk (point) and Qikkertaq (island), but also their singular places, like Angutausugivik (the place where he thought he was a big man; Wheeler 1953). Similarly, prior human and human-like inhabitants and their traces were sometimes subsumed in existing cognitive tropes, and sometimes given novel names and readings. Thus the same Tunit stories recur throughout the Eastern Arctic, reflecting a distinctive style of thought about the ubiquitous evidence of prior Dorset settlement, but room was also made in local cosmogonies for entirely new sorts of beings, like the Innu of the interior, or the powerful deity Torngâsok of the Torngat Mountains coast (Taylor 1997).

The encounter with novel peoples and biomes frequently demanded such novel concepts and practices. Labrador had an archaeologically complex history of repeated colonization and abandonment by an alternating array of First Nations (Maritime or Labrador Archaic, Intermediate Indian, Recent Indian or Innu) and Paleoeskimo (Independence I, Pre-Dorset, Groswater, Middle Dorset, Late Dorset) groups (Fitzhugh 1977 and 1997; Loring 2002). While the Paleoeskimo traces would have been a mostly familiar, even reassuring, confirmation of durable Inuit historical models forged in the Arctic Archipelago, the traces of Amerindians must have been astonishing, reflecting a disturbingly discordant occupational history based on alien spatial, social, and technological templates. In effect, different people had lived in the same places with radically different models of both what constituted a living and what constituted a place. The landscape and biota were similarly novel. For example, moving south along the Atlantic coast Inuit would have encountered not merely willow and alder thickets but increasingly dense stands of spruce. Forest likely presented a silent challenge to Inuit understandings of how people could make their way in the world. Beyond the novel landscapes to which the new arrivals had to quickly accommodate themselves, the Inuit colonists of Labrador ultimately became embroiled in the production of new histories of encounter and conflict. Innu still occupied some of these places, and within decades of the Inuit arrival Europeans began exploring and raiding north along the coast, establishing seasonal commercial outposts in southern Labrador (Tuck and Grenier 1981; Grenier et al. 2007). Inuit pioneers were drawn into an intricate, millennia-long dialogue on society and nature. The settlement of Labrador exposes the diversity of people, things, and processes that local imaginaries must reconcile.

Environmental Imaginaries

Like those they study, archaeologists have repeatedly revised their approach to the environment. The arrangement of archaeological study areas by ecological zone—arctic, subarctic, northwest coast, eastern woodlands, etc.—preserves the legacy of early twentieth century environmental determinist thinking about the land, which accorded primary importance to the scale and nature of food production as understood by Euro-Americans (Holmes 1919). The varying importance accorded to the environmental constraints and opportunities faced by a distinct array of societal types—bands, tribes, chiefdoms, states—reflects the mid-century allowance of cultural ecologists for the character of particular sorts of groups' adjustments to their environment (Steward 1955). Not merely the source of food, but how it was produced, stored, and distributed, and by whom, assumed critical significance, and these factors were seen to be at least in part the legacy of historical processes that had progressively transformed people's relationship to the land and its resources. For evolutionary ecologists, the quantified details of resource abundances, and the contextual harvesting decisions that are seen to follow from them, have been of key importance (Broughton and O'Connell 1999).

Missing in all of these approaches is recognition that prior harvesting decisions and frameworks are adjusted to a current situation through an ongoing and creative process of accommodation and invention. Individuals are not locked into a rigid environmental understanding; a fluid reality forces them to constantly arrive at novel solutions to harvesting problems. The archaeological record of inhabitants' spatial organization appears to be in particularly rapid flux in northern Labrador during the period of Inuit arrival in the region, and there are very few grounds for anticipating precisely how colonists would have reacted to the unusual situation in which they found themselves. Environmental areas, cultural ecology, and evolutionary ecology assume stable cultural boundaries and understandings, not movement, discovery, and invention. There is little reason to expect that Inuit would have driven south of the treeline into already occupied territory.

Different occupants of northern Labrador read and utilized the landscape in profoundly different ways, and consequently left different sorts of material traces. In each instance archaeologists are confronted with a record of exploration and colonization that was subject to a shifting set of rules that were mostly foreign in origin, having congealed in the disparate ecological milieus from which the new arrivals had come. Amerindian groups, who appear to have made only seasonal forays into far northern Labrador, beyond the major chert outcrop at Ramah Bay (Loring 2002; Tuck 1975), originated further south in mainland North America and would have been accustomed to a more diverse terrestrial fauna and flora (for example, access to substantial stands of timber). Paleoeskimos and Inuit likely both arrived from the biotically simpler Canadian Arctic islands with a focal orientation to marine mammals, but radically different types of equipment (and correlative needs or expectations, for example of Paleoeskimos for knappable cryptocrystalline stone) and patterns of cooperation. Europeans staged their exploration, seasonal harvesting, and, ultimately, settlement of Labrador from an enormous distance, with the advantage of deep reserves of labour and equipment, but the disadvantage of dissonant environmental understandings and slim local knowledge. In each case, the cognitive resources and social needs of the colonists appear to have been as significant as the material environment itself for shaping the record they produced. Although for the most part the ecological setting fluctuated only gradually, according to very long-term cycles (deglaciation, Holocene warming and cooling, the century-long cycles of game peaks and crashes), the styles of knowing and using it were diverse.

The assumption adopted here is that particular societies have distinctive modes of social, economic, and cultural organization that mediate their relationship to the world around them, including, not incidentally, what is considered the world around. What is taken as the *boundary* between the social and the natural is peculiar to particular worldviews, and even to the subject positions of particular groups or individuals. For example, the notion that the seasons are changing in northeastern North America in September or October is constructed, in part, from non-environmental facts, including the return to work from summer vacations, the return of students to school, tree viewing by tourists, personal observations of calendrical change, and perhaps changing patterns of interaction with family, friends, and co-workers. These more-or-less orchestrated social events complement and give substance to changes in the atmosphere and biosphere—make them socially and personally *real*. The change of seasons means something radically different depending on one's social and personal understandings, one's actions, and the actions of those around. The actual environmental cues may not be readily recognizable to someone who has never been to this part of the world before, at least at this time of year. Local Aboriginal peoples in the past would have experienced and understood changes in the biophysical world—such as reddening foliage—in a profoundly different way. They may, for example, have felt deeply implicated in these changes through their participation in significant economic and ritual acts, such as harvests, hunts, and festivals

As archaeologists, we use various terms for talking about different aspects of people's lives, but these terms are frequently incommensurate with people's own experience of the world. The notion that land, ice, sea, atmosphere, fauna, and flora constitute a sphere or spheres wholly distinct from, and even opposed to, the human is not universal. Inuit, for example, saw the world as being arranged in different ways than did Western scientists, with an array of planes of existence and conditions for moving between them (Saladin D'Anglure 1986). A host of complex beings and simple creatures inhabited the land, sea, and air that we might not recognize as real at all, and the behaviour of various edible creatures was articulated with the human in unusual ways. For example, the well-known corpus of Sedna beliefs represents a folkloric map of relations amongst different sorts of humans (male/female, young/old, child/parent, married/unmarried, Inuit/qallunat, etc.), animals (dogs, sea birds, sea mammals), hybrid creatures (dog-human, bird-human), and deities (Sedna) and their mediation by different landscape (mainland, island, air, sea), weather (stormy, calm), and technological (umiak, iglu) contexts. Their repetition in social settings (storytelling, performances, shamanic séances), embedding in language and place names, and depiction in art rooted this distinctive worldview in habitual practices and understandings. The particular understanding held at a given moment of interactions amongst people, deities, biota, and landscape across a network of inhabited places can be considered a group's environmental imaginary, or ecoreality (Whitridge 2004).

There is no reason to expect that local ecorealities were homogeneous. Inuit likely held widely varying understandings of their world, depending on their position within it and their personal history. Women's and men's histories were distinct on a host of scales, from daily routines and paths of movements to entire lives, based on their different task obligations, systems of interaction amongst themselves and with others, and experience of their own and others' bodies. Children understood the creatures of which they heard stories, or that they encountered, differently than did elders with a lifetime of experience watching, harvesting, and otherwise using and interacting with animals. Ecoreality names a dimension of understanding of the world that certainly varied amongst individuals (according to knowledge, experience, values, roles, etc.) but likely also achieved a certain consistency with respect to nameable (and hence typically interacting) categories of individuals, from gender and age cohorts to groups of co-resident families, named culture groups, and larger linguistic entities. It would be possible to take some element of this world and examine it from the distinct perspectives of various social groups. Polar bears, for example, are represented archaeologically by bones, artifactually altered teeth (pendants, whetstones), hair, hide, and representations in various media (e.g., wooden toys, ivory amulets, decorated tools, engraved depictions). These contain information bearing on the interactions of different people (men, women, children, shamans, etc.) with living bears (while hunting, travelling, in the settlement), various dead bear parts (meat, bones, teeth, hide), and the idea of bears (for example as animals, food, supernatural creatures, or figures in myth and stories), in various natural (ocean, sea ice, land) and built (kitchen, house, settlement) settings. Alternatively, we could take a particular group of people (e.g., women, children, or the occupants of a house, settlement, or region) and examine their set of understandings of various environmental phenomena within a particular place-time. This is the approach adopted here:

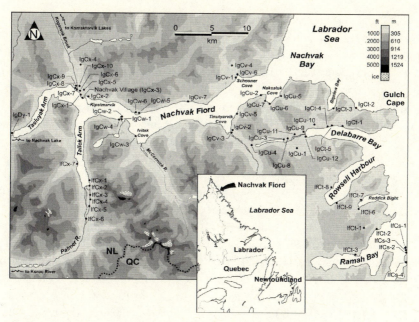

Figure 1. *Archaeological sites in the Nachvak Fiord region.*

some of the rudiments of the Inuit environmental imaginary at Nachvak Fiord during the sixteenth and seventeenth centuries are explored below.

Nachvak Fiord Case Study

Nachvak Fiord is situated at the southeastern corner of the North America Arctic, only a couple of hundred kilometres north of the treeline at Napaktok Bay (Figure 1). It is a deep, for the region, east-west trending fiord that cuts some 45 kilometres into the northern Labrador coast at about 59° N. The steep fiord walls are patchily covered with sedges, mosses, and willow, and there are relatively few areas that appear readily suitable for human settlement. In most places the walls rise precipitously to an elevation of 1000 metres or more, with broader areas of level ground confined mostly to the mouths of river valleys that enter the few bays. Before the over-hunting of the nineteenth century, bowhead whales entered the outer fiord in late fall (bowhead bone and baleen occur at Inuit sites throughout the fiord), and walrus could be found there in late winter (Brice-Bennett 1977). Now only solitary minke whales are regular summer visitors, and occasionally small groups of ringed and harp seals; herds of migratory harps pass through in late fall. Ringed seals would have been accessible throughout the fiord during the winter period of stable ice cover. A polynya in the inner reaches of the fiord, at the junction of Tallek and Tassiuyak Arms, was likely a major attraction for past occupants of the area (Kaplan 1983); the main pre-contact Inuit winter village is situated on a terrace directly adjacent to it, and traces of a string of prior occupations of the area occur on the terrace and nearby. Arctic char are abundant in summer, as they school along the coast before ascending streams to winter, and portions of the George River caribou herd were likely harvested not far inland, around the Komaktorvik Lakes, in late summer and early fall.

The first people to arrive in the area were the Maritime or Labrador Archaic, who explored north as the Holocene ice sheets receded during the later sixth millennium BP (Fitzhugh 1997). A significant outcropping of high quality chert at numerous locations between Nachvak and Saglek Bay, centred on a "quarry bowl" at intervening Ramah Bay, likely continued to draw Maritime Archaic and Intermediate Indian summer visitors over the next few millennia. Certainly, traffic in this material encompassed much of the northeastern North American seaboard between the fifth and first millennia BP (Loring 2002). Pioneering Arctic Small Tool tradition groups moving south into Labrador (Hood 2000) appear to have made sporadic use of the area, though not the Ramah chert, not long after 4000 BP, while later Paleoeskimo populations embraced this raw material and had a more visible presence in the region. A substantial Middle Dorset occupation dating to around 1500 BP occurs at Tinutyarvik Cove, towards the mouth of Nachvak, and traces of a sparse, seasonal Late Dorset presence occur further in the fiord.

At some point during the later fifteenth century Inuit groups moved south along the Labrador coast, establishing permanent regional occupations of varying sizes in a number of fiord systems before the arrival of Europeans (Schledermann 1971; Kaplan 1983). Evidence of an earlier arrival and contact with resident Late Dorset (Fitzhugh 1994) is equivocal (Park 2000) and made somewhat unlikely by recent re-dating of the initial Inuit colonization of the Canadian Arctic (McGhee 2000; Whitridge 1999a). Staffe Island, Komaktorvik, Nachvak, Uivak, Hebron, Napaktok, Okak, and other village sites likely emerged as recurrent wintering locations in the late pre-contact era, with anywhere from five to twenty sod, stone, and whale bone winter dwellings each housing half a dozen to a dozen people. The initial arrivals were likely refugees from the Central and High Arctic, or perhaps groups bumped by them, pushed south by deteriorating harvesting opportunities at the beginning of the Little Ice Age (Whitridge 1999a). Sporadic contact with Europeans exploring north along the newly encountered coast began in the early sixteenth century, and by the seventeenth century Inuit groups from Killinek to the Strait of Belle Isle were avid users of metal, beads, and other European commodities, although only the southerners had good access to these wares through direct contact with the newcomers (Jordan and Kaplan 1980; Kaplan 1985; Kaplan and Woollett 2000; Woollett 2003). During the 1600s Nachvak became a site of occasional consumption of European goods by resident Inuit who likely obtained them through down-the-line trade with central and southern coastal groups. The emergence of large, multi-family winter houses, and a major residential shift from the inner fiord settlement of Nachvak Village (IgCx-3) to the more coastally oriented Kongu (IgCv-7), probably reflect, in part, intensifying interaction with British, French, and Dutch traders during the eighteenth century.

Nachvak was first investigated by the Smithsonian Institution's Torngat Archaeology Project in the late 1970s (Fitzhugh 1980; Fitzhugh et al. 1977, 1978; Kaplan 1980). After a twenty-five-year hiatus, large-scale feature investigations were conducted between 2003 and 2006 at sites IgCx-3 and IgCv-7 by Memorial University of Newfoundland's Archaeology Unit. Four houses have been excavated at the pre-contact site of IgCx-3, and middens adjacent to communal houses have been tested at the contact-era site IgCv-7. IgCx-3, consisting of about fourteen winter houses and associated midden deposits, appears to have been abandoned by 1700; a small collection of nails, a single glass sherd, and a trade bead are the only indications of access to European materials. IgCv-7, on the other hand, has produced little to suggest a pre-contact presence; it appears to represent a new winter village established at about the time that IgCx-3 was abandoned, likely to better position Inuit for the emerging indigenous trade in European commodities (e.g., Haven 1773a, b; Curtis 1774), and perhaps even to directly intercept European coastal traffic. With the establishment of a Hudson's Bay Company post at Kipsimarvik in 1869, Inuit settlement appears to have returned to the inner fiord; both the joint Euro-Canadian/Inuit community there and the large village of Ivitak (IgCw-1), immediately across the fiord, were occupied during the late nineteenth and early twentieth centuries. IgCx-3 provides a useful starting point for thinking about pre-contact Inuit conceptions of northern Labrador's land-, sea-, and icescapes, and it is the focus of subsequent discussion.

The Archaeology of Environmental Imaginaries at Nachvak

From the perspective of environmental imaginaries, Nachvak is interesting for a number of reasons. First, its period of prehistoric occupancy is relatively well constrained archaeologically because of the late arrival of Inuit in the area and the appearance, within decades, of European explorers. Northern Labrador was rapidly resettled soon after the onset of the Little Ice Age (LIA), at which time it represented a huge, sparsely inhabited region with relatively abundant resources (bowhead whales, walrus, small seals, caribou, char). This means, second, that the arrival of Inuit at Nachvak was part of a colonizing movement more than two centuries more recent, hence potentially more accessible archaeologically, than the initial Inuit settlement of the Eastern Arctic, with which it affords a productive contrast. Third, the colonization of Labrador was likely associated with a severe disruption, in part LIA-mediated, of prior ecological models. If Inuit had come to possess a relatively stable set of understandings and representations of the Eastern Arctic environment, it was likely impossible to transfer these directly to northern Labrador in any substantially intact fashion in the fifteenth century. Fourth, the long history of prior occupation of the region by Amerindians and Paleoeskimo groups can be regarded as both an important resource for newly arrived Inuit (in terms of the value of a record of prior settlement for guiding, or at least influencing, resettlement and resource use) and a productive set of contrasts for archaeological analysis. Although organic preservation is often poor, it would still have been possible to discern the very different social and technical resources that underpinned the contrasting networks of harvesting, travel, and settlement locations. Fifth, although it is only one of many occupied fiords along the north coast, Nachvak is unusual because of the inland situation of the main pre-contact winter village and because the Inuit deity Torngâsok was reputed to live in the mountains on the north side of the fiord. The interior location of site IgCx-3 presents an interesting contrast to the situation at the neighbouring winter villages of Komaktorvik (at the mouth of a fiord issuing into Seven Islands Bay) and Ikkusik (on an island in Saglek Bay, at the head of a network of fiord arms), both of which provided readier access than Nachvak to the outer fiord and *sina* (floe edge) but poorer access to interior travel and harvesting opportunities. Together these establish Nachvak as a unique, and in many ways uniquely informative, archaeological case study.

As the abode of Torngâsok, Nachvak occupies a pivotal place in Labrador Inuit cosmology. Although there were locations, such as Saglek, that appear to have been more productive for the marine mammal harvesting that anchored Inuit economy and that supported correlatively larger pre-contact populations (Haven 1773a, b; Curtis 1774; Kaplan 1983), the tradition that a powerful and petulant supernatural being occupied Nachvak draws attention to indigenous understandings of the northern Labrador lifeworld. The entire region was named and assimilated into Inuit understandings; fiords, islands, settlement sites, and topographic features are individuated in local stories (Wheeler 1953). Nachvak, however, is reputed to be a big place (Gary Baikie, personal communication, 2003): significant, and not a little dangerous. Its situation also varies from the pattern for other major winter villages.

Figure 2: *Base of toy soapstone pot from House 12, IgCx-3, with incised design resembling mountains.*

While most are located close to the outer coast, tacitly emphasizing winter access to ringed and bearded seal, Nachvak is located some 30 kilometres inland of the fiord mouth. It is well-positioned for ringed seal hunting at the polynya, and for travel to the interior to recover cached caribou or harvest timber along the Koroc valley, but it seems inappropriately distant from the fall whaling grounds and opportunities for winter walrus and seal hunting at the floe edge.

Geographically, the situation of Nachvak implies an attempt to balance interior harvesting, cache-retrieval, and inter-regional travel with outer-coastal harvesting, a possibility that was typically foregone in other fiord systems. One result of this emphasis is the unusually mountainous quality of the local backdrop; people made their winter home in the centre of a landscape in which the Torngats rise steeply from the ocean to peaks of over 1600 metres (the highest in northeastern North America south of Baffin Island). Outer fiord winter settlements, in contrast, typically open out onto an icescape with little vertical relief. The situation of being ringed by tall mountains appears to be documented in a design scratched into the base of a toy soapstone pot from House 12 (Figure 2), which depicts a line of simple triangular peaks that resembles the surrounding terrain (and especially the regular saw-toothed array at nearby Ramah Bay; see Figure 3). Figurative art or decoration of any kind is rare in the Nachvak assemblage. Although

Figure 3: *Skyline at mouth of Ramah Bay, looking southeast.*

pots (both full size and miniature) often exhibit an incised groove on the upper face of the rim and one or more grooves around the adjacent upper edge of the exterior, this is the only specimen with incised lines on the base. The distinctiveness of the Nachvak landscape seems to have been reiterated in a common element of local material culture, and, based on the contrast between the careful craftsmanship of the pot and the impromptu scratching of the design, perhaps by a later user of the object rather than its manufacturer. Women and/or children entered into a discourse linking landscape, gendered labour, and foodways (and whatever other magical, decorative, or play associations such objects may have possessed) through the medium of an imaginary landscape.

At a smaller scale, the main pre-contact winter village is distinctively positioned on a ten-metre-high terrace facing the junction of the fiord arms, rather than immediately adjacent to the fiord (and a regular source of freshwater from one of the brooks that enter the ocean on either side of the point). This may be due to the winter build-up of freshwater ice on Kogarsok Brook that makes the more obvious coastal location inappropriate. In any case, occupants of the village had an excellent view out over two major fiord arms and the leads that formed there some winters. The village is composed of clusters of single- and two-family houses and likely reflects a complex palimpsest of the changing family composition of the community. Some houses were substantially remodelled and may have been wholly or partially abandoned for some of the life of the settlement. House 2, for example, had two compartments that were likely both occupied during the early period of site occupation and then abandoned, whereas only one of its compartments seems to have been reoccupied during the period leading up to village aban-donment (Whitridge 2008).

Individual houses either have a single platform or, like House 2, are bifurcated, with two more-or-less identical living areas attached to a single tunnel. Each house or living area includes a raised, stone-edged sleeping platform, paved floor, and stone lamp stand, and most also have small niches or extensions. A superstructure composed of whale bone and/or wood was likely tied together with bowhead baleen and covered with hides and sod. The lamp stands typically incorporate a single bowhead vertebra, as they do at the contemporaneous site of Ikkusik (Schledermann 1971, 75). The houses, then, organize a sheltered social space in a repetitive, highly conven-tional fashion and make relatively conspicuous and deliberate reference to the importance of whales. Vertebrae not only represented useful construc-tion elements and tools (they were used in unmodified form as chopping blocks at both House 2 and Ikkusik) but also invoked the centrality (perhaps declining) of bowheads in Eastern Arctic economies and invested women's domestic workspace with cetacean symbolic associations. These associations would appear to be closely related to the whale-woman association marked by the incorporation of bowhead skulls in the detached kitchens of Classic Thule–phase winter houses in the Central Arctic (Whitridge 2004). They also seem to tangibly cite the Inuit story of a woman who married a whale and made a home in its body (Sheppard 1998). Bowhead whales, a key pre-contact Inuit prey species in many parts of the North American Arctic for centuries (McCartney 1980; Savelle and McCartney 1994; Whitridge 1999b), represented a fertile nexus of domestic meanings even as economic reliance on them waned. Houses helped "house" these meanings and provided space for formal age and gender groupings involving work, rest, eating, and sleep. These living arrangements, mostly inherited from Classic Thule–phase antecedents in the Central Arctic, changed in significant ways when people assembled into multi-family houses in Labrador in the early eighteenth cen-tury (Whitridge 2008).

At the level of household artifact assemblages, the northern Labrador material stands out for the overwhelming importance of stone. The assem-blages are dominated by ground slate for various styles of men's and women's knives, harpoon head end blades, and lance blades; nephrite for drill bits, knives, and occasionally end blades; and soapstone for lamps and pots. Whale bone, baleen, and wood appear to have been in regular use, along with lesser amounts of antler and bone, but uneven preservation makes these difficult to quantify. Considering the importance of caribou in the food-bone assemblages from some of these houses, the apparent paucity of antler tools is difficult to explain. However, the absence of flaked chert is even more surprising. Nachvak Fiord sits at the northern edge of an extensive intermittent outcropping of Ramah chert that continues south for tens of kilometres almost to Saglek (Lazenby 1980; Nagle 1984; Loring 2002). This was one of the most widely exchanged raw materials in prehistoric eastern North America, and it dominates pre-contact Amerindian and Paleoeskimo tool assemblages throughout Labrador. Although Inuit groups made extensive use of cherts for knife and harpoon blades in the Western Arctic (see, for example, Giddings and Anderson 1984), and during the initial stage of expansion east (Arnold 1986), they seem to have effectively discarded this material in favour of slate, nephrite, iron, and copper by the time they reached the Central and Eastern Arctic (Whitridge 2002). Strikingly, the Inuit settlers of Labrador clung to a distinctive set of cultural identifiers in the face of an attractive local alternative.

Conclusion

If we cannot begin to see the world through indigenous eyes, then what are we doing as archaeologists? Are we talking only to each other about our fascinations or, worse, serving some insidious political purposes of which we are mostly unaware? Although there are undoubtedly sensible patterns to be adduced through conventional archaeological approaches, we should also be prepared to think and talk in different ways. Inuit moving south into Labrador exemplify this need: people with a distinct and local understanding of North Atlantic land-, sea-, and icescapes adapted their understandings and practices to a dramatically new physical and social environment, which they assimilated and ultimately reinvented in the course of constructing a new system of liveable places. Nachvak came to be understood as the abode of a powerful deity, Torngâsok, and the land and sea were progressively marked with the stories, memories, and physical traces that people's lives produce in their wake, some of which were radically different from modern ones. These understandings and practices and things, not to mention the land and sea, were themselves in flux. The movements of game were learned, new sources of stone were discovered, Europeans arrived, whales and walrus disappeared, and conflicts arose between converts and traditionalists. The troublesome details of people's lives at a particular time and place dissolved into the flow of history.

Acknowledgements

An earlier version of this paper was presented at the NABO conference "The View from Here: History and Ecology of the North Atlantic Region" held at Université Laval, Québec, 20–24 September 2006. Thanks very much to Jim Woollett for the invitation to participate in the session "Colonisation of

Landscapes and Anthropogenic Change in Northern Landscapes," and to Social Sciences and Humanities Research Council of Canada, Canadian Foundation for Innovation, Wenner-Gren Foundation for Anthropological Research, J.R. Smallwood Foundation and Institute for Social and Economic Research at Memorial University, and the Newfoundland and Labrador Provincial Archaeology Office (PAO) for funding various aspects of the Nachvak research. The Torngâsok Cultural Centre, PAO and Parks Canada provided permission to conduct this research, and of course the work could not have been accomplished without the numerous field assistants from Nain and Memorial University who carried on through weather, bears and the inevitable logistical delays and made the fieldwork a true pleasure. Finally, I am grateful to David Natcher, Larry Felt, and Andrea Procter for their patience and encouragement with the manuscript. Photos and map by Peter Whitridge.

References

Arnold, Charles D. 1986. "In Search of the Thule Pioneers." In *Thule Pioneers*, edited by E. Bielawski, C. Kobelka, and R. Janes, 1–93. Occasional Paper No. 2. Yellowknife: Prince of Wales Northern Heritage Centre.

Brice-Bennett, Carol, ed. 1977a. *Our Footprints Are Everywhere: Inuit Land Use and Occupancy in Labrador*. Nain: Labrador Inuit Association.

Broughton, Jack M., and James F. O'Connell. 1999. "On Evolutionary Ecology, Selectionist Archaeology, and Behavioral Archaeology." *American Antiquity* 64, 1: 153–65.

Curtis, Roger. 1774. "Particulars of the Country of Labradore, Extracted from the Papers of the Lieutenant Roger Curtis, of his Majesty's Sloop the Otter, with a Plane-Chart of the Coast." *Philosophical Transactions of the Royal Society* 64: 372–88.

Fitzhugh, William. 1980. "Preliminary Results of the Torngat Archaeological Project." *Arctic* 33: 585–606.

_____. 1994. "Staffe Island I and the Northern Labrador Dorset-Thule Succession." In *Threads of Arctic Prehistory: Papers in Honour of William E. Taylor, Jr.*, edited by David Morrison and Jean-Luc Pilon, 239–69. Hull: Canadian Museum of Civilization, 1994.

_____. 1997. "Biogeographical Archaeology in the Eastern North American Arctic." *Human Ecology* 25, 3: 385–418.

Fitzhugh, William, Richard H. Jordan, and Steven Cox. 1977. "1977 Field Season Summary Report." Report on file with the Provincial Archaeology Branch, St. John's, Newfoundland and Labrador.

Fitzhugh, William, Richard H. Jordan, Steven L. Cox, Christopher Nagle, and Susan A. Kaplan. 1978. "Report to the Newfoundland Museum on the

Torngat Archaeological Project 1978 Field Season." Report on file with the Provincial Archaeology Branch, St. John's, Newfoundland and Labrador.

Giddings, J. Louis, and Douglas D. Anderson. 1986. *Beach Ridge Archeology of Cape Krusenstern*. Publications in Archaeology 20. Washington, DC: National Park Service, U.S. Department of the Interior.

Grenier, Robert, Marc-André Bernier, and Willis Stevens, eds. 2007. *The Underwater Archaeology of Red Bay: Basque Shipbuilding and Whaling in the 16th Century*. Ottawa: Parks Canada Publishing and Depository Services.

Hamilakis, Y., M. Pluciennik, and S. Tarlow, eds., 2002. *Thinking through the Body: Archaeologies of Corporeality*. New York: Kluwer Academic/Plenum Publishers.

Hamilton, Sue, and Ruth Whitehouse. 2006. "Phenomenology in Practice: Towards a Methodology for a 'Subjective' Approach." *European Journal of Archaeology* 9, 1: 31–71.

Haven, Jens. 1773a. "A Brief Account of the Dwelling Places of the Eskimaux to the North of Nagvack to Hudson Straits, Their Situation and Subsistence." Unpublished translation by James Hiller on file at the Centre for Newfoundland Studies, Memorial University of Newfoundland, St. John's.

_____. 1773b. "Extract of the Voyage of the Sloop George from Nain to Reconnoitre the Northern Parts of Labradore in the Months of August and September, 1773." Copy of manuscript on file at the Centre for Newfoundland Studies, Memorial University of Newfoundland, St. John's.

Holmes, W.H. 1919. *Handbook of Aboriginal American Antiquities*. Washington, DC: Government Printing Office.

Hood, Bryan. 2000. "Pre-Dorset/Maritime Archaic Social Boundaries in Labrador." In *Identities and Culture Contacts in the Arctic*, edited by Martin Appelt, Joel Berglund, and Hans Christian Gullov, 120–28. Copenhagen: Danish National Museum and Danish Polar Center.

Jahn, R.G. , P. Devereux, and M. Ibison. 1996. "Acoustical Resonances of Assorted Ancient Structures." *Journal of the Acoustical Society of America* 99, 2: 649–58.

Jordan, Richard H., and Susan A. Kaplan. 1980. "An Archaeological View of the Inuit/European Contact Period in Central Labrador." *Études/Inuit/Studies* 4: 35–46.

Kaplan, Susan. 1980. "Neo-Eskimo Occupations of the Northern Labrador Coast." *Arctic* 33, 3: 646–58.

_____. 1983. "Economic and Social Change in Labrador Neo-Eskimo Culture." PhD diss., Bryn Mawr College.

_____. 1985. "European Goods and Socio-economic Change in early Labrador Inuit Society." In *Cultures in Contact: The Impact of European Contacts on Native American Cultural Institutions A.D. 1000–1800,* edited by William Fitzhugh, 45–70. Washington, DC: Smithsonian Institution Press.

Kaplan, Susan A., and Jim M. Woollett. 2000. "Challenges and Choices: Exploring the Interplay of Climate, History, and Culture on Canada's Labrador Coast." *Arctic and Alpine Research* 32, 3: 351–59.

Lazenby, M.E. Colleen. 1980. "Prehistoric Sources of Chert in Northern Labrador: Field Work and Preliminary Analysis." *Arctic* 33, 3: 628–45.

Loren, Diana DiPaolo. 2008. "Beyond the Visual: Considering the Archaeology of Colonial Sounds." *International Journal of Historical Archaeology* 12: 360–69.

Loring, Stephen. 2002. "'And they took away the stones from Ramah: Lithic Raw Material Sourcing and Eastern Arctic Archaeology." In *Honoring Our Elders: A History of Eastern Arctic Archaeology*, edited by William Fitzhugh, Stephen Loring, and Daniel Odess, 163–85. Washington, DC: Arctic Studies Center, Smithsonian Institution.

McCartney, Allen P. 1980. "The Nature of Thule Eskimo Whale Use." *Arctic* 33, 3: 517–41.

McGhee, Robert. 2000. "Radiocarbon Dating and the Timing of the Thule Migration." In *Identities and Cultural Contacts in the Arctic*, edited by Martin Appelt, Joel Berglund, and Hans Christian Gulløv, 181–91. Copenhagen: Danish National Museum and Danish Polar Centre.

Nagle, Christopher L. 1984. "Lithic Raw Materials Procurement and Exchange in Dorset Culture Along the Labrador Coast." PhD diss., Brandeis University.

Park, Robert W. 2000. "The Dorset-Thule Succession Revisited." In *Identities and Cultural Contacts in the Arctic*, edited by Martin Appelt, Joel Berglund, and Hans Christian Gulløv, 192–205. Copenhagen: Danish National Museum and Danish Polar Centre.

Petrone, Penny, ed. 1988. *Northern Voices: Inuit Writing in English*. Toronto: University of Toronto Press.

Rockman, Marcy. 2003. "Knowledge and Learning in the Archaeology of Colonization." In *Colonization of Unfamiliar Landscapes: The Archaeology of Adaptation*, edited by Marcy Rockman and James Steele, 3–24. New York: Routledge.

Saladin D'Anglure, Bernard. 1986. «Du foetus au chamane: la construction d'un "troisième sexe" inuit, » *Études/Inuit/Studies*, 10, 1–2: 25–114.

Savelle, James M., and Allen P. McCartney. 1994. "Thule Inuit Bowhead Whaling: A Biometrical Analysis." In *Threads of Arctic Prehistory: Papers in Honour of William E Taylor Jr.*, edited by D. Morrison and J-L Pilon, 281–310. Archaeological Survey of Canada Mercury Series Paper 149. Hull: Canadian Museum of Civilization.

Scarre, Chris, and Graeme Lawson, eds. 2006. *Archaeoacoustics*. Cambridge: McDonald Institute for Archaeological Research.

Schledermann, Peter. 1971. "The Thule Tradition in Northern Labrador." MA thesis, Memorial University of Newfoundland.

Sheppard, W.L. 1998. "Population Movements, Interaction, and Legendary Geography." *Arctic Anthropology* 35, 2: 147–65.

Skeates, Robin. 2008. "Making Sense of the Maltese Temple Period: An Archaeology of Sensory Experience and Perception." *Time and Mind* 1, 2: 207–38.

Steward, Julian H. 1955. *The Theory of Culture Change.* Urbana: University of Illinois Press.

Stewart, Andrew, Darren Keith and Joan Scottie. 2004. "Caribou Crossings and Cultural Meanings: Placing Traditional Knowledge and Archaeology in Context in an Inuit Landscape." *Journal of Archaeological Method and Theory* 11(2): 183-211.

Sturtevant, W.C. 1980. "The First Inuit Depiction by Europeans." *Études/Inuit/Studies* 4: 47–49.

Taylor, J. Garth. 1997. "Deconstructing Deities: *Tuurngatsuak* and *Tuurngaatsuk* in Labrador Inuit Religion." *Études/Inuit/Studies* 21, 1–2: 141–58.

Tilley, Christopher. 1994. *A Phenomenology of Landscape: Places, Paths, and Monuments.* Oxford: Berg.

Tuck, James A. 1975. *Prehistory of Saglek Bay, Labrador: Archaic and Palaeo-Eskimo Occupations.* Mercury Series, Archaeological Survey of Canada No. 32. Ottawa: National Museum of Man.

Tuck, James A., and R. Grenier. 1981. "A Sixteenth-century Basque Whaling Station in Labrador." *Scientific American* 245: 125–36.

Wheeler, E.P. 1953. *List of Labrador Eskimo Place Names.* Bulletin No. 131, Anthropological Series No. 34. Ottawa: National Museum of Canada.

Whitridge, Peter. 1999a. "The Construction of Social Difference in a Prehistoric Inuit Whaling Community." PhD diss., Arizona State University.

_____. 1999b. "The Prehistory of Inuit and Yupik Whale Use." *Revista de Arqueología Americana* 16: 99–154.

_____. 2002. "Gender, Households, and the Material Construction of Social Difference: Metal Consumption at a Classic Thule Whaling Village." In *Many Faces of Gender: Roles and Relationships Through Time in Indigenous Northern Communities* , edited by L. Frink, R. Shepard, and G. Reinhardt, 165–92. Boulder: University Press of Colorado.

_____. 2004. "Landscapes, Houses, Bodies, Things: 'Place' and the Archaeology of Inuit Imaginaries." *Journal of Archaeological Method and Theory* 11, 2: 213–20.

_____. 2008. "Reimagining the Iglu: Modernity and the Challenge of the Eighteenth Century Labrador Inuit Winter House. *Archaeologies* 4, 2: 288–309.

Witmore, C.L. 2004. "Four Archaeological Engagements with Place: Mediating Bodily Experience through Peripatetic Video." *Visual Anthropology Review* 20, 2: 57–71.

Woollett, James M. 2003. "An Historical Ecology of Labrador Inuit Culture Change." PhD diss., City University of New York.

_____. 2007. "Labrador Inuit Subsistence in the Context of Environmental Change: An Initial Landscape History Perspective." *American Anthropologist* 109, 1: 69–84.

CHAPTER 3

Southern Exposure: The Inuit of Sandwich Bay, Labrador

Lisa Rankin, Matthew Beaudoin, and Natalie Brewster

The Inuit presence in Labrador was not restricted to the North, and while the recently established boundaries of Nunatsiavut define a modern geopolitical unit and represent a "new chapter" in Labrador Inuit history, they do not fully demonstrate the breadth of Inuit influence in the historical development of southern Labrador, a region generally considered to be outside the core Inuit settlement zone. Nevertheless, a lengthy and significant Inuit presence in southern Labrador is now being documented by both historical and archaeological research. This is not altogether unexpected, as it was to southern Labrador that the Inuit first travelled to retrieve desirable European commodities from seasonal European whaling stations, and much of the early contact between Inuit and Europeans took place in the south before the establishment of Moravian missions in the north. Ultimately, many Inuit chose to remain in the south, often marrying European settlers. In this manner Inuit of southern Labrador played a significant role in the emergence of new economic and cultural traditions that are now associated with Inuit-Métis society in the south. The blended culture pattern that emerged from the union of Inuit and European populations maintained strong ties to Inuit traditions, and it is the enduring legacy of Inuit of southern Labrador that has defined the Inuit-Métis culture from the eighteenth to the twenty-first century.

Ongoing historical and archaeological investigations associated with the Porcupine Strand Archaeology Project in the Sandwich Bay region of Labrador have begun to shed light on the rich Inuit history south of Nunatsiavut. This research aims to help resolve the timing and nature of early Inuit settlement in southern Labrador, an issue that has been the focus of academic debate for some time. The long-term impact of the southern Labrador Inuit is also being examined in relation to the development of the Inuit-Métis population in this region.

At Issue: The Nature of the Inuit Presence in Southern Labrador

As early as the sixteenth century, Basque and Breton fishermen and whalers were operating in the vicinity of southern Labrador. Europeans would occasionally encounter Inuit in southern Labrador, and from 1588 sporadic references to these encounters have been recovered from historical documents (Stopp 2002). Whether Inuit travelled south specifically to acquire European goods or whether their presence in the south was part of their general expansion along the Labrador coast is not yet understood, but historical documentation indicates that both Inuit and Europeans were present in southern Labrador by the sixteenth century. The nature of Inuit settlement in southern Labrador does not appear to have been questioned by the early explorers, whalers, and fishermen, who wrote largely about the nature of the encounters between the two populations, which often resulted in violent action by one or both groups. However, these early European populations were seasonal visitors to the Labrador coast, and the permanence and nature of Inuit settlement in the south may not have been of great concern to them.

European concerns changed following the Treaty of Utrecht in 1713, which gave France the right to establish shore-based fishing premises, and ultimately settlements, along the southern coast of Labrador and to thereby take advantage of a wider variety of seasonally abundant resources. To maximize their profits, the French first encouraged trade with Inuit, who were able to provide valuable commodities such as whale bone, baleen, and seal and eider down. This trade ensured Inuit participation in the growing global economy (Auger 1991, 9; Kaplan 1983, 165–68; 1985, 58; Trudel 1978, 103–04; 1980, 137; Zimmerly 1975, 46–47). But European settlement in the south made life more complicated for Inuit because they had to compete directly with the French, who chose to establish their settlements at profitable seal-hunting locales (Auger 1991, 28–30; Trudel 1978, 117–118). Documentation from this period makes frequent reference to Inuit attacks (Stopp 2002, 80–81), and there were regular requests to the French government to send troops and establish forts along the southern coast to discourage Inuit raids.

Likewise, the English, who gained control of the southern Labrador coast after the fall of New France in 1763, were concerned for the safety of their seasonal fishing fleets when they encountered Inuit. The initial response of the British was to ban permanent European settlement in the region. This was done largely to minimize competition for lucrative fishing grounds between permanent settlers and seasonal fishers, but the ban also aimed to improve relations with Inuit by establishing a trade protocol for items such as furs and oils and to thereby decrease hostile encounters that threatened the seasonal cod fishery (Auger 1991, 10; Brice-Bennett 1981, 12–13; Loring and Cabak 2000, 4–5; Hiller 1977, 84; Kaplan 1983, 169; 1985, 64; Zimmerly 1975, 41). Nevertheless, it soon became apparent that there was money to be made in other seasonal industries, such as salmon fishing and sealing, and within a few years English merchants began to re-populate the coast, albeit with annual re-supply and staff from Britain. By 1771 the British had allowed Moravian missionaries to establish permanent stations in northern Labrador in order to convert Inuit to Christianity while drawing them north toward European goods and away from English activities in the south. By the time permanent European settlement was firmly established along the southern coast in the nineteenth century, most Inuit had withdrawn to the northern mission stations, and an understanding of the early Inuit tenure in southern Labrador began to fade, only to re-emerge as the focus of academic debate in the late twentieth century ("The Inuit of Southern Québec-Labrador" 1980).

At issue in this debate was the timing and permanency of Inuit settlement south of Hamilton Inlet. Scholars wondered whether Inuit presence in southern Labrador was seasonal, and, if so, whether it was undertaken for the limited purpose of meeting and trading with European fishermen, or perhaps for stealing from them or pilfering their camps ("The Inuit of Southern Québec-Labrador" 1980; Stopp 2002, 72). By 1885 entomologist and paleontologist A.S. Packard had already presented documentary evidence that Inuit had once been very numerous in southern Labrador and the Gulf of St. Lawrence (1885). The early opposing view, presented by W.G. Gosling in his 1910 history of Labrador, claimed that Inuit were not present at all in the Strait of Belle Isle region before the appearance of Europeans, and after that only on a seasonal basis, for the sole purpose of trade (18).

The more recent debate has tended until recently to favour the view presented by Gosling. In 1974 J. Garth Taylor indicated that there was insufficient archival and archaeological evidence to judge whether Inuit who were encountered in southern Labrador during the early European expansion there were permanent residents or simply seasonal visitors. In the eighteenth century, however, he noted that very few Inuit wintered south of Hamilton

Inlet, with the exception of a few families who resided in Table Bay (1974, 6–7). With regard to the possibility of a pre-European Inuit presence in southern Labrador, Taylor stated in 1980 that there was little evidence for any Inuit activity in southern Labrador prior to European contact (193). This view was echoed by most archaeologists of the time, as typified by Richard Jordan (1977, 43; 1978, 176), who pointed to a lack of Thule or Inuit winter houses in the Strait of Belle Isle as evidence that the Inuit ventured south of Hamilton Inlet only in the summer.

In 2002 Marianne Stopp revisited this issue and noted that the documentary evidence suggested an Inuit presence in southern Labrador from the mid-seventeenth century that was comparable to that in northern Labrador: a year-round, multi-activity use of the area in keeping with mobile northern forager strategies rather than seasonal, special-purpose visits. The archaeological evidence, while not plentiful, also indicated year-round occupation. In Stopp's opinion, the combination of archival and archaeological evidence made "a good case" for year-round Inuit residence in southern Labrador and along the Quebec north shore from the mid-1500s to the mid-1700s (2002, 96). This was somewhat at odds with the conclusions of the only in-depth archaeological study conducted by Reginald Auger (1991), which concluded that there was no archaeological evidence for Inuit settlement in the Strait of Belle Isle prior to the 1700s. Nevertheless, his excavation of a sod house at Chateau Bay did provide evidence of Inuit winter residence in the 1760s.

As Stopp's article was being published, the Porcupine Strand Archaeology Project began work in the Sandwich Bay region. At Snack Cove, on the outer coast of Sandwich Bay, the project recovered evidence of multi-season Inuit occupation in southern Labrador during the mid-seventeenth century (Brewster 2006, 2008; Rankin 2004, 2006, 2009a). Simultaneous excavations at North River recovered evidence of nineteenth century Métis settlement that was strongly influenced by Inuit traditions (Beaudoin 2008). It thus seems that emerging archaeological data support the notion advanced by Stopp that the early Inuit presence in southern Labrador may have been comparable in nature to that further north, and its influence as enduring.

The Sandwich Bay Region

At thirty kilometres long and twenty kilometres wide, Sandwich Bay is the second largest bay on the Labrador coast. It is located approximately sixty-five kilometres south of Hamilton Inlet, the region considered by some to be the southern limit of year-round Inuit settlement (Jordan and Kaplan 1980, 39). The bay opens up into a region that contains several diverse ecological landscapes, including the rocky headland of Hare Harbour to the southeast

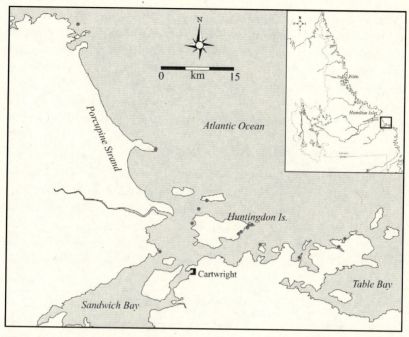

Figure 1. *Map of Sandwich Bay region.*

and a sixty-kilometre-long stretch of sandy beach known as the Porcupine Strand to the north that links Sandwich Bay to Hamilton Inlet (Figure 1). There are also three major rivers in this region: the Paradise and Eagle Rivers, which drain into the base of Sandwich Bay, and the North River, located just north of the bay mouth at the base of the Porcupine Strand. These three rivers not only are prime salmon-spawning rivers but also were regularly used throughout the historic era as travel routes into the interior. The shoreline of the greater region is flanked by islands that provide access to the outer coast.

Aside from salmon there is a wide diversity of animal resources available in this region, including grey, harbour, harp, ringed, hooded, and bearded seals, several species of whale, black bear, and polar bear, caribou, wolf, fox, several small fur bearing mammals, and at least 250 species of birds (King 1983; Peterson 1966; Spiess 1993; Todd 1963). A variety of marine and freshwater fish can be found, including important species such as members of the cod family, salmon, capelin, Arctic char, and sculpin. Plant species including blueberries, crowberries, and cloud berries, along with lichen, cover large swaths of ground in this forest-tundra zone, but large stands of white and black spruce are also present. Most resources are abundant between spring and fall. However, several species over-winter in the region, and local polynyas and ice-edge hunting allow access to marine resources throughout the year. As a result, Inuit travelling to and settling in this region would have encountered a rich ecosystem, though one subject to extreme seasonal fluctuation. While heavily forested in parts, the physical landscape and environment would not have been considerably different from that which they encountered elsewhere in Labrador, particularly in Hamilton Inlet.

Archaeology of the Inuit in Sandwich Bay

Data gathered from the Newfoundland and Labrador provincial archaeology office site record database, publications, and archived field notes refer to the discovery of twenty-nine Inuit sites in the Sandwich Bay region that date from the mid-sixteenth to late nineteenth century. In reality, few of these sites have been subject to in-depth investigation, and their classification as Inuit sites remains tentative at best. For example, several sites have

Table 1. *Confirmed Inuit sites in the Sandwich Bay region.*

Site	Evidence
GbBi-19	Boulder tent rings, stone caches, hunting blinds, rock crevice burials
F1BF-02	Boulder houses, boulder caches, graves, stone fox trap
FkBg-03	Sod houses (semi-subterranean with entrance passages)
FkBg-34	Tent rings, possible sod houses
FkBf-01	Tent rings, cache
FkBf-02	Tent ring, caches, fox trap
FkBe-01	Tent rings with intact hearths
FkBe-03	Sod houses (semi-subterranean with entrance passages), cache, burials
FkBe-06	Tent rings with intact hearths
FkBe-08	Cache, fox trap, box hearth
FkBe-16	Burial
FkBd-10	Stone fox trap
FkBd-20	Sod houses (semi-subterranean filled by an old growth of trees)
Cape Porcupine	Sod house, earthenware pottery sherd
Dumpling Island	Sod house, Inuit-carved bone pendant

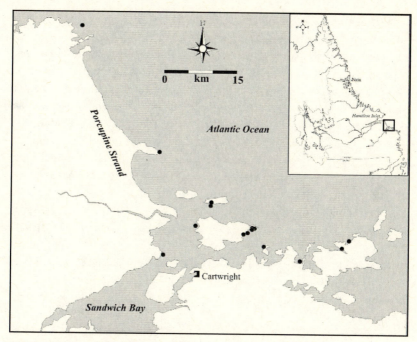

Figure 2. *Map of confirmed Inuit sites in Sandwich Bay region.*

been categorized as Inuit because they contain European material culture manufactured prior to the European settlement of Sandwich Bay in the late eighteenth century, while others have been referenced as Inuit solely on a single Inuit-style feature, such as a boulder storage cache. While future excavation of these sites may well prove that they were settled by Inuit occupants, the possibility that they result from European or even Innu activity remains. As a result, they have been removed from the current analysis. This leaves fifteen sites from which to evaluate Inuit settlement of Sandwich Bay (see Table 1 and Figure 2).

The fifteen sites span the length and breadth of the Sandwich Bay region and are most heavily concentrated on the islands and outer headlands. It is interesting to note that no Inuit sites have been recorded inside Sandwich Bay proper, but this area is heavily forested and, as a result, has not been the subject of intensive archaeological survey. Nevertheless, a full range of Inuit activities can be associated with the sites that have been recorded, including spring-through-fall settlement (tent rings), fall/winter settlement (semi-subterranean sod and boulder dwellings), hunting activities (fox traps and blinds), storage (caches), and burials.

Dating these sites is difficult, and in most cases dates must remain speculative until further investigation is conducted. Several sites, however, are suggestive of particular periods and appear to indicate the continued presence of Inuit in the Sandwich Bay region over several centuries. The site of Cape Porcupine, though perhaps the least understood, offers great potential for an early date. In 2003 the Porcupine Strand Archaeology Project noted a single semi-subterranean sod house here while conducting a helicopter survey. No further research was undertaken at this locale, but in 2009 Canadian Armed Forces personnel conducting munitions sweeps on the cape collected a single fragment of earthenware pottery in proximity to this house (Figure 3). The pottery has since been submitted for analysis by mass spectrometer, in hopes of verifying pottery type, source, and age. However, it is believed that the sherd is most likely to be a portion of Pabu-Guingamp earthenware manufactured in Brittany in the late seventeenth or early eighteenth century. Its association with the Inuit house on Cape Porcupine suggests that it was acquired by Inuit in the Strait of Belle Isle or the Newfoundland Petit Nord, which were frequented by Breton fishermen at this time (Peter Pope, pers. comm. 2009).

Several other sites provide some evidence of continued Inuit settlement in the region. William Fitzhugh's 1986 archaeological survey located two boulder houses at FlBf-02 in Baird Cove that were similar in style to Inuit houses recorded at Black Island in Hamilton Inlet that dated to the seventeenth and eighteenth centuries (Fitzhugh 1989, 168). At FkBg-03, in Indian Harbour, the remains of four semi-subterranean sod houses with long entrance passages have been found (Rankin 2009b). Archaeological testing undertaken in one of the structures revealed an iron spike and seal bone. The shape and size of the houses vary, suggesting that the site was re-visited over time. Two shallow houses measuring approximately five metres wide by four metres long have entrance passages approximately five metres long that join together. These structures closely resemble the Thule structures illustrated by Susan Kaplan (1983, 221), and it is presumed that they are the earliest structures at the site. The two other houses are much bigger (eight metres long and six metres wide) and have a rectangular form. They also appear to have shorter entrance passages, approximately three metres in length. The size and shape of these larger houses, along with the presence of at least one historic European artifact, suggest that they date to the late eighteenth century (see Kaplan 1983, 230–236). Excavation that began at this site in 2009 should add further detail. Finally, at FkBf-1 on Huntingdon Island, the remains of a nineteenth-century ceramic sherd were found in association with tent rings and a hearth, suggesting that Inuit occupation in Sandwich Bay persisted for some time.

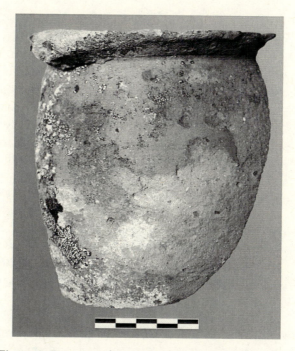

Figure 3. *Breton earthenware potsherd, Cape Porcupine.*

No other area in the Sandwich Bay region has the density of Inuit settlement that is found on the seaward end of Huntingdon Island. Here a series
of five Inuit sites are dispersed over the landscape. A further four sites are
located in nearby Hare Harbour. While more archaeological survey has been
undertaken in this part of Sandwich Bay than in other locales, it is unlikely
that these two clusters of sites are anomalous, given that over half of the
confirmed Inuit settlements are located here. In this part of Sandwich Bay,
the shallow marine shelf emerges from the present beach terrace and rapidly
gives way to a deep sea channel. Together, these geological features provide
easy access to the diversity of marine life traditionally exploited by the Inuit.
As well, the Hare Harbour sites are situated to take advantage of a small over-
land portage to Table Bay. This route would have provided faster and safer
access to more southerly regions than rounding the Cape North peninsula by
sea. Finally, this area may have been strategically selected for settlement by
Inuit during the contact period because it would be the first point of contact
for Inuit in the Sandwich Bay region wishing to trade among the European
ships entering or passing the bay.

For these reasons the Porcupine Strand Archaeology Project selected two Inuit sites from the eastern limits of Huntingdon Island to be extensively examined. Between 2003 and 2005 three semi-subterranean Inuit sod houses were excavated at Snack Cove 3 (FkBe-3), as was a single large tent ring from the nearby settlement of Snack Cove 1 (FkBe-1). The investigation of these sites has revealed much of what we know about Inuit settlement of the region.

FkBe-3 is a large settlement containing a minimum of four semi-subterranean sod-walled houses, a series of kayak supports, rock-walled and subterranean caches, and nearby boulder burials. Excavation of three of the houses revealed three single room dwellings of similar design all oriented toward the beach (Figure 4). Each house was approximately six metres wide (side wall to side wall), and three metres long (front to back). They were lined with flat paving stones and had been roofed with timber and sods. Sleeping platforms varied in number and position between houses (one rear platform in Houses 1 and 2, and a rear and side platform in House 3). All the houses contained a long, straight entrance passage with cold trap. These entryways were approximately five metres in length and emerged from the centre of the house (Figure 5). None of the houses had outdoor middens, but all three contained interior wall middens, as well as other interior features such as storage niches, and either lamp stands or sooty residues from lamp use. Generally, the houses look very much like pre-contact Thule dwellings from northern Labrador as well as houses found in Hamilton Inlet at Eskimo Island 3, which date to the seventeenth century (Kaplan 1983, 220–31).

Semi-subterranean dwellings were generally occupied between fall and spring. Thus far, faunal analysis of approximately 2500 animal bones excavated from Houses 1 and 2 has been completed and suggests that these houses were occupied largely during the autumn. The collection was dominated by juvenile harp seal, fox, caribou, and ptarmigan, all species that are abundant during the fall. The best evidence is provided by the juvenile harp seal, who would have migrated south past Snack Cove in the autumn towards their winter breeding grounds. No newborn harp seal were recovered, thereby reducing the likelihood of a spring occupation of these dwellings.

Material culture recovered through excavation includes traditional Inuit artifacts such as ground stone end blades and several worked bone items (Brewster 2006, 23). However, these objects were recovered alongside a minimal number of European items, many of which were modified into traditional Inuit tools. For example, several iron nails had been fashioned into end blades, while other metals had been used as ulu blades that were fitted with whalebone handles (Figure 6). Pottery fragments appear to have been used as oil lamps (Brewster 2006, 26). The inclusion of European items

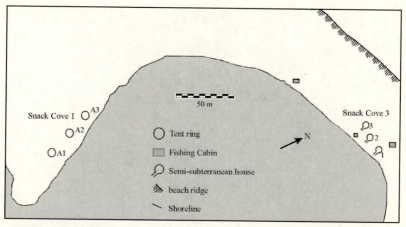

Figure 4. *Map of Snack Cove 3.*

in the material cultural assemblage indicates a post-contact date, but the presence of traditional stone and bone implements, the modification of European materials to suit traditional needs, and the limited number and variety of European items (fewer than 150 items combined from the three houses) suggest the site was occupied in the early post-contact period, prior to regular interaction with Europeans.

Figure 5. *Photo of House 3, Snack Cove 3, after excavation.*

Figure 6. *Ulu recovered from House 2, Snack Cove 3,*
with whale bone handle and iron blade.

Radiocarbon dates run on organic material recovered from Houses 1 and 2 place site occupation between the mid-fifteenth and seventeenth centuries, but carbon-dating material from this time period, and within this region, presents its own set of problems. The marine reservoir effect, the probable presence of contaminants such as seal fat on organic materials, the regular use of driftwood for hearths and construction, and Inuit use of curated bone objects and wood all contribute to the difficulties of acquiring reliable dates (Rankin 2009a, 17). As a result, several dating methods were combined to situate the period of occupation at Snack Cove 3: radio carbon dates, manufacture dates for European pottery, and chronologies of Inuit architecture styles (Brewster 2006, 27–28; Kaplan 1983, 220–50). Together these techniques suggest an occupation date between CE 1625 and CE 1650 and place Snack Cove 3 within the early contact period.

On a cobble ridge approximately 250 metres north of Snack Cove 3 are the remains of three Inuit tent rings that make up the site of Snack Cove 1. Originally found by Fitzhugh in 1986, the Porcupine Strand Archaeology Project excavated a single tent ring (Tent Ring A1) at this site in 2004 (Fitzhugh 1989) (Figure 7). Structure A1 measures 12.5 metres by 6 metres and is divided into two unequal-size areas or rooms by an arc-shaped line of rocks. The largest segment contains a U-shaped hearth and a small segment of slab floor representing an activity area. The smaller room has no visible features. The dwelling resembles the tent structures dating to the Early Period (CE 1450–1700) of Thule/Inuit culture history that were recorded on Sculpin Island near Nain (Fitzhugh 1989; Kaplan 1983). Structure 15 at Sculpin Island was also divided into two rooms and appears to have been used in a similar fashion, with one room reserved for sleeping and the other used as working and living space (Kaplan 1983).

Because Snack Cove 1 is located on a cobble beach terrace and was primarily a surface site, few artifacts or faunal remains were recovered. The hearth feature did include mussel shell and a few seal and ptarmigan bones. The two artifacts recovered under the tent floor had leached into the cobbles beneath the structure and were found by carefully removing the surface boulders during excavation. The first artifact was a lead pendant similar to those found by James Bird (1945) in association with a grave at Iglosoataligarsuk in the Hopedale region. Unfortunately, Bird's material was not well dated, so the artifact offers little help in dating Snack Cove 1. The other artifact was a fragment of a harpoon fore shaft worked from mammal bone. Together the artifacts and fauna tell us little about the daily lives of the occupants, but the ephemeral quality of the tent ring and the appearance

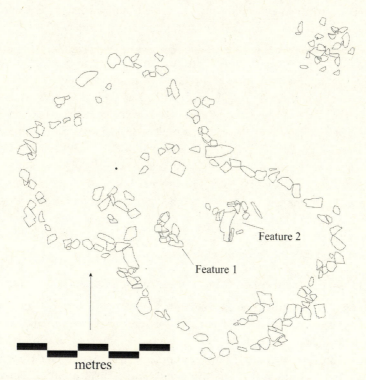

Feature 2

Feature 1

metres

Figure 7. *Plan of Tent Ring A1 at Snack Cove 1.*

of mussel shell confirm warm-season occupation (April through October). The form and layout of the tent ring suggest that the structure was erected between CE 1450 and 1700, while the presence of a lead pendant indicates a date toward the end of this period. Fitzhugh (1994) was able to extract carbon samples from the U-shaped hearths in structures A1 and A3 that returned dates between CE 1333 and CE 1637, but given the aforementioned problems with radio carbon dating Inuit settlements on the Labrador coast, these dates are of little use on their own.

Since both Snack Coves 1 and 3 contain minimal amounts of contact period material, traditional tool forms, and architectural elements indicative of the seventeenth century, it seems plausible that Snack Coves 1 and 3 were inhabited by the same population that occupied the sites sometime between CE 1625 and CE 1700 (Brewster 2006, 34). This group likely moved from the warm-season tent rings into the semi-subterranean houses in the autumn, spending several months on Huntingdon Island before moving elsewhere or to snow houses for the winter months. The broad range of features associated with the two settlements suggests that the primary activities were undertaken during their stay, including hunting for land and sea mammals, fishing, storing surplus, and, more rarely, burying those who had passed away. The occupants of the Snack Cove sites continued to use traditional materials to create their toolkit, but they were also exploiting European material that was re-worked into traditional forms. There is nothing to indicate that the European goods were acquired through formalized trade (for example, there are no trade beads present), and the items recovered could have been easily scavenged. It is therefore not likely that Inuit of Snack Cove chose to inhabit the locale for the specific purpose of trading with Europeans, since foreign materials were not present in abundance. It is more likely that the area was, by the seventeenth century, part of the greater Inuit settlement system. In fact, the data from these two sites, combined with archaeological survey data from other sites in the vicinity, suggests that Inuit were regular occupants of the Sandwich Bay region by the mid-seventeenth century and that they could be found in the region throughout the annual cycle.

European Exploration and Settlement of Sandwich Bay

Beginning in the late seventeenth century, Europeans ventured northwards in exploration of the Labrador coast and made several reports relating to Inuit in Sandwich Bay. In 1694 Louis Jolliet made his second of two voyages to Hamilton Inlet and noted Inuit encampments in the Sandwich Bay region (Delanglez 1948; Stopp 2002). In 1743 Louis Fornel made a similar journey and referred to the entire coast between Alexis Bay and Hamilton Inlet as

La Coste des Eskimaux, distinguishing Inuit occupants of that region from the inhabitants of the French and Jersey fishing stations located south of Cape Charles (Stopp 2002, 76). His narratives also describe Inuit in Hare Harbour portaging from the Sandwich Bay region over the peninsula to Table Bay to avoid the dangerous sea surrounding Cape North (Handcock 2007, 13).

By 1775 merchant and adventurer George Cartwright had established several premises in the Sandwich Bay region. His journals make many references to Inuit in Sandwich Bay with whom he traded, visited, and occasionally camped. John Kennedy (1995, 84) notes that Cartwright failed to state whether this population was permanent or perhaps just drawn there by Cartwright's presence. Many Inuit travelled south during this period to acquire firearms, which were not supplied by the Moravians in the north until 1780 (Kaplan 1983, 171). Ultimately, relations between Cartwright, his men, and Inuit women they encountered in Sandwich Bay resulted in several offspring (Kennedy 1995, 44). It is not known if these offspring were the women who married the first generation of permanent British settlers in the early nineteenth century (Kennedy 1995, 44), but it was about this time that the Inuit-Métis society that continues to dominate the cultural landscape in this region was established.

The permanent European settlement of southern Labrador (without legislated re-supply from Britain) began between 1830 and 1870, when the merchants began to voluntarily provide their former servants with the necessary supplies for fishing, trapping, and sealing on credit (Kennedy 1995, 72–73). Reports indicate that very few European women resided in Labrador at this time (Thornton 1977). Bishop Field, who visited the southern coast between Battle Harbour and Sandwich Bay in 1848, recorded only one English woman in the region. Therefore, the men generally took Inuit or Inuit-Métis wives. These wives may well have been drawn from the resident population of Inuit that was present in the region during Cartwright's time in Sandwich Bay, but other possibilities exist: enclaves of Inuit may have been established in the south after they were banished from Moravian mission stations due to moral infractions; Inuit may have voluntarily ventured south from northern or central Labrador to populate the region; or Inuit middlemen positioned to take advantage of earlier European trade protocols may have chosen to remain in the south after the establishment of the mission stations (Kennedy 1995, 84). David Anderson (1984, 37) also mentions that, until 1869, Inuit brought from Nain were hired to work for merchants such as Hunt in Sandwich Bay because the resident population was not large enough to sustain the economic viability of trading posts. Whatever the situation,

E. Feild (1848a) records that "many of the occupants of Sandwich Bay are pure Eskimaux, but the majority are Anglo-Eskimaux." As a result, the prayers and hymns of church service in the summer of 1848 were conducted predominantly in Inuktitut (Feild 1848b).

The Archaeology of the Inuit-Métis in Sandwich Bay

In 2001 and 2002 the Porcupine Strand Archaeology Project tested a sod dwelling (FkBg-24) located near the mouth of North River at the southern end of the Porcupine Strand (Rankin 2002, 2003). The material culture recovered from the test units indicated a late-nineteenth-century occupation. Further research suggested that the house belonged to Charles Williams, a settler from Plymouth, England, whose family was listed as the only residents of North River on Reichel's 1872 map of the region. Williams was believed to have married twice before his death in 1879 at the age of seventy-one. A marriage licence located in the Anglican Archives at Memorial University lists Mr. Williams as a widower when he married Mary McPherson, a local woman of Scottish and Inuit parentage, in August of 1848 on Dumpling Island. This union suggests that the Williams/McPherson family was one of the earliest ethnically mixed families in the region. Tombstones in the North River cemetery indicate that the couple had several children and stayed in this location until both Charles and Mary had passed away (Beaudoin 2008).

In 2007 the Williams home was excavated in order to gain insight into the culture patterns of the early Inuit-Métis families in the region (Beaudoin 2008). The excavation garnered data concerning the architecture, foodways, and domestic life of the household and demonstrated that British and Inuit traditions were amalgamated. Unexcavated, the surface of the dwelling looked much like any Late Period Inuit house, with high-banked sod walls surrounding a rectangular house floor. Upon excavation, it was determined that the house was actually built in a European tradition. Measuring ten metres by four metres, the house had a timber frame held together with iron nails and spikes. Sods had been used to cover the exterior for insulation. There was at least one glass window and a single ground-level door with an iron latch in the southern wall. A large midden, laden with the remains of seal and caribou, as well as fish and small mammal, was found immediately outside the doorway. A saw pit was visible to the rear of the structure. The house interior contained a single room with no evidence of partitions, but various features and activity areas were present. An iron stove had been placed on a platform in the centre of the north wall. Concentrations of artifacts, including barrel hoops, chest strapping, and large numbers of faunal remains, were found in the east end of the structure, which was used for

Figure 8. *Inuit Métis house at North River after excavation. Stone feature furthest from camera is the foundation for a stove.*

storage and likely sleeping, while the west end of the structure contained a cellar pit and open work space littered with glass beads (Beaudoin 2008) (Figure 8).

The material culture assemblage included 6158 items. This was used to date the occupation of the structure from the mid-to-late nineteenth century, consistent with the documentary evidence. A knife handle engraved with the letters "WI" (Figure 9) helped to confirm that this was the Williams home. The artifacts were used to interpret the daily activities of the householders, which generally broke down along gender lines. For example, the remains of at least four different guns, a pressure activated leg-trap, fishing gear, and whale bone sled runners found in the home were interpreted as men's items used in the procurement of subsistence resources and trade commodities (Beaudoin 2008). Overall, few items associated with male tasks were recovered (approximately 7 percent of the assemblage). This is likely because men worked away from the home much of the time hunting, fishing, and trapping, and most of their gear would have been stored closer to the locations in which they were used (Beaudoin 2008).

The house, once constructed, appears to have been the realm of the female members of the household, who remained home to raise children when their husbands were away. Most of the material culture recovered inside the dwelling reflects their domestic roles. Domestic items constituted approximately 50 percent of the total assemblage and included items related to food preparation and consumption, such as ceramic dishes (several of which were repaired using mending holes), cutlery, and cooking pots (Beaudoin 2008). Hollowware bowls and mugs dominated the identifiable ceramic collection

Figure 9. *Broken knife from Inuit Métis house at North River.*

(51 percent), suggesting a preference for liquid-based meals such as soups and stews (Otto 1977; Loring and Cabak 2000). Flatware, at 7 percent, was poorly represented. Several pieces of worked antler were also present, with many of them functioning as pot handles. Another significant female task was the manufacture, mending, and adorning of clothing. Items representing this activity included thimbles, buttons, beads, fabric, and decorative pendants.

By comparing the architecture, organization of internal and external space, artifacts, and fauna recovered from FkBg-24 to the archaeologically documented Inuit and European sites dating to the eighteenth and nineteenth centuries in coastal Labrador, it is possible to suggest a hybrid culture pattern for this Inuit-Métis family. The architectural traditions used at the Williams home were largely European: timber framing and floors, internal cellars, and latched, ground-level doorways are found at a variety of nineteenth-century European homes on the Labrador coast (Burke 1991; Temple 2006). This is not surprising, given that the construction of the home was likely undertaken by Williams. Nevertheless, FkBg-24 had a large midden outside the entry-way. This feature has not been documented at any of the European sites in Labrador, but is common at Inuit sites through the nineteenth century (Auger 1991; Cabak 1991; Wollett 2003). Furthermore, the Williams house lacked the internal partitioning generally found in European structures, which is uncommon in Inuit dwellings from the period (Auger 1991; Schledermann 1972; Woollett 2003). Given that Inuit-descendent women managed the home, the latter features likely reflect their ideal use of domestic space.

The assemblage of domestic artifacts is also much more in keeping with assemblages recovered from late-eighteenth and nineteenth-century Inuit dwellings in Labrador. By this time, Inuit-occupied houses had begun to show the influence of European commodities, tastes, and values (Whitridge 2008), but the domestic assemblage remained distinct from those found in European households, suggesting that Inuit domestic traditions were not simply abandoned but were adapted to accommodate new circumstances (Cabak 1991).

For example, the abundance of hollowware vessels found in both the Williams residence and at contemporary Inuit sites indicates a preference for liquid-based meals such as soups and stews. This demonstrates continuity with Inuit foodways, which relied on similar meals prepared in soapstone bowls for group consumption (Loring and Cabak 2000). The use of mending holes to repair broken crockery also has antecedents in Inuit tradition (Jurakic 2007). Finally, the quantity of glass beads found inside the house suggests that, like Inuit women elsewhere in Labrador, the women of the Williams home chose this adornment for embroidery to indicate their status (Beaudoin 2008). The domestic items recovered from FkBg-24 therefore reflect the tasks and choices of the women of the household and suggest that they were maintaining the domestic traditions learnt from their Inuit mothers. It is not known if the women directly selected the goods to be brought into the household, but Melanie Cabak (1991) reports that Labrador Inuit women were shrewd bargainers who conducted the majority of trade with the merchants. If the women in the Williams household were able to select their own domestic items, it may help to explain the retention of Inuit traditions reflected in the assemblage.

The tools associated with male activities largely mirror those seen at other European sites (Beaudoin 2008). However, evidence of trapping during this period has been recorded at only one other site to date—the Inuit site of Tuglavina (Schledermann 1972). Trapping gained greater economic significance during the nineteenth century, when both Inuit and settler families participated in this industry. The use of whale bone sled runners, which facilitated work on the traplines, suggests that the male occupants of the Williams home were adopting local Inuit technologies to aid their economic pursuits.

The faunal remains recovered from the house and associated midden reflect the procurement and consumption patterns of the entire household and suggest that seal and land mammals were most significant to the family's diet. The percentage of different species recovered at FkBg-24 was similar to faunal assemblages recorded at Inuit sites and reflects the Inuit subsistence pattern (Auger 1991; Beaudoin 2008; Wollett 2003). This is distinct from the subsistence assemblages from European settlements on the Labrador coast, which indicate a preference for domesticated animals and wild birds (Burke 1991). The Williams family was no doubt trading valuable subsistence commodities such as salmon to the merchants and subsisting on other wildfoods that they were able to hunt and gather. This process ensured that their diet was more closely aligned with Inuit foodways, and, as stated above, the preparation of these local foods also allowed the women of the home to maintain their Inuit traditions.

The excavation at FkBg-24 demonstrates the importance of both English and Inuit traditions in the daily life of the Inuit-Métis in southern Labrador. The cultural influences break down largely along gender lines. The activities performed by men, while informed by local Inuit knowledge, are more in keeping with European customs, and the tasks performed by women are strongly influenced by Inuit tradition. The persistence of the Inuit culture pattern is most obvious in the domestic realm, where Inuit-descendent women ensured that Inuit traditions were passed to their children. In this manner, Inuit culture continued to be a prominent component of southern Labrador society.

Conclusion

The results of research undertaken by the Porcupine Strand Archaeology Project, when combined with other archaeological and historical data, suggest that Inuit have had a significant presence in the Sandwich Bay region since the early seventeenth century and prior to European settlement in the region. The permanency of this settlement can be debated, as many different Inuit families may have travelled to and resided in the region over time. However, Stopp (2002) indicates that "permanency" was not a significant component in the lives of Labrador Inuit prior to nineteenth-century mission settlement. Before this time, Inuit, like other hunting/fishing/foraging people, made frequent excursions to different regions for differing purposes throughout the year. Even so, there is mounting evidence that Inuit of Sandwich Bay were able to fulfill many of their annual requirements within the region.

The Inuit way of life changed considerably during their occupation of Sandwich Bay in response to the social and economic circumstances they faced. The earliest settlements, like those at Snack Cove, mirror those in northern Labrador. While Inuit may have expanded into the south to acquire European iron and other items, the location and temporary nature of the early occupations appears to have resulted predominantly from a desire for access to local, seasonally abundant natural resources. By the early eighteenth century, Inuit in Sandwich Bay were well positioned to take advantage of trade opportunities resulting from the French occupation of the southern coast. Between the establishment of British rule in 1763 and the development of northern Moravian mission stations soon after, settlement in southern Labrador may have become more precarious for Inuit. Distanced from the British occupation, Sandwich Bay may have become a safe haven for those Inuit who did not wish to settle permanently in the north. These Inuit quickly took advantage of the trade opportunities that presented themselves in this region with the arrival of Cartwright, seemingly spending much of the year in the vicinity of his settlements. Permanent European and British settlement of the Labrador coast in the nineteenth century brought a new set of opportunities, and once again Inuit adapted to the new circumstances rapidly, marrying settlers and pursuing economic opportunities provided by local merchants. Throughout it all, many Inuit traditions were maintained, as exemplified by the domestic practices of the Williams household.

Inuit adaptation to historical circumstances in Sandwich Bay is no less of an achievement than that witnessed in the north, nor is their adjustment to the cultural adaptations that must have taken place as their Thule ancestors encountered new situations while colonizing the Arctic generations earlier. Resilience is a hallmark of Inuit culture, and the contemporary Inuit-Métis who now occupy Sandwich Bay represent the enduring legacy of this culture in southern Labrador. They continue to demonstrate the importance of Inuit culture in the development of the southern coast.

Acknowledgements

We would like to thank the editors of this volume for allowing us to contribute and for all their work bringing it to fruition. We also acknowledge the generous support of the Social Sciences and Humanities Research Council of Canada, the Northern Scientific Training Program and the Provincial Archaeology Office of Newfoundland and Labrador, and the NunatuKavut Community Council. Finally, none of this work would have seen the light of day if not for the assistance of the fantastic archaeology crews associated with our work in Sandwich Bay. Any errors or omissions remain our responsibility. Maps and photos by Lisa Rankin.

References

Anderson, David. 1984. "The Development of Settlement in Southern Coastal Labrador with Particular Reference to Sandwich Bay." *Bulletin of Canadian Studies* 8, 1: 23–49.

Auger, Reginald. 1991. *Labrador Inuit and Europeans in the Strait of Belle Isle: From the Written Sources to the Archaeological Evidence.* Nordicana 55. Quebec City: Centre d'Études Nordiques, Université Laval.

Beaudoin, Matthew. 2008. "Sweeping the Floor: An Archaeological Examination of a Multi-ethnic Sod House in Labrador (FkBg-24)." Master's thesis, Memorial University of Newfoundland.

Bird, Junius B. 1945. *Archaeology of the Hopedale Area, Labrador.* Anthropological Papers of the American Museum of Natural History 39, 2. New York: American Museum of Natural History.

Brewster, Natalie. 2006. *The Inuit in Southern Labrador: The View from Snack Cove.* Occasional Papers in Northeastern Archaeology No. 15. St. John's: Copetown Press.

_____. 2008. "The Archaeology of Snack Cove 1 and Snack Cove 3." *North Atlantic Archaeology* 1: 25–42.

Brice-Bennett, Carol. 1981. "Two Opinions: Inuit and Moravian Missionaries in Labrador 1804–1860." Master's thesis, Memorial University of Newfoundland.

Burke, Charles. 1991. "Nineteenth Century Ceramic Artifacts from a Seasonally Occupied Fishing Station on Saddle Island, Red Bay, Labrador." Master's thesis, Memorial University of Newfoundland.

Cabak, Melanie. 1991. "Inuit Women as Catalysts of Change: An Archaeological study of 19th Century Northern Labrador." PhD diss., University of South Carolina.

Delanglez, Jean. 1948. *The Life and Voyages of Louis Jolliet (1645–1700)*. Chicago: Institute of Jesuit History.

Feild, E. (Bishop). 1848a. "Visitation to Sandwich Bay, Autumn 1848." Report on file with Hans Rollmann. St. John's: Memorial University of Newfoundland.

_____. 1848b. *The (Newfoundland) Times*. 21 October 1848.

Fitzhugh, William. 1989. "Hamilton Inlet and Cartwright Reconnaissance." In *Archaeology in Newfoundland and Labrador 1986: Annual Report #7*, edited by J. Callum Thomson and Jane Sproull Thomson, 164–81. Historic Resources Division, Newfoundland Museum. St. John's: Department of Municipal and Provincial Affairs.

_____. 1994. "Staffe Island 1 and the Northern Labrador Dorset-Thule Succession." In *Threads of Arctic Prehistory: Papers in honour of William E. Taylor, Jr.*, edited by David Morrison and Jean-Luc Pilon, 239–68. Mercury Series No. 149, Archaeological Survey of Canada. Ottawa: National Museum of Man .

Gosling, W.G. 1910. *Labrador: Its discovery, Exploration and Development*. Facsimile edition. Alston Rivers, London: Elibron Classics.

Handcock, Gordon. 2007. "A Cartographic and Toponymic Analysis of the Jens Haven Maps of Coastal Labrador, 1765." In *The 1765 Map of Jens Haven: Linguistic, Toponymic, and Geographical Studies*, edited by Hans Rollmann, 1–23. Report on file. Goose Bay: Labrador Métis Nation.

Hiller, James. 1977. "Moravian Land Holdings on the Labrador Coast: A Brief History." In *Our Footprints Are Everywhere: Inuit Land Use and Occupancy in Labrador*, edited by Carol Brice-Bennett, 83–94. Nain: Labrador Inuit Association.

Jordan, Richard. 1977. "Inuit Occupation of the Central Labrador Coast Since AD 1600. In *Our Footprints Are Everywhere: Inuit Land Use and Occupancy in Labrador*, edited by Carol Brice-Bennett, 43–48. Nain: Labrador Inuit Association.

_____. 1978. "Archaeological Investigations of the Hamilton Inlet Labrador Eskimo: Social and Economic Responses to European Contact." *Arctic Anthropology* 15, 2: 175–85.

Jordan, Richard, and Susan Kaplan. 1980. "An Archaeological View of the Inuit/ European Contact Period in Central Labrador. *Études/Inuit/Studies* 4, 1–2: 35–45.

Jurakic, Irena. 2007. "Up North: European Ceramics and Tobacco Pipes at the Nineteenth-century Contact Period Inuit Winter Village Site of Kongu (IgCv-7), Nachvak Fiord, Northern Labrador." Department of Anthropology. St. John's: Memorial University of Newfoundland.

Kaplan, Susan. 1983. "Economic and Social Change in Labrador Neo-Eskimo culture. PhD diss., Bryn Mawr College.

_____. 1985. "European Goods and Socio-economic Change in Early Labrador Inuit Society. In *Cultures in Contact,* edited by William Fitzhugh, 45–69. Washington, DC: Smithsonian Institution Press.

Kennedy, John C. 1995. *People of the Bays and Headlands: Anthropological History and the Fate of Communities in the Unknown Labrador.* Toronto: University of Toronto Press.

King, Judith E. 1983. *Seals of the World.* 2nd edition. Oxford: Oxford University Press.

Loring, Stephen, and Melanie Cabak. 2000. "A Set of Very Fair Cups and Saucers: Stamped Ceramics as an Example of Inuit Incorporation." *International Journal of Historical Archaeology* 4, 1: 34–52.

Martijn, Charles A. 1980. "The Inuit of southern Quebec-Labrador." Études/ Inuit/Studies 4, 1-2.

Otto, John Solomon. 1977. "Artifacts and Status Differences: A Comparison of Ceramics from Planter, Overseer and Slave Sites on an Antebellum Plantation." In *Research Strategies in Historical Archaeology,* edited by Stanley South, 91–118. New York: Academic Press.

Packard, A.S. 1885. "Notes on the Labrador Eskimo and their Former Range Southward." *American Naturalist* 19: 471–81, 533–560.

Peterson, Randolph, L. 1966. *The Mammals of Eastern Canada.* Oxford: Oxford University Press.

Rankin, Lisa. 2002. *The Porcupine Strand Archaeology Project: Interim Report on the 2001 Field Season.* On File, Provincial Archaeology Office. St. John's: Department of Tourism, Culture and Recreation.

_____. 2003. *The Porcupine Strand Archaeology Project: Interim Report on the 2002 Field Season.* On File, Provincial Archaeology Office. St. John's: Department of Tourism, Culture and Recreation.

_____. 2004. *The Porcupine Strand Archaeology Project: Interim Report on the 2003 Field Season.* On File, Provincial Archaeology Office. St. John's: Department of Tourism, Culture and Recreation.

_____. 2006. *The Porcupine Strand Archaeology Project: Interim Report on the 2004 Field Season.* On File, Provincial Archaeology Office. St. John's: Department of Tourism, Culture and Recreation.

_____. 2009a. *An Archaeological View of the Thule/Inuit Occupation of Labrador.* Goose Bay: Report on File with the Labrador Métis Nation.

_____. 2009b. *The Porcupine Strand Archaeology Project: Interim Report on the 2006 Field Season.* On File, Provincial Archaeology Office. St. John's: Department of Tourism, Culture and Recreation.

Schledermann, Peter. 1972. "The Thule Tradition in Northern Labrador." Master's thesis, Memorial University of Newfoundland.

Spiess, Arthur. 1993. "Caribou, Walrus and Seals: Maritime Archaic Subsistence in Labrador and Newfoundland." In *Archaeology of Eastern North America: Papers in Honour of Stephen Williams,* edited by James B. Stoltman, 73–100. Archaeological Report No. 25. Jackson, MS: Department of Archives and History.

Stopp, Marianne. 2002. "Reconsidering Inuit Presence in Southern Labrador." *Études/Inuit/Studies* 26, 2): 71–106.

Taylor, J. Garth. 1974. *Labrador Eskimo Settlements of the Early Contact Period.* Publications in Ethnology No. 9. Ottawa: National Museums of Canada.

_____. 1980. "The Inuit of Southern Quebec-Labrador: Reviewing the Evidence." *Études/Inuit/Studies* 4, 1–2: 185–93.

Temple, Blair. 2006. "'Their House is the Best I've Seen on the Labrador': A Nineteenth-century Jersey Dwelling at L'Anse au Cotard." In "From Arctic to Avalon: Papers in Honour of Jim Tuck," edited by Lisa Rankin and Peter Ramsden, special issue, *Canadian Journal of Archaeology* 31, 2: 43–52.

Thornton, P.A. 1977. "The Demographic and Mercantile Bases of Initial Permanent Settlement in the Strait of Belle Isle." In *The Peopling of Newfoundland,* edited by J.J. Mannion, 152–83. Newfoundland Social and Economic Papers No.8. St. John's: ISER Books.

Todd, W.E. Clyde. 1963. *Birds of the Labrador Peninsula and Adjacent Areas.* Toronto: University of Toronto Press.

Trudel, François. 1978. "The Inuit of Southern Labrador and the Development of French Sedentary Fisheries (1700–1760)." In *Canadian Ethnology Society, Papers from the Fourth Annual Congress, 1977,* edited by Richard J. Preston, 99–120. Mercury Series, Canadian Ethnology Service, Paper No. 40. Ottawa: National Museum of Man.

_____. 1980. «Les relations entre les Français et les Inuit au Labrador Méridional, 1660–1760.» *Études/Inuit/Studies* 4, 1–2: 135–46.

Whitridge, Peter. 2008. "Reimagining the Iglu: Modernity and the Challenge of the Eighteenth Century Labrador Inuit Winter House. *Archaeologies* 4, 2: 288–309.

Woollett, James. 2003. "An Historical Archaeology of Labrador Inuit Culture Change. PhD diss., City University of New York.

Zimmerly, David William. 1975. *Cain's Land Revisited: Culture Change in Central Labrador, 1775–1972.* Newfoundland Social and Economic Studies No. 16. St. John's: ISER Books.

CHAPTER 4

Abandoned and Ousted by the State:
The Relocations from Nutak and Hebron, 1956-1959

Peter Evans

Contemporary visitors to north-coast communities are often struck by the impact Euro-Canadian and settler modes of life appear to have had upon Labrador Inuit culture and identity, and many outsiders naturally assume that this is the result of three centuries of their political and cultural hegemony. In fact, it is a relatively recent influence, rooted in processes that emerged only after Newfoundland confederated with Canada in 1949. The memories of Inuit and the memoranda of administrators reveal that Confederation inaugurated a period of state-sponsored welfare administration that altered nearly every aspect of the Inuit culture that arose out of the nineteenth century. This period's most devastating impact was felt within the political system that had animated Inuit community life prior to Confederation.

Although Inuit exercised their autonomy by voting overwhelmingly to join Canada in 1949, Confederation marked a turning point in Inuit-Kablunaat relations. Through a series of manoeuvres by provincial and federal bureaucrats, Inuit were omitted from the Terms of Union and entered Confederation with their rights in a suspended state under the administration of the province. Adrian Tanner observes that Labrador Inuit probably lost most in the Confederation process because they had more autonomy to lose:[1] although British and Newfoundland confederates promoted self-determination as a critical component of the decolonization process,[2] Labrador

Inuit of the 1940s had already been negotiating greater self-determination for several decades. Inuit adults had voted in local elders' elections for a generation. The elders, with their *maligaksait*, their written community and environmental laws,[3] and together with local white patrons and middle-men on town committees, constituted a more advanced form of social and political governance than was found in much of rural Newfoundland. Men's meetings—enlivened with Inuit political rhetoric, consensual decision-making, and written issuances—were a highly developed Inuit institution by the time of Confederation.[4]

For Inuit, the arrival of the modern liberal welfare state appeared as it had to Aboriginal people elsewhere in Canada—as an uneven assortment of useful assistance programs attached to a sublime managerial power that spread into every corner of their world. In Labrador, the centrepiece of the state's efforts to manage and improve the lives of Aboriginal people involved reconfiguring the distribution of people across the landscape. In the latter half of the 1950s, Newfoundland, Canadian, and private health and religious charitable patrons such as the International Grenfell Association and the Moravian Mission, withdrew public and social services from the coastline north of Nain—the historic stronghold of independent Inuit, yet a region they regarded as isolated from the technological and cultural mainstream—effectively ousting them to more southerly communities.[5]

In 1956 the Division of Northern Labrador Affairs (DNLA), a branch of the Newfoundland government's Department of Public Welfare, closed its trading operations at Nutak in Okak Bay. Some 200 Inuit found themselves with no choice but to follow administrators' wishes and move southward, where the materials for new public welfare houses were awaiting them at Nain, Hopedale, Makkovik, and North West River. A few families, preferring the familiar environment of the north, migrated instead to Hebron, a community 130 miles north of Nain. Nutak's closure isolated Hebron even farther from the network of services—shipping, mail, education, nursing—that the state was centralizing farther south. Hebron's new isolation led to the second step of the resettlement program. In 1959 the Moravian Mission withdrew its missionary from Hebron; this was followed soon after by an announcement that the provincial government would close its store and withdraw its services. In October of 1959 the last of the community's roughly 300 people were ousted and travelled south to Nain, Hopedale, and Makkovik, where many were given shelter much as their Nutak brethren had been. Still others took shelter in tents and makeshift dwellings constructed of scrounged materials, or in emergency shelters provided by the American military.

In the twenty-first century, as a result of indigenous activism and court decisions,[6] states and third parties are much more aware of their obligation to consult with Aboriginal peoples over decisions that might affect their rights. In the 1950s, however, many administrators went about their work blithely ignorant of Aboriginal opinions. A spirited high modernism drove the state's approach to developing Canada's North and the social and economic lives of its residents. The dominant, though not universally shared, ideology of politicians and civil servants alike held that the route to salvation for those up to now outside the state's lure and pull was through centralized resettlement, the provision of health and social services, and the creation of modern forms of employment. Social planners perceived Inuit dilemmas as essentially problems of "social engineering" that could be solved by knowledgeable "experts." In the most disastrous of such schemes, James Scott observes, experts rejected older, more established models of living as well as local knowledge as outmoded, backward, and regressive.[7] Unfortunately, such new schemes and strategies typically produce outcomes that are the polar opposite of intentions.

The immediate and long-term social effects of the ousting of northern Inuit from Hebron and Nutak have been apparent to generations of north-coast residents and visitors. Several academic research programs and government commissions have illuminated different aspects of the relocations' impacts, although the full scope of the cumulative social and economic outcomes would be extremely difficult to gauge. This paper builds on important work on the Labrador Inuit relocations done by Shmuel Ben-Dor;[8] John Kennedy;[9] and Carol Brice-Bennett,[10] among others. Ben-Dor and Kennedy did ethnographic field studies ten years apart that charted the ethno-political effects upon Inuit and settler identity and socio-economic success in Makkovik. Terje and Anne Brantenberg analyzed some of the same processes at work in Nain during the early 1970s.[11] Donald Snowden, the head of the Royal Commission on Labrador, took a personal interest and held interviews with and surveys of relocated Inuit in 1973 and 1974. The commission addressed the relocations in its final reports and defined the central failure of the relocation program as a failure to consult with Inuit.[12] Twenty years later, Brice-Bennett produced a report on the administrative history and socio-economic and ecological outcomes for the federal Royal Commission on Aboriginal Peoples.[13] In its final analysis, the Royal Commission reiterated that a lack of consultation and consent were failures of relocation schemes everywhere.[14] Nain's OKalaKatiget Society has contributed an important body of documentary work describing the personal impacts of the relocations upon the lives of Inuit.[15]

That the relocations disrupted ecological relationships between people and the environment of northern Labrador is widely acknowledged and has been written about by numerous researchers.[16] Less understood are the ideological assumptions and misconceptions about Inuit identity, culture, and northern ecology that lurked behind the relocations, as well as the mechanics of the relocations—how the state and other agencies framed, portrayed, or socially constructed the northern Inuit population and landscape in such a way as to make relocation appear inevitable, even self directed. The mid-century mark signalled the end of a golden age in Inuit politics, a period that had begun with the creation of Inuit community elders councils at the turn of the twentieth century and concluded with Confederation in 1949. The resettlement programs marked a decisive series of events in this process, events made possible only by the total exclusion of Inuit from decisions about their destiny. Such exclusion from decision making became commonplace in the decades that followed—at least until the gradual resolution of land claims in the 1990s.

This chapter distils the results of my primary and secondary source research into one small facet of the relocations: the mechanics of the state's overthrow of indigenous Inuit political institutions via an ideologically driven program of coerced resettlement. Through a careful reading and analysis of the existing literature surrounding the Labrador relocations, community interviews conducted in 1999 and 2006–2007, and extensive on-site reviews of archival materials—contained primarily in the files of both the federal Northern Affairs administration (Library and Archives Canada, RG85 series) and the provincial Department of Welfare (housed at the Provincial Archives of Newfoundland and Labrador), among others—a picture emerges of how, in the 1950s, the state barred or restricted Inuit from all discourse concerning their future in order to engineer radical solutions consistent with a then-dominant Westernized worldview founded on an inevitable trajectory of modernization.

The "Eskimo Problem" in the Canadian Arctic

It is instructive to view the Northern Labrador relocations within the wider context of federal-provincial-Inuit relations, as well as in the context of relocations elsewhere in the Canadian Arctic. Major studies of relocation policies in the eastern and central Arctic have not mentioned the Labrador relocations.[17] Likewise, regional literatures examining the Labrador relocations have not connected the events of 1956–1959 with federal programs in other areas of the Arctic.[18] Although administrative histories differ over the vast Arctic, Kablunaat officials focused in on a similar range of social problems and solutions during the 1950s.

Governments began to replace the older, established patrons of and brokers to the Inuit, the churches and traders, in the 1950s, as the entirety of the
vast Canadian North came increasingly under the purview of Canadian and
provincial administrations. New administrations identified and then experi-
mented with a range of instruments to solve perceived social and economic
problems in Inuit communities, from development of cottage industries to
welfare state initiatives; however, manipulation of Inuit community life in the
form of resettlements, relocations, and community planning emerged as the
preferred policy direction in the early 1950s and remained so into the 1960s.
The federal government made a series of well-documented Inuit relocations
between 1953 and 1960. According to Alan Rudolph Marcus, the 1953 Grise
Fiord/Resolute relocation and the 1957 relocation of the Ahiarmiut were
motivated in part by officials' determination to sever "dependency relationships Inuit had developed with whites."[19]

Relief payments and indigence were the primary social problem occupy-
ing federal administrators in the Canadian Arctic of the 1950s, but other
social facts of Inuit life competed for their attention, notably assimilation,
restlessness, housing difficulties, cleanliness concerns, and the unreliability of game.[20] All these concerns played upon non-Aboriginal notions of
Inuit as noble hunters and happy gatherers and together formed what was
often called "the Eskimo Problem." The broad outlines of these concerns
were shared across administrative lines in Labrador, with some regional
variations. Newfoundland officials found common cause with the Canadians
over relief, for instance, or "white man's handouts." Both believed it was
morally degrading to Inuit, destroying the formerly happy, proud, independent-
spirited hunting people and sapping them of their drive and ambition at the
same time that it drew upon public funds. Labrador field staff complained
frequently about relief rolls, "indigence," and "loafing."[21] Max Budgell, the
Nutak depot manager in the 1950s, complained of great increases in the
Inuit assistance bill, "loafing" around the post, and consumption of too many
"non-essentials."[22] The depot manager at Hebron complained that "no one
cares to trap for a living" because "everyone concerned is in receipt of some
kind of assistance."[23] "If poverty was a disease," Marcus observes of the di-
lemma administrators faced, "then the cure—relief payments—was equally
undesirable."[24]

For the Canadian Arctic, federal administrators vacillated between two
seemingly opposing answers to the "Eskimo problems" of indigence, moral
degradation, dependence, and hunger: relocation to urban centres in the
south, or dispersal to scattered communities across the Arctic.[25] At a pivotal
1952 "Conference on Eskimo Affairs"—the first conference drawing together

agencies to develop a new direction for northern policies—federal officials agreed to "assist the natives to continue to follow their traditional way of life as hunters,"[26] that is, to "keep the 'native' native" amidst the rapid changes unfolding in postwar society.[27] Relocation was conceived as a method of moving people from areas considered overpopulated or wanting in resources to thinly populated or richer regions.[28] Utopian notions of the Arctic environment and the Inuit ability to transfer their skills from region to region were evident in the first relocation conducted under this policy shortly afterward, at Grise Fiord and Resolute.

In the 1950s observers began to suggest that an originally balanced Inuit physical and social environment had been so badly "disturbed" by Europeans that Inuit were unable to adjust their social and hunting habits to it.[29] The American geologist E.P. ("Pep") Wheeler opined as much to federal officials in late 1951: "Before we modified his environment, the Eskimo was sufficiently well adjusted to it so that his life was essentially successful and happy," he wrote. "We have supplied him with white man's goods to such an extent that he can no longer do without them, much as the wiser ones would like to do now. Older Eskimos have told me with regret of the days when their fathers went into the store and carried out their winter's supplies in a fold of their parkas."[30]

Harold Horwood, Confederation-era provincial politician and writer, advanced a more pessimistic view of Labrador Inuit capacity to adapt to culture change.[31] The main threat facing Inuit was, in Horwood's view, their rapid cultural and ethnic "degradation," a process that the Cold War had increased by positioning American radar sites near Hopedale and Hebron. Culture change or reorganization, as Horwood called it, was difficult for the Inuit. It was "attended by social maladjustment, emotional disturbance, and insanity," a condition he attributed to children in boarding schools whom he had seen with "malady adjustment altogether out of proportion to what could be considered normal."[32]

> The tendency for Labrador Eskimos to become white men in habits and ways of thought has been accelerated. The tendency for them to become white men in fact, by inter-breeding, has probably not slowed down. Both tendencies have been given a shove forward by the arrival of hordes of Americans in Northern Labrador. As white civilization advanced northward, Eskimo civilization has retreated before it. That has been true both in Eastern and Western North America. It has been true in Labrador, where there is now no real Eskimo settlement south of Nain…. The Eskimo culture—what

little there is left of it—is caught in the middle, and must inevitably disappear within the next few years.[33]

Inuit populations were in various states of flux across the Arctic of the 1950s, migrating between the spaces of the dying fur economy and those of undefined newer modes of subsistence and production. In Canada, officials cited the movement of populations from areas of supposed "want" to areas of plenty as justification for coerced relocations to the high Arctic (c. 1953). In Labrador in the post-war decade, there was migration around three locales: Hebron and other northern Inuit migrated to the Okak Bay area, Nain Inuit migrated to Hopedale, and Inuit from along the coast migrated to Goose Bay. The impression left upon administrators was that Inuit were rejecting Hebron's isolation and lack of trees and turning away from hunting and fishing to become wage labourers. However, federal and provincial administrations misrepresented the seasonal nature of the migrations. They shared a language that eventually described relocations as "migrations" or "assisted moves." Marcus notes that this reformist language allowed the planners to make migration a metaphor for self-directed social reform.[34]

At the same time, Happy Valley–Goose Bay was emerging as an important post-war military base and the regional centre for coastal Labrador. It exercised a powerful pull on Inuit and administrators alike. Some Inuit migrated yearly for employment to Happy Valley and North West River, while others went to live there more permanently. In the summer of 1955, for instance, eight families from Cape Harrison, Nain, and Nutak moved south to seek wage labour in Happy Valley–Goose Bay.[35]

The Ethnicity Question

A conversation between Ottawa and St. John's commenced following Confederation regarding the status, identity, authenticity of, and responsibility for Labrador's "aborigines,"[36] and concerning the distribution of non-Aboriginal settlers in Inuit space. In order to map out a solution to the "Eskimo Problem," provincial and federal officials needed first to collect and classify Inuit and Innu population data. Federal officials felt they required better census data on Labrador's population to determine ethnicity and constitutional entitlements, and they were sceptical of data provided to them by their provincial counterparts, pointing out discrepancies between it, the 1945 census, and other federal sources.[37] In 1950 the Newfoundland Rangers were dispatched to gather more precise data on Innu and Inuit ethnicity and movement. Families were enumerated as normal by household, along with age, household relation, location, and place of origin; but the census also included a category to describe individuals' racial makeup by percentage of Eskimo or Indian.[38] It is unclear whether these percentages were self-reported or based on the observations of the rangers. In 1951 Canada undertook the first comprehensive survey of the Arctic population, intended to provide a foothold in their new northern social policy interests. Labrador Inuit, for the first time, were given a separate heading in its summary pages.[39] This action both related Labrador Inuit to their kin across the Arctic in questions of policy and also created grounds on which to compare and contrast ethnicity. The survey gave a total Inuit population of 9,493 in the four Arctic regions: eastern Arctic (4,858), western Arctic (1,999), Quebec (1,789), and Labrador (847). Federal and provincial officials grappled with the interpretation of the data, as it would affect funding levels to the province, and a provincial "enumeration," conducted for funding purposes, boosted these numbers to 1400 in Labrador.[40]

The discrepancies between the different results meant little, according to Jenness; instead, they "strengthened the conviction, held now by the federal government as well as by the authorities in Newfoundland, that it was impossible to distinguish accurately the 'aborigines' of the region from the 'whites,' and that in matters of health and relief, at least, no attempt should be made to separate them."[41] For federal officials, this was the principal consideration informing deliberations over Labrador Aboriginals, and officials framed and reframed the question concerning Inuit ethnicity in their policy deliberations. A typical memorandum distributed to policy makers offered an analysis of the 1951 census:

> In any consideration of this problem it is well to bear in mind that the population of Northern Labrador is a mixture of races, Eskimo, Indians, whites, and mixed blood. This mixing has been going on for about 200 years so that it is most difficult to determine who is a full-blood Eskimo.... If an ethnologist were employed as a census taker he might produce different figures. At many points any medical, educational or other welfare facilities provided for Eskimos or Indians would be used by those elements of the population who are admittedly a provincial responsibility' and the racial dividing line between federal and provincial responsibility is difficult or impossible to define.[42]

1951 Ad Hoc Funding Agreement

Canada created the Interdepartmental Committee on Newfoundland Indians and Eskimos as a forum in which to workshop its obligations toward Innu and Inuit. It was a federal counterpart to the provincial Labrador North Development Committee, formed at about the same time. For the next few years, until the establishment of the Eskimo Affairs Committee in 1952, the interdepartmental committee functioned as the most powerful forum for federal views on Labrador. In April 1950 it met for the first time in the offices of the Privy Council.[43]

Ottawa agreed to cover relief payments to Indians and Inuit, to cover transportation and hospital costs for Natives, and to partly underwrite the cost of an X-ray survey of the Native population as the first step in an aggressive anti-tuberculosis campaign. The Indian Affairs branch of the Department of Citizenship and Immigration provided $40,000 to reimburse Newfoundland for expenses on Indians and $25,000 for Eskimos. The different amounts reflected federal scepticism about the racial identity of the Inuit population.[44] Monies to cover relief costs were ad hoc funds, recoverable from Ottawa on the submission of semi-annual lists of relief payments to Aboriginals. Canada's obligation, as bureaucrats understood or admitted it in negotiations, was a limited one. Canada was unconvinced about the Aboriginal identity of northern Labradorians, and unconvinced about its obligations under Confederation, and sought to avoid being drawn into the position of providing services to settlers through monies intended for Aboriginals.

The X-ray survey program, supported by the Indian Health branch of the Department of National Health and Welfare and conducted by the International Grenfell Association (IGA) in the summer of 1951, had lasting effects on the development discourse concerning Aboriginals. While development and welfare specialists debated what to do for Aboriginals, the health agencies—led by P.E. Moore in Ottawa and Drs. Curtis and Paddon with the IGA—were moving a plan of action forward. Compared with the northern social agencies, which were in states of transition in Ottawa and St. John's and fractured by a range of opinions, from preservationist to integrationist, these were much older, established bureaucracies. The physicians shared a common set of medical, professional, and policy concerns that allowed them to advance their plans to the top of the agenda. The X-ray program, once underway, had a more pronounced effect on debates; the IGA's X-ray program peered into the bodies of Inuit children and adults, pathologizing their lifestyles and placing tuberculosis squarely at the centre of a knot of related concerns—from housing to diet to transportation.[45]

After the 1951 census, Canada and the province exchanged information, views, and emissaries for several years in order to arrive at a
more stable funding arrangement. Correspondence from the files of the
Interdepartmental Committee and later from the Eskimo Affairs Committee
shows the Canadian position was underpinned by several ideas; among
them: scepticism about the ethnicity of Labrador Aboriginals, concern about
Newfoundland's accounting, and concern over the size of projects proposed
for a relatively small Aboriginal group. In early 1953 negotiations were taken
over by a group of high-level "closers." Federal Cabinet established an ad hoc
Cabinet committee to coordinate the end of negotiations with similarly high-
level Newfoundlanders. Several versions of the proposed agreement moved
back and forth. Finally, in March 1954, Secretary of State Jack Pickersgill
concluded negotiations in Newfoundland with senior ministers of Health
and Welfare and Premier Smallwood over the agreement. The three-point
funding formula to come into effect 1 April 1954 agreed: "1. The Federal
Government to assume 66.66 percent of agreed capital expenditures on
Eskimo account and 100 percent of agreed capital expenditures on Indian account in the fields of welfare, health and education; the aggregate cost to the
Federal Government not to exceed $200,000."[46] In addition, Canada agreed
to cover *all* health costs for ten years, and to underwrite the cost of a ten-year
anti-tuberculosis campaign, including transportation and hospitalization of
the sick. Finally, the agreement shifted responsibility for "all financial and
administrative responsibilities for the Indian, and Eskimo population of
Labrador, including relief, but excluding those matters mentioned in (1) and
(2) above, and all federal benefits, such as family allowance and old age pensions…for relief back onto the Province would assume other costs."[47]

The funding scheme—66.66 percent for Inuit accounts and 100 percent
for Innu—reflected federal beliefs that the Labrador Aboriginal population
was tiny, and well established on the path to assimilation either through
intermarriage with European settlers or economic migration. These beliefs
were summed up in correspondence between W.E. Harris and Herbert L.
Pottle during negotiations in 1952–1953:

> There are three main considerations which prompted my colleagues
> to approve the sort of arrangement which we contemplate. The first
> of these is that there is no legal requirement for the Federal Gov-
> ernment to assume any responsibility whatsoever, either financial
> or administrative, in regard to the residents of Northern Labrador.
> The second is that, even if the Federal Government agreed to as-
> sume continuing responsibility in some form for the residents of

Northern Labrador, it could not in practice do so with propriety as it appears to be virtually impossible to determine who is an Eskimo and who is not. Finally, notwithstanding the two considerations set out above, the Federal Government is appreciative of the fact that there is a job to be done in Northern Labrador (particularly in regard to the alarmingly high incidence of tuberculosis) and it is, therefore, prepared to assist the Government of Newfoundland with its Northern Labrador program.[48]

Discussing Labrador's Eskimo Problem

The funding program created a fertile environment for the emergence of expert voices in the spheres of health, welfare, and economic development, each offering solutions to the problems facing "the Eskimo," and each arguing on behalf of their own agency's vision.

Walter Rockwood, northern Labrador's most prominent provincial bureaucrat and the director of the Division of Northern Labrador Affairs, argued against relocations. Rockwood's writing depicted the Inuit in a "stage of transition" from "primitive culture" to the society of tomorrow, and envisioned the job of government as assisting Inuit to adjust to the rapid changes. Yet he sometimes admitted to seeing a limited range of options for the future of Inuit culture. "For good or ill, the Labrador Eskimos have developed beyond the raw meat eating, snow igloo, blubber lamp stage and are intent on adopting the White Man's culture to the fullest degree possible in the environment," he wrote.[49]

Rockwood defined the main problem as "the attainment of a solid economic base on which a better society can be built"[50] and sketched an overview of Labrador's industrial potential in forestry, mining, and hydro. His concluding paragraph contained all the beliefs informing administrators' views on northern development and Inuit acculturation in the 1950s: in the inevitability of the future; in the ability of technology to overcome isolation; in the need for state services in health and social services; and in the danger technological modernity represented to semi-traditional Inuit groups:

> But one fact seems clear—civilization is on the northward march, and for the Eskimo and Indian there is no escape. The last bridges of isolation were destroyed with the coming of the airplane and the radio. The only course now open, for there can be no turning back, is to fit him as soon as may be to take his full place as a citizen in our society. There is no time to lose. No effort must be spared in the fields of Health, Education, Welfare, and Economics. If industrial

development comes first to South and Central Labrador, the North will provide some shelter to the people concerned, but if it should break in full fury into their immediate environment effective steps will have to be taken to protect them during the next two or three decades of the transition period.[51]

Rockwood's cautious approach, however, was pushed aside by influential medical voices. First, in early 1955, an influential essay written by Dr. Anthony Paddon circulated widely among Newfoundland and Canadian officials. The minister of Public Welfare, Herbert L. Pottle, and MLA Fred Rowe distributed it among their counterparts in Ottawa. In it, Paddon argued forcefully for "radical and different thinking" on the Eskimo problem: The solution, Paddon wrote, was to resettle "all the people north of the Kiglapaits…into one modern planned community in an approved site," where "the various community needs of education, health, trading facilities, communications etc.…could be provided for at reasonable cost." The new model community would be located within the treeline, still north of Nain, at either Pussekartok or Tessiujuk. This community would be rigorously ordered, "planned from the ground up," "subject to rigid guidance, probably by an appointed committee representing the various agencies in the town, such as school, church, trading post, medical personnel etc."[52]

Paddon interpreted all health problems among the Hebronimiut as public health issues flowing from the lack of trees in the area. Fuel was related to all other problems. It forced people to live in crowded conditions, which created ideal conditions for the spread of infectious diseases and increased inbreeding and other problematic conditions. The essay was written in provocatively descriptive terms. Both the Nutak and Hebron Inuit, he wrote, "live lives of degrading squalor and poverty, and must endure conditions fortunately rare in this nation today." Because they have little access to firewood for fuel, the Hebronimiut "in general are verminous, apt to be covered with sores and ulcers, and to harbour and spread tuberculosis."[53] Finally, he pointed to the migration of a few families to Nutak in the previous five years as proof that Inuit wanted to move. The remainder needed to be gradually enticed south: "The Eskimo may talk about what he will or will not do, but he looks to the white man to provide economic leadership. The prospect of their own church in the Nutak area, and of a community hall complete with 'movies' and of a school would be irresistible to most of the people remaining at Hebron. They will move, if a community is established for them."[54]

Paddon's argument was a rejection of dispersionist notions, which sought to encourage Inuit to retain traditional movement and smaller settlements, although it maintained their presence in the North. Admitting there was some foundation to dispersion, he wrote, however, that "carried to its logical conclusion it would scatter the population abroad into every creek and run that might produce a few seals or ptarmigan." Instead, he argued that the new community should be situated in the familiar North, as a model northern community.

> The old Eskimo way of living off the land by hunting is irretriev-
> ably lost. There are many who urge a program to bring the Eskimo
> back to living by the harpoon. With the increasing scarcity of game
> and seals this would be impossible. The only future for the Eskimo
> lies in community life, better education, and gradual adaptation
> to Canadian life. Amalgamation of the Eskimos in the Nutak area
> would give rise to a strong community, with a reasonable standard
> of health, an adequate education system, facilities for entertainment
> of the people, and the resources of church, village government,
> good communications, reduced transportation costs and easier
> administration generally.[55]

Paddon's essay was seized upon and circulated by social reformers in the provincial government. "The statements made by Dr. Paddon are so serious that I feel that his memorandum should be given the most serious consideration by the Department or Departments concerned and should then be followed by consideration at Cabinet level," wrote Fred Rowe the following month.[56]

While in Ottawa to attend a federal-provincial conference in the fall of 1955, Rowe handed Gordon Robertson copies of a letter written by the superintendent (general) of the International Grenfell Association, Charles S. Curtis.[57] Dr. Charles Curtis, Dr. Anthony Paddon's superior, had made a visit to the coast as far north as Nain that spring, on Paddon's invitation, to see the work underway on the new Nain nursing station. For medical administrators of the 1950s, travel and modern transportation framed a vision of a more accessible North, and they believed health and social problems were ultimately rooted in housing conditions. *Vision* played a vital role in articulating a link between transportation, health, housing, and social problems. Curtis was appalled by what he called the "most deplorable and appalling" living conditions of Inuit in Nain. He juxtaposed the view of Nain from a distance with its appearance up close and his growing sense of revulsion as the *MV Cluett* drew nearer. His disgust is palpable, and his tone that of the morally indignant professional:

As one approaches, by sea, the village of Nain from a distance has the appearance of a neat, well-painted settlement. But as you approach nearer you can see a definite line of demarcation between where the white settlers—the police, Missionary, and storekeeper—live, and the appalling slum area where the Eskimos live.... The Eskimo house is a hovel sometimes covered with tarred paper but more often not.

Only one house I saw had a porch on it with a door. The filth is disgraceful. There is no attempt at sanitation—the sewerage is thrown out the door and eaten by mangy dogs and pups which infest the area. With the exception of one house, of an Eskimo who is away working at Hopedale, there is no house in the Eskimo settlement but what would be condemned by health authorities as unfit for human habitation. Dr. Paddon wished me to go north to Nutak and Hebron with him as he said conditions were worse there than at Nain. But I did not wish to see anything worse than what I saw at Nain....

I understand from the Department of Indian Affairs that the Dominion Government is allocating $200,000.00 a year for ten years for the health, education and, I presume, better houses for the Eskimo. Surely, along with any attempt to treat any disease among these people should go, hand in hand, a complete investigation of living conditions and economic conditions and money should be spent in moving them to better surroundings and in building better houses as soon as possible.

It seems to me that there is no unity of action, no comprehensive plan and while, at St. Anthony, we are treating them and doing thorocoplasties excising lesions, we are sending them back to hovels with no futures.[58]

Curtis's letter proposed a radical solution to the knot of medical/social problems evident to the gaze of outsiders: the resettlement of the Inuit from the Okak and Hebron areas—not just their reestablishment in a model Arctic community in Okak, but a wholesale removal southward. He called for a meeting with staff in the provincial Departments of Health and Welfare, MLA Rowe, and Dr. Moore of the federal Indian Health Services to work out a method to execute his plan:

1. To bring the Eskimo at Hebron and Nutak south where there is fuel.

2. To appropriate a percentage of Federal Government Grant of $200,000.00 for a housing project and make plans for building some houses next summer.

3. To ascertain if some solution can be found to better the deplorable economic and living conditions of the Eskimo.[59]

His letter, once widely distributed throughout the provincial and federal systems, had a mobilizing effect on the agencies responsible. Both administrations were shifting their gaze away from dispersionist notions toward a plan to centralize the populations. Newfoundland officials were ideologically closer than their federal counterparts to articulating a radical resettlement program, and hardly required this encouragement: at the meetings of the Northern Labrador Affairs Committee, Rowe called for the immediate closing of the Nutak depot and the resettlement of its residents.[60]

The Labrador Conference

The expertise of brokers and patrons operates best in zones of exclusion, where Aboriginal people can be spoken about without the interference of their presence. Nutak's closure was theorized at a special gathering of politicians, bureaucrats, patrons, and experts from 13 to 16 February 1956. The Labrador Conference, as it was called, brought together all the government agencies formerly related only through correspondence, with development, health, and other "experts" to define and seek solutions to the development and social "problems" affecting the North.[61] No Aboriginal people were invited to attend the conference, although it was reported that "lumbermen, fishermen, business men" attended. The Moravians represented the Inuit, and Father Cyr, the Roman Catholic priest from Davis Inlet, represented the Innu. Non-Aboriginal local governments, including the committee from Happy Valley—then so young it did not even warrant a council—were invited and attended, but no Inuit elder was even asked.[62] Although heralded as "a new concept in government,"[63] the Labrador Conference was undoubtedly inspired by the similarly influential federal Eskimo conference held in Ottawa in 1952, which resulted ultimately in the high Arctic relocations. At one level, conferences demonstrate to a public—in this case, a southern public—that government is capable of understanding and tackling an issue. They create a forum in which experts can be seen naming and classifying a social problem while elected officials go to work upon solving it. Because they are also events—newsworthy ones—the policy directions that flow out of them have a momentous, optimistic feeling. However, framing the social life of a people in a "problem/solution" discursive setting is itself highly problematic, bound to produce solutions that are further problems.[64] Perhaps it is no surprise that both federal and provincial conferences gave rise to relocations: as James Scott has argued, the abstraction of problems from their environment and local knowledge is a requirement for social engineering schemes to proceed unopposed. In this way, they subvert possible resistance.

Ironically, as the conference structure isolated Native voices from the centre of decision making, the social and spatial problem of "isolation" loomed large over the conference discussion. Welfare services, mail, communications, wharves, roads, transportation, and resettlement formed an inter-related series of discussions at all three conferences, and they seeded resettlement and centralization schemes for both Labrador's and Newfoundland's outports.[65] In press releases before the conference, Rowe established that "special emphasis" would be placed "on the implementation of the health, welfare, and educational programme of the Indian and Eskimo citizens of Northern Labrador. Included in this will be the possibility of a re-settlement and re-housing programme."[66]

The International Grenfell Association used the forum to reinforce their message that public health was at the centre of all other socio-economic concerns: "It was pointed out that infant mortality which was as high as 40% at Nain several years ago has been reduced to 6%, but that at Hebron it is still very high. This condition, it was stated, depends very largely on the nutritional state of the mother and the new born child."[67] Inuit faced what administrators saw as a diminished natural world. Caribou populations were "discouraging." Fur was a write-off. Northern Labrador's cod were "small and thin and inferior to fish caught in more southern waters," and only a limited, heavily subsidized fishery was possible in the Nain area, which would "ultimately absorb all the fishermen of the Nain, Nutak, and Hebron districts." Ironically, the sole bright spot was the Arctic char fishery: "centred mainly in the Hebron district, [it] is the one fishery which appears to offer some prospects for economic operation."[68]

Although the conference looked to wage employment in heavy industries to completely eclipse hunting and fishing, the attendees admitted that rumours of employment in base construction at Goose Bay and Hopedale were greater than the actual employment possibilities. Furthermore, the kinds of industries they discussed were the same cottage industries—arts, handicrafts, carving—that had been promoted by a succession of agencies. Mining, however, offered the promise of an industrial future, and the attendees believed that Labrador's hidden resources would be "similar to Northern Ontario."[69] The conference produced a buoyant optimism among its followers around mining. In a fateful coincidence, while attendees were in

St. John's to attend the conference, Brinex/Brinco announced it had discovered uranium near Makkovik. The ground soon shook with rumours of
future progress and wages for all.[70]

Closing Nutak

Buoyed by the emotion and optimism of the conferences, the provincial government's Northern Labrador Affairs Committee reached a decision to close
the Nutak trade depot.[71] Later, at a 26 April meeting of the executive council
of the Newfoundland government, the closure of the Nutak depot was approved. It was further ordered that "all Eskimo families living in the Nutak
area [be] transferred to Nain or some point further south in Labrador."[72]

The money for the resulting housing project was to come from the 1954
final agreement with Canada to improve social and health conditions for
Newfoundland's Aboriginal citizens. The Department of Welfare estimates
for that year had gone forward with an amount of $90,000, and Andrews
wanted federal assurance that Canada would share the costs of the houses.[73]
The Federal Treasury Board agreed and established an important principle
that, given their influence over discharging the Crown's relationship to Inuit,
was tantamount to creating a policy of relocation and centralization: "The
meeting discussed various types of projects that might be worth-while. It
was generally agreed that no federal assistance should be given towards
works at any point north of Nain. Nain will be a staging point to which the
older persons from more northern points will be brought and from which
the younger persons will be taken to points in the Melville Lake area where
employment possibilities are much better. Provision of housing at Nain to
encourage the older persons to come there would be a reasonable project for
federal assistance."[74]   .

The official justification for Nutak's closure was that "there were no services or facilities except those operated by the Department of Public Welfare."
Closure of the station and transfer of the people southward would concentrate residents in communities "where churches, schools, medical services
and other facilities already existed."[75] It was not the lack of these services
per se that led to the envisioning of its closure, but the negative social effects
that arose from their lack. Religious and government administrators feared
the deteriorating social conditions at Nutak, which they blamed on a rising
level of resistance to Mission and store policies and a breakdown in social
society.[76] "The point is that the closing of Nutak depot was brought about at
least as much by social factors as for economic reasons. It must also be
remembered that there was a serious feud between rival factions (shots were
fired in the direction of the depot in December 1953, and a woman was

murdered in February 1954) and several families left Nutak and settled at North West River before the decision was taken to close the depot."[77]

The mechanics of relocating the Nutak Inuit created the context for questions about the capacity of the receiving communities to manage their own affairs. Rockwood, the lone sceptic about social engineering among the various administrators, was concerned about the detailed administration required to execute a project involving the Inuit moving themselves south-ward and constructing their own homes. In the spring of 1956 Rockwood circulated a memo calling for the formation of an inter-agency committee to "regulate the transfer of people from Nutak to Nain, Makkovik, and North West River." The committee—made up of missionaries, depot managers, Dr. Paddon, and Rockwood, with no Nutakmiut representative—acted as "a selection committee" to determine the destination community of each Nutak family. "Families were to be placed where it was believed they had the best chances for adjustment," Rockwood wrote to Andrews, and "housing assistance would be distributed as agreed by the committee."[78]

At Nain, the main destination of the Nutak relocatees, the relocation would exacerbate infrastructural needs and services there—"e.g. drain-age, fire prevention, garbage disposal, sewerage, local roads, water supply, animals at large," Rockwood wrote. "In addition some measure of control would be necessary in respect to the new housing units," he indicated, and proposed a new form of community governance: "a Village or Community Council," consisting of Reverend Peacock, depot manager H.M. Budgell, the nurse, Dorothy Jupp, the RCMP Officer (J. Matthiason) or his successor, and Martin Martin to represent the Nain Inuit community. A few weeks later, Julius Ford, a settler, was added to the committee. The committee included no representatives of the Nutak Inuit, and some of its business would have normally fallen on the elders. It was made up mostly of patron agencies with some local representation.[79]

Although the creation of this village council constituted the only formal consultation attempted with the receiving communities, it illustrates how the mechanics of the relocations were antagonistic toward the older forms of Inuit government, which had arisen from the Moravian-Inuit encounter and had deep roots in local history. This antagonism was particularly pronounced toward the elected *AngajokKauKatiget*, or community elders' councils. The exclusion of Nutak Inuit from the decisions affecting their community was even more extreme than the exclusion of the Hebron Inuit three years later. Nutak, as indicated earlier, was not a Moravian community in the sense of the other stations; its focus was the trade depot. Yet in 1955, Nutamiut had worked to build a small church at Nutak and a handful of houses had gone up, although the missionary complained of some "disharmony" in the congregation.[80] Although a community governed by elders was emerging in the 1950s, it was not sufficiently developed to gather and express the feelings for or against the move with the same intensity as at Hebron. It was because of their loose institutional organization that the Moravians, and therefore, later, the government, considered the Nutak population troublesome. No *katimak* or similar public event was offered to Nutak Inuit. Inuit were simply informed of the depot's closing in the spring of 1956 and offered some of the details of the planned housing project:

> It was in the winter when we went to buy our grub from Nutak. We were in Umiagajak at the time. My father was told by the store manager Max Budgell, Sam Lyall was the interpreter, that we will have to move and that we could go anywhere we wanted to; he also told my father even when the supply boat came after ice break-up that it wouldn't take no more groceries, he said we would starve.[81]

> I still think about it. I don't know why they relocated us. I think it could have been better if we were told exactly why we had to move, with translators available. There was a lack of communications on the government's side. I also know that there was a meeting in the Moravian church in Hebron, but there were no meetings of such in Nutak, we were just told to move. No explanation whatsoever.[82]

The closure of the Nutak DNLA depot in the spring of 1956 uprooted more than 200 people, mostly Inuit and fourteen settlers, making up approximately thirty-eight families. Quotas were put on how many families could go to each community: four families went to North West River, four to Makkovik, and the remainder to Nain.[83]

The Hebron Elders Speak Out

Nutak's closure set in motion an exclusionary logic that led ultimately to Hebron's closure as well. Within the stultifying logic of isolation that closed Nutak, Hebron was now 150 kilometres from its nearest neighbour, Nain, and therefore more easily problematized by administrators as a peripheral and remote place. In the words of Walter Rockwood, "After Nutak was abandoned, Hebron seemed more isolated than ever."[84] Hebron, however, was unlike Nutak in its constitution and arrangement. Hebron Inuit shared a sense of place that contradicted the perception administrators held of them as a disparate, composite population. This sense of place was rooted in the Inuit traditional economy and their long-term use and occupancy of the region, but Inuit also had a long relationship with what modern services Hebron offered—church, school, hall, trade store—and the physical presence of the community was the centre for the network of families and harvesting relationships that spread out into the nearby bays and headlands.

At the centre of the Hebron community sat powerful elders' institutions that mediated between Inuit and European-Canadian concerns. Unlike other areas in the eastern Arctic, where governments were beginning to coerce Inuit into centralized communities without consultation,[85] Hebron Inuit made their feelings known to administrators, and to posterity, via a letter dispatched in 1956. In August of that year, the Hebron *AngajokKauKatiget* (community elders) and *Kivgait* (chapel servants) called a meeting to decide on a course of action. The letter was destined for Rowe, the minister for Public Welfare, whom the elders rightly figured to be the boss of Labrador affairs. The elders had experienced, several years previously, the difficulty of attempting to communicate with the government in their second language, so they brought their letter to the Hebron missionary, Rev. Hettasch, for translation:

> Dear Dr. Rowe,
>
> We Hebron People have heard that Hebron is to be closed, but we have not been told enough about it. And we would like to know if this is correct or not, so that we may be ready for it.
>
> Thus we anxiously beseech you, though we do not want to be moved from our land and customs with all our doings and fame hunting as this seems the best for us. The seal-hunt and trouting and deer-hunt and others which all are good for our livelihood, and it would seem that we would suffer hardships (in moving south) until such time that we can be assured of having steady work with good wages for our livelihood; when such a good time comes it should not be too bad to move.
>
> Also if we are promised good houses in exchange, we would agree to move.
>
> Even although we do not want to move we are glad to be able to let you know our ideas on it.
>
> And finally we would be thankful to know from you what your definite plans are for us here.
>
> I as the official writer of the decision of the Hebron Men's Meeting greet you (Levi Nochasak, William Millie, Hebron Elders).[86]

Brice-Bennett points out that important nuances of the elders' thinking were probably lost in translation, perhaps due to the Hebron missionary's imperfect rendering of their petition into English, his second language: the letter, as translated by Reverend Hettasch, eerily mirrored the beliefs of the Mission and government officials on the subjects of jobs and houses. Moreover, its precepts were accepted by the government as the official feelings of the elders.[87]

The elders' plea to have their opinions considered and to participate in the decisions concerning Hebron garnered only vague promises by the government to inform them of their destiny when the time was right. Several weeks later, Rowe dispatched a telegram to Levi Nochasak, Hebron's principal chapel servant and elder: "Your letter has been received," it began. "I am referring it to the proper authorities for careful consideration. You may rest assured of our deep concern for the welfare of all our friends in Hebron. You will be receiving more details later."[88] More than a month later, Rowe's deputy, Andrews, wrote, informing the elders that "no overt action to compel the Hebron people to leave their homes is being contemplated," but venturing that they would be given a year's notice should conditions change. "We agree that the attitude adopted at the meeting, and as expressed in your letter is reasonable and logical, and you may rest assured that only when steady work is assured elsewhere will the People be expected to move," he wrote.[89]

The elders' letter made it difficult for the usual patrons and experts to attempt to speak of "the Eskimo" to decision makers. When Reverend Peacock tried to tell the minister for Welfare that the opposition to moving among the Hebronimiut was based on "uncertainty rather than unwillingness," Rockwood pointed to the Inuit letter: "We have the views of the people concerned as expressed in their letter to Hon Dr F.W. Rowe, dated August 9th. They do not wish to leave their homes, hunting, and fishing grounds at this time for fear of suffering hardship. They say that when they can be assured of having steady work with good wages they will be prepared to move."[90] But Rockwood's voice, like the elders', was gradually excluded from the centres of power and influence as the discourse about Hebron's future continued to shift. After Nutak's closure, Rockwood mounted a spirited, measured defence of Hebron as a successful resource-based economy before his boss, the influential Welfare deputy minister, and pushed a cautious approach among other bureaucrats and officials. To close Hebron soon "would be taking a leap in the dark," Rockwood wrote, "[and] I think the letter from Hebron means the same thing, when the time is ripe the Hebron people and many of the Nain folk will move of their own accord." Rockwood argued that those relocated from Nutak should be carefully observed to see how they "are assimilated at

Nain and other communities" and to assess the real employment prospects at Makkovik, Hamilton Inlet, and Cartwright before any further decisions were made regarding Hebron.[91]

Reverend Peacock attempted to reach beyond Rockwood to Premier Joey Smallwood himself. Sometime in 1957—the precise date is uncertain— Peacock, F.C.P. Grubb, who had at one time been the Hebron missionary, and regional IGA director Dr. Paddon turned to Smallwood's new Island Outport Resettlement Program to make an appeal for Hebron's closure, even though the program did not expressly include northern Labrador. In a perfect synthesis of patronage and totalizing bureaucracy, the government's program invited officials to submit suggestions for resettlement of fishing outports to the provincial Department of Community and Social Development by way of a simple official form, the "Form Requesting Resettlement." Superficially, the form may have looked like an instrument for the government to engage with the public, allowing people and communities to direct their own relocations; in practice, only administrators or elites had access to it. Each official had to identify himself, and his "Position or Appointment," and fill out three tables: "Name of settlements you think should be vacated (In order of priority)"; "No. of families involved (approximate)"; and "the reasons why you think the settlement should be vacated." Paddon wrote: "Unfit for human habitation. Existence pauperizing the people of Hebron, wasting money and resources," and recommended a relocation stretched over several summers. "Recommendations: Move 8–10 families 1958—repeat in 59—vacate town and close station (except possibly for trout fishery in summer in 1960)."[92] Peacock made a more expansive argument:

> Hebron is approximately 150 miles from the nearest Eskimo settlement and is about 30 miles from the nearest source of fuel (wood). Every year people have to go farther for wood and must spend most of their time in the winter fetching fuel. The health in this remote settlement is poor. Moravian records show that the infant mortality is appallingly high, the highest on the Coast. The incidence of T.B. is higher than on other Eskimo stations. The cost both to Mission and Government in maintaining this settlement is high. The trout fishery could just as easily be prosecuted from Nain. If Hebron were closed the folk could be spread out among other villages to their own advantage. To further education, to improve health and create better social conditions it would be wise to close Hebron. Furthermore to close Hebron would be to save man-power and money. The People of Hebron can never hope to make a decent living in their

present community. I believe that they should be gradually moved out of this depressed area to places where better economic conditions prevail.[93]

For many years, Mission superintendent Peacock lobbied the British Mission Board to transfer the church's headquarters from Nain to Happy Valley–Goose Bay. At first the board only reluctantly consented to station a missionary there,[94] but it later capitulated to his request to transfer the headquarters too. Not surprisingly, Peacock soon received an official "call" to act as the new Happy Valley missionary.[95] He lobbied aggressively to close the Hebron mission and wore down opposition among his field staff and the Mission board. At a field conference in the summer of 1958, with two visitors from the Mission board in attendance, a vote was taken to withdraw the Hebron missionary. The minutes from the conference record, "Closure of Hebron: The proposed closure of Hebron mission station, which was the unanimous recommendation of the field conference, was in view of the urgent reasons there set forth accepted by BMB, to take place in August 1959. It was agreed that M. Rockwood, Director of Northern Labrador Affairs for the Canadian Govt [sic] be notified of this decision."[96]

The Moravians' decision to abandon the Hebron mission put new pressure on the provincial government to rule on the fate of the community's other services. It also placed the government in a difficult position: in his 30 October 1956 letter to the Hebron Inuit, after all, Deputy Minister of Welfare Andrews had promised Inuit they would be given a year's notice should the community be uprooted.

In December 1958 the new minister for Public Welfare, S.J. Hefferton, recommended that the province announce in early 1959 that the depot would be closed in August 1960, and that a housing program costing $90,000 be added into the budgets for that year, with an additional $15,000 to upgrade the DNLA's store and landing facilities in Makkovik; the money would be partly sought from the federal government (the original post-confederation funding agreement that funded the Nutak closure had run out). The executive council of the government agreed to this, and Cabinet ordered the Hebron depot closed.[97] The original date given for the closure of the depot was August 1960.[98]

With the processes that would result in the relocation well underway, official attention turned to the mechanics of the relocation. Because Inuit had been excluded from the conversation regarding Hebron's fate, officials carefully constructed announcements to convince Inuit of the good sense of vacating Hebron. Different claims and traditions of rhetoric—religious, political, medical, judicial—competed with one another as church and state agents tried to distance themselves from the coming relocation and disavow responsibility for it. These announcements were highly ceremonial and recalled the ceremonies of possession enacted by European travellers in the first days of contact with North American indigenous nations. The Moravian missionary at Hebron attempted to disclose the Mission's imminent departure several times over the coming year, but each time found the Inuit response underwhelming. Their muted reception underlines the Inuit sense of Hebron as a place of an enduring collection of ecological, economic, civic, religious, and family associations. While Christianity still held a privileged sphere in Inuit culture, the idea of community had outgrown the religious form of the nineteenth and early twentieth century. It is almost certain that Inuit did not react to either the first or second announcement because they were more concerned about the trade store, a vital component of their economic, environmental, and social relationships. Further, Inuit recognized the pre-eminent authority of the *AngajokKauKatiget* and *Kivgait*; the elders had been assured by the government that they would receive fair warning of decisions and would not be compelled to leave until jobs and houses were available.

A Contested Meeting: Easter, 1959

There is no account in Inuit oral history of any important announcement regarding Hebron's closure prior to the meeting that occurred on 10 April 1959, an event that would come to symbolize administrators' abandonment of their historic engagement with Inuit in Labrador. That morning two planes landed at Hebron. One, a single-engine Otter, carried Walter Rockwood, director of Labrador Affairs. The other, a single-engine Beaver, held Moravian superintendent F.W. Peacock and the Nain missionary Revered F.C.P. Grubb, the International Grenfell Association's Dr. Anthony Paddon, and a young RCMP officer new to the coast, Walter Shupe. According to Rockwood, they met with Rev. Hettasch, the Hebron missionary, soon after landing to discuss how the government's announcement of the depot's closure and the relocation of its citizens should take place.[99] Hebron did have a meeting hall, which, like the hall at Nain, had been constructed through great effort of the local elders and people. It had only been completed in the fall of 1957, with its official opening in the new year of 1958.[100] The mechanics behind the choice of the church as a site of the meeting are not known and are in fact the subject of much speculation, but according to Walter Shupe, it was the only building of sufficient size.[101] According to Rockwood, after the people arrived, Peacock confirmed the Mission's closure as announced at the Easter

Love Feast earlier by Rev. Hettasch. Rockwood then delivered a telegram from his deputy minister:

> Rev. Peacock confirmed the Mission's decision as announced earlier by Rev. Hettasch, following which I read the telegram received from you on March 25th as follows:
>
> > "YOU MAY INFORM HEBRON PEOPLE THAT FOLLOW-ING THE WITHDRAWAL OF THE MORAVIAN MISSION GOVERNMENT OF NEWFOUNDLAND WILL ASSIST FAMILIES TO MOVE TO COMMUNITIES SOUTH OF NAIN AND THAT THE SUPPLY DEPOT WILL BE CLOSED."
>
> Rev. Peacock left Hebron again the following day, but I remained there until April 15th for further discussions with Rev. S.P. Hettasch, Mr. T. Baird, Depot Manager, and the Elders.[102]

The accounts of Walter Rockwood and Reverend Hettasch (below) are reminiscent of the earliest encounters between British traders and the Inuit, where declarations of the Crown's wishes to trade with the Inuit were read aloud for a gathering of the people, or of encounters between early Moravians and Inuit, where declarations of land charters were read amid pageant, prayer, and song. The declaration is meant to illustrate the authority for the action it announces, even if the message is only vaguely understood by the audience. As Reverend Hattasch describes the announcement,

> After a brief discussion of the situation a message from the Govern-ment was read, effecting the closing of Hebron also by the Govern-ment. After this the bells were rung and all the people gathered in Church, where first we sang a hymn, then Br. Peacock spoke a few words, followed by the message from the Government read out by the Government agent, which was then translated to the people, and we closed with a prayer and a hymn. This relieved a tension which had existed for long time, not a tension of joy for the move so much, but it relieved the tension of uncertainty.[103]

Inuit oral tradition came to locate the meeting as the moment of their dispossession, when it became impossible to speak to the power arrayed around them because of the social mores that governed behaviour inside the church. This realization evolved over time as Hebronimiut sought to explain their own silence—their apparent lack of resistance—to themselves. The earliest recorded interviews with Hebron and Okak relocatees were gathered for the Royal Commission on Labrador in 1973 and 1974. Later interviews come from the preparation of the Inuit use and occupancy study,[104] an Inuit-made television documentary by OKalaKatiget, a report to federal Royal Commission on Aboriginal Peoples,[105] and interviews conducted by this author in 1999, 2003, and 2006–2007. In interviews, two residents remembered the situation:

> I don't think there is one person who is satisfied from those who have been moved from there. There is not one of us who can move to another place on our own before the white man helps us. Our white men didn't tell us, a lot of us don't know why we were moved, I can say we just went along. Not very many know the reasons.[106]

> They had to move out because they had, that they was doin' it. They didn't want to move but they had to, on account of that there was going to be nothing there. There's no stores or not going to be nothing there, no ministers or anything. Just the people alone.[107]

Later oral histories, collected in the late 1970s and after, focus more on the cultic nature of the church site and the expectation of silence before God and minister that made it impossible for Inuit to speak against the relocation. Inuit have cited both religious observance and observance of the Moravian civil order as reasons for the silence that enveloped them. One interviewee explained, "We wanted to speak out but we couldn't because we were in the church. Only the minister could speak in the church, that's why we couldn't do anything about it.... We couldn't say anything in the church because that's where we sang and had meetings. Even if we wanted to speak we weren't supposed to. That's why we couldn't do anything about relocating."[108]

Administrators made little effort to convey the reasons for their abandonment of Hebron as a community, and little was understood. Among the older Inuit, the justifications offered by the officials are remembered with apparent scepticism: "I remember that there was a meeting held by Hettasche, Peacock, Rockwood, and Dr. Paddon. We had a community hall, but the meeting was held at the Moravian Church. They didn't say why [it was held there]. We knew that in the church, we couldn't say anything. I guess that is the reason why the meeting was held at the church."[109] The silence is made up of several different tensions between the cultures of Inuit and administrators as well as tensions inherent within Inuit culture itself. External authority was not new to Labrador Inuit, and Inuit were not as inclined to feelings of awe in the presence of Kablunaat officials as is frequently reported in other areas of the eastern Arctic. *Ilira*, in this context, is not a fear of Kablunaat power as such, but a fear of distinguishing oneself from the social milieu by speaking up. However, as a kind of pageant, the meeting brought together the most powerful external forces in Inuit affairs at that time and displayed them in one symbolically loaded location. Recently, retired RCMP officer Walter Shupe recalled how, as a newly arrived constable at Nain, he was ordered north to attend the meeting and asked to stay behind afterward to ensure no difficulties arose as a result of it. He says that his superiors did not anticipate a show of Inuit resistance: "I don't think there was ever any concern that there was going to be a confrontation about it, ... and me going up there for that purpose, but maybe someone had that in their mind that it was. I got the impression that the government was making this decision and that was the bottom line."[110] Shupe described the meeting as "a one-way conversation, and it was all down."[111] In the several days he spent in Hebron after the other administrators had left, however, there were telltale incidents of drunkenness in the community: "There was certainly a lot of drinking. Myself and John Piercey, we had no place to arrest anybody and we just handled it the best we could. We tried to tell them, 'Look this is the thing that's going to happen and you're not doing anything better for yourself by being this way, and I'm not going to charge you but I don't want to see it happening again.'"[112] Drinking was just one of the many small acts of resistance that followed the administrators' unilateral decision to withdraw their services from Hebron and oust its residents. Nevertheless, the missionary departed in August 1959, followed in October by the Grenfell mission nurse. Finally, on 5 October, the provincial government's vessel *Treppasey* transported the last of Hebron's Inuit, and what belongings they could carry with them, southward.

Much has been written about the impacts of the relocation upon the lives of the relocated Inuit and the environment of Northern Labrador. Ben-Dor, Kennedy, and Brice-Bennett have all noted that the ecological impacts of the relocation scheme are at the centre of a knot of socio-economic effects that have spiralled outward with the passage of time. Northern Inuit were thrown into new environments where their lack of local ecological knowledge and social access made it difficult to achieve the same levels of success and happiness they had known at Okak and Hebron. Resident Inuit and settlers, neither of whom had been consulted about receiving the relocated Inuit, had prior access to the best fishing and sealing areas, employed different technologies, and had different customary laws to regulate harvesting. At Makkovik, this problem was greatest. Though it had a few Nutak residents, Makkovik was a settler community in genesis and organization, operating according to European-style proprietary regimes. The sudden presence of hundreds of new residents led to stresses upon local resources in the areas of the receiving communities, undermining the carrying capacities of those environments[113] and affecting every aspect of community economy—the ability of people to make a living, spiritually and economically, from the land. Depopulating the coast north of Nain isolated Inuit from the richest bioregion in Labrador. Returning to their traditional hunting and fishing camps now required arduous and expensive travel. The greatest impacts of being abandoned by the state and ousted from their homeland were revealed behind closed doors—in the inadequate houses, diminished lives and economies, and personal psychologies of northern Inuit. Tragically, as Brice-Bennett told the Royal Commission on Aboriginal Peoples in 1994, the true cost of displacement for northern Inuit revealed itself in higher mortality rates in the ensuing years at Nain, Hopedale, and Makkovik, as the ousted families struggled to orient themselves in new environments and grappled with poverty.

The exclusion of Inuit voices from the discourse concerning the fate of northern Labrador's communities made possible their ousting from the Okak and Hebron environments. This was a startling reversal of fortune for a community with a robust political tradition and a history of engaging as equals with outsiders. Northern Inuit soon sought political solutions to the difficulties they were experiencing. Former Okak residents petitioned the government for a new community in 1963. By the early 1970s, new forums for discussing and dealing with painful issues were emerging in politics and local media, especially at Nain, where many relocated families had migrated in defiance of the logic of relocation, in order to be closer to friends, family, and their old homes. The grievances of northern Inuit were foundational to the establishment of the Labrador Inuit Association (LIA) in 1973, and a demand for a new community north of Nain was for many years an intrinsic piece of the LIA's negotiations with the Crown. But the Inuit/Euro-Canadian front is by no means the only one on which northern Inuit have had to negotiate; indeed, as the works of Ben-Dor and Kennedy have shown, the relocations created a complicated ethno-political scene in northern Labrador. The relocation was not a priority for the LIA, and it eventually disappeared from the treaty table. That changed somewhat in 1999, when a group of surviving relocatees formed a committee to push their agenda. The Hebron committee organized an emotional reunion at Hebron in August 1999 and eventually won modest compensation and an apology from the government of Newfoundland. (Canada, apparently unaware of its own archives, denied any involvement.) The words of Newfoundland's apology are inscribed on a plaque at Hebron, today a UNESCO World Heritage site and a gateway to the new Torngat National Park. Such gestures, alongside treaty making itself, however important they may be in the difficult work now called *reconciliation*, remain largely rhetorical unless matched with a commitment from the

Crown and other agencies to fully engage with, and respect the autonomy of, Inuit. The development of Nunatsiavut will demonstrate whether or not we have moved beyond the failings of the 1950s.

Notes

1 Adrian Tanner, "The Aboriginal Peoples of Newfoundland and Labrador and Confederation," in "Confederation," special issue, *Newfoundland and Labrador Studies* 14, 2 (1998): 238.

2 Robert Holland, "Newfoundland and the Pattern of British Decolonization," in "Confederation," special issue, *Newfoundland and Labrador Studies* 14, 2 (1998): 141.

3 The literal meaning of *maligaksait* is "things to follow." See August Anderson, William Kalleo, and Beatrice Watts, eds., *Labradorimi Ulinnaisigutet* (Nain: Torngasuk Cultural Centre, 2007), 127.

4 Helge Kleivan, *The Eskimos of Northeast Labrador: A History of Eskimo-White Relations 1771–1955* (Oslo: Norsk Polarinstitutt, 1966), 78.

5 There are a number of terms that can be accurately applied to these events, including *resettlement, relocation, eviction,* and *displacement. Relocation* has the most currency in literature and among Inuit survivors. I use all these terms, but have lately adopted the verb "oust" (following Kim Beazley), which is more common in global south studies. See Kim Beazley, "Interrogating Notions of the Powerless Oustee," *Development and Change* 40, 2 (2009): 219–48.

6 Delgamuukw v. British Columbia, 1997 CanLII 302 (SCC), [1997] 3 SCR 1010, <http://canlii.ca/s/pbse> retrieved on 2011-10-18; Haida Nation v. British Columbia (Minister of Forests), 2004 SCC 73 (CanLII), [2004] 3 SCR 511, http://canlii.ca/s/qppg (accessed 18 Oct. 2011).

7 James Scott, *Seeing Like a State: How Certain Schemes to Improve the Human Condition Have Failed* (New Haven, CT: Yale University Press, 1998).

8 Shmuel Ben-Dor, *Makkovik: Eskimos and Settlers in a Labrador Community* (St. John's: Institute of Social and Economic Research, Memorial University: 1966), and "Inuit-Settler Relations in Makkovik, 1962," in *The White Arctic*, ed. Robert Paine (St. John's: Memorial University of Newfoundland, 1977), 306–325.

9 John C. Kennedy, "Northern Labrador: An Ethnohistorical Account," in *The White Arctic*, ed. Robert Paine (St. John's: ISER Books, 1977), 264–305; also Kennedy, "Local Government and Ethnic Boundaries in Makkovik, 1972," in the same volume (359–375); and Kennedy, *Holding the Line: Ethnic Boundaries in a Northern Labrador Community* (St. John's: ISER Books, 1985).

10 Carol Brice-Bennett, ed., *Our Footprints Are Everywhere: Inuit Land Use and Occupancy in Labrador* (Nain: Labrador Inuit Association, 1977); Brice-Bennett, *Dispossessed: The Eviction of Inuit from Hebron, Labrador* (Happy Valley: Labrador Institute of Northern Studies, 1994); and Brice-Bennett, "The Redistribution of the Northern Labrador Inuit Population: A Strategy for Integration and Formula for Conflict," *Zeitschrift für Kanada-Studien* 14, 2 (1994): 95–106.

11 See the following articles, all in Paine's *The White Arctic*: Terje Brantenberg, "Ethnic Values and Ethnic Recruitment in Nain" (326–343) and "Ethnic Commitments and Local Government in Nain, 1969–1976" (376–410); Anne Brantenberg, "The Marginal School and the Children of Nain" (344–358). Much of the work in this era was associated with ISER's "Identity in the East Arctic" project.

12 Royal Commission of Labrador, Volume 6 (St. John's: Queen's Printer, 1974).

13 Brice-Bennett, *Dispossessed*.

14 Department of Indian and Northern Affairs, *Royal Commission on Aboriginal Peoples* (Ottawa: Government of Canada, 1996).

15 See the films *The Relocation of Hebron* (1987) and *Imprisoned in Our Hearts* (2000); the magazine *Honouring Our Elders* (2004); and the magazine *Kinatuinamut Ilingajuk*, issues from 4 February 1976, 28 March 1980, 6 March 1981, January 1988, Summer 1993, Winter/Spring 1998, and Fall 1999.

16 Ben-Dor, *Makkovik*; Brice-Bennett, *Footprints*, *Dispossessed*, and "Redistribution"; Kennedy, *Holding*; and Anthony Williamson, "Population Movement and the Food Gathering Economy of Northern Labrador," Master's thesis, McGill University, 1964.

17 David Damas, *Arctic Villagers, Arctic Migrants* (Montreal and Kingston: McGill-Queen's University Press, 2002); Alan Rudolph Marcus, *Relocating Eden: The Image and Politics of Inuit Exile in the Canadian Arctic* (Hanover and London: Dartmouth College, University Press of New England, 1995); Frank Tester and Peter Kulchyski, *Tammarniit (Mistakes): Inuit Relocation in the Eastern Arctic 1939–63* (Vancouver: University of British Columbia Press, 1994).

18 Ben-Dor, *Makkovik*; Brice-Bennett, *Footprints*, *Dispossessed*, and "Redistribution"; Kennedy, *Holding*; also Williamson, "Population."

19 Marcus, 196.

20 Marcus, 43.

21 These concerns had prompted the Northern Labrador Trading Operation, the DNLA's predecessor, to relocate the Davis Inlet Innu band to the Okak Bay area in 1948.

22 Max Budgell, Nutak Depot Manager, to Trade Supervisor, 19 June 1951, GN 56/2 Box 63, Provincial Archives of Newfoundland and Labrador (PANL). The Division attempted to limit the consumption of "non-essentials," and Budgell attempted to enact work-relief schemes, but the programs did not take off.

23 Walter Rockwood, Director, Division of Northern Labrador Affairs, to Ted Baird, Hebron Depot Manager, 22 April 1958, GN 56/2 Box 82, PANL.

24 Marcus, 44.

25 Diamond Jenness, *Eskimo Administration III: Labrador* (Montreal: Arctic Institute, 1965); also Damas; Tester and Kulchyski; Marcus.

26 Eskimo Affairs 1952, 4; qtd. in Marcus, 48.

27 In May 1952, at the suggestion of the reformist RCMP officer and bureaucrat Henry Larsen, the federal government held an inter-agency "Conference on Eskimo Affairs" (Marcus, 25), which inaugurated Canada's new interest in Inuit social policy. The conference was essential for the government to be seen as tackling "the problem" Farley Mowat and Richard Herrington had publicly identified. The federal conference, Marcus says, defined the "Eskimo problem" as having

three sides: an unstable economy, poor health, and dependence on government benefits (Marcus, 26). Although there was no single policy that emerged from the federal conference, it resulted in the striking of the Eskimo Affairs Committee, composed of representatives of all the federal departments touching on areas of northern policy. As spaces for information gathering and exchange, conferences were exclusive to Euro-Canadian bureaucrats, as was the committee they spawned: no Inuit appeared before the Eskimo Affairs Committee until 1959 (Marcus, 27).

28 Marcus.

29 Euro-Canadians believed the poverty of Inuit social and economic fortunes was reflected in depressed environmental conditions. The unreliability of game was a prime motivator in the federal government's policy initiatives in the 1950s. In Labrador, officials expressed similar concerns in the same time period. Walter Rockwood had arrived at this conclusion during his years as government agent (1942–1945) and reiterated this fact in 1955: the Inuit household and social economy was dependent on a balance of land animals and fish, but seal was the pillar and staple of the whole thing, and for several years ending in 1955, the seal fishery had been in perceived decline. Walter Rockwood, *Memorandum on Wildlife as Affecting the Food Supply of Northern Labrador*, 26 January 1955, GN 56/2 Box 63, PANL. "The staple meat diet of the Northern Labrador people, Eskimos and Settlers as well as for their beasts of burden, the dogs, have always been the seal, and this supply appears to become more and more precarious each year," Rockwood wrote. "Man cannot live by fish alone, and when people state, as I have heard them do, that the people are starving what they really mean is that their diet is lacking in meat and fats which the rigorous climate demands."

30 E.P. Wheeler, *Report on Labrador Eskimo*, 1951. RG 85 Vol. 2079, 1006-5, Part 2. Library and Archives Canada.

31 Although Horwood had helped create the DNLA, it became one of the principal targets of his newspaper column and other writings as soon as he had left government.

32 Harold Horwood, "Policy in Labrador Part II," Political Notebook, *St. John's Evening Telegram*, 1952.

33 Harold Horwood, "Policy in Labrador Part I," Political Notebook, *St. John's Evening Telegram*, 1952.

34 Marcus, 219.

35 Walter Rockwood reported that they were living with relatives, or in tents on one of the islands: "These people have no money to buy building materials with which to build new homes," he wrote. (Walter Rockwood to RL Andrews, Deputy Minister of Public Welfare, 10 March 1955, MG 908 Box 2, Special Reports, PANL. The Moravian Mission, the International Grenfell Association, and the Department of Welfare monitored the migration to Goose Bay and sought to control movement in and out of the north coast, in case it "got out of hand," by coordinating their management of Inuit movements southward and the houses they would live in when they got there. Social housing programs emerged as an instrument of liberalization and social control, through which officials could influence Inuit behaviour.

36 Jenness, 76.

37 See, for instance, Paul Pelletier, Memorandum for the Interdepartmental Committee on Indians and Eskimos, 3 April 1950, RG 85 Vol 2079 1006-5, LAC.

38 Ranger F. Cheeseman to Chief Ranger, St. John's, re: Census of Indians and Eskimos, 24 June 1950, GN31/2 Box 117, File 628.2, PANL.

39 Previously, in 1949, James Cantley had included Labrador Inuit under the heading "New Quebec," which was made up of Nunavik and Labrador (Marcus, 39).

40 Jenness, 76. The Mission, provincial government, and International Grenfell Association often had different views on what an Inuk was, and within the federal system different agencies had divergent interpretations on the same census material.

41 Ibid.

42 Paul Pelletier, Memorandum on Labrador Indians and Eskimos (Federal Responsibility), 1953. RG 85, Vol. 2079, 1006-5, Part 3. LAC.

43 Paul Pelletier, Memorandum for the Interdepartmental Committee on Indians and Eskimos, 3 April 1950, RG 85 Vol. 2079 1006-5, Part 1A. LAC. In attendance were NA Robertson, Secretary to Cabinet (Chair), D.M. McKay, Citizenship and Immigration, A.B. Hockin from Finance, Dr. Moore from National Health and Welfare, J.G. Wright and James Cantley from Resources and Development, C.K. Grey, the Deputy Commissioner of the RCMP, and Paul Pelletier from the Privy Council, who chaired the Committee (Report of the Interdepartmental Committee on Newfoundland Indians and Eskimos, 18 April 1950, RG 85 Vol. 2079 1006-5, Part 1A. LAC).

44 P.E. Moore, Director, Indian Health Services, 19 June 1950, Memorandum to Deputy Minister, National Health, re: Indians and Eskimos in Newfoundland, RG 85 Vol. 2079, 1006-5 Part 1A, LAC. See also Jenness, 75; Kennedy, *Holding*, 282.

45 Paddon felt that Nutak's poor housing conditions had reached a crisis with the arrival of the Hebron families: "Now one can say that the populations are huddled into the houses in the Nutak area. The overcrowding must be seen to be believed," he wrote. Paddon believed the housing conditions were related directly to tuberculosis rates at Nutak and Hebron, which he claimed were "worse than anywhere else in Labrador, and probably in the province." Families gathering together in small houses at Nutak were creating conditions for a rapid transmission of the disease. "Overcrowding amongst Eskimos is not a racial habit, but the result of coldness, of inadequate building materials and inadequate technological knowledge, and above all the result of lack of material or the money to purchase it" (Dr. W.A. Paddon, International Grenfell Association, to Deputy Minister of Natural Resources, 14 July 1951, PANL).

46 Secretary of State J.W. Pickersgill to Herbert L. Pottle, Minister of Public Welfare, 12 April 1954. Re: Labrador Indians and Eskimos. RG 85 Vol. 2079, 1006-5 Part 4, LAC. Also MG 908 Box 1 File 6, Provincial Archives of Newfoundland and Labrador. Canada arrived at the $200,000 figure based on a suggested capital program of expenses submitted by Newfoundland during discussions in 1952 (W.E. Harris to Herbert L. Pottle, 19 May 1953, RG 85 Vol. 2079, 1006-5 Part 3, LAC).

47 Secretary of State J.W. Pickersgill to Herbert L. Pottle, Minister of Public Welfare, 12 April 1954. Re: Labrador Indians and Eskimos. RG 85 Vol. 2079, 1006-5 Part 4, LAC. Also MG 908 Box 1 File 6, Provincial Archives of Newfoundland and

Labrador. Family allowance and OAP became available for distribution and management by RCMP between 1945 and 1948 in the Eastern Arctic (Marcus, 21).

48 W.E. Harris, Minister of Citizenship and Immigration, Ottawa, to Herbert L. Pottle, Minister for Public Welfare, Province of Newfoundland, 28 March 1955, MG 908 Box 1 File 6, PANL.

49 Walter Rockwood, Memorandum on General Policy in Respect to the Indians and Eskimos of Northern Labrador, 1955, RG 85 Vol. 2079 1006-5 Part 5, LAC: 3; a draft version of this memorandum can be found in GN 56 Box 2, "File—Policy General," Provincial Archives of Newfoundland and Labrador.

50 Ibid.

51 Ibid., 6–7.

52 Dr. Anthony Paddon, "Community Aspects of Health and Welfare in Northern Labrador," 27 February 1955, Collection 077 1.01.022, Centre for Newfoundland Studies, Memorial University, 5. This suggestion resurrected a proposal the Moravians had discussed among themselves throughout much of the 1940s, but had abandoned for lack of resources.

53 Ibid., 1.

54 Ibid., 3.

55 Ibid., 2.

56 F.W. Rowe, MLA for Labrador, to H.L. Pottle, Minister for Public Welfare, 8 March 1955, Collection 077.1.01.022, Centre for Newfoundland Studies, Memorial University.

57 Copy of a letter from Dr. Charles S. Curtis to Dr. Leonard Miller, NF Deputy Minister of Health (August 23, 1955). RG 85 Vol. 2079, 1006-5 Part 4, LAC: 2. Like Paddon's essay on community redevelopment, Curtis's letter appears to have been highly influential on decision makers. Copies of the letter were found by this author in all archives visited, including federal, provincial, and Moravian archives.

58 Copy of a letter from Dr. Charles S. Curtis to Dr. Leonard Miller, NF Deputy Minister of Health, 23 August 1955, RG 85 Vol. 2079, 1006-5 Part 4, LAC, 2-3.

59 Ibid., 3.

60 *Periodical Accounts of the Work of the Moravian Missions* (Second Century) (London: Trust Society for the Furtherance of the Gospel, 1956), 25; in Kennedy, 278.

61 In attendance were representative bureaucrats and politicians from provincial and federal departments, including the federal representatives for Labrador, T.W.G. Ashbourne and H. Batten, provincial MLAs, the speaker of the House of Assembly, and a large contingent of federal senior civil servants, including the deputy ministers of Welfare and Transport, as well as Gordon Robertson, the deputy minister of Northern Affairs and National Resources. Federal representatives were there in a "consultative capacity" only, an arrangement that mirrored the opaqueness of the federal-provincial agreements (J. Lesage to F.W. Rowe, 30 January 1956, RG 85 Vol 2079 1006-5, LAC).

62 "Conference on Labrador Affairs," *News and Views on Welfare II* (Department of Public Welfare, St. John's, 1956), MG 895, PANL.

63 "Editorial," *News and Views on Welfare I* (Department of Public Welfare, St. John's, 1956), PANL MG 895.

64 Piers Vitebsky, "National Discussion and Local Actuality," *Manchester Papers on Development* 2.2: pp. 1-12 (1986), 11; in Marcus, *Relocating*, 27.

65 "Roads and more roads are needed everywhere, in order to bring people out of the isolation which they have suffered down through the years. However, to connect every settlement would be a tremendously costly business and, perhaps, it would not be necessary. It was pointed out that all over Newfoundland people are scattered in small communities. There were good reasons for them settling in these places originally but these reasons no longer exist. If fishermen are to be making a living out of the industry they must be near to markets for their fish. In the old days fishing was done from small boats, but the trend now is to larger boats with modern facilities. The setting up of small settlements has meant doubling and trebling of churches, schools, halls, as well as public facilities. If the people were moved to larger centres they could take advantage of facilities which exist in those places and there would not be need for connecting roads. These larger places could provide health and welfare services, as well as educational facilities and would make it easier and more economical to operate transportation and mail services. The government, it was pointed out, is prepared to help people who want to move from small to large centres, but there are certain unalterable conditions; the chief is that all people of the small settlement must want to move" (Department of Public Welfare, *News and Views on Welfare I* (Department of Public Welfare, St. John's, 1956), MG 895, PANL).

66 Press and Radio Release (Office of the Minister of Public Welfare, St. John's, 6 February 1956), Collection 077 1.01.010, Centre for Newfoundland Studies, Memorial University.

67 Government of Newfoundland, Labrador Conference, 13–16 February 956, RG 85 Vol. 2079. 1006-5 Part 4, Library Archives Canada, 11.

68 Ibid.

69 Iron Ore mining was already underway in western Labrador at Knob Lake and Lake Wabush.

70 The influence of exploration on the closings has not been noted in literature before, but Inuit oral history remembers it.

71 *Periodical Accounts of the Work of the Moravian Missions* (Second Century) (London: Trust Society for the Furtherance of the Gospel, 1956), 25; in Kennedy, *Northern Labrador*, 278. Representatives of all the major government departments as well as charitable patrons sat on this committee, including the Superintendent of the Moravian Mission.

72 Minutes of the Executive Council, 26 April 1956; in Brice-Bennett, *Dispossessed*, 41.

73 R.L. Andrews, Deputy Minister of Public Welfare, St. John's, to Gordon Robertson, Deputy Minister of Northern Affairs, 19 April 1956, RG 85 Vol. 2079, 1006-5 Part 4, LAC.

74 F.A.G. Cunningham, Memorandum for the Deputy Minister. Re: Federal Assistance for Capital Expenditures by Newfoundland on Eskimo and Indian Account, 28 May 1956, RG 85 Vol. 2079, 1006-5 Part 4, LAC.

75 Government of Newfoundland, Department of Public Welfare Annual Report, March 1960. In Jenness, 81. See also "Northern Labrador Affairs in Retrospect," 1961, MG 908 Box 2, Special Reports file.

76 There were a number of events at both Nutak and Hebron, in addition to those mentioned by Rockwood, that jarred the sensibilities of administrators and led

them to regard the communities as problematic. Peter Evans, *Transformations of Indigenous Resistance and Identity in Northern Labrador,* unpublished PhD Dissertation (2011 forthcoming, Magdalene College, University of Cambridge). See Chapters 4 and 5 for a description of protests at Hebron in 1934, outbreaks of "madness" at Hebron in 1938, a suspicious death at Nutak in 1946, and trade disputes in 1946 and 1951.

77 Walter Rockwood, Director, Northern Labrador Affairs, Memorandum, Request by Former Residents of Nutak to Establish a New Depot in the Okak Bay Area, 28 June 1963, GN 56/2 Box 11 File "Okak Bay." PANL.

78 Walter Rockwood to R.L. Andrews, "Community Governance in Northern Labrador," 1959, MG 908, Box 2 Special Report File, PANL.

79 Ibid.

80 *Periodical Accounts of the Work of the Moravian Missions* (Second Century) (London: Trust Society for the Furtherance of the Gospel, 1955)', 43.

81 Tom Uvloriak, in discussion with the author and Wilson Jararuse, 1999.

82 Susie Onalik, in discussion with the author and Wilson Jararuse, 1999.

83 Walter Rockwood, Division of Northern Labrador Affairs Annual Report, 1956, MG 908 Box 1 File 5, PANL, 6. See also GN 56/2 File "Population – Nutak," PANL.

84 Walter Rockwood, *Northern Labrador Affairs in Retrospect*, 1961, MG 908 Box 2 Special Reports. PANL: 4

85 See Damas, 100.

86 Levi Nochasak, William Millie, Hebron Elders, "Petition of the Hebron People to Government in St. John's," 9 August 1956. Addressed to Dr. F.W. Rowe, Minister of Mines and Resources. Translation by Rev. Sigfried Hettasch of an original in Inuktitut contained in the same file. Government of Newfoundland. Collection 077: 1.01.020, Centre for Newfoundland Studies, Memorial University.

87 Brice-Bennett 1996, 73–74, translation by Rita Andersen.

88 F.W. Rowe, Minister of Education, Government of Newfoundland, to Levi Nochasak, Church Elder, Hebron, 31August 1956, Collection 077: 1.01.020, Centre for Newfoundland Studies, Memorial University.

89 R.L. Andrews to Levi Nochasak and William Millie, Hebron Elders, 30 October 1956, MG 908 Box 1 File 4, PANL.

90 Walter Rockwood, Director, Division of Northern Labrador Affairs, to R.L. Andrews, Deputy Minister of the Department of Public Welfare, 1958, "Proposed Closing of Hebron," MG 908 Box 1 File 4, PANL.

91 Ibid.

92 W. Anthony Paddon, MD, International Grenfell Association, Form Requesting Resettlement, 1957, RG Stacey Collection, Centre for Newfoundland Studies, Memorial University. Found at *No Great Future: Government Sponsored Resettlement in Newfoundland and Labrador since Confederation:* http://www.mun.ca/mha/resettlement/documents_1.php

93 Reverend F.W. Peacock, Superintendent, Moravian Mission,"Form Requesting Resettlement," 1957, RG Stacey Collection, Centre for Newfoundland Studies, Memorial University. Found at *No Great Future: Government Sponsored Resettlement in Newfoundland and Labrador since Confederation:* http://www.mun.ca/mha/resettlement/documents_1.php

94 British Mission Board, BMB Minute Book 16, 22 November 1956, 165. Moravian Church Archives, Muswell Hill, London.

95 British Mission Board, BMB Minute Book 17, 14 April 1957. Moravian Church Archives, Muswell Hill, London.

96 British Mission Board, BMB Minute Book 17, 31 October 1958, 137. Moravian Church Archives, Muswell Hill, London.

97 Minutes of meeting, 30 December 1958 (in Brice-Bennett, *Dispossessed*, 49–52).

98 Walter Rockwood, Director, Division of Northern Labrador Affairs, to R.L. Andrews, Deputy Minister of the Department of Public Welfare, 1 May 1959, "Re: Closing of Hebron," MG 908 Box 1 File 4, PANL .

99 Walter Rockwood, Director, Division of Northern Labrador Affairs, to R.L. Andrews, Deputy Minister of the Department of Public Welfare, "Re: Closing of Hebron," 1 May 1959, MG 908 Box 1 File 4, PANL.

100 *Periodical Accounts of the Work of the Moravian Missions* (Second Century) (London: Trust Society for the Furtherance of the Gospel, 1958), 33; 1959, 50.

101 Walter Shupe, interview with author, ND 2006.

102 Walter Rockwood, Director, Division of Northern Labrador Affairs, to R.L. Andrews, Deputy Minister of the Department of Public Welfare (n.d. 1958), "Proposed Closing of Hebron," MG 908 Box 1 File 4, PANL.

103 *Periodical Accounts of the Work of the Moravian Missions* (Second Century) (London: Trust Society for the Furtherance of the Gospel, 1960), 17.

104 Brice-Bennett, *Our Footprints*.

105 Brice-Bennett, *Dispossessed*.

106 Jusiah Ittulak, interview by William Kalleo, 1973, GN 142 Box 18, PANL.

107 Sampson Andersen, interview by William Kalleo, 1973, GN 142 Box 18, PANL.

108 Johannes Semigak, OKalaKatiget 1987. OKalaKatiget Society Collection, Nain, Labrador.

109 Sabina Nochasak, in discussion with the author and Wilson Jararuse, Hopedale, 1999.

110 Walter Shupe, in discussion with the author, 2006.

111 Other administrators who dealt closely with Inuit, including Ted Baird, the DNLA store manager, were aware that the church meeting defied the usual methods of Inuit decision making. "There was no community meeting as such that they normally would have concerning such an event. They were just told and it happened," he told the Royal Commission in 1994. "It was a terrible injustice" (quoted in Brice-Bennett, *Dispossessed*, 77).

112 Walter Shupe, in discussion with the author, 2006.

113 John C. Kennedy, *Brief to the Royal Commission* (St. John's: Institute for Social and Economic Research, 1973), 9.

CHAPTER 5

Tracing Social Change Among the Labrador Inuit: What Does the Nutrition Literature Tell Us?[1]

Maura Hanrahan

Inuit believe that you are literally the food you eat. One way to better know Inuit, then, is to understand what they eat, how their eating habits and patterns changed, and, crucially, why. An exploration of the relevant nutrition literature can enhance our understanding of the Labrador Inuit and their history.

This chapter relates the nutrition-related literature to three phases of social change as experienced by the Labrador Inuit: disruption, adaptation, and, finally, transformation (during which the epidemiologic transition occurs). Social change and food practices are intertwined, and changes in food practices are associated with health effects. As we trace the development of each phase of social change—disruption, adaptation, and transformation— through the food-related literature, we learn how social change affects food acquisition, consumption, and meaning in Labrador Inuit society. At the same time, nutrition studies can help us locate where Inuit communities are in their journey through these phases; they help demonstrate, for example, that since the early part of the twentieth century the Labrador Inuit have been in the transformation phase and are undergoing the epidemiologic transition, a phase in human development characterized by a sudden increase in population growth rates brought about by improved health care, followed by a re-levelling of population growth from subsequent declines in procreation rates.

This chapter grows out of a critical review of the Labrador Inuit–specific and related nutrition literature. The review was carried out as part of a larger review of all nutrition-related literature pertaining to Newfoundland and Labrador from 1630 to 2000, culminating in the 2001 publication of the annotated bibliography, *A Veritable Scoff: Sources on Foodways and Nutrition in Newfoundland and Labrador*.[2] In addition, it relies on other literature, such as references to missionary accounts, that provides information on Inuit diet and food practices. Given the significant time the author has spent in Labrador to conduct food-related and other studies,[3] the paper is also informed by participant observation.

Indigenous People and Social Change

Perhaps no population in North America has experienced such rapid social change as the indigenous peoples of Canada's North.[4] In Labrador, this includes the Inuit, the Métis, and the Innu. The social change experienced by indigenous peoples has usually been imposed by outside forces, including explorers, early settlers, missionaries, and colonial and post-colonial governments. Indigenous peoples are forced to react, using their own agency as best they can as they adapt to change. Indigenous people in what is now Canada have become part of the Fourth World—internally colonized people with continuing political aspirations, many of whom still live on their traditional land or, more accurately, a reduced portion of this land. As ways of life changed, so did nutritional habits and nutritional status.[5] The indigenous situation is markedly different from those of other populations in Canadian society that are undergoing social change, such as immigrants who often voluntarily came to Canada.

According to Peter Bjerregaard and T. Kue Young,[6] who studied Inuit health throughout the circumpolar region, Inuit patterns of social change are characterized by three phases, all of which are initiated by the arrival of Europeans to Inuit land. The first is the initial period of profound and disruptive change, which I shall call "disruption." It usually begins with the first major epidemic, which causes havoc in Inuit communities as young and old die in numbers larger than any ever seen by the Inuit. This phase lasts until the traumatized Inuit convert to Christianity, with its promises brought by missionaries.[7] In West Greenland, disruption began in 1734 with a smallpox epidemic and lasted until Danish missionaries baptized Greenland Inuit through the first half of the nineteenth century.[8] The Inuit of the Mackenzie River delta were faced with an onslaught of diseases during this phase, including tuberculosis, syphilis, smallpox, diphtheria, and influenza. As a result, their numbers declined from approximately 2500 people to only 130 over a sixty-year period.[9] This phase may be lengthy, lasting several decades or more.[10]

The second phase is, in the words of Bjerregaard and Young, "a period of relative stability and adaptation," which I shall refer to as "adaptation." It is most clearly delineated in Greenland, which the Danish government, through the Royal Greenland Trade Department, kept isolated for decades. Broadly, this phase lasted until the middle of the twentieth century, varying widely from one Inuit region to another. During this period, the Labrador Inuit continued to rely mainly on traditional foods, as we shall see, but were also becoming familiar with introduced foods, such as the root vegetables grown by the Moravian missionaries on the north coast. The Hudson's Bay Company and other traders became established at North West River, Cartwright, and other Labrador communities, with the result that Inuit and Inuit-Métis traded for or purchased imported foodstuffs like sugar and coffee. However, the mass influx of commercial food products had yet to occur.

The third phase is a time of more complex and intense transformation with the outcome of national and global integration, according to Bjerregaard and Young and M.H. Wahdan. I shall call this phase "transformation." Bjerregaard and Young (both research physicians) claim that, in the last half-century or so, "all Inuit communities...have completed the transformation from relatively isolated self-reliant communities based on hunting and fishing that existed at the time of contact."[11] In fact, Inuit are integrated in some ways, but not all, since, as we shall see, some of their food practices are remarkably persistent, and in some jurisdictions there are factors that facilitate cultural persistence (e.g., the land claims process in Canada). Further, the epidemiologic transition and the transformation phase are more complex than Bjerregaard and Young's description indicates.

The epidemiologic transition may never be complete, because it is not necessarily unidirectional; in the words of Wahdan, the epidemiologic transition is "a continuous transformative process, with some (infectious) diseases disappearing and others appearing or re-emerging."[12] During the transformation phase, multiple changes happen at a rapid pace; these include economic, technological, and social change leading to new economies; population growth, caused, in this case, by influxes of non-Inuit; transformed housing, clothing types, and hunting styles; and language loss. The resulting acculturative stress can negatively impact mental health and cause increases in violence, suicide, and substance abuse.[13] Changing patterns in physical health are also associated with acculturative stress. Some of these patterns are associated with altered diets, others with improved health care (e.g., large numbers of people no longer die of infectious diseases). Note that for Inuit this acculturation is largely involuntary; they have even been called "specta-tors" to the social change of the transformation phase.[14]

The epidemiologic transition is a process indigenous people undergo during the transformation phase. As populations undergo the epidemio-logic transition, they generally become healthier and their life expectancy increases; infant mortality falls and more people survive to adulthood.[15] There is a fundamental change in the main determinants of health and a shift in the primary causes of death from infectious to non-infectious diseases. Populations experience higher rates of chronic degenerative diseases, such as cancer, cardiovascular diseases, and type 2 diabetes. There is also a rise in non-fatal but disabling conditions, such as osteoarthritis.

Before Disruption: Labrador Inuit in the Pre-contact Period

Labrador is a large northern territory of boreal forest and sub-arctic tundra that constitutes the mainland portion of the eastern Canadian province of Newfoundland and Labrador. There are currently (as of 2011) about 7000 Labrador Inuit, nearly half of whom live on the coast abutting the Labrador Sea, part of the north Atlantic Ocean. The Labrador Inuit are the direct de-scendants of the Thule who migrated across northern Canada from Alaska about 1200 CE. The Labrador Inuit share many customs and cultural prac-tices with Inuit in the other three Inuit regions of Canada (as defined by the Inuit Tapiriit Kanatami [ITK], the national organization for Inuit): Nunavik, Quebec; Nunavut, Canada's third territory; and Inuvialuit, northwestern Canada. There are linguistic similarities among all these groups, although Labrador Inuktitut is an endangered language and spoken in only a few of the communities on Labrador's north coast, most notably Nain and Hopedale. In addition to their links within Canada, the Labrador Inuit are also connected to Inuit worldwide through their membership in the Inuit Circumpolar Conference (ICC), the international Inuit body, which draws from Russia (especially Chukotka), Greenland, and the United States as well as Canada. The Labrador Métis remain outside the ICC and are not part of the land claim that led to the formation of Nunatsiavut.

Like most indigenous peoples who have an integral relationship with the land and sea, Labrador Inuit practise a seasonal round of economic activities that provide the means to stay alive but also are imbued with cultural and social meaning. Historically, large gatherings of up to 200 people took place in summer when Inuit fished salmon and caught Arctic char using weirs or spears. Food, mainly fish that was dry-cured, was relatively abundant during the short summer season. In late summer, Inuit moved inland to hunt cari-bou, drying and storing much of the meat for the winter, when food scarcities were not uncommon. By early fall, Inuit were living in small family groups; they dispersed to better take advantage of sparse resources. In late fall, Inuit hunted migrating harp seals, and in winter they caught and ate ringed seal, walrus, and seabirds, such as murre. Labrador Inuit lived in sod houses in winter and skin tents in summer, building *igloos* (snow houses) when they travelled to access food resources during the snowy months.

The whale hunt was economically and socially important until the late 1800s, when it declined because of over-harvesting by Europeans and possibly because of climate changes. Seasonal delicacies that added variety to the Inuit diet included *sablalik*, a partly predigested mixture of blubber, berries, and trout roe; *utjak*, or seal flippers; and *uinastika*, dried caribou stomach. Seal and caribou were the most highly prized of all food. The primary nutritional problem facing the Inuit was shortage of food, not nutritional deficiencies. When energy needs were met, nutritional adequacy was assured through the consumption of all animal parts. In addition to animal flesh, organs, blood, fat, and bones were used as food. There was significant seasonal variation in food availability: a "scattered feed meal of ducks and a scattered meal of seals and a feed of mussels, and a feed of winkles [periwinkles] and a feed of *conyucks* [seaweed]or whatever" made up the diet during a southern Labrador spring.[16]

The 1845 Moravian missionary report from Nain describes a winter famine that led to the deaths of some Inuit who went inland in search of trout.[17] In times of severe food shortage, Inuit resorted to eating sea grass, foxes, and mussels. The diet was high in protein, relatively low in carbohydrates, moderately high in fat, and rich in minerals, B vitamins, and most fat-soluble vitamins. While understanding of the traditional Inuit diet is still evolving, there is a consensus among dieticians that the Inuit diet provided all the essential nutrients.[18]

There is no word for nutrition in any of the Inuit languages. The Inuit concept of nutrition involved consuming all parts of the animal, eschewing any waste whatsoever (a practice that may be rooted in occasional experiences of food shortage). Inuit ate not just seal meat but also seal blubber, intestine, blood, and liver. Inuit believed that the food one eats in childhood becomes part of one and, as such, is necessary through life.

The First Phase of Social Change: Disruption

The arrival of Europeans in the New World is central to the first phase of social change, disruption. This phase is often marked by an epidemic, deadly to many in the population, including elders, who are the source of prestige and knowledge for Inuit and other indigenous peoples. The death of elders speeds up social change, since sources of knowledge transfer and social control are now absent; this is especially true if there are a number of fatalities at once, particularly for small groups. Missionaries are present, offering hope for the next life and sometimes sustenance for this one, so often it is at this time that indigenous people are Christianized.

Owing to their easterly location, Labrador Inuit had contact with Europeans beginning almost as early as the permanent presence of Europeans in the Americas.[19] Between 1500 and 1771 CE, Labrador Inuit–European relations were mainly hostile, although peaceful trade did occur, especially in southern Labrador, where Inuit traded with seasonal fishermen from Europe. In 1767 three traders and twenty Inuit were killed at Cape Charles, while nine more Inuit were taken prisoner. Seven Moravian missionaries (part of a Czech-German Christian sect) were killed on the north coast in 1752, preventing Christians from getting a toehold in Labrador. The missionaries' luck changed in 1771 when they succeeded in establishing their first permanent station at Nain, in northern Labrador, a summer gathering place for Inuit. Missions were also set up at Okak, the largest mission (1776), Hopedale (1782), Hebron (1830), Makkovik (1896), and other places. The first baptism took place in 1776 and was followed by the "awakening" of 1799–1804 at Hopedale, Nain, and Okak, which was triggered by game scarcities. The awakening was the conversion of many northern Labrador Inuit to Christianity. Given the large numbers of baptisms during the awakening, it is likely that influential shamans (*angakkuk* or *angnatok*) converted at this time. The Moravians undermined the role of shamans and Inuit spiritual practices but did not entirely eliminate them; in 1811 two missionaries noted the use of a raven's claw by Uttakiyok, an Inuk, as protection from dangerous spirits while travelling.[20]

It was during the disruption phase that diseases foreign to the Labrador Inuit were introduced; these would have an effect on the population in the next phase, adaptation. Given the Moravians' early preoccupation with establishing themselves, initiating trade, and providing food for themselves in a strange climate, it is reasonable to conclude that the Inuit diet remained largely unchanged during the disruption phase.

The Second Phase of Social Change: Adaptation

Fiercely independent, the Labrador Inuit resisted the Moravians' efforts to turn them into cod fishermen—at least for many decades. Cod fishing was viewed as the work of women and elders. The Moravians had a financial interest in transforming the Inuit economy; they were traders as well as missionaries and knew that they would do well brokering cod sales in Europe.

They received subsidies from their church's headquarters in Europe but, like Moravian missionaries worldwide, were expected to and needed to supplement this income through their own economic activities. (Missionary trade was managed by the Society for the Furtherance of the Gospel in London.)

The Inuit continued to hunt caribou, which necessitated seasonal movement. Their movement to the coast to catch salmon, char, and seals was dictated by the seasons. They did not settle year-round in Nain, Hebron, Nutak, or any of the other Moravian mission stations, which were clustered on the north coast. Many were, however, eager to return for Christmas and Easter church services. The missionaries' goal was to have them stay at the stations through the post-Christmas and Lenten period, but this proved difficult.

The Moravians rejected as congregants the trickle of "settlers" to the coast. These men, mainly trappers and traders from Scotland, Norway, England, and Wales, joined Inuit groups and married Inuit women. The Moravians would not admit settlers or their half-Inuit children, whom they called "southlanders" and "half-castes," to their congregations, believing them to be a negative and corrupting influence on the Inuit. Some Inuit families were less Christianized than others, and, given Moravian disapproval of settlers, it was likely the less Christianized families who absorbed the European men. In 1850 the Moravians realized that they would have to be as inclusive as the Inuit if they hoped to maintain and increase their congregations; as a result, they finally admitted the settlers. They did not, however, establish mission stations on the south coast or even on the southern part of the north coast; they remained in Makkovik and further north.

The Inuit household economy remained relatively intact in the early Moravian era. The missionaries' effect on Inuit food consumption would have been somewhat limited, given that the majority of Inuit continued their version of seasonal transhumance. It is likely that the diets of the missionaries and their families changed the most, since they had left an agrarian society and market-based economy in Europe. Their attempts to engage in farming—building small kitchen gardens at the mission stations—met with limited success in this geophysical environment. Indeed, in September 1876 a missionary's child died "of a complaint which is new in Labrador as far as we know; it appears to be a form of scurvy."[21]

But change was occurring, albeit slowly, throughout the adaptation phase, partly as a result of periods of food shortage, such as the 1845 famine. Some Inuit went inland for trout and died there of starvation. Inuit began consuming foodstuffs imported by the Moravian missionaries and eating the vegetables cultivated by the missionaries, although the Europeans did not necessarily encourage the practice. One missionary wrote in a private letter dated 1857, "it would seem as if they became more and more dissatisfied with the means of sustenance providentially assigned to them, and acquired a greater taste for European articles of diet, such as flour, pork, tea, sugar, etc. We often protest against this, but the poor people think we do so because we begrudge them these things."[22] The missionaries may have been on the right track; according to Kuhnlein, introduced foods can provide energy and variety but those most often consumed are not good sources of nutrients, resulting in an overall decline in diet quality.[23]

The main threat to Inuit health, however, was an increase in infectious diseases such as influenza, whooping cough, dysentery, and typhoid. By 1868 these diseases had caused a significant decline in the (northern, Moravianized) Inuit population. A missionary wrote, "This results mainly from the mortality arising from frequently recurring malignant epidemics. It seems clear that the people's power of endurance under the hardships of their daily life are [sic] diminishing. This may be attributed to the use of foreign articles of diet instead of the flesh and fat of seals."[24] Threatened mainly by infectious rather than chronic diseases, Labrador Inuit were not yet undergoing the epidemiologic transition, and they would not for some time to come.

In 1900 the most common new diseases were also infectious: tuberculosis and syphilis.[25] Samuel King Hutton, one of only two physicians ever hired by the Moravian missions, worked at the Okak hospital from 1903 to 1908. Hutton's description of the Inuit diet in a 1909 monograph[26] shows that pre-contact foods remained important, especially the seal, followed by caribou. Inuit also ate walrus, bears, foxes, and sea birds, as well as tiny snow bunting. Trout and cod were not preserved in salt, which was the European practice at the time. Sculpin tails, mussels, and sea urchins were also consumed—all of this in marked contrast to the preferred Moravian diet of grains, domesticated meats, and vegetables from their kitchen gardens.

Hutton stressed that scurvy was still unknown among the Inuit of northern Labrador, but he noted that some of those further south who lived among settlers had experienced it. There was no rickets among the Inuit either, Hutton observed, attributing this to the Inuit practice of breast-feeding infants up to two years. In contrast, settler children frequently had rickets. Chronic alcoholism was unknown, although there were occasional incidents of drunkenness. The Inuit population was severely impacted by the Spanish influenza of 1918–1919; most of the inhabitants of Hebron died, as did all the men of Okak (which was abandoned after the epidemic) and many Inuit-Métis in Cartwright.

The Third Phase of Social Change: Transformation

For reasons that are not entirely clear, the Inuit became more involved in fishing through the 1800s; at the same time, Newfoundland families from the island's northeast coast began fishing in Labrador in large numbers each summer. The expanding Inuit cod fishery was one of the signals that the days of the adaptation phase were numbered and the Inuit were about to enter the transformation phase. The fishery was characterized by a barter system in which merchants outfitted fishermen each spring and then traded winter supplies, mainly foodstuffs, for fish.[27] The appearance of *kallak*, a deficiency disease observed by J.M. Little in Labrador and on Baffin Island in 1917, might be associated with an increasing Inuit dependence on cod.[28] *Kallak* was characterized by pustule-like lesions on the skin, intense itching, and secondary infection. Little wrote: "while it may occur at any time of the year, if they have plenty of seal flesh to eat, they don't have *kallak*. Most of the cases, as well as the worst cases, and the epidemics, occur in the autumn after they have been living almost exclusively on a fish diet, and especially after a failure of the berry crops.... [I] found the best treatment to be in the addition of seal meat and berries to the diet."[29] Little was surprised to find so few deficiency diseases, which points to the nutrient-adequacy of their traditional diet.

Another indication of change was the increasing dominance of the fur trade, spearheaded by the expanding Hudson's Bay Company (HBC), which required specialization rather than the occupational pluralism the Inuit practised through the seasons. The Moravians had always had an extremely difficult time raising sufficient funds for their mission stations; as the HBC expanded, the Moravians stopped trading altogether. The missionaries' trading style had been liberal, allowing the Inuit to continue subsistence activities, but the HBC's approach was more rigid. Cod fishing had been confined to July and August, but the fur trade took up many more months of the year. Now the Inuit were involved in a specialized economy and had much less opportunity for hunting and fishing.[30] This made the Inuit dependent on imported foodstuffs, in a place where shipping was unreliable due to sea ice and harsh weather conditions.

By 1928 the Inuit diet was significantly altered: carbohydrate intake had increased to 50 percent while protein and fat intake had decreased to 25 percent, causing havoc to dental health.[31] L.M. Waugh described the dental health of the Inuit of Makkovik and Hopedale as "deplorable,"[32] with common problems of decay, caries, and alveolar abscess. With every Inuit under age twelve showing heavy deposits of calculus resulting in periodontal disease,

Inuit dental health was worsening with each generation, Waugh concluded: "Teeth, in some of the Eskimo, under twenty years of age, were decayed to the gum line, and the root further hollowed out by caries.... Some of the old natives had very good teeth."[33] Waugh noticed that Inuit further north in Hebron ate fewer carbohydrates and had better dental health. The solution, he wrote, was "a native diet based on protein...eaten almost entirely raw."[34] In 1921 V.B. Appleton reported constipation, gastro-intestinal disorders, poor teeth, amenorrhea, night blindness, tuberculosis, "nervous instability," psychosis, and "under-nourishment," all of which were prevalent during the closed navigation period.[35] These problems disappeared with "proper diet," Appleton concluded. The presence of these conditions indicated that the epidemiologic transition had begun. Waugh and Appleton articulated a theme that would be repeated through the twentieth century: that Inuit were better nourished by their indigenous diet.

But the Inuit diet was a mixed one by this time, consisting of traditional land and sea-based foods as well as imported foods. Paulus Maggo, an Inuit hunter born in 1910, learned about wildfood procurement from his father, although imported foods were also part of the family diet. Maggo's lifelong preference was for Inuit food. Food shortages, at least on occasion, continued to be part of the Inuit experience: "I am not saying that we had everything but when wildlife was plentiful, we never went hungry."[36]

American dieticians Helen Mitchell and Marjorie Vaughn also did comparative studies of the (mainly southern) Labrador and northern Newfoundland diets, in 1929. They identified general malnutrition, poor teeth, and chronic constipation as common health problems, with vitamin intake being quite low. They concluded that the Labradorians were in better health than the Newfoundlanders. Irish nutritionist W.R. Aykroyd was in St. Anthony, Newfoundland, at the same time; he, too, concluded that dental health was poor, except among those Inuit who continued their traditional foodways.[37] As others had, Aykroyd noted that rickets was uncommon among Inuit, which he oddly (in this cold and wet climate) attributed to plenty of sunlight, as well as to the use of fresh livers as a tonic in Labrador. It is possible that continuity in the Inuit diet, as described by Maggo, played a protective role here.

"Store-bought" (imported) foods were crucial to the Inuit and Inuit-Métis by the Great Depression of the 1930s. By then, the household economies of many Labrador families were integrated into trapping and other, mainly seasonal, wage-paying work, and their supplies came from the HBC and other traders. Several accounts by Inuit-Métis women[38] demonstrate the reliance on purchased foods during the 1930s. Joanne Martin of Cartwright wrote, "When Jim worked for the Hudson's Bay Company, salmon collecting, mending twine, and all that, in the fall he'd bring home what we called our winter supplies. There'd be flour, butter, molasses, hard bread, pork, beef, beans, peas, rice, rolled oats. There was no such thing as apples or oranges them times. We had dried apples and dried apricots. There was no such thing as canned fruit, meat or soup.... Later we began to get tinned meat. In 1938 corned beef was 15¢ a tin. That's the first time I can remember."[39] While Elizabeth Goudie, a trapper's wife, and Millicent Blake Loder, a trapper's daughter, refer to their apparently ample consumption of wildfood in the post–World War I era, it seemed that this food was being replaced by mainstream foodstuffs.

By 1935, on the margins of the capitalist economy of the Great Depression, many Inuit were forced to rely on welfare. In response to the conditions facing the Inuit, the Newfoundland government sent members of its Newfoundland Ranger force to Labrador, where they distributed relief.[40] The rangers' other duties included enforcing the game laws set down by the Newfoundland government, something that was entirely alien to the Inuit. With the war-time construction of a large military base at Goose Bay in central Labrador, hundreds of Inuit and Inuit-Métis left the coast and became almost completely absorbed in the wage economy, albeit mainly in low-paying jobs.

The twentieth century brought the Inuit intensely into the transformation phase, not just in Labrador but throughout the North. Inuit had to contend with a dizzying array of changes: the forced relocation of some of their communities in the 1950s; the resettlement of others; the militarization of Labrador and the Labrador economy, especially during World War II; the entrenchment of wage labour; technological changes in housing, communications, and transportation; the imposition of government rules and regulations regarding land use and wildlife (e.g., hunting restrictions); the mechanization of the cod fishery; and the transfer of education from the Moravians to provincial authorities, who applied the general curriculum in English, not Inuktitut, which led to ongoing language loss. Massive changes in Inuit diet and foodways occurred in Labrador as well as in the Northwest Territories and what is now Nunavut; this was a time when many Inuit were induced to leave their hunting camps for permanent settlements. According to Otto Schaefer, in the mid-1950s in the territories there was a drastic shift to bottle and cereal feeding infants, an increase in sugar consumption, and much more reliance on nutritionally inferior imported food products, the intake of which was well above the Canadian average.[41] Many of these changes proved detrimental to Inuit health as chronic but not necessarily life-threatening diseases (then called "civilization diseases") emerged, among them obesity, gall bladder disease, diabetes, atherosclerosis, and hypertension.[42]

In Labrador, the next spate of (university-sponsored) nutrition-related studies did not occur until the last two decades of the twentieth century. The largest of these was the Labrador Food Study (1984–1985), which focused on "country food" in five Inuit/Inuit-Métis communities (Nain, Makkovik, Rigolet, Black Tickle, and St. Lewis).[43] The Labrador Food Study was based on dietaries with consumption measured in *avoir dupois* weights (pounds). This and other studies did demonstrate some persistence in Inuit foodways, well into the transformation period. Hunting was still practised by most families,[44] "rabbits" (Arctic hare) and "partridge" (willow ptarmigan) being the chief sources of wild meat in southern Labrador, since caribou and porcupine had disappeared from the area.[45]

The studies from this period clearly show that Labrador Inuit and Inuit-Métis faced many food challenges, with food access and quality figuring prominently among them. While Inuit continued to hunt, this activity required the presence of an adult male as well as cash income. The demise of dog-teams for travel, caused by the gradual adoption of gas-fuelled snowmobiles for hunting, necessitated a heavy capital investment. Inuit cash incomes were low, however, with only 32 percent of household income in the form of wages, followed by 27 percent in transfer payments (social assistance and unemployment insurance), with subsistence making up the rest.[46] Although Inuit were now part of the wage economy, those living in coastal Labrador in particular remained on its periphery.

Meanwhile, Inuit had to contend with high living costs, including food expenditures. In 1974 an adequate diet for a "moderately active man" cost $11.40 per week in the Inuit-Métis communities of Cartwright, Port Hope Simpson, and Mary's Harbour; this was significantly higher than the province's average cost of $10.66.[47] The Inuit diet had changed substantially, with an increasing reliance on imported foodstuffs, yet, quite naturally, many Inuit did not know how to prepare such foods as pasta or dried peas.[48] They substituted domesticated meats for wildfood, favouring chicken first, then pork chops and ground beef, although these meats were not as nutrient-dense as seal or caribou. Now that they were mainly consuming a standard North American diet, Inuit nutrition was further compromised by low fruit intake and very low vegetable intake.[49] Worryingly, with carbonated beverages available year-round, there was an observable rise in sugar consumption, linked to obesity.[50] Inuit were now eating high-carbohydrate diets leading to excess glucose, also linked to obesity.[51]

Dieticians were also concerned about calcium intake, especially for preg-
nant and lactating Inuit mothers who no longer chewed animal bones.[52] The
muscles of many wild birds and animals had higher calcium content than the
chicken, pork, and ground beef that the Inuit increasingly relied upon. Inuit
in coastal and central Labrador were also following European trends in infant
care, which resulted in low breast-feeding rates and a reliance on evaporated
milk formula without supplementation. Inuit mothers reported a decline in
breast-feeding support from their partners and, in 1998, had a breast-feeding
rate of 18.2 percent at birth, the lowest of all Inuit in Canada.[53] Finally, food
security in some communities remains compromised by a lack of water access.
There is no running water and no readily available source of potable water in
Black Tickle, a former summer station where Inuit-Métis were forced to live
year-round in the 1960s. Residents must travel by boat and snowmobile to access water, incurring costs much higher than water taxes in most of Canada.
Given the necessity of purchasing home-heating fuel in the Labrador climate,
food is the most elastic budget element, resulting in poor nutrition and occasional hunger.[54] Low income was also a factor in the change from iron-fortified
baby formula to evaporated milk formula; as a result, Inuit infants were getting
limited iron.[55]

The first nutrition education program began on Labrador's north coast in
1981, prompted by the growing reliance on imported foods, high prices, and
weather-related transportation problems.[56] But clearly much more was needed, including the development of food classifications, culturally appropriate
food guides, and consumer education.[57] Little had changed in the 1980s when
dieticians carried out the Labrador Food Survey and observed large numbers
of dental caries linked to consumption of carbohydrates, just as Waugh had
seen some seventy years before.[58] Dieticians had at that point already been ad-
vocating for decades for more nutrition education in Labrador.[59] Meanwhile,
electronic media in the form of radio and television had come to both the
north and south coasts, bringing into people's homes advertising for foods
that were not necessarily needed by communities. Elsewhere, electronic media in particular convinced people that such food products were necessary.[60]
It is likely that this happened among the Labrador Inuit, as indicated by the
widespread presence of junk food like packaged cheesies and chocolate bars.

Further changes occurred as the twentieth century approached. Chief
among them was the ground fish moratoria of 1992, which led to closed fish
plants and general unemployment in the artificially large communities created
by relocation and resettlement. The ground fish moratoria further curtailed
seasonal movement based on natural resource use by Inuit. Meanwhile, the
Labrador Inuit Association (LIA) was engaged in a land claims struggle that

lasted thirty years and eventually led to limited self-government. Progress for the Labrador Métis Nation (LMN) has been slower, partly but not entirely because the LMN's claim was submitted much later than the LIA's.

Conclusion

Within developed countries and within developed regions, there may be social classes or social groups whose vulnerability remains during a more general epidemiologic transition; clearly, indigenous people, including the Labrador Inuit and Inuit-Métis, are among these groups. While tuberculosis is rare in urban Canada, it has re-emerged in some indigenous communities, including Hopedale, Labrador, where a six-year-old girl died of the disease in 2006. Tuberculosis seems to have been present for at least the past couple of decades; in 1990 Maureen Baikie wrote that tuberculosis "caused a great deal of concern" among the Labrador Inuit.[61]

The sedentarization of the Inuit has resulted in overcrowding in many coastal villages and homes, providing opportunities for the easy transmission of infectious diseases. While often viewed as a positive development in the literature, since there is an implication that all now have access to the basic necessities of life,[62] the epidemiologic transition is likely a mixed experience for indigenous people like the Inuit and Inuit-Métis. The multi-dimensional nature of the transition should be considered and monitored by health care providers and policy makers as well as indigenous leaders. In addition, the epidemiologic transition as a concept should be deconstructed from a Fourth World perspective; through this lens, it may be seen as a colonialist construct with limited use for indigenous people.

Social change is key to the epidemiologic transition. Social change is not necessarily negative, but it is likely to be negative when imposed by outside forces and when those affected by change are able to influence it only minimally or not at all. Some changes in Inuit health have been positive. Mortality rates among modern Inuit have declined in all age groups, and, while they still exist, infectious diseases no longer pose the threat they once did. Infant mortality has also declined. In addition, there has been a long-term decline in lung cancer among Inuit women, who may have previously increased their risk of developing the disease by tending seal oil lamps at close range, exposing themselves to carcinogens released by hydrocarbons. However, Inuit infant mortality rates remain two to three times the national average, and Inuit health status is still relatively low compared to that of other Canadians; this is true overall and within age and gender groups.[63] Further, these physical health improvements have probably been at the expense of mental and social health.

For better or worse, it is clear that Inuit, including the Labrador Inuit and Inuit-Métis, are well into the transformation phase of social change and are undergoing the epidemiologic transition. Chronic diseases—obesity, diabetes, atherosclerotic heart disease, hypertension, gall bladder disease, dental caries, and others—have emerged among Inuit across the circumpolar region, including Labrador. These diseases are associated with a certain "lifestyle" in modern society (although this term is depoliticized, ignoring the context of indigenous lives and communities)[64] and were once known by the term "businessmen's diseases" and by similar terms that alluded to the social-class dimension of health status; Weiss et al. call these diseases "New World Syndrome."[65] The presence of such diseases among the Labrador Inuit raises questions about quality of life, mastery, and cultural continuity. Further, Inuit society today is characterized by high rates of violence, suicide, accidents, and substance abuse.[66] Although I have heard individual Inuit blame themselves for their problems, particularly in the case of addictions, these phenomena occur among people throughout the Fourth World, a fact that points to the effects of social, economic, and political change as well as subsequent severe acculturative stress.

Acknowledgements

I would like to thank Marg Ewtushik (my co-author on *A Veritable Scoff: Sources on Foodways and Nutrition in Newfoundland and Labrador*); the Department of Health, Government of Newfoundland and Labrador, who helped fund book publication; the Division of Community Health and Humanities, Faculty of Medicine, Memorial University, who provided in-kind support; Memorial University, which was another source of funding for the original research; the library staff at Memorial University; the Food Security Network of Newfoundland and Labrador; and last, but certainly not least, the people of Coastal Labrador, who inspired me to carry out this project and others.

Notes

1   This chapter was published originally in *Food, Culture and Society* 1, 3 (2008): 315–33. We are grateful to the journal's editors for allowing us permission to include this paper in the present volume.

2   Maura Hanrahan and Marg Ewtushik, eds., *A Veritable Scoff: Sources on Foodways and Nutrition in Newfoundland and Labrador* (St. John's: Flanker Press, 2001).

3   Maura Hanrahan, "Industrialization and the Politicization of Health in Labrador Métis Society," *Canadian Journal of Native Studies* 20, 2 (2002): 231–50; Maura Hanrahan, *Brooks, Buckets, and Komatiks: The Problem of Water Access in Black*

Tickle (St. John's: Faculty of Medicine, Memorial University of Newfoundland, 2000).

4   Otto Schaefer, "Changing Dietary Patterns in the Canadian North: Health, Social and Economic Consequences," *Canadian Dietetic Association Journal* 38, 1 (1977): 17.

5   Ibid., 17.

6   Peter Bjerregaard and T. Kue Young, *The Circumpolar Inuit: Health of a Population in Transition* (Copenhagen: Munksgaard, 1998).

7   This phase is depicted in the 2006 Inuit film *The Journals of Knud Rasmussen*, co-directed by Norman Cohn and Zacharias Kunuk.

8   A. Keenleyside, "Euro-American Whaling in the Canadian Arctic: Its Effects on Eskimo Health," *Arctic Anthropology* 27, 1 (1990): 1–19.

9   Ibid.

10 Bjerregaard and Young; Keenleyside; W.H. Oswalt, *Bashful No Longer: An Alaskan Eskimo Ethnohistory, 1778–1988* (Norman: University of Oklahoma Press, 1990).

11 Bjerregaard and Young; Keenleyside; Oswalt, 228.

12 M.H. Wahdan, "The Epidemiologic Transition," *Eastern Mediterranean Journal* 2, 1 (1996): 9.

13 J.W. Berry, "Acculturation and Adaptation: Health Consequences of Culture Contact among Circumpolar Peoples," *Arctic Medical Research* 49 (1990): 142–50.

14 Bjerregaard and Young; Keenleyside; Oswalt, 228.

15 Wahdan, 8–20.

16 Lawrence Jackson, *Bounty of a Barren Coast: Resource Harvest and Settlement in Southern Labrador, Phase One* (Calgary: PetroCanada Explorations, 1982), 126.

17 G. Johnson, "Nutritional Deficiency Diseases in Newfoundland and Labrador: Their Recognition and Elimination" (unpublished paper, n.d., c. 1980).

18 Mary G. Alton Mackey, "The Impact of Imported Foods on the Traditional Inuit Diet," *Arctic Medical Research* 47 (Supp. 1, 1988): 128–33.

19 One of the challenges with the early literature is explorers' tendency to confuse First Nations people (the Labrador Innu) with the Inuit. Both were called "natives" or "savages" and there are many references to "Eskimeaux-Indians".

20 Benjamin Kohlmeister and George Kmoch, *Journal of a Voyage from Okkak, on the Coast of Labrador, to Ungava Bay, Westward of Cape Chudleigh Undertaken to explore the Coast, and visit the Esquimaux in that unknown Region* (London: W. McDowell, 1814), 36.

21 Johnson, 3.

22 Ibid., 2–3.

23 Harriet V. Kuhnlein and Nancy J. Turner, *Traditional Plant Foods of Canadian Indigenous Peoples: Nutrition, Botany and Use*. Vol. 8, Food and Nutrition in History and Anthropology (Philadelphia: Gordon and Breach Science Publishers, 1991).

24 Johnson, 3.

25 Author unknown, "Inuit," *Encyclopedia of Newfoundland and Labrador* 3 (St. John's: Newfoundland Book Publishers, 1991), 63.

26 Samuel K. Hutton, *A Thesis on the Health and Diseases of the Eskimos* (Derby: James Harwood, 1909).

27 Newfoundlanders called this the "truck system."

28 J.M. Little, "An Eskimo 'Deficiency Disease,'" *Boston Medical and Surgical Journal* 176, 18 (1917): 642–43.

29 Ibid., 643.

30 For this reason, the Innu wisely resisted involvement in the fur trade, preferring to concentrate on their traditional caribou hunt and other hunting activities.

31 L.M. Waugh, "Nutrition and Health of the Labrador Eskimo with Special Reference to the Mouth and Teeth," *Journal of Dental Health* 8 (1928): 428–29.

32 Ibid., 428.

33 Ibid., 428.

34 Ibid., 429.

35 V.B. Appleton, "Observations of Deficiency Diseases in Labrador," *American Journal of Public Health* 11 (1921): 617–21.

36 Paulus Maggo, *Remembering the Years of My Life: Journeys of an Inuit Hunter*, ed. Carol Brice-Bennett (St. John's: Institute of Social and Economic Research, Memorial University of Newfoundland, 1999), 87.

37 W.R. Aykroyd, "Beriberi and Other Food–Deficiency Diseases in Newfoundland and Labrador," *Journal of Hygiene* 30 (1930): 357–86; W.R. Aykroyd, "Vitamin A Deficiency in Newfoundland," *Irish Journal of Medical Sciences* 28 (1928): 161–65.

38 Millicent Blake Loder, *Daughter of Labrador* (St. John's: Harry Cuff Publications, 1989); Elizabeth Goudie, *Woman of Labrador* (Agincourt, ON: Book Society of Canada, 1983); Joanne Martin, "We Knew Hard Work, Them Days," *Stories of Early Labrador* 2, 1 (1976): 41.

39 Martin, 41.

40 Although a complete discussion is beyond the scope of this paper, it is interesting that in many ways (such as social control through imposing "law and order") the roles of the Newfoundland Rangers in Labrador paralleled those of the withdrawing Moravians.

41 Schaefer, 17.

42 Ibid., 17–25.

43 The Innu (First Nations, formerly "Indian") community of Davis Inlet, now resettled to nearby Natůashish, was also included in the study.

44 Mary G. Alton Mackey and Robin D. Orr, "Country Food Use in Makkovik, Labrador, July 1980 to June 1981," *Proceedings of the Sixth International Symposium on Circumpolar Health*, edited by R. Fortune, special issue of *Circumpolar Health* 84 (1985); Mary G. Alton Mackey, *Country Food Use in Selected Labrador Coast Communities, Comparative Report, June–July 1980 and June–July 1981* (St. John's: Faculty of Medicine, Memorial University of Newfoundland, 1984); Mary G. Alton Mackey, *An Evaluation of Household Country Food Use, Black Tickle, Labrador, July 1980–June 1981* (St. John's: Faculty of Medicine, Memorial University of Newfoundland, 1984); Mary G. Alton Mackey, *An Evaluation of Household Country Food Use, Makkovik, Labrador, July 1980–June 1981* (St. John's: Faculty of Medicine, Memorial University of Newfoundland, 1984); Mary G. Alton Mackey, *An Evaluation of Household Country Food Use, Nain, Labrador, July 1980–June 1981* (St. John's: Faculty of Medicine, Memorial University of Newfoundland, 1984); Mary G. Alton Mackey, *An Evaluation of Household Country Food Use, St. Lewis, Labrador, July 1980–June 1981* (St. John's: Faculty of Medicine, Memorial University of Newfoundland, 1984).

45 Jackson, 126.

46 Mary G. Alton Mackey and K.M. Boles, *The Birthing of Nutrition Education in Labrador: A Summary Report* (Goose Bay, Labrador: Labrador Institute of Northern Studies, Memorial University of Newfoundland, n.d., c. 1984).

47 Central Statistical Services, Executive Council, *Cost of Basic Diets in Newfoundland and Labrador, 1974* (St. John's: Nutrition Division, Department of Health, Government of Newfoundland), 9.

48 Mackey, "Impact," 128–33.

49 Ibid.

50 Ibid.

51 Author unknown, "Background Submission: Nutritional Value of Country Foods," *EIS Military Flight Training: An Environmental Impact Statement on Military Flying Activities in Labrador and Québec: Submissions 1-6* (Ottawa: Department of National Defence, Government of Canada).

52 Ibid.

53 E. McKim, M. Laryea, S. Banoub-Baddour, K. Matthews, and K. Webber, "Infant-feeding Practices in Coastal Labrador," *Journal of the Canadian Dietetic Association* 59, 1 (1998): 41; Mary G. Alton-Mackey and Robin D. Orr, "Infant Feeding Practices in Metropolitan, Urban and Small Communities in Newfoundland," *Journal of Canadian Dietetic Association* 39 (1978): 236.

54 Hanrahan, *Brooks*.

55 McKim et al., 35–42.

56 Mackey and Boles.

57 Some of this is being done, e.g., Inuit versions of Canada's food guide, published by Health Canada, Government of Canada.

58 Mackey and Orr, "Country Food Use"; Mackey, *Country Food Use in Selected Labrador Coast Communities, Comparative Report*; Mackey, *Evaluation of Food Use, Black Tickle*; Mackey, *Evaluation of Food Use, Makkovik*; Mackey, *Evaluation of Food Use, Nain*; Mackey, *Evaluation of Food Use, St. Lewis*.

59 Mackey and Boles; Mackey, "Impact," 128–33.

60 Wahdan, 8–20.

61 Maureen Baikie, "Perspectives on the Health of the Labrador Inuit," *Northern Perspectives* 18, 2 (1990), http://www.carc.org/pubs/v18no2/index.html.

62 Wahdan, 8–20; Richard G. Wilkinson, "The Epidemiologic Transition: From Material Scarcity to Social Disadvantage?" in *Population and Society: Essential Readings*, ed. Frank Trovato (Don Mills, ON: Oxford University Press, 2002), 107–16.

63 Inuit Health Status (Ottawa: Health Canada, 2000), http://www.hc-sc.gc.ca/ahc-asc/media/nr-cp/2000/2000_20bk2_e.html.

64 K.M. Weiss, R.E. Ferrell, and C.L. Harris, "A New World Syndrome of Metabolic Diseases with a Genetic and Evolutionary Basis," *Yearbook of Physical Anthropology* 27 (1984): 153–78.

65 Ibid.

66 Baikie.

CHAPTER 6

The More Things Change: Patterns of Country Food Harvesting by the Labrador Inuit on the North Labrador Coast

Lawrence Felt, David C. Natcher, Andrea Procter, Nancy Sillitt, Katie Winters, Tristan Gear, Darren Winters, Susan Nochasak, Sheldon Andersen, Rose Ford, Holly Flowers, Susan Rich, and Roland Kemuksigak

This chapter reports on a recent collaborative participatory action study (Kemmis and McTaggart 2000; Reason and Bradbury 2001; Couglan and Brannick 2007) on country or wildfood harvesting in the five north central Labrador communities of Nain, Hopedale, Postville, Makkovik, and Rigolet. It is best understood as an Inuit-initiated and -directed attempt to provide a more quantitative Inuit voice to the level and relevance of country food utilization in response to Section 12.4.6 of the Labrador Inuit Land Claims Agreement, which seeks to establish an Inuit Harvest Level that "Shall be as accurate a quantification as possible of the amount of a species or population of wildlife or plant required by Inuit for the Inuit Domestic Harvest" (210).

While information sources such as Inuit knowledge and historical information are also encouraged in the agreement, the new government of Nunatsiavut was interested in developing a capacity to carry out research based on "Western" science to supplement the more traditional Inuit voice grounded in Inuit cosmology and ontology. The reasoning for such a strategy was simply that, since the co-management boards mandated by the agreement were heavily premised on Western science, in order to protect Inuit subsistence interests, their leadership would need to understand Western science and develop the capacity to express it as something of a second voice of their own. Rather than denigrating or devaluing more traditional knowledge, development of this additional voice was believed to strengthen the relevance of traditional knowledge and therefore build Inuit-made management solutions derived from both voices. Given the very high priority Inuit negotiators placed upon protecting and preserving wildfood harvesting activities for its citizens (See Procter this volume; Brice-Bennett 1997), it was felt such an approach was essential.

Change and Continuity in Subsistence Inuit Harvesting

The last fifty years have brought profound political, socio-economic, demographic, and cultural changes to the Inuit and Kablunangajuit (settlers living on the Labrador coast, many of whom have intermarried with their Inuit neighbours, see Ben-Dor 1966; Kennedy 1977, 1982, 2009) who form the beneficiaries of Nunatsiavut. Settlement is now more geographically compressed to five communities, located in what is best considered the central Labrador coast, as a result of largely coerced resettlement from more northerly settlements of Nutak, Hebron, Ramah, and other settlements (Evans this volume; Brice-Bennett 1994; Royal Commission on Labrador 1974; Kennedy 1985). Outmigration from the coast has resulted in a large proportion of Nunatsiavut citizens now residing completely outside the land claims settlement and Inuit lands areas (Community Accounts 2006; Government of Nunatsiavut 2008). As of 2008, approximately 40 percent of beneficiaries under the agreement resided in the Upper Lake Melville area, including the towns of Happy Valley–Goose Bay, North West River, and Mud Lake.

While these communities are still geographically remote in the sense that no roads link them to larger Canadian populations, larger and more powerful ships bring supplies for nearly six months of the year, and new airports link communities to each other and more southerly areas on a daily basis. Forms of state presence are now more visible and palpable to people as well. Government offices administering a wide array of programs have emerged in every community, often staffed by more southerly, non-Aboriginal immigrants, and state-sponsored initiatives to bring modern technology through television and Internet reach virtually every household in the region. Economically, modern industrial job opportunities have increased with resource development such as at the Voisey Bay nickel mine, just southwest of Nain. The buzz and scurry of resource exploration is widespread, with the pulsating noise of overhead helicopter blades common in every coastal community. While unemployment remains crushingly high, particularly in winter, wider opportunities for wage labour have grown to the point that it is now the largest source of household income (Community Accounts 2006).

Such change has arguably altered attitudes and behaviours toward a wide range of activities, including, potentially at least, food preferences and nutrition. There is plentiful, though largely anecdotal, suggestion of such a shift toward new types of food and beverage. Every community has at least one modern, larger groceteria where southern foods are prominently displayed for much of the year. Their desirability is seductively communicated in gala store advertisements and backed up by an incessant media campaign that stresses the modern, convenient benefits of processed food.

And yet, many of the old ways, particularly those associated with the harvesting and curing of wild or country food, remain evident, oftentimes in stark juxtaposition to the processed southern foods. Caribou and caribou parts such as ribs and quarters are frequently seen hanging on ropes outside houses or in sheds as residents return home from the central supermarket laden with highly processed foods indistinct from those found in any North American supermarket. Char and other fish are buffeted by strong breezes as they are dried for the long winters, and berry picking is still a very public and popular form of provisioning. But are these instances of traditional food utilization merely vestiges of increasingly marginalized traditional preferences and behaviours, more for sport and recreation than nourishment, or do they remain a critical part of a 4000-year survival strategy large numbers of residents continue to pursue? Our own experience clearly suggests that subsistence provisioning remains an important strategy of household and community survival. Moreover, research from Nunavut and other northern locations shows a strong continuity of country food subsistence harvesting (NWMB 2004; Alaska Fish and Game 2010; Naves 2009). Thus, the question is not so much whether country food provisioning is dying out, but rather how strong it remains within the context of the changes that are so clearly visible.

The Emergence of Modern Wildlife Management

Before the presentation of any analysis of the scale and intensity of country food harvesting, a brief digression about the study and its place in larger wildlife management among Aboriginal peoples in more remote regions is useful. For countless generations, Labrador Inuit, like all other Aboriginal peoples of the North, pursued a life founded upon subsistence wildlife harvesting (Brice-Bennett 1977; Usher 1982; Northland Associates 1986) largely unencumbered by state regulation and management (Ames 1977). Over the last forty years the situation has significantly changed, with greater and greater state intervention taking place in the name of resource conservation. In place of traditional knowledge as the primary basis for understanding the health of resources, scientists and managers stress the need to calculate resource population levels, human demands on those resources, and the ongoing capacity of the land and/or water to maintain the resources in light of human demands. Once sufficient information becomes available, probability statistics are used to chart population dynamics for any given resource. From these population estimates, replete with their confidence intervals and other elements of modern probability, permissible harvests are calculated and allocations distributed to various harvesting groups. As a result of several important judicial decisions, in Canada populations with officially designated Aboriginal or First Nations status are awarded first harvest priority after conservation concerns have been addressed.

The seeming legitimacy of this process has been so compelling that Aboriginal groups, as they struggle to gain control over country food harvesting, have been required to participate in, if not fully embrace, this approach even as they oft-times struggle with how it might co-exist with the traditional knowledge and understanding that guided and informed their harvesting practices for centuries. As a result, Aboriginal peoples today have largely become an integral and integrated part of the modern management process in the myriad initiatives they have developed in collaboration with state management agencies. Thus, it is common for Aboriginal groups, as they strive for a greater say in managing those living, renewable resources that are so critical to them, to collect particular types of information in scientifically mandated ways. That information can then either be given to state resource scientists or used for their own creation of management initiatives, in those instances in which they have been able to secure considerable control over resource management of particularly important species . Such collaborative management arguably reaches its most mature form when formalized, legally binding agreements (for example, land claims agreements) are reached between Aboriginal people and the larger states of which they are part, thereby establishing ownership, management, and benefits for people with historic associations to terrestrial as well as aquatic territories, and the living and non-living resources located within them.

The Labrador Inuit Land Claims Agreement (LILCA) signed in 2003 between the Labrador Inuit Association, representing the Inuit people of Labrador's north coast, and the governments of Canada and Newfoundland and Labrador is a particularly good example of such an agreement, as are similar agreements with Quebec and central Arctic Inuit organizations. While there are important differences between these three land claims

agreements, all establish some collaborative structure of resource management and bestow upon the respective Inuit peoples important roles in the
collection of scientifically sound information and in the promulgation of
management plans, which use that scientific information along with traditional knowledge and any other sources. This particular orientation to
resource management is further reinforced by the imposition of a government structure that largely mirrors those of the more dominant parties in
the agreement. Thus, the agreement creating the Labrador Inuit government
of Nunatsiavut in December of 2005 resulted in a structure built around a
bureaucracy replete with deputy ministers, assistant deputy ministers, and
directors housed in departments such as Renewable Resources, Industrial
Development, Health, and Education. The adoption of such a government
organization was said to be necessary if ongoing collaboration and cooperation was to occur on a "government to government" basis. The result was the
creation of an Aboriginal government, Nunatsiavut, largely indistinguishable, at least in structure, from the modern state through which it had been
negotiated. An important potential consequence of such an outcome is that
the process of resource management, even where Aboriginal influence and
power is significant, may become largely indistinguishable from the processes of other state resource management agencies.

To manage living, renewable resources, the agreement established an
independent tri-partite co-management resource agency, the Torngat
Secretariat, entrusted with the sustainable management of approximately
147 renewable plant, animal, and marine animal resources. The secretariat's
creation reflects a hard-fought victory by Inuit negotiators to convince the
government that country food harvesting was an ongoing and important
foundation of Inuit life, and one not likely to disappear, as earlier com-
mentators had sometimes suggested it might with accelerated resource
development and modernization in the region (Hefferton 1959; Rockwood
1955). The secretariat's mandate is to manage in such a way as to ensure that
domestic harvest levels for Inuit beneficiaries are protected in a sustainable
fashion.

The secretariat is composed of an executive office composed of an executive director, resource biologists and necessary administrative support
personnel, and two parallel co-management boards. One board is entrusted
with management of wildlife and plants, while the other oversees fisheries
and associated marine mammals. Each board comprises seven individuals:
three appointed by the government of Nunatsiavut, two by the province of
Newfoundland and Labrador, and one by the government of Canada. A
neutral chair is the final appointee. Initially, a former Canadian fisheries

manager was appointed chair of the fisheries board and a provincial wildlife biologist of the plants and wildlife board. The promotion of Inuit subsistence harvesting is each board's primary objective, consistent with conservation and a precautionary approach to wildlife management. The mandate also includes management of respective habitats upon which species are dependent (LILCA 12.1.1). Utilizing a wide array of information from scientific studies of specific resources, current and projected domestic harvest levels for specific species, and traditional sources of knowledge from Inuit harvesters themselves, each board is mandated to manage in such a way as to ensure that Inuit domestic harvests are protected. Where evidence suggests overharvesting may be occurring, each board has the legal right to recommend to the relevant Canadian or provincial minister that an Inuit Domestic Harvest Level (IDHL) be established. Such an IDHL shall be "as accurate a quantification as possible of the amount of a species or population of wildlife or plant required by Inuit for the Inuit domestic harvest" (LILCA 12.4.6).

It was clear to Nunatsiavut leadership that a current estimate of Inuit harvests for a wide range of plants and animals was particularly critical. While several earlier estimates of Inuit subsistence harvesting were available, most were a decade or more old and incomplete in their coverage (Mackey and Orr 1988; Usher 1982; Northland Associates 1986; Williamson 1997). Within this context, the then director of Renewable Resources for Nunatsiavut approached Drs. David Natcher and Lawrence Felt in 2006 concerning the possibility of establishing a base line of current subsistence harvest levels for a number of keystone species of importance to Labrador Inuit. With funding support from the Canadian Wildlife Service to ensure harvest information of several birds of interest to them, a contract was formally negotiated in May of 2007 to (among several other areas of research) develop and implement a study of current (2007) harvest levels for twelve selected animals, though for three sea birds (terns, gull, and guillemot) only information on egging harvest was collected. Species selected for study included the Canada goose; black duck; common eider; white-winged, black, and surf scoters; Arctic char; Atlantic salmon; and caribou. Given the importance of egg collection as a subsistence activity, eider, gull tern, and guillemot egging were also included. To be credible, the study needed to meet criteria of scientific rigour and comprehensiveness. As part of the contract between Memorial University and the government of Nunatsiavut, ownership of all data collected as well as subsequent reports and presentations was to rest with Nunatsiavut, with provision for shared authorship and professional publication opportunities with the Memorial researchers.

Research Design and Methodology

Given the importance of establishing Aboriginal harvest levels as an initial step towards some variety of co-management, it is not surprising that studies and methodologies doing so are numerous (Usher and Wenzel 1987; Naves 2009; NWMB 2004; Fall 1990, among many others). Several instruments have been used to collect harvest information, including calendars, personal logbooks, and various surveys using some form of memory recall. To maximize representativeness, a variety of sophisticated multi-stage sampling frames have been employed. The Nunavut Wildlife Management Board (NWMB) harvest study and a recent study undertaken by the Alaskan Department of Fish and Game, Subsistence Division (Naves 2009), illustrate more complex sampling strategies.

The study reported in this chapter uses a research design founded on a memory recall data collection strategy in which harvesters are asked to remember the number of animals of a specific species harvested during the last year. Validity and reliability are assessed through a number of data triangulation and "ground truthing" strategies (Webb et al. 1999). To assist respondents, the previous year was broken down into four segments corresponding to local definitions of seasons, coloured photographs of selected animals were provided, and local names were listed in English and Inuktitut. Local residents of each community were hired as research assistants and underwent a five-day training session in interviewing techniques and data recording. Adjustments in questions, wording, local nomenclature of species, and related issues were made through public community meetings, discussions with individual harvesters, and interviewer input during training sessions. The final information collection instrument was then pilot-tested by research assistants and a small number of Inuit officials before its final use. To facilitate data entry and portability to other computer software, the final instrument was constructed in Excel-based form.

The limited number of communities (five) and relatively small number of households (fewer than 800 in total) allowed for a household population saturation strategy (HPSS) in which attempts were made to interview all beneficiary households in the five coastal communities. In each community, a map was created in which researchers located beneficiary households and assigned each a unique identification number. Interviewers were instructed to interview households randomly and to interview primary harvesters for each species in the household. Where more than one harvester was present, efforts were made to interview all. Up to three attempts were made to contact and complete interviews. Due to movement to and from communities, refusals, and other difficulties in locating relevant household members, completed interviews varied between 70 and over 90 percent of community households, with an overall mean completion percentage, weighted by size of community, of 80 percent. To cover the large number of Nunatsiavut beneficiaries residing outside the coastal settlement area in the nearby area of Upper Lake Melville, a 20 percent random sample of households there was enumerated using a household beneficiary list provided by the Nunatsiavut government.

To assess harvest estimate validity, a number of triangulation and post-collection public information-sharing strategies were utilized. Data triangulation involves attempts to find additional, independent data sources in support of collected data values. Post-collection strategies are typically referred to as "ground truthing" and involve sharing findings with those providing the information and those knowledgeable of the situation for review and assessment. The major form of data triangulation utilized was to compare our estimates of Atlantic salmon and Arctic char harvests with those independently made by personnel of the Canadian Department of Fisheries and Oceans (DFO), the federal department charged with stock assessment for those species. In this comparison, survey estimates and ones made by DFO for Atlantic salmon were generally within 5 percent of each other. The major ground truthing exercise was to hold public meetings in each community, during which findings were summarized and residents encouraged to engage in discussion of the estimates. Private commentary was also encouraged. In addition, large posters of findings were produced and given to local Inuit Community Governments with encouragement to provide any comment. Feedback was requested on general findings as well as extreme or outlying instances in the community distributions for each of the surveyed species. In addition, Nunatsiavut conservation officers living, and often born in, each community were privately asked to comment on general findings and distributional outliers for the community in which they resided. No substantial criticisms of resulting estimates were provided as a result of these consultative processes.

Participation in Subsistence Harvesting for Selected Wildfoods

Table 1 provides an overview of harvest participation in the 2007 harvest survey by community and species. It is important to note that this data represents a single year only as well as a limited, though locally important, listing of species. As we briefly discussed regarding caribou harvest in Hopedale, actual harvest levels may vary considerably annually based on changes in the availability of wild animals as well as residents' financial resources and time. When deviations from annual harvests are known, they are indicated, as we have done with Hopedale. As part of data collection, respondents were asked whether the year in which they harvested was typical and, if not, why this was the case. Most residents reported 2007 as a fairly typical year for other species, but it is acknowledged that "typical" may have considerable variability in its meaning to respondents.

Table 1: *Household Participation by Community and Species, 2007.*

	Rigolet		Makkovik		Postville		Hopedale		Nain		ULM	
	N	%	N	%	N	%	N	%	N	%	N	%
Geese	33	45%	32	37%	32	57%	39	35%	85	40%	37	33%
Black Duck	37	50%	26	30%	27	48%	28	25%	61	29%	28	25%
Eider	33	45%	22	26%	26	46%	41	36%	62	30%	4	4%
Surf Scoter	28	38%	5	6%	14	25%	21	19%	5	2%	23	21%
Black Scoter	1	1%	17	20%	20	36%	10	9%	10	5%	9	8%
WW Scoter	0	0%	1	1%	5	9%	1	1%	11	5%	2	2%
Eider eggs	9	12%	32	37%	24	43%	58	51%	76	36%	1	1%
Tern eggs	24	32%	29	34%	5	9%	65	58%	73	35%	1	1%
Gull eggs	18	24%	1	1%	12	21%	4	4%	3	1%	1	1%
Guillemot eggs	1	1%	6	7%	0	0%	10	9%	37	18%	0	0%
Atlantic salmon	54	73%	56	67%	45·	80%	31	27%	5	2%	99	88%
Arctic Char	21	28%	65	76%	40	71%	74	65%	160	76%	15	13%
Caribou	20	27%	37	43%	25	45%	33	29%	114	54%	66	59%

Harvest participation is defined as harvest of at least one animal of at least one species by a surveyed household. Using this definition, participation varied by community from 73 percent to 92 percent, with an overall, unweighted average of 85 percent of households. The table reveals considerable intra-community variation in household participation with respect to species. Variation by species can be read down the table. In Rigolet, for example, participation in goose hunting stood at 45 percent, black duck 50 percent, common eider duck 45 percent and Atlantic salmon 73 percent. Conversely, harvesting black scoter, white-winged scoter, guillemot eggs, and caribou involved 1 percent, 0 percent, 1 percent, and 27 percent of households respectively. Other locations display similar patterns of intra-community variation. In the most northerly community of Nain, fully 76 percent of households harvest Arctic char, making it a keystone species. In fact, only caribou comes close to such participation, and it involves only slightly more than half of all households at 54 percent. Goose harvesting is third at 40 percent. Variation appears as well when communities are compared with each other. Reading across the table, for example, eider eggs are an important country food in Makkovik, Postville, Hopedale, and Nain with 37 percent, 43 percent, 51 percent, and 36 percent respectively, while in Rigolet only 12 percent of households harvested any eider eggs.

Graph 1 summarizes this intra-community variation for six sea bird species, while Graph 2 does the same for Atlantic salmon, Arctic char, and caribou. Most likely due to its more southerly range, Atlantic salmon is a major country food in the more southerly communities of Rigolet, Postville, and Makkovik, as well as Upper Lake Melville, at 73 percent, 67 percent, 80 percent, and 88 percent respectively, but is at only 27 percent and 2 percent in more northerly Hopedale and Nain. With regard to caribou, all communities have substantial numbers of households participating in the harvest, though Rigolet and Hopedale percentages are somewhat lower at 27 percent and 29 percent respectively. Rigolet's lower participation rate is most likely a result of its being generally too far south for residents to regularly access the George River caribou herd that provides most of the animals for harvest. However, a limited number of households do traverse long distances to the north and west to intercept George River animals.

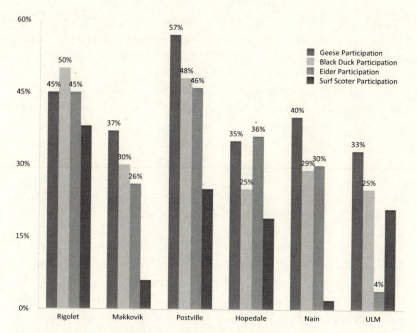

Graph 1: *Percent Variability in Sea Bird Harvesting by Community, 2007.*

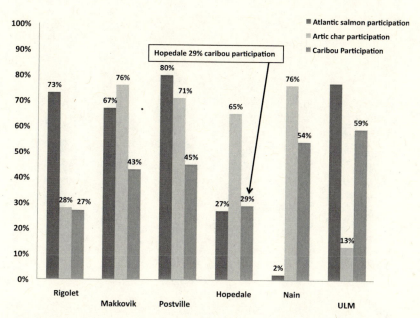

Graph 2: *Percent Variability in Caribou, Salmon, and Char Harvesting by Community, 2007.*

Larger caribou harvests for that community only occur when members of the George River herd migrate into southerly areas more readily accessible to the community. The 29 percent participation in Hopedale is likely a deviation from traditional practices; residents informed us that caribou did not migrate as close to the community in 2007, limiting access and necessitating more costly excursions to the interior for harvest. While no comprehensive explanation of other differences in species harvested is offered in this chapter, reasons most likely reflect temporary lack of resource availability in nearby land and/or marine environments (as with Hopedale caribou), change in harvester access to financial and/or time resources, or longer-standing historical variations in availability (for example, the low participation in Atlantic salmon harvesting in Nain, which lies just north of the historical limits of that species' distribution).

While direct harvest participation is an important measure of wildfood utilization in a community, it is not the most inclusive. Households may be unable or uninterested in harvesting yet receive portions of other household harvests for their own use or distribution. A total of fifty-five households from all six communities reported receiving at least one wild species listed while doing no harvesting of their own. Reasons offered by non-harvesting households included distance of the resource from the community, cost of

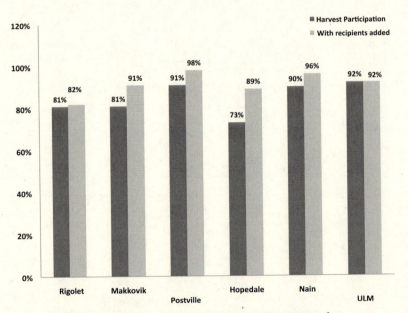

Graph 3. *Combined Participation in Subsistence Harvesting by Community, 2007.*

technology such as boats, nets, snowmobiles, or all-terrain vehicles, time demands, absence due to wage labour, and physical handicaps associated with older age. Such linking of harvesting and recipient households forms a number of distinct, bounded networks in each community (see Natcher, Felt, and Procter in this volume). When recipient and harvesting households are linked in this way, the total percentage of households benefitting from wildlife harvesting is even greater. Graph 3 presents these new percentages.

Postville emerges as the most inclusive community, with 98 percent involvement. Nain and Makkovik, due to their larger numbers of recipient-only households, show the largest increase in participation from subsistence activities.

One further comment concerning combined participation harvesting profiles is worth noting. Several researchers (Magdanz et al. 2002; Wolfe 1987) have reported on a particular type of participatory distribution in their work with Alaskan Inuit. In this work, approximately 30 percent of households were found to act as "super harvesters," supplying the vast majority of wildfood for much of the community, even though the percentage of harvesting households harvesting any single species could vary considerably. Graph 4 assesses the validity of the super harvester with data from this research.

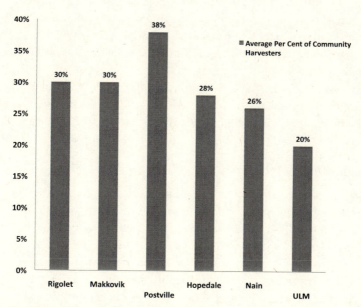

Graph 4. *Mean Percentage of Harvesters of All Species Pooled by Community, 2007.*

It summarizes the average percentage of households supplying all types of country food reviewed in the study. The percentage is calculated by taking an average of all harvesting rates of species studied and calculating a grand mean per community. When harvest participation values for all species are pooled and divided by the number of species, the percentage of households involved ranges between 38 percent and 20 percent, with an average of exactly 30 percent. Postville displays the greatest percentage of harvesters at 38 percent, and the more urban community of Upper Lake Melville is lowest at 20 percent. Most communities appear to have a limited number of what might be termed *keystone species*, those of such cultural, spiritual, economic, and nutritional importance and availability that a majority of households participate in harvest. Examples include Arctic char in Nain (76 percent, from Table 1) and Atlantic salmon in Rigolet and Postville (73 percent and 80 percent respectively, from Table 1). Having said this, it does not seem unreasonable to suggest that a pattern similar to that found in Alaska operates on the north coast of Labrador as well.

The small number of wildfoods reported here represents a limited sample of the multitude available to Labrador Inuit. While several of the more important species, such as caribou, geese, various species of saltwater duck, Arctic char, and Atlantic salmon, are covered in the present study, public consultations suggested a number of important species, including ring seal, partridge, rabbit, wild berries, and other fish species, that are not. It does not seem unreasonable, therefore, to expect that as more species are added to any investigation, the participation rate is likely to further increase from its already high level.

Participation in country food harvesting does not necessarily tell us directly about total harvest levels, and in many respects it is the total number rather than the participation that is critical to understanding the importance of subsistence food in Inuit life. It is to these levels that we now turn.

Reported and Projected Harvests

Table 2 summarizes recorded harvest levels by species and community for a one-year period commencing in late fall of 2006 and continuing to early fall the following year. Two values are provided for each species, the actual reported total harvest (Column HT in the table) and an extrapolated or projected total harvest (Column PT) based on the percent of households surveyed in each community. Thus, if the reported number of animals for a given species was based on 50 percent of households being interviewed in a community, the projected harvest would be exactly twice that value. Such extrapolation assumes that those not included in data collection do not dif-

Table 2. *Estimated and Projected Harvests by Species and Community, 2007.*

Species	Rigolet HT	Rigolet PT	Makkovik HT	Makkovik PT	Postville HT	Postville PT	Hopedale HT	Hopedale PT	Nain HT	Nain PT	ULM HT	ULM PT
Geese	187	246	189	240	148	187	184	214	390	450	152	760
Black Duck	266	350	169	215	211	267	199	231	220	254	169	845
Eider	312	411	446	567	235	297	780	907	369	426	18	90
Surf Scoter	248	327	27	34	101	128	188	219	32	37	167	835
Black Scoter	40	53	176	224	150	189	90	105	38	44	62	310
White Wing Scoter	0	0	4	5	16	20	27	31	26	30	15	75
Eider egg	134	177	641	815	347	438	107	124	2136	2465	11	55
Gull egg	633	834	826	1050	81	102	190	221	1269	1464	12	60
Tern egg	1530	2016	4	5	274	346	4	5	91	105	0	0
Guillemot egg	8	11	89	113	0	0	72	84	910	1050	0	0
Salmon	500	659	350	445	293	370	197	229	135	156	630	2810
Arctic char	363	478	2097	2666	1070	1352	3651	4246	9888	11410	153	765
Caribou	64	84	195	248	132	167	205	238	580	669	190	900

fer substantially from those included. Since interviewers were residents of the community where harvest occurred and knew all residents, they, along with local conservation officers, were able to make assurances that our assumption of *ceteris paribus* was reasonable.

As a general rule, reported harvests follow a similar pattern to participation rates, with those communities possessing higher participation rates for particular species also amassing higher harvest levels for that species. To take the most contrasting example, it will be recalled that Nain had 76 percent of its households harvesting Arctic char while the corresponding figure for Upper Lake Melville was 13 percent. Reading Table 2 across, harvesting households in Nain landed 9,888 char while those in Upper Lake Melville recorded 153 char.

Graphs 5 through 10 compare reported harvest levels for adult Canada geese and eider ducks (the two most commonly hunted adult species), egg harvests for eider, gull, and tern, and Atlantic salmon, Arctic char, and caribou by community of harvester residence. As was the case with participation rates, there is considerable variability both within and between communities with regard to harvest levels. For geese, harvest levels are nearly twice that of other communities, with the others all displaying reported harvest levels between 150 and 200 birds. Eider ducks and their eggs are particularly sought in Nain, as are tern eggs, whereas tern eggs appeared to dominate egg harvesting in Rigolet.

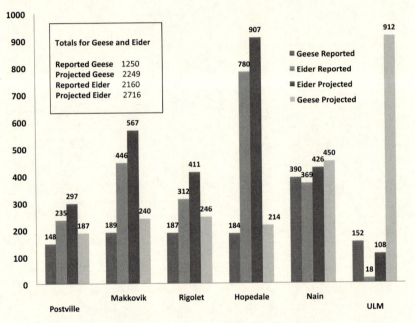

Graph 5. *Reported Harvests of Geese and Eider by Community, 2007.*

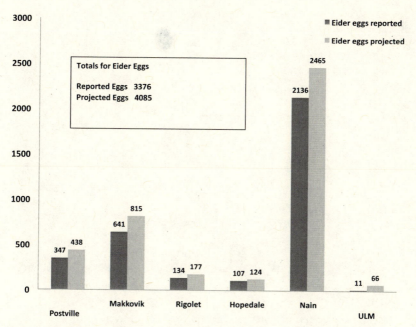

Graph 6. *Reported and Projected Egg Harvests for Eider by Community,*
2007.

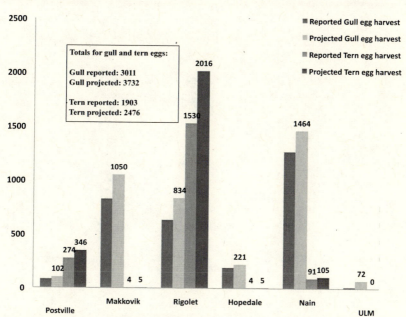

Graph 7. *Reported and Projected Egg Harvests for Gull and Tern*
by Community, 2007.

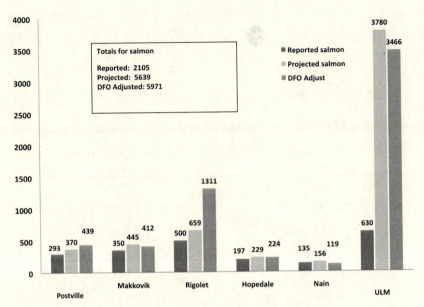

Graph 8. *Reported and Projected Harvests for Atlantic Salmon by Community, 2007.*

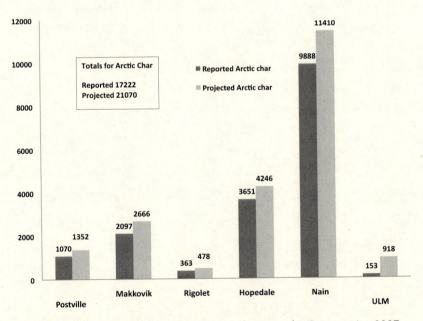

Graph 9. *Reported and Projected Harvests for Arctic by Community, 2007.*

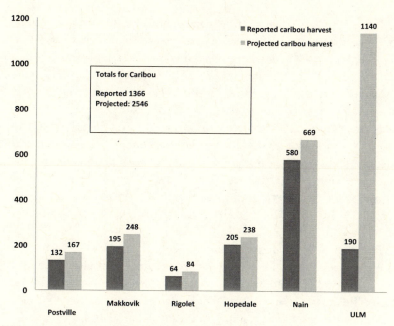

Graph 10. *Reported and Projected Harvests for Caribou by Community, 2007.*

Atlantic salmon dominate fishing harvests in Rigolet and Upper Lake Melville, while, due to its more northerly location, in Nain they are of relatively minor importance. For comparison, federal government estimates of Atlantic salmon landings are also provided. As indicated in the beginning of this chapter, these independent estimates are quite close to our own. Arctic char are the most important fish in our list in the more northerly communities of Nain and Hopedale. Finally, caribou harvests are quite consistent in number of animals for four of the sites, with Nain reporting over twice as many as any other community, and Rigolet reporting the least harvested number. As indicated previously, these differences reflect a number of factors, including the differing populations of the various communities and local availability of resources. A more useful comparison is to calculate mean values per household for each community and its associated measures of dispersion of standard deviations and standard errors. Table 4 makes this comparison and is discussed shortly.

Table 3 combines harvests for all species for which data was collected and provides an overview of reported and projected harvests for all communities. As such, it provides the most complete overview of reported and estimated total harvests for all species investigated for all communities.

In interpreting these harvest levels, one should be cautioned that in addition to a very substantial difference in participation rates in char harvesting there is also a considerable discrepancy in household sample size between communities. In Nain, 220 households were interviewed, compared to a random sample of 100 in Upper Lake Melville. In Postville, only 56 households were interviewed out of approximately 76. To make such comparisons more understandable, a useful procedure is to calculate mean harvests for all active harvesters in each community along with dispersion measures of standard deviations and standard error. This provides a more rigorous means for comparison while allowing the use of standard errors to calculate confidence intervals, an estimate of statistically significant differences between various means. Table 4 summarizes mean harvest levels by species and community for 2007.

While the study was designed to interview all households in each community, household selection within each community was determined on a random basis from a map in which all households were assigned a unique number. This allowed the final households interviewed to be treated as a randomly drawn sample. As a result, various inferential statistical techniques could be utilized in analysis. Of particular use were 95 per cent confidence intervals for determining deviation from true population averages. These

Table 3. *Reported and Projected Total Harvests for All Species, 2007.*

	Reported	Projected
Geese	1250	1648
Black Duck	1234	2162
Eider	2160	2698
Surf scoter	763	1579
Black scoter	556	924
WW scoter	88	162
Eider egg	3376	4074
Gull egg	3011	3732
Tern egg	1903	2476
Guillemot egg	1079	1257
Salmon	2105	4669
Char	11231	13276
Caribou	1366	2306

Table 4. *Means, Standard Deviations and Standard Error Measurements of Selected Species by Community.*

Community	Geese	Black Duck	Eider	Eider egg	Gull egg	Tern egg	Salmon	Char	Caribou
Rigolet									
Mean	2.690	3.660	4.390	1.890	8.920	52.640	9.090	5.120	0.920
Std dev.	5.935	8.764	1.498	1.963	20.423	67.865	2.145	17.112	2.109
St. error	0.87	0.776	1.165	4,000	6.325	20.000	1.789	14.629	0.410
Makkovik									
Mean	2.200	1.97	5.19	7.45	9.8	0.06	5	24.38	2.270
Std dev.	4.765	0.678	1.291	1.927	26.981	0.478	3.102	31.088	3.767
St. error	0.50	0.580	1.117	1.620	2.694	0.047	0.372	4.231	0.389
Postville									
Mean	2.640	3.770	4.200	6.20	1.450	4.890	5.23	19.11	2.36
Std dev.	3.348	1.019	9.145	1.417	5.258	13.61	2.66	25.223	3.324
St. error	0.449	0.956	1.116	1,316	0.673	1.746	0.405	3.313	0.435
Hopedale									
Mean	2.630	1.760	6.900	0.950	1.690	0.05	1.740	43.99	1.810
Std dev.	4.389	4.811	2.325	3.086	4.761	0.215	3.965	56.769	4.267
St. error	0.425	0.833	1.055	0.287	0.879	0.048	0.317	6.866	0.385
Nain									
Mean	1.870	1.050	1,770	10.220	6.68	0.48	0.71	47.310	2.780
Std dev.	4.221	2.354	3.932	25.713	11.922	3.902	2.127	61.156	4.828
St. error	0.285	0.158	2.65	1.566	0.835	0.264	0.150	4.389	0.350
ULM									
Mean	1.380	1.540	0.160	0.100	0.110	0.000	6.120	1.350	1.680
Std dev.	2.604	0.324	0.098	1.334	1.455	1.455	2.088	5.638	1.673
St. error	0.239	0.301	0.900	0.128	0.140	0.190	0.358	0.597	0.151

intervals can then be used to construct error box charts, which can be used to determine which means are statistically different from each other for each species. Graph 11 shows such an error box plot for eider eggs. The vertical axis to the left scales the mean harvest level for the species by community. In the graph, it is denoted by the circle in the middle of each vertical line. The top and bottom bars of each line represent the upper and lower 95 percent

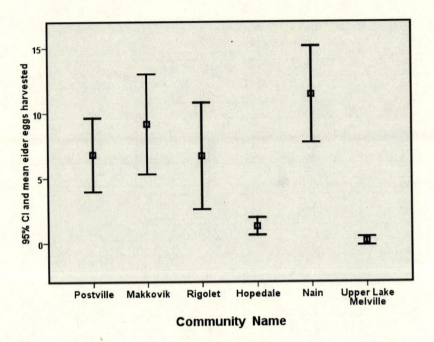

Graph 11. *Box Error Plot for Mean Eider Eggs Harvested.*

confidence limits of the true, but unknown, mean harvest for each community. The smaller the vertical length of the bar, the more tightly packed is the sampling distribution. One can detect visually which mean values are statistically different from each other at 95 percent confidence by seeing which do not have overlap in their distributions with others. In this case, Hopedale and Upper Lake Melville overlap with each other but not with any other communities, meaning that they are not statistically different from each other but are from the other four communities. As might be expected, these same two communities also differ statistically in their mean harvest levels of adult eiders.

Error box plots were constructed for all species. For each species, statistically significant mean differences were found. For example, Hopedale, Nain, and Makkovik differ from other communities with respect to Arctic char harvest, and only Upper Lake Melville differs from other communities in mean caribou harvests. While we offer no specific explanations for these differences, earlier explanations of factors associated with either the animals themselves or possible social and economic factors of harvesters likely explain them.

Seasonal Variation in Harvesting

Harvesting of the species examined in this chapter occurs throughout almost the entire year, although certain species, regardless of the community where they are harvested, tend to be harvested at approximately the same time. There are, however, some exceptions. While our annual division does not allow as precise a specification of harvest time as would be ideal, even that division of the year into five "seasons" reveals some unsurprising differences between species. Egging, for example, occurs in late spring, and seabird harvesting in late fall as well as spring. Graphs 12 and 13 summarize seasonal distribution for selected seabird harvesting, geese, and eider. As can be seen from Graph 12, there is some seasonal difference in harvesting patterns for geese. Hopedale and Postville harvesters have a late fall/early winter season that appears not to be shared by other communities. It should be understood, however, that only a few weeks might separate a late October from an early November harvest, and, given our division of months, any difference might be more apparent than real. Only a longer time series of data with finer temporal scaling could address this issue.

It would seem that seasonal variation can to some extent be explained with regard to eider ducks. In particular, Hopedale concentrates eider

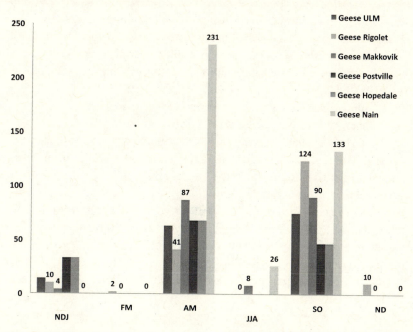

Graph 12: *Canada Goose Harvesting by Community and Time of Year, 2007.*

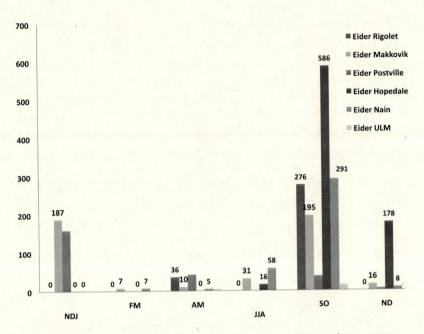

Graph 13: *Eider Duck Harvesting by Community and Time* of Year, 2007.

harvesting during summer in a way no other communities does. (However, our caveat about seasonal variation with geese may also apply here.) With the exception of the communities of Postville and Makkovik, harvesting is concentrated on either side of the summer season, offering the possibility, at least, that the graphs overstate any temporal difference.

Caribou provide a seemingly stronger case for seasonal variation. Graph 14 presents the seasonal harvest of caribou by community.

As can be seen, harvest is most widely distributed in Nain, with harvests occurring throughout the year, though concentration is in late fall and winter. Once again, depending upon the time of month in which actual harvest occurs, the range of harvesting time may actually be considerably shorter than it appears. More specific temporal categories are necessary to resolve this issue, as are multiple years of information in order to differentiate annual variations from clearly delimited differences. At this time, we can offer this discussion of seasonal variation as a useful direction for further research. We will also make a further comment about seasonal variation over time in the next section.

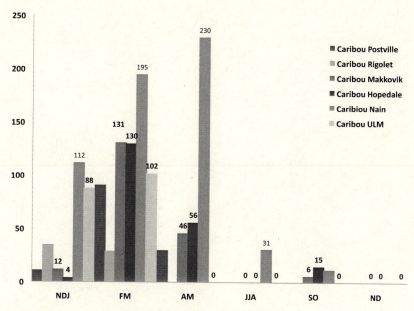

Graph 14. *Caribou Harvest by Season and Community.*

Historical Continuity in Harvesting

A premise underlying this chapter, and indeed the results of our study, is that subsistence harvesting remains an important component of Inuit life, particularly on the north central Labrador coast. Where possible, we have compared our harvest estimates with others compiled in earlier years (see Natcher et al. 2009). According to these earlier assessments, harvest levels appear to be similar in 2007, and in some cases current harvest estimates exceed earlier ones. We were fortunate to acquire a copy of the data from one of the earlier more comprehensive studies in the region (Mackey and Orr 1988), which allowed us to more systematically examine harvest continuity in our research. In fact, several of the communities in that study are the same as in this study. The percentage of households in this particular work is quite comparable to ours, and while there is some demographic variability between our study and the Mackey and Orr one, the households in Nain, Rigolet, and Makkovik are fairly comparable, considering the two sets of research were done approximately twenty-five years apart. Rigolet and Makkovik, in particular, are quite comparable, with similar proportions of households and total population included. Graph 15 compares estimates from the Mackey and Orr study with ours for Atlantic salmon, a keystone species for each community.

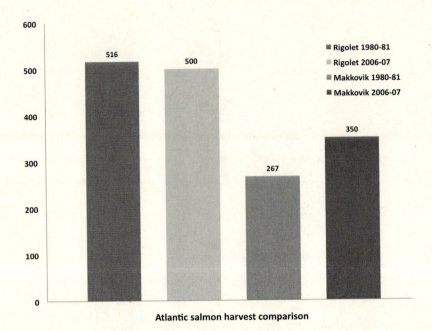

Graph 15. *Salmon Harvest by Community, Rigolet and Makkovik 1981 to 2007.*

Graph 15 compares total harvests reported for each community for roughly similar numbers of households. In Makkovik approximately 267 Atlantic salmon were reported harvested in 1981, compared to 350 in 2007. For Rigolet, the numbers were 516 and 500 respectively. Graph 16 summarizes the harvest by season. While the majority of the harvest occurs during June, July, and August for both time periods, there is a wider seasonality in the earlier period. This is likely a result of changes in Atlantic salmon management. In 1981 salmon fishing berths were more likely to be further extended off headlands in order to intercept the largest number and size of fish, and there was a commercial gillnet fishery harvesting upwards of 500 metric tonnes. As well, there were no restrictions or quotas for household consumption. Finally, there was a well-known run of large salmon late in the fall, and those salmon were often taken as a main holiday meal. While the run of large salmon probably remains, none of the other conditions do. In response to outcries from other parts of Atlantic Canada, the Labrador commercial fishery was closed in 1998 and a seven-fish limit was imposed on each household.

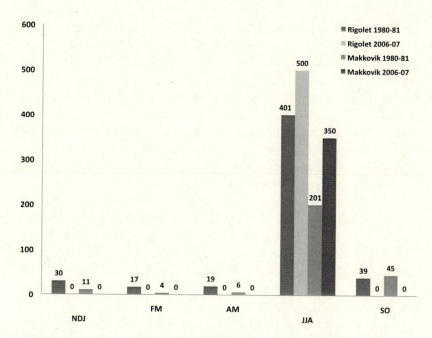

Graph 16. *Salmon Harvest by Seasonality, Rigolet and Makkovik 1981 and 2007.*

These changes most likely account for the elimination of the late fall/early winter fishery, though it is interesting to speculate on whether or not the issuing of seven-fish household quotas might have encouraged a more concentrated fishing effort. This is also an interesting and important area of investigation for how management initiatives may indirectly affect subsistence harvesting patterns. Comparisons with a number of other species in the Mackey-Orr study result in similar findings. In combination with the other estimates provided by Peter Usher (1982), T. Williamson (1997), and Carol Brice-Bennett (1977, 1986), there is extremely strong support for the general argument that subsistence harvesting remains a significant and important component of coastal Inuit life.

Conclusion

Inuit residents of Labrador's north central coast, and particularly those living in the more interior administrative centre of Happy Valley–Goose Bay, have experienced and subsequently adopted into their everyday lives many elements associated with contemporary modern society. Yet much of their lives and everyday activity remains synchronized to the rhythms of the land and sea, and through this synchronization an ongoing continuity with the past is reinforced. This is illustrated by Inuit residents' maintenance of a flexible and adaptive strategy of subsistence provisioning within a wider cultural, spiritual, economic, and nutritional milieu. This adaptation to the wider natural environment as a source of renewable resources has always been and continues to be flexible and dynamic. Residents respond to the cycles of specific animal abundance resulting from natural population cycles, environmental changes that affect availability at particular locations and times, and the matrix of economic and temporal opportunities and constraints within which individuals and households must weigh decisions about the extent, type, and duration of country food harvest intention.

Approximately 85 percent of households are active harvesters in that at least one animal from those species studied is harvested. In fact, most households participate to a greater extent than this minimalist definition. When households that do not harvest but receive country foods are included, the percentage is between 2 and 8 percent higher. As we have indicated elsewhere (Natcher et al. 2009), these harvests represent a very significant economic and nutritional contribution to Inuit households.

Continuity with past harvesting has been demonstrated in several ways, despite limited systematic information on past harvest levels as a result of diverse estimating methodologies and sampling procedures as well as a limited number of reference years. The clearest and most comprehensive comparison is provided in the work of Mary Alton Mackey and Robin Orr for three of the coastal communities examined in the early 1980s. With access to their original data, we were able to develop comparable estimates for several species at the community level. After adjusting for changes in number and characteristics of households in these communities, we found evidence suggesting a generally clear continuity in harvesting. In fact, our estimates for Atlantic salmon suggest slightly more salmon are being harvested for subsistence use in 2007 than they were in 1981, though the former year has been locally regarded as a very good year for that species, and we have no comparable estimate of abundance for 1981. Other, less systematic estimates of keystone species such as caribou by Usher (1982), of seabirds by Northland Associates (1986), and of several other species by Williamson (1997) and Brice-Bennett (1986) suggest a similar continuity.

In light of these findings, it is worth revisiting the theory briefly discussed early in the chapter: that a possible decline in country food subsistence harvesting results as cultural, economic, and technological elements of what is generally referred to as "modernization" become entrenched in isolated community and household life. This theory suggests that hunting, fishing, berry picking, and other foraging activities may continue, but they can be described as "recreational" in their extent and harvest, and in the cognitive understanding of them; the justification for them can be found in the social benefits they grant participants. Some recent research has argued that this is, in fact, the case on the Labrador coast (See Montevecchi et al. 2008).

A variation on this view is that technological improvements in harvesting equipment, secured through greater access to wage labour and resulting higher incomes, combined with increased population growth (and possibly environmental change affecting habitat), has led to lesser abundance and an obsolescence of much of the traditional knowledge that informed earlier subsistence harvesting. The result is less dependence on traditional subsistence harvesting and possibly less overall interest in harvesting more generally (Kennedy 2007). While our data does not offer any systematic response to these arguments, particularly the cognitive understandings in which any harvesting activity might occur, we would offer the following points. One must be extremely cautious in attributing any particular cognitive understanding to any foraging activity. Traditional subsistence harvesting always contained important social, cultural, and spiritual understandings for Inuit people (Smith 1991). The increase in sophisticated technological tools such as snowmobiles and all-terrain vehicles (ATVs) may indeed impart a strong social dimension to contemporary foraging practices. This need not undermine the view that the harvesting documented here is widely seen by harvesters as an important activity critical to the reproduction of household life.

Similarly, we urge some caution in contending that many species traditionally harvested are no longer available and that traditional knowledge is lacking for species that heretofore were not extensively exploited or are immigrants to habitat niches previously occupied. Several respondents in the coastal communities offered similar comments about a few species, including harp and hood seals, walrus, polar bear, and cod. Despite this observation, each of the communities possesses what we have termed keystone species, which 50 percent or more of households harvest, and most of these have long been harvested by community members. Atlantic salmon, Arctic char, caribou, eider ducks, and eggs are among the most common examples. Many community residents, particularly elders, possess extensive traditional knowledge of these species and the wider ecosystem in which they reside.

Traditional knowledge is generally holistic, adaptive, and integrative (Neis and Felt 2000). It is sensitive to complex temporal and spatial cycles as well as year-to-year variation resulting from a wide range of natural and anthropogenic changes and interventions. Given the extensive and historically maintained harvest levels documented in this chapter, it would appear as if traditional knowledge, at least for these species, is still widely held and contemporarily informing. Thus, while we would not necessarily contradict the assertions outlined above nor deny their accuracy in describing some species, more extensive investigation would seem required before generalizing too widely.

Believing that wildfood and the foraging activities associated with their utilization spoke to their very survival as a distinct people, Labrador Inuit activists emphasized the continuing salience of wildfood to the social, cultural, spiritual, economic, and nutritional dimensions of Inuit life and lobbied successfully to ensure that subsistence activities were a prominent part of land claims negotiations and the subsequent land claims agreement. Our examination of subsistence wildfood harvesting reaffirms the soundness of that insight and subsequent strategy. Despite the incursion of many elements of modern life into coastal communities and households, subsistence harvesting continues to be a dynamic and flexible activity critically relevant, if not essential, for life in the Labrador context.

References

Alaska Fish and Game. 2010. Summary papers found at http://www.subsistence.adfg.state.ak.us/geninfo/publctns/articles.cfm.

Ames, Randy. 1977. *Social, Economic, and Legal Problems of Hunting in Northern Labrador.* Nain: Labrador Inuit Association.

Ben-Dor, Shmuel.1966. *Makkovik: Eskimos and Settlers in a Labrador Community.* St. John's: ISER Books.

Brice-Bennett, Carol. 1986. *Renewable Resource Use and Wage Employment in the Economy of Northern Labrador.* St. John's: Royal Commission on Employment and Unemployment, Newfoundland and Labrador.

_____. 1977. *Our Footprints Are Everywhere: Inuit Land Use and Occupancy in Labrador.* Nain: Labrador Inuit Association

_____. 1994. *Dispossessed: The Eviction of Inuit from Hebron, Labrador.* Happy Valley: Labrador Institute of Northern Studies.

Couglan, D., and T. Brannick. 2007. *Doing Action Research in Your own Organization.* Thousand Oaks, CA: Sage Publications.

Fall, James A. 1990. "The Division of Subsistence of the Alaska Department of Fish and Game: An Overview of its Research Program and Findings." *Arctic Anthropology* 27, 2 :68–92.

Government of Canada. 1993. *Agreement between the Inuit of the Nunavut Settlement Area and Her Majesty in Right of Canada.* Ottawa: Indian and Northern Affairs Canada and Tungavik Federation of Nunavut.

_____. 2006. *Agreement between Nunavik Inuit and Her Majesty the Queen Concerning Nunavik Land Claims.* Ottawa: Indian and Northern Affairs Canada.

_____. 2005. *Agreement between the Inuit of Labrador and Her Majesty in Right of Canada (Labrador Inuit Land Claims Agreement).* Ottawa: Indian and Northern Affairs Canada, Government of Newfoundland and Labrador and Labrador Inuit Association.. Queen's Printer: Ottawa and Labrador Inuit Association, Nain, Labrador.

Government of Newfoundland and Labrador. 2006. *Community Accounts.* http://www.communityaccounts.ca/communityaccounts/onlinedata/getdata.asp. St. John's.

_____. 1974. *Report of the Royal Commission of Labrador.* Vol. 6. St. John's: Dollco Printing, 1974.

Hefferton, S.J. (Minister of Public Welfare, Government of Newfoundland). 1959. Letter to Minister of Citizenship and Immigration, Ottawa, 26 March 1959. In *The Administration of Northern Labrador Affairs*, Appendix 1. St. John's: Government of Newfoundland (Department of Public Welfare), 1964.

INAC (Indian and Northern Affairs Canada). Labrador Inuit Land Claims Agreement. 2003. Ottawa: INAC.

Kemmis, S., and R. McTaggart. 2000. "Participatory Action Research." In *Handbook of Qualitative Research*, 2nd ed., edited by N.K. Denzin and Y. S. Lincoln, 567–605. Thousand Oaks, CA: Sage Publications.

Kennedy, John C. 1977. "Northern Labrador: An Ethnohistorical Account." In *The White Arctic: Anthropological Essays on Tutelage and Ethnicity*, edited by R. Paine. St. John's: ISER.

_____. 1982. *Holding the Line: Ethnic Boundaries in a Northern Labrador Community.* St. John's: ISER Books.

_____. 2007. "New Foods, Lost Foods: Local Knowledge about Changing Resources in Coastal Labrador." In *Resetting the Kitchen Table: Food Security, Culture Health and Resilience in Coastal Communities*, edited by Christopher Parrish et. al., 87–98. New York: Nova Science Publishers.

_____. 1995. *People of the Bays and Headlands: Anthropological History and the Fate of Communities in the Unknown Labrador.* Toronto: University of Toronto Press.

_____. 2009. "Two Worlds of Eighteenth-Century Labrador Inuit." In *Moravian Beginnings in Labrador: Papers from a Symposium Held in Makkovik and Hopedale*, edited by H. Rollman, 23–36. St. John's: Newfoundland and Labrador Studies.

Mackey, Mary G. Alton, and Robin Orr. 1988. "The Seasonal Nutrient Density of Country Food Harvested in Makkovik, Labrador." *Arctic* 41, 2: 105–09.

Magdanz, James, S. Charles, J. Utermohle, and R.J. Wolfe. 2002. *The Production and Distribution of Wild Food in Wales and Deering, Alaska.* Technical Report 259. Juneau: Division of Subsistence , Alaska Department of Fish and Game.

Montevecchi, W.A., H. Chaffey, and C. Burke. 2007. "Hunting for Security: Changes in the Exploitation of Marine Birds in Newfoundland and Labrador." In *Resetting the Kitchen Table: Food Security, Culture Health and Resilience in Coastal Communities*, edited by Christopher Parrish et. al., 99–114. New York: Nova Science Publishers.

Natcher, David C., Lawrence Felt, Andrea Procter, and Government of Nunatsiavut. 2009. "Monitoring Food Security in Nunatsiavut, Labrador." *Plan Canada.* 49, 2: 52–54.

Naves, Liliana C. 2009. *Alaska Migratory Bird Subsistence Harvest Estimates, 2004–2007*. Technical Paper 349. Anchorage: Alaska Department of Fish and Game, Subsistence Division.

Neis, Barbara, and Lawrence Felt. 2000. *Finding Our Sea Legs: Linking Fishery People and Their Knowledge with Science and Management*. St. John's: ISER Books.

Northland Associates. 1986. *Native Waterfowl Harvest in Coastal Labrador*. Prepared under Supply and Services Canada Tender: KL 103-0-0398.

Nunavut Wildlife Management Board (NWMB). 2004. Nunavut Wildlife Harvest Study. NWMB. Nunavut, Canada. http://www.nwmb.com/english/resources/harvest_study/NWHS%202004%20Report.pdf.

Nunatsiavut, Government of. 2008. Distribuition of Nunatsiavut Beneficiaries by residence. Beneficiary Office, Government of Nunatsiavut: Nain.

Reason, P., and H. Bradbury, eds. 2001. *Handbook of Action Research: Participative Inquiry and Practice*. Thousand Oaks, CA: Sage Publications.

Rockwood, W.G. 1955. *Memorandum on General Policy in Respect to the Indians and Eskimos of Northern Labrador*. St. John's: Department of Public Welfare.

Smith, E.A. 1991. *Inujjuamiut Foraging Strategies: Evolutionary Ecology of an Arctic Hunting Economy*. New York: Aldine De Gruyter.

Usher, Peter J. 1982. *Renewable Resources in the Future of Northern Labrador*. Nain: Labrador Inuit Association.

Usher, Peter J., and George Wenzel. 1987. "Native Harvest Surveys and Statistics: A Critique of Their Construction and Use." *Arctic* 40, 2: 145–60.

Webb, Eugene, D.T. Campbell, R.D. Schwartz, and L. Sechrest. 1999. *Unobtrusive Measures*. Thousand Oaks, CA: Sage Publications.

Williamson, T. 1997. *From Sina to Sikujâluk: Our Footprint. Mapping Inuit Environmental Knowledge in the Nain District of Northern Labrador*. Nain: Labrador Inuit Association.

Wolfe, Robert J. 1987. "The Super-household: Specialization in Subsistence Economies." Paper presented at the 14th annual Meeting of the Alaska Anthropological Association, March 17–21. Anchorage, Alaska.

CHAPTER 7

The Social Organization of Wildfood Production in Postville, Nunatsiavut

David C. Natcher, Lawrence Felt, Jill McDonald, and Rose Ford

As described in the preceding chapters, the Nunatsiavummiut have, over the course of several centuries, been challenged by profound social, economic, and environmental change. Arguably the only constant during this time has been change itself. Yet, despite the enormity of these disruptions, Nunatsiavummiut have successfully maintained a lasting relationship with the Labrador environment through hunting, fishing, and gathering of resources from the land and sea. Today, as in the past, Nunatsiavummiut harvest, process, distribute, and consume considerable volumes of wildfoods annually (as discussed in detail in the preceding chapter). Collectively, these activities have come to be known as "subsistence," and together they make up an essential component of Nunatsiavummiut culture.

The term *subsistence* has been defined as the local production and distribution of resources (Lonner 1980) where the objective is neither total self-sufficiency nor capital accumulation, but rather a continuous flow of goods and services (Sahlins 1971). Stuart Marks (1977) expands upon this definition by noting that subsistence, as a specialized mode of domestic production, also entails the transmission of social norms and cultural values, or what Walter Neale (1971) refers to as the non-monetary value of wildlife harvesting. In this way, one's participation in subsistence activities is fundamental to maintaining the social and cultural continuity of one's household and community (Freeman 1986, 29).

It has been suggested, however, that due to the increasing importance of money in Inuit communities, divisions and social tensions are arising in ways that are challenging traditional forms of subsistence production. For example, James Ford and his colleagues (2008) have found that sharing practices among some Inuit families have come under increasing stress, with younger family members showing reluctance to share with others or requesting payment before exchanges occur. These conditions are causing divisions within community social networks and are devaluing traditional forms of Inuit socialization (Hund 2004, 1). As a result, "the functioning of social networks have been affected by a decrease in importance of the extended family unit, the emergence of inter-generational segregation, a decline in the practice of traditional cultural values, and a concentration of resources in fewer hands" (Ford et al. 2008, 54).

Notwithstanding these findings, others have observed that, despite the importance of money in contemporary Inuit economies, the customary social relationships long inherent in these subsistence-oriented systems remain intact (Wenzel et al. 2000, 2). Jack Kruse (1991), for example, notes that among the Inupiat in Alaska, the cultural values associated with subsistence production have not been diminished by the wage economy; instead, wage earning has actually allowed for the continuation of harvesting activities and in some cases has strengthened the social networks supporting them. Rather than subverting subsistence production, the wage economy provides an economic basis to support wildlife harvesting, thereby invigorating social institutions and perpetuating traditional values within communities (Wheelersburg 2008, 170). In their examination of contemporary food sharing networks in the Inuit community of Holman, Peter Collings et al. (1998) found that despite the growth of the wage economy, food sharing patterns between Holman households were very much consistent with patterns described in the early 1900s, where kinship served as the central and determining factor for exchange. Similarly, Heather Meyers et al. (2008, 129) found that among the Nunavut communities of Cambridge Bay, Pond Inlet, and Clyde River, sharing relationships remain important to ensuring community stability and solidarity among family social connections.

In response to these somewhat divergent views, this chapter, and the research that informed it, set out to examine the contemporary (2006–07) social organization of wildfood production in the Nunatsiavut community of Postville. In this context, wildfood production involves the harvest, distribution, and receipt of wildfoods within households and multi-household networks. Drawing on information gained through household surveys, this chapter provides a contemporary portrait of the Postville subsistence economy and demonstrates the inherent complexity and blend of activities that together compose most Postville household economies.

Postville, Nunatsiavut

Postville is a relatively small, predominantly Inuit community of approximately 240 persons. Located on the north shore of Kaipokok Bay, approximately fifty-one kilometres inland from the Labrador coast, it is surrounded by a low, rugged, and rocky landscape. Postville's more immediate environment is sparsely forested by spruce, fir, birch, juniper, and alder willows, dispersed amongst numerous ponds, creeks, and streams.

Prior to community settlement (pre-1941), an estimated forty-one Inuit and non-Inuit residents lived in scattered homesteads along the coast of Kaipokok Bay (Ames 1977). Families generally maintained two dwellings, a summer house on the shore of the bay, located near the mouths of rivers or streams with convenient access to salmon- and cod-jigging grounds, and an inland residence, used primarily during the winter, that was located close to trapping and hunting areas (Ames 1977, 235). With the exception of caribou hunting, which occurred further inland, most household subsistence activities were carried out within the general area of these seasonal dwellings.

In 1837 a Quebec merchant named D.D. Stewart established a trading business at the present site of Postville. Postville, or the "Post" as it was originally called, gradually became a more established seasonal site of occupation for bay residents. Although the community has been inhabited since the late 1830s, year-round settlement of Postville did not occur until roughly a century later, when, in 1941, the construction of the Pentecostal church was completed.[1] While most residents of the bay were slow to abandon their traditional homesteads, the construction of the Postville school, together with the encouragement of the Newfoundland government that all school-age children attend, was, by 1946, sufficient motivation for most residents of the bay to relocate to town.

In the immediate years following settlement, the land use patterns and means of livelihood for most Postville residents changed very little. During this time residents continued to use their traditional family hunting and trappings areas. However, as more time was spent in their new community surroundings, land use patterns began to shift, with proximity to Postville

---

1 Postville is unique among Nunatsiavut communities in that the predominant religion remains Pentecostalism. Most Inuit from other communities consider themselves to be Moravians.

being the most important factor in the selection of hunting areas. Postville hunters were now choosing to remain closer to home and to make only occasional trips to traditional family areas (Ames 1977, 227). One result of this shift in territorial use was that hunters from the entire community were now exploiting areas that in the past had been used almost exclusively by individual families, thereby placing more pressure on local resources. The changes in community land use also influenced the prey choice of Postville hunters. Prior to community settlement, the primary species harvested tended to be fur-bearing animals, seals (with an emphasis on harp), caribou, and cod. After settlement the primary species harvested were salmon, char, caribou, and migratory birds. During the summer and early fall Postville residents would set nets for Atlantic salmon. Before the practice was made illegal, residents would also "bar-off" salmon-spawning creeks and streams in order to ensure a large catch (Ames 1977, 231). Netted incidentally with salmon, char also made an important contribution to the community food harvest. Migratory birds were another primary subsistence species and served as an important source of fresh meat in the fall and, prior to the introduction of game laws, in the spring, when residents also gathered eggs. Caribou were by and large the most important terrestrial source of meat for Postville residents. Beginning in January or February, when there was sufficient snow for inland travel, hunters would pursue caribou through the month of April or as long as snow conditions and the presence of caribou would allow (Ames 1977, 225). While all these species served as important subsistence food sources for community members, it remained necessary for Postville residents to adjust to seasonal changes and subsequent fluctuations in resource availability. In fact, given the variability that characterizes the Labrador environment, flexibility in harvesting strategies was perhaps the single most important adaptive feature for all residents of the coast (Natcher et al. 2009). This adaptive capacity was particularly important given the limited wage-earning opportunities available to Postville residents.

Since its establishment in the 1940s, wage-earning employment in Postville has been sporadic at best. From 1946 to 1957 logging and mill operations provided some seasonal employment. However, by 1956 mill operations were abandoned, and in 1957 the mill facility was destroyed by fire. While these changes could have been potentially disastrous, the Postville economy was only marginally affected. This was due in part to the seasonal nature of mill operations and to the fact that Postville residents never developed a complete dependency on the wage-earning economy. Rather, wage earning was used simply to supplement and support more reliable subsistence activities (Ames 1977).

In addition to finding occasional wage-earning opportunities, Newfoundland's confederation into Canada in 1949 provided Postville residents with family allowances, welfare payments, and unemployment insurance. As described by Randy Ames (1977, 210),

> Men would earn unemployment stamps by cod fishing in the summer and, more recently, by salmon fishing. Fishermen who failed to earn the required number of stamps during the summer could often make up the balance that was required by working at some of the short-term construction projects carried out in the fall. If a man then failed to earn the required number of unemployment stamps, he was still entitled to welfare benefits. The premiums were too small to support a family, but they supplemented land-based activities. A man may trap and collect welfare or unemployment insurance at the same time.

In 1974 more secure employment became available when a shipyard was established in Postville. On average, shipyard operations employed sixteen men, or nearly two-thirds of the eligible male workforce (Ames 1977). Those who did not find employment with the shipyard took advantage of other occasional and seasonal employment opportunities in construction, roadwork maintenance, and salmon fishing. Yet for all these wage-earning opportunities, Postville residents saw them, like the logging and mill enterprises, as fleeting, while the harvesting of wildlife resources would remain the cornerstone of the Postville economy.

Methodology

To understand the contemporary social organization of wildfood production in Postville today, a social network analysis was employed. This involved examining the extent to which households and multi-household networks participate and cooperate in the production of wildfoods. To access this information, a survey was designed to systematically gather information on the harvest, use, and distribution of wildfoods, specifically Atlantic salmon, char, caribou, waterfowl, and eggs. Several factors contributed to our choosing to focus on these species. First, Ames (1977) identified these species as being the most important subsistence food sources to Postville residents following community settlement (post-1941). Nunatsiavut government representatives and Postville residents also identified these species as being the primary species targeted by community harvesters today. Second, as an outcome of the comprehensive land claims, the Nunatsiavut government has entered into a co-management relationship with the provincial and federal governments for the administration of fish and wildlife. As part of that co-management process, a determination of the annual allowable harvest for these species will soon be necessary. Prior to those levels being agreed upon, it was necessary to identify the current level of domestic use among Nunatsiavut households (Inuit Domestic Harvest Levels). The findings of this research are contributing to that determination.

During the summer and fall of 2007, a community researcher (R. Ford) administered surveys during face-to-face interviews in residents' homes or other convenient locations. In total, fifty-six out of seventy-seven Postville households were surveyed (73 percent coverage). From the household perspective, we identified: 1) household demographic information; 2) the total amount of wildfoods harvested over the course of the previous year (2006–2007); 3) the amount of time male and female heads-of-households allocated to wage earning and wildlife harvesting (in weeks per year); and 4) household development stages. As defined by James Magdanz et al. (2002), these development stages include: 1) Inactive Single Parent/Retired Elder/ Inactive Single Households (single grouping); 2) Developing Households (households with heads twenty to thirty-nine years of age); 3) Mature Households (households with heads forty to fifty-nine years of age); 4) Active Elder Households (households with heads sixty years of age or more and still actively harvesting); and 5) Active Single Person Households.

From the multi-household network perspective, we identified cooperation (giving/receiving) among Postville households, the social relationships that frame those sharing networks, and the total amount of wildfoods being exchanged between households over the course of the previous year. Additional household economic data were derived from the Community Accounts Database. Community Accounts is a provincially supported Internet-based data retrieval system that serves as a single comprehensive source for key social, economic, and health data and indicators for Labrador communities.

Postville's Subsistence Economy (2006–2007)

Based on the results of our surveys, an estimated 91 percent, or seventy out of seventy-seven Postville households, participated in subsistence production.[2] This includes the harvest, distribution, and/or receipt of wildfoods. In

---

2 During the time of this survey there were seven non-local teachers residing in Postville. While no distinction was made in our survey, these households may represent a significant percentage of Postville's non-harvesting households.

nearly all cases the production of wildfoods served as an important component of household economies. The total Postville harvest in 2006–2007 was an estimated 167 caribou, 187 geese, 901 ducks, 886 eggs, 370 salmon, and 1,352 char. This harvest equates to an edible food weight of approximately 13,509 kilograms of wildfood, or 175 kilograms of wildfood per household and 56 kilograms for every Postville man, woman, and child. It is important to emphasize that this harvest represents only a portion of all the species used by Postville households during the course of the year, for reasons noted above. If we were to include all species harvested, for instance marine and other terrestrial mammals, the total Postville harvest would undoubtedly be greater. Nonetheless, in terms of replacement value—the cost of purchasing the equivalent amount of store-bought food in Postville—the harvest of these species equates to roughly $150,497, or $1,954 per household (see Table 1).

Table 1. *Postville Wildfood Harvest.*

Species	Total Harvest	Edible Food Weight Conversion (kg)	Total Edible Food Weight (kg)	Grocery Replacement	Store Cost	Replacement Costs
Caribou	167	68	11,356	Ground Beef	$9.47/kg	$107,541.32
Geese	187	.96	180	Chicken	$9.75/kg	$1,755.00
Ducks	901	.45	405	Chicken	$9.75/kg	$3,948.75
Eggs	886 (74 doz)	.14	124	Eggs (doz)	$3.87/doz	$286.38
Salmon	370	1.6	592	Fish (fresh fillets)	$25.60/kg	$15,155.20
Char	1,352	.63	852	Fish (fresh fillets)	$25.60/kg	$21,811.20
Total			13,509			$150,497.85

In terms of harvesting effort, considerable time is being devoted to subsistence activities. During 2006–2007, Postville male heads-of-households were engaged in subsistence activities an average of 47.19 weeks per year, while female heads-of-households participated in subsistence activities an average of 37.7 weeks per year (Table 2). This is not to suggest that this amount of time was devoted exclusively to subsistence harvesting, but rather that subsistence activities (harvesting, processing, sharing) occurred during this number of weeks. Comparing the time spent in harvesting in 2006 with seasonal round data derived from Ames (1977), it appears that Postville harvesters are devoting more time to subsistence harvesting today than in the past. As shown in Table 3, household harvesting effort has been extended for each of the four species identified.

Table 2. *Postville Seasonal Round 1960, 1977, 2007.*

Species	Year	Jan	Feb	Mar	April	May	June	July	Aug	Sept	Oct	Nov	Dec
Caribou	2007	———	—	—								—	—
	1977	———	—										
	1960	——	—										
Salmon	2007							—	—				
	1977								—			—	
	1960								—			—	
Char	2007							—	—				
	1977								—	—			
	1960							—					
Waterfowl	2007	—				—	—				—	—	
	1977												—
	1960					—	—					—	

The harvest of wildfoods among Postville households is not uniform. Rather, household harvesting levels are generally consistent with the 30:70 rule (Wolfe 1987), where 30 percent of households harvest approximately 70 percent of the total community harvest. Variability between household harvest levels has in other cases (Magdanz et al. 2002) been attributed to varying stages of household development. That is, as households mature, their social configuration goes through normative cycles of development. As developing households mature their labour force presumably increases in age, number, and harvesting ability. For a period of time mature households have the means (i.e., labour) to participate in a full range of harvesting activities, thereby securing a greater volume of wildfoods. In time, the children of mature households leave to establish their own households, thereby perpetuating their own normative cycle of household development. Depending on the health and social configuration of the remaining household members, wildlife harvesting may begin to decline. There are also those households that fall outside the normative development cycle, for instance those with single parents, individuals with disabilities, or elders who may no longer have the capacity to engage in harvesting activities. It would be expected that those households would produce limited amounts of wildfoods.

In Postville, the overall frequency of household types were: Inactive Single Parent/Retired Elder/Inactive Single Households (n=7); 2) Developing Households (n=30); 3) Mature Households (n=26); 4) Active Elder Households (n=10); and 5) Active Single Households (n=4).

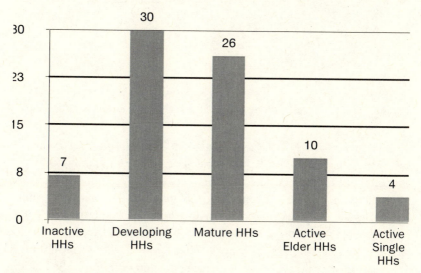

Figure 1: *Household Development Types.*

Among these households, the highest producers of wildfoods were Developing Households, with a total harvest of 8,241 kilograms of edible food weight, followed by Mature Households (3,512kg), Active Elder Households (1,621kg), and Active Single Households (135kg). The only non-producing households were Inactive Single Parent-Retired Elder-Inactive Single Households (n=7).

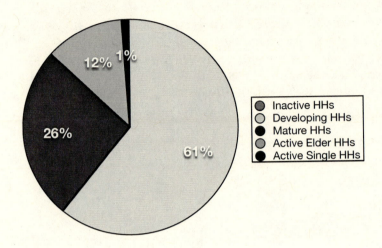

Figure 2. *Total Harvest Among Household Types (% of Edible Food Weight).*

Although relatively consistent with the 30:70 rule, it was the Developing rather than the Mature Households that were, in terms of food weight, the predominant harvesters. The disparity between Developing and Mature Households harvest levels can be attributable to the harvest of caribou, where Developing Households harvested 102 caribou (food weight of 6,936 kg) compared to thirty-one caribou (food weight of 2,108 kg) harvested by Mature Households. This may suggest that some degree of specialization is occurring, in which younger hunters are pursuing caribou while Mature Households concentrate their harvesting efforts on waterfowl, salmon, and char. This may also be an indication of cooperation between households.

Food Sharing

Prior to relocating to Postville from their family homesteads, it was necessary for residents of Kaipokok Bay to adjust their subsistence strategies in response to temporal and spatial variations associated with resource availability, for instance the annual migration of caribou, salmon, and waterfowl. While this often involved harvesting the species most readily available, food sharing between households also helped to minimize the unanticipated impacts of change and reduced the consequences of environmental and economic strain on individual households (Nelson, Natcher, and Hickey 2008). After people settled in Postville in the 1940s, food sharing remained important due to the continuing need to adapt to fluctuations in wildlife populations, as well as the need to cope with a variety of new influences associated with community living, such as the requirement for income to support subsistence activities, population change, and constraints imposed by wildlife regulations. As in the past, the basic purpose of sharing wildfoods remained the same: to maximize the overall well-being of the household.

Based on the results of our survey, food sharing is widely practised among Postville households, with 77 percent, or fifty-nine out of seventy-seven households, engaged in food sharing networks. Figure 3 shows twenty-nine Postville households that make up four food sharing networks, each varying in social complexity. These networks are delineated on the basis of cooperation in wildfood distribution between households. For example, Network I reflects a relatively simple network comprising a parent-children network headed by an inactive male and a female elder (grandparents). Network II is headed by active elders (grandparents), with a son serving as a male head-of-household for a Mature Household and three grandchildren heading Developing Households of their own. Active male and female elders again head Network III, with children heading one Mature and two Developing Households. In this network food sharing occurs between sibling and parental households as well as between three non-kin related households (two Developing and Mature). Last, Network IV consists of thirteen Postville households and an additional eight non-local households. Of all the networks examined, Network IV represents the most complex network in operation. However, Network IV shares many of the same attributes as Networks I, II, and III. Specifically, Network IV is headed by elders whose children and grandchildren compose a large (consisting of seven households) food sharing network, including an Inactive Single Female Household. However, Network IV differs in the inclusion of a second affinal household of active elders (in-laws of married son). Last, Network IV is involved in an extensive network of non-local households (i.e., households residing outside of Postville). In each of the networks described, kinship is to a large extent the defining factor for food exchange. While sharing does occur outside kinship networks, such non-related household networks occur far less frequently (12 percent of all exchanges).

Based on our survey results, together with conversations with community members, it is clear that the exchange of wildfoods unites households on economic and social grounds. This form of generalized reciprocity (Sahlins 1971) not only facilitates the distribution of food as an economic resource but also affirms personal relationships and the social networks that support them. By encompassing important social dimensions, food sharing and norms of reciprocity entail broader conceptions of social responsibility and account for an entirely different set of motivations that extend beyond

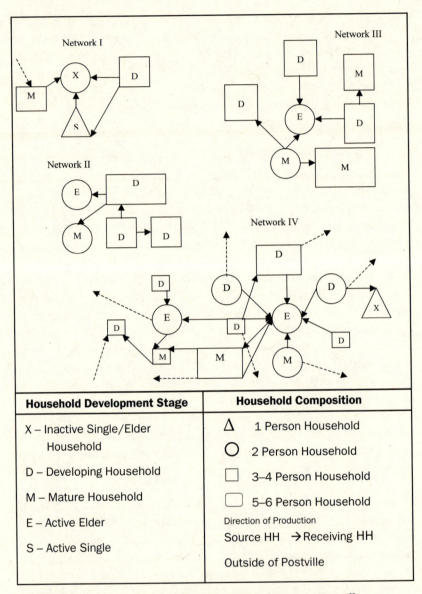

Household Development Stage	Household Composition
X – Inactive Single/Elder Household	△ 1 Person Household
D – Developing Household	○ 2 Person Household
M – Mature Household	☐ 3–4 Person Household
E – Active Elder	▢ 5–6 Person Household
S – Active Single	Direction of Production Source HH → Receiving HH Outside of Postville

Figure 3. *Social Organization of Wildfood Distribution in Postville.*

economic rationality. Thus, by embodying both social and economic attributes, food sharing continues to represent a defining feature of the Postville economy.

Economic Optimization

As mentioned in the introduction, considerable academic debate exists concerning the effect of the wage economy on subsistence production. Some argue that wage earning has displaced traditional forms of wildfood production and exchange, while others argue that participation in the wage economy actually facilitates and is increasingly necessary for the harvest of wildfoods, and in some cases has strengthened communal social networks. Keith Hart (2006, 22) attributes much of this debate to the tendency to compartmentalize subsistence and wage economies into distinct "sectors," as if subsistence and wage economies functioned in different places, like agriculture and manufacturing or Western and traditional knowledge. While the distinction between subsistence and wage economies may be useful in analytical terms, Postville's involvement in subsistence and wage economies is best seen as occurring along a continuum, with participation measurements at varying points on the scale. As reflected in Table 5, both male and female heads of households allocate considerable time to wage earning and subsistence harvesting.

Table 3. *Postville Time Allocation in Economic Production.*

	Wage Earning		Harvesting	
	Male	Female	Male	Female
Weeks per Year	29.85	32.80	47.19	37.70

As this allocation of time indicates, the economic make-up of most Postville households is quite heterogeneous and includes a blend of economic activities. Some household members participate in subsistence harvesting, some receive government transfer payments (employment insurance, social assistance, pensions), and others are involved in full and/or seasonal wage-earning labour. Community members move along an economic continuum that reflects a range of circumstances, with most households participating simultaneously in multiple economic activities. Figure 4 illustrates the mix of economic activities that occur within a single, relatively simple household network.

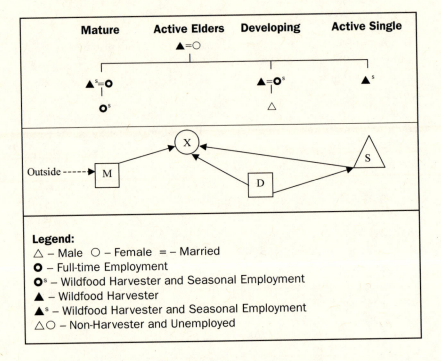

Figure 4. *Network Characteristics (Network I from Fig. 3).*

It is hopefully clear from Figure 4 that "dwelling and family are not congruent" (Magdanz et al. 2002, 3). In this case, an elder couple lives alone; their oldest son with his wife and teenage daughter occupy a neighbouring home and maintain a connection with their adult son, who lives in Makkovik; a daughter with her husband and young son reside in a third house; and their single unmarried grandson occupies a fourth house. Each of these households, while separate, constitutes part of a core family network interacting primarily through subsistence and wage-earning activities. Extending beyond the physical confines of a single or even multiple dwellings, this social network represents an unbounded organization of economic activities based on established kinship relationships (Jorgenson 1984).

Rather than choosing to participate exclusively in any one form of economic activity, most Postville households attempt to find a balance, with household incomes derived from multiple sources. For example, in 2006 the primary employers in Postville were the Torngat Housing Corporation, the Inuit community government, and Torngat Fisheries. Seasonal employment opportunities were found in road maintenance and short-term construction projects. The personal income per capita in Postville was $18,400,[3] adjusted to $12,400 after accounting for tax and inflation. During the time in which our harvest survey was conducted (2006–2007), the unemployment rate for Postville was 28.6 percent, with seventy individuals, or approximately 50 percent of Postville's available labour force, collecting Employment Insurance (Community Accounts). The average benefit for those individuals collecting Employment Insurance was $8,000. Accounting for other forms of government transfers—Canada Pension, Old Age Security, Employment Income Support Assistance—Postville's total self-reliance ratio in 2006 was 76.4 percent; in other words, 23.6 percent of per capita income came from government transfers (Community Accounts).[4] Rarely a means in itself, wage earning enables Postville households to have greater access to wildfoods—either through the direct harvest or through exchange networks. For most Postville households, wage labour (in various forms) is used to support the harvesting activities of other family members. In fact, households with the greatest access to wage income, and thereby the financial means to purchase the necessary equipment to harvest effectively, tend to produce, consume, and distribute significantly more wildfoods than households with limited or no access to wage-earning opportunities.

L. Robbins and F.L. Little (1988) have noted that few subsistence-oriented households are able to function without the contributions of others—whether in terms of harvesting or by gaining access to the wage economy. This is true for Postville, where the need for wildfoods and wage income serves as strong motivation for the cooperation that unites households and communities.

Conclusion

For nearly seventy years, the Postville economy has involved a complex combination of occasional and seasonal employment, government social assistance, and subsistence harvesting activities. In many ways the Postville economy can be seen as one of optimization (Nuttall et al. 2005), where community members exploit a range of opportunities that together contribute to

---

3 For the Province of Newfoundland and Labrador, the personal income per capita was $22,900.

4 The self-reliance ratio is a measure of the community's dependency on government transfers. The higher the percentage of income that comes from transfers, the lower the self-reliance ratio.

an overall livelihood strategy. Despite suggestions that wage earning is transforming, and in some cases displacing, the subsistence economy, the harvest of wildfoods in Postville has remained resilient in times of change and continues to be integral to the health and well-being of community residents. Our research reveals that fishing, hunting, and collecting wild resources makes an important contribution to the economies of many, if not most, Postville households. Today, as in the past, the harvesting and distribution of wildlife resources not only fulfills important economic and nutritional needs but also strengthens and perpetuates social networks by linking individuals and households in Postville. It also appears that, given the frequency with which wildfoods are shared beyond Postville households, food sharing contributes to the maintenance of community networks throughout the Nunatsiavut settlement region. Given that subsistence and wage-earning activities are intrinsically linked, it will be critical for the Nunatsiavut government to implement appropriate policies that promote equitable linkages between the two. This will be a necessity if the Nunatsiavut government hopes to strengthen rather than hinder the economies of Nunatsiavut communities in the future.

References

Ames, Randy. 1977. "Land Use in the Postville Region." In *Our Footprints Are Everywhere: Inuit Land Use and Occupancy in Labrador*, edited by Carol Brice-Bennett, 205–38. Nain: Labrador Inuit Association.

Collings, Peter, George Wenzel, and Richard G. Condon. 1998. "Modern Food Sharing Networks and Community Integration in the Central Canadian Arctic." *Arctic* 51, 4: 301–14.

Community Accounts. N.d. St. John's: Economics and Statistics Department of Finance, Government of Newfoundland and Labrador.

Ford, James D., Barry Smit, Johanna Wandel, Mishak Allurut, Kik Shappa, Harry Ittusarjuat, and Kevin Qrunnut. 2008. "Climate Change in the Arctic: Current and Future Vulnerability in Two Inuit Communities in Canada." *The Geographical Journal* 174, 1: 45–62.

Freeman, Milton M.R. 1986. "Renewable Resources, Economics and Native Communities." In *Native Peoples and Renewable Resource Management*, edited by J. Green and J. Smith, 23–37: Edmonton: Alberta Society of Professional Biologists.

Hart, Keith. 2006. "Bureaucratic Form and the Informal Economy." In *Linking the Formal and Informal Economy—Concepts and Policies*, edited by Basudeb Guha-Khasnobis, Ravi Kanbur, and Elinor Ostrom, 21–35. Oxford: Oxford University Press.

Hund, A. 2004. "From Subsistence to the Cash-Based Economy: Alterations in the Inuit Family Structure, Values, and Expectations." Paper presented at the annual meeting of the American Sociological Association, San Francisco, CA. http://www.allacademic.com/meta/p108826_index.html

Jorgenson, Joseph G. 1984. *Effects of Renewable Resource Harvest Disruptions on Socioeconomic and Sociocultural Systems: Norton Sound.* Social and Economic Studies Program Technical Report No. 90. Anchorage: United States Department of Interior, Minerals Management Service Alaska, OCS Region.

Kruse, Jack. 1991. "Alaska Inupiat Subsistence and Wage Employment Patterns: Understanding Individual Choice." *Human Organization* 50, 4: 317–626.

Lonner, Thomas D. 1980. *Subsistence as an Economic System in Alaska: Theoretical and Policy Implications.* Technical Paper No. 67. Anchorage: Alaska Department of Fish and Game, Division of Subsistence.

Magdanz, James S., Charles J. Utermohle, and Robert J. Wolfe. 2002. "The Production and Distribution of Wild Food in Wales and Deering, Alaska." Technical Paper No. 259. Juneau: Alaska Department of Fish and Game, Division of Subsistence.

Marks, Stuart S. 1977. "Hunting Behavior and Strategies of the Valley Bisa in Zambia." *Human Ecology* 5, 1: 1–36.

Meyers, Heather, Stephanie Powell, and Gerard Duhaime. 2008. "Food Production and Sharing in Nunavut: Not Only Discourse, But Reality." In *Arctic Food Security*, edited by Gerard Duhaime and Nick Bernard, 121–38. Edmonton: Canadian Circumpolar Institute Press.

Natcher, David C., Lawrence Felt, Andrea Procter, and the Nunatsiavut Government. 2009. "Monitoring Food Security in Nunatsiavut, Labrador." Special issue, *Plan Canada* 49, 2: 52–55.

Neale, Walter C. 1971. "Monetization, Commercialization, Market Orientation, and Market Dependence." In *Studies in Economic Anthropology*, edited by G. Dalton, 25–29. Washington, DC: American Anthropological Association.

Nelson, Mark, David C. Natcher, and Clifford G. Hickey. 2008. "The Role of Natural Resources in Community Sustainability." In *Seeing Beyond the Trees: The Social Dimensions of Aboriginal Forest Management,* edited by David C. Natcher, 38–49.Concord, Ontario: Captus Press.

Nuttall, Mark, Fikret Berkes, Bruce Forbes, Gary Kofinas, Tatiana Vlassova, and George Wenzel. 2005. "Hunting, Herding, Fishing and Gathering: Indigenous Peoples and Renewable Resource Use in the Arctic." In *Arctic Climate Impact Assessment*, 649–90. Cambridge: University of Cambridge Press.

Robbins, L., and F.L. Little. 1988. "Subsistence Hunting and Natural Resource Extraction: St. Lawrence Island." *Society and Natural Resources* 1: 17–29.

Sahlins, Marshall. 1971. "The Intensity of Domestic Production in Primitive Societies: Social Inflections of the Chayanov Slope." In *Studies in Economic*

Anthropology, edited by G. Dalton, 30–51. Washington, DC: American Anthropological Association.

Stanek, Ronald T., Davin L. Holen, and Crystal Wassillie. 2007. "Harvest and Uses of Wild Resources in Tyonek and Beluga, Alaska, 2005–2006." Technical Paper No. 321. Anchorage: Alaska Department of Fish and Game, Division of Subsistence.

Wenzel, George W., Grete Hovelsrud-Broda, and Nobuhiro Kishigami. 2000. "The Social Economy of Sharing: Resource Allocation and Modern Hunter-Gatherers." SENRI Ethnological Studies 53. Osaka, Japan: National Museum of Ethnology.

Wheelersburg, Robert P. 2008. "The Need to Conduct Studies of Swedish Saami Reindeer-Herder Subsistence Behaviours: A Case of Indigenous Resource-Use Rights." *The Northern Review* 28: 161–80.

Wolfe, Robert W. 1987. "The Super-Household: Specialization in Subsistence Economies." Paper presented at the 14th Annual Meeting of the Alaska Anthropological Association, Anchorage, Alaska, 22–25 March.

CHAPTER 8

Nunatsiavut Land Claims and the Politics of Inuit Wildlife Harvesting

Andrea Procter

Wildlife harvesting has always been of fundamental importance to Labrador Inuit, both as a source of sustenance and as a source of trade goods. Many species, including seal, whale, walrus, caribou, Arctic char, cod, and Arctic fox have for centuries provided Inuit with food, clothes, tools, household materials, fuel, and products for trade with other Aboriginal groups and with European merchants. The choice of species and pattern of Inuit harvesting have varied over time and with changes in the global economy, but Inuit have retained the cultural and economic value of their reliance on wildlife.

For the past 250 years, outside interests have increasingly interfered with, undermined, or ignored the importance of Inuit harvesting activities. Ever since Moravian missionaries arrived in Labrador in the mid-1700s, outsiders have pursued their own self-interest and employed ever-changing ideas about "ideal" Inuit livelihoods and society to influence Inuit economic and cultural practices. The form of this interference by missionaries, traders, organizations, and governments has fluctuated, but its presence has been constant. Depending on prevailing ideas about how Inuit should best support themselves, these groups alternately encouraged Inuit to retain their self-sufficiency by maintaining a diverse harvesting economy, or supported Inuit in more extensive participation in global trading networks or industrial wage labour. By the 1970s, Inuit were so exasperated with this outside interference in all aspects of their lives, including harvesting, housing, health, education, and economic issues, that they decided to assert their rights to govern their society and the lands and resources of Nunatsiavut by filing a land claims proposal. Land claims negotiations continued for thirty years, and the Labrador Inuit were eventually successful in establishing their resource and governance rights. Nonetheless, Inuit negotiators had to struggle against entrenched assumptions about what constitutes "Inuitness"—assumptions that were similar to ideas used in the past in efforts to influence Inuit livelihoods.

This chapter examines how ideas about "ideal" Inuit livelihoods and society were influential in historical attempts to regulate Inuit economic activities, and how these ideas still permeate Inuit-government relationships by manifesting themselves in the Labrador Inuit Land Claims Agreement (INAC 2005). The final agreement, signed in 2005, affirms Inuit harvesting rights and governance, but it also demonstrates how the politics of the recognition of Inuit rights can be restricted to simplified and limited definitions of Inuit economic and social activities. Although the land claims process uses more subtle means, it continues the practice of outside agencies attempting to control Inuit and their resources. Despite this, however, Labrador Inuit are working within the confines of the final agreement and the possibilities that it does offer in order to determine their own futures.

Wildlife Harvesting in Nunatsiavut: Historical Attempts at Control

> *Since time immemorial, the Labrador Inuit have used the resources from our land to survive. This survival stemmed from the cultural and customary law practices and the traditional method of hunting, fishing, and gathering. Since Confederation, federal and provincial laws and regulations have been imposed upon us. These laws and regulations have been drafted by governments who had no knowledge of, or respect for, the aboriginal rights of the Labrador Inuit, nor for our absolute dependency upon the land and its resources for our survival. These factors have led to increasing frustration, and mistrust toward governments and others.* (W. Andersen 1990)

Wildlife harvesting has always been a fundamental component of Labrador Inuit livelihoods, and it continues to play an important role in the culture, economy, and diet of Inuit today (Brice-Bennett 1977; Natcher and Felt this volume). Harvesting practices for both subsistence and trade needs have overlapped since well before the first Europeans arrived in Labrador in the 1500s; wildlife has been a source of livelihood through food, the domestic use of animal products, and the trade and sale of furs, meat, and other materials (Kaplan 1983). Over the years, the interrelationship between subsistence and commercial activities has become increasingly complex as Inuit involvement in the global economy has increased and new dynamics among wage labour, cash, global markets, and harvesting have developed (Wenzel et al. 2000; Natcher 2009). Since the arrival of outside agencies in Labrador in the eighteenth century, various interests have attempted to control Inuit involvement in these global networks. Driven by imperial, colonial, or commercial motivations, these agencies have thereby tried to guide the social transformation of Inuit by influencing their harvesting strategies.

Moravian missionaries made the first major attempt at social transformation in the late 1700s when, supported by the British Crown, they established missions on large land grants in northern Labrador. These missions were intended to attract and isolate Inuit, through what historian James Hiller (1971) calls a "containment policy," in order to protect the Inuit from unscrupulous traders and convert them to Christianity, as well as to prevent them from further disrupting the lucrative British fishery to the south. The missionaries encouraged Inuit to settle at these missions, and to trade with them, but they struggled to find a suitable economic base for the more sedentary life that they were trying to create (Brice-Bennett 1990; Hiller 1967, 1971). They soon realized that they could not require that converts live at the villages year-round if the mission stations were to be financially viable—both because they could not afford to feed everyone in the settlements, and because they would be thereby reducing their supply of animal products for the trade that supported the Mission (Hiller 1971). The missionaries therefore revised their tactics and instead encouraged Inuit to continue to support themselves (and the Mission) by harvesting food (and trade products), but to minimize their movements by spending some of the year at the missions. Missionaries would later frame this approach as one of cultural protection, although it was originally driven by the Mission's economic circumstances: "The Moravians tried to preserve the Eskimos [sic] in their old mode of living and not to introduce trade goods which would lead to the downfall of the Eskimos" (Peacock 1959, 63), as a Moravian minister explained in 1959. "[They] endeavoured as far as possible, to encourage the Eskimos to pursue their natural mode of life and to hunt seals" (77). The missionaries "have instilled habits of morality and clean living, and have weeded out habits that are bad and harmful, they have urged the people to keep closely to their native foods and habits of life, and clothing; in a word, their policy has been to make the Eskimo a better Eskimo" (Hutton 1912, 337).

The missionaries attempted to change Inuit economic behaviour that conflicted with their own goals by criticizing Inuit sharing practices and values. The value of sharing is intrinsic to a nomadic hunting lifestyle, but it was seen by the missionaries as antithetical to settled life in the Mission and to the Moravian goals of "civilizing" Inuit with the doctrines of Protestantism and capitalist ethics. "Rational" economic behaviour, according to the missionaries, included the individual accumulation of goods for future use, and the Inuit ethic of sharing was seen as irrational and wasteful, as well as bad for the trading business (Kennedy 1977; Kleivan 1966). Inuit often reacted to these arguments, as they did to many other imposed practices and ideologies, with tacit disapproval, and they continued to uphold the fundamental value and the practice of sharing (Hiller 1967; Kennedy 1977; Kleivan 1966; Brice-Bennett 1990; Natcher et al. this volume).

In the mid-1800s, Moravian missionaries, intent on keeping Inuit even closer to the mission stations, encouraged them to start fishing commercially for cod, an activity that would provide them with the cash to pay for the supplies needed for winter sealing activities. The Moravians also introduced seal nets to increase the efficiency of the commercial seal harvest. The Mission traded the seal products, and Inuit kept the meat, skins, and oil for domestic purposes. By the end of the century, the cod and seal fisheries played a fundamental role in both Inuit livelihoods and Moravian trade. Inuit continued to hunt, gather, and fish other species for their own sustenance in addition to participating in these commercial harvesting activities, and the missionaries encouraged a diverse economy by providing equipment and a market for a wide variety of Inuit goods (Brice-Bennett 1990).

In the 1900s global market fluctuations and the influence of traders on harvesting decisions resulted in some profitable years, but they created many more periods of considerable economic and social hardship. In 1926, for example, when the Hudson's Bay Company leased trading rights from the Moravian Mission, it encouraged Inuit to increase their white fox trapping activities and to limit the time afforded to subsistence harvesting. Fox are unlike seals or cod in that they do not also provide domestic food, and so when the fox pelt markets dropped in the 1930s, many Inuit were left without a source of income or food, and without the equipment needed to pursue other species. When the Hudson's Bay Company closed many of its stores in northern Labrador in 1942, the provincial government took over trade on the coast and initiated a new era of renewed support for a diversified economy through increased seal netting and by encouraging families to stay on the land (Brice-Bennett 1986). However, dropping prices for cod and diminished markets for seal products and fur pelts after World War II hampered these efforts and left many Labrador families in severe economic straits.

In the wake of these economic crises, the Newfoundland government intensified its presence in Labrador and joined the Moravian missionaries in the attempt to shape Inuit livelihoods. The prevailing notions among these agencies about what constituted suitable Inuit economic activity, and whether Inuit should be more self-reliant or more involved in global trading systems, influenced the trading opportunities and equipment that they offered to Inuit. At times during the early to mid-twentieth century, the Mission, the government trading operation, and other traders used economic and social pressure to persuade Inuit to pursue commercial species, such as cod or white fox, in order to supply the trading business and earn credit. At other times, they encouraged Inuit to pursue a more diverse harvesting strategy in order to maintain their self-reliance. These influences undoubtedly affected Inuit greatly in their harvesting decisions, but Inuit also based their choices on global market conditions, species availability, equipment, alternative economic opportunities, and other social factors.

The uncertainty and the hardships created by a reliance on turbulent global markets for fish and fur led many people to view the wage labour opportunities from the region's new industrial developments as potential alternatives to participation in the renewable resources economy. Governments and other organizations debated how Inuit should be incorporated into "modern" Canadian society and provided with a more stable economic basis than the harvesting economy had afforded (Jenness 1965). The advent of transfer payments and federal funding for Aboriginal communities in Labrador in the 1960s also led to governmental concerns about Inuit dependency on the public purse and the necessity of developing more secure sources of livelihoods.

Many policy makers in this era saw the harvesting of country food as a remnant of "pre-modern" times in Labrador (Hefferton 1959; Rockwood 1955). Although the Moravians and, for a time, the provincial government had supported a diverse economy of harvesting for both food and commercial products, modernization ambitions in Labrador in the mid-twentieth century resulted in increased attempts to provide Inuit with wage labour opportunities that would keep them in settlements, where they could also be provided with education and health services. "Both the Eskimos [sic] and the Indians have been encouraged and assisted in hunting and fishing," wrote the minister of Public Welfare in 1959, "but we regard these activities as 'holding operations' until the economy in the area becomes more diversified. However, with the development of the mineral resources of Labrador, there is hope that some progress in this direction will be possible" (Hefferton 1959: 97–98). As the director of the provincial Department of Northern Labrador Affairs argued in 1955, "For the Eskimos, Indians, and half-breeds of Northern Labrador, the days of the primitive hunting economy are numbered.... The needs of the Eskimo [include] a vigorous Health, Education, and Welfare programme to fit him for the society of the future" (Rockwood 1955, 10). Modernization would provide the government with the dual benefits of creating "productive" and sedentary citizens and (the less articulated benefit) of removing people from land, thus potentially making it available for development (Tester and Kulchyski 1994).

Although many policy makers discounted the economic viability of the subsistence[1] (i.e., non-commercial) hunting and fishing economy during this period and attempted to persuade Inuit to pursue other economic activities, both subsistence and commercial harvesting continued to be fundamental sources of livelihood for Inuit and foundations of cultural vitality. Despite attempts by the government to regulate Inuit activity, the extent, economic value, and social importance of subsistence harvesting remained largely invisible to bureaucratic methods of data collection and understanding (Kulchyski and Tester 2007). This invisibility helped to maintain the flexibility of harvesting and sharing activities and to preserve the vitality of culturally driven practices, but it also served to support the perspective among policy makers that subsistence harvesting was economically irrelevant.

The fundamental importance of subsistence and commercial harvesting to Inuit continued, despite all attempts to "modernize" the north coast and all impacts of these policies on harvesting. In the early 1970s, although the cod fishery was in decline, the market price of sealskins reached an all-time high, and harvesting was, for a while, a self-sufficient way of life. However, by the late 1970s and 1980s, the animal rights movement had caused the sealskin markets to collapse, and the price of equipment and fuel had risen to levels that made it almost impossible for someone without a source of cash income to hunt or fish (Williamson 1997; Brice-Bennett 1986). Many populations of important species were declining, including cod, char, salmon, and seals, although the number of sports hunting and fishing camps in the area was growing.[2] Increasing levels of government regulation also meant that the

---

1 "Subsistence" harvesting refers here to harvesting that provides food and other products for the sustenance of families and sharing networks, as opposed to providing explicitly for markets. However, the distinction between subsistence and commercial harvesting is often blurred, as harvesters may participate in both practices simultaneously.

2 In 1976 Bill Edmunds of the Labrador Inuit Association reported that there were forty-three sport fishing camps in Labrador, and that fewer than six of them were run by Labradorians (LRAC 1976).

cost for licences and the limitations placed on harvesting activities presented Inuit with significant barriers to making a living (Ames 1977).

These challenges to their livelihood, coupled with the threat of industrial development to the traditional land-based economy in the Nunatsiavut region in the 1970s, galvanized Inuit to reassert control over their own political and economic possibilities. Foreign and Canadian fishing fleets had already destroyed cod stocks off the coast by the 1970s, and uranium exploration in the Makkovik/Postville area, offshore drilling for oil and gas, and plans for national parks in northern and central Labrador were perceived as further attempts by outside interests to claim local resources, potentially harm the environment, and inhibit Inuit pursuit of their own livelihoods. These activities, as well as the national movement for the recognition of Aboriginal rights, spurred Inuit to initiate both political and economic strategies of increased self-determination.

The Aboriginal rights movements and court decisions of the 1960s and 1970s regarding Aboriginal rights resulted in the federal government agreeing to fund and administer a land claims process. In Labrador, the Inuit created the Labrador Inuit Association (LIA) in the early 1970s and submitted a land claim proposal in 1977. The land use and occupancy study for the land claim, *Our Footprints Are Everywhere*, documented the depth of Inuit knowledge about the environment, as well as the Inuit's proven success in managing the harvest through cultural governance (Brice-Bennett 1977). The LIA also funded research on how Inuit could become more self-reliant economically while maintaining a way of life that valued and included harvesting (see, for example, Ames 1977; Usher 1982). In order to negotiate for adequate support for a harvesting economy, the LIA explored the possibility of institutionalizing Inuit customary laws, including those concerning harvesting and sharing. Inuit negotiators put great effort into developing the case for incorporating Inuit law into the land claims agreement, but they encountered great reluctance on the part of the province to accept non-codified laws, and more generally to relinquish any sort of real authority over resources to Inuit (A. Procter field notes 2008).

Efforts to negotiate support for Inuit harvesting in the land claim talks were generally buoyed by the development, during the negotiation period (1977–2005), of legal consensus in Canada about the Aboriginal right to harvest. Existing Aboriginal rights were enshrined in the Canadian Constitution in 1982, and the Supreme Court of Canada's *R. v. Sparrow* decision of 1990 recognized the Aboriginal right to hunt and fish in traditional territories for food and ceremonial purposes, and limited the right of governments to control this harvesting. Aboriginal harvesting for food was acknowledged as having priority over sports or commercial use, although conservation and safety concerns override all harvesting rights (Imai 2008).

Many of the Inuit concerns about their harvesting rights were therefore resolved by legal developments in the rest of Canada while they were at the negotiation table, but other concerns remained in question. The Canadian judiciary generally recognized the importance of protecting Inuit livelihoods only as far as subsistence harvesting needs extended. Commercial rights to harvest were not granted the same recognition as subsistence rights. The courts recognized an Aboriginal right to commercial hunting or fishing in only a handful of cases across the country, and these cases either involved a treaty right (e.g., the *R. v. Marshall* decision in Nova Scotia in 1999) or succeeded in proving that commercial activities had been central to the Aboriginal culture in question before contact with Europeans.[3] The rights of Labrador Inuit to subsistence harvesting were therefore protected under these legal developments, but their right to make a living from harvested resources was not so obviously recognized.

Away from the negotiation table, Inuit efforts at developing a viable economy for the Labrador north coast have consistently, although by no means exclusively, focused on harvesting activities. With the decline of the cod fishery in the 1960s and 1970s, the coastal industry turned to salmon and char. In the late 1970s Inuit formed the Torngat Fish Producers Co-operative Society in an attempt to regain local control over resources, and the co-op has since worked on expanding the fishery to include scallop, crab, turbot, and shrimp. In the early 1980s, with caribou numbers high, the provincial government returned to the possibility of a sports hunt, and this time, the Labrador Inuit Development Corporation responded by initiating an Inuit commercial hunt, amid great controversy about the cultural appropriateness of such an activity. The new industry provided much-needed employment and provided country foods to regional and provincial markets (Notzke 1994). After a few years, however, the hunt was cancelled due to inspection regulation issues, and it has remained closed since. The development of a renewed seal fishery based in Rigolet has also been discussed recently, and Inuit organizations have initiated community freezer programs, in which country foods are collected centrally and then given to residents who need them. When the land claims negotiations were finally resolved, these attempts to maintain a resilient harvesting economy were bolstered by the

---

3   The *R. v. Van der Peet* case of 1996 outlined this test to determine which activities could be recognized as Aboriginal rights (Imai 2008).

final agreement's recognition of Inuit rights and Inuit involvement in wildlife management.

The Labrador Inuit Land Claims Agreement

The Labrador Inuit Land Claims Agreement, when it was finalized in 2005, reflected Inuit political and economic interests in maintaining and supporting a harvesting economy. Under the agreement, the Inuit of Nunatsiavut possess specific harvesting and management rights, jurisdiction over some areas of land, and a degree of control over governance issues. The agreement specifies that people who live in the communities of the Labrador Inuit Settlement Area (LISA) have the right to harvest wildlife in LISA without licences and generally without quotas, up to their level of need, but with very specific conditions.

The agreement addresses many Inuit concerns by acknowledging the economic needs of Inuit and the cultural importance of subsistence harvesting. It outlines harvesting jurisdiction for the Nunatsiavut government and establishes co-management boards and procedures for the inclusion of Inuit and Inuit knowledge in resource management. It also confirms the pre-eminence of subsistence harvesting over sports hunting, and, notably, provides Inuit with some rights to commercial harvesting.

The agreement, however, continues the trend of attempting to influence the role of harvesting in Inuit society by delineating some very specific limitations to recognized Inuit rights. In order to attain official recognition of their rights, Inuit negotiators had to conform to requirements and limitations as determined by the federal and provincial governments in their land claims negotiation policies. These limitations defined what the governments would recognize as specifically Aboriginal, and therefore what would be accepted as a potential area in which to negotiate Aboriginal rights. In terms of harvesting, the land claims process employs this politics of recognition to influence and control the kinds of economic activities that are recognized as Inuit. Based in large part on the desire of the judiciary and the federal government to limit and define Aboriginal rights in order to protect non-Aboriginal interests, the politics of recognition employs many of the same ideas that other groups have used in Labrador to influence Inuit harvesting activities in the past.

This section describes the negotiated role of Inuit in the governance of harvesting, and then examines how the legacy of ideas used in historical attempts at economic and social control continues to impact the politics of recognition and the future of harvesting in Nunatsiavut.

Inuit Involvement and Knowledge in Harvesting Governance

The face of wildlife management has changed with the creation of Nunatsiavut. Inuit now participate on co-management boards for wildlife and plants, the fisheries, Torngat Mountains National Park, and land use planning in LISA. The Torngat Wildlife and Plants Co-Management Board recommends the total allowable harvest for caribou and migratory birds, and decides on the total allowable harvest for all other species for the settlement area. The Nunatsiavut government (NG) has the jurisdiction to regulate some harvesting activities, including all harvesting on Labrador Inuit Lands, and it has greater involvement in advising and consulting with the provincial and federal governments on fish and wildlife issues.

With this newly affirmed Inuit jurisdiction, however, comes the requirement that the NG collect information for use in justifications for decisions or for recommendations to other governments. Depending on the species or issue involved, the onus may be on the NG to provide certain types of information, as outlined in the final agreement,[4] to provincial or federal ministers in order to substantiate recommendations for the ministers' final decisions. The NG must therefore monitor the harvesting activities of their constituents and solicit information from them that for years Inuit have refused to offer to other government officials.[5] This information may then be shared with other governments in order to influence the final decisions of the provincial or federal ministers.

---

4 For example, the final agreement (INAC 2005) outlines the appropriate information needed (from the NG) to justify (to the Department of Fisheries and Oceans) a decision about domestic harvest levels for fish: "13.6.6: The Inuit Domestic Harvest Level is an estimate of the quantity of a species or stock of Fish or Aquatic Plant in the Labrador Inuit Settlement Area needed annually by Inuit for their food, social and ceremonial purposes that is based on all relevant available information, including:

   a) any data that may be compiled on an ongoing basis by the Nunatsiavut Government using Inuit traditional knowledge;

   b) any data that may be compiled on an ongoing basis by the Nunatsiavut Government during monitoring of the Inuit Domestic Fishery;

   c) historical data;

   d) information on variations in the availability and accessibility of the species or stock of Fish or Aquatic Plant; and

   e) information that may be provided by the Nunatsiavut Government about the nutritional, social and ceremonial importance of the species or stock of Fish or Aquatic Plant to Inuit."

5 Very few people, for instance, submitted information to the provincial government on their wildlife harvesting licence returns in the 1970s (Ames 1977), and the situation is no different today.

Inuit harvesting activities will therefore be increasingly monitored and supervised, often by Inuit bureaucrats themselves, in order to provide justifications to the Nunatsiavut and other governments. Subsistence harvesting, once almost invisible to governmental agencies, will now be thoroughly documented as the NG takes on the information-gathering role (Scott 1998; Kulchyski and Tester 2007; Sandlos 2007). The Inuit and the provincial and federal governments have thus all benefited in some way from the land claims agreement negotiations. While the Inuit have gained greater influence and control, the other governments are closer to achieving their long-standing surveillance goals by influencing and supporting Inuit participation in harvesting management, information collection, and enforcement in Nunatsiavut. Labrador Inuit are assuming and even augmenting the administrative duties of previous governments, but perhaps with this change in the face of wildlife management will also come a change in the priority and understanding given to Inuit concerns and approaches.

Livelihoods and Inuit Harvesting

One of the most blatant examples of outside interference in Inuit livelihoods, from the Inuit point of view, was the provincial government's historical indifference to the vital role of harvesting for Inuit livelihoods. Restrictive harvesting regulations "hamper[ed] their pursuit of an adequate living" and were often designed for sports hunters or for Newfoundland conditions (Ames 1977, 1). In response to these concerns, and based on legal decisions such as *R. v. Sparrow*, the land claims agreement gives priority to Inuit subsistence harvesting over the activities of sports hunters and fishermen if conservation limits need to be established (INAC 2005, 12.5.3). The economic interests of the existing outfitters are protected in the agreement, however, as it ensures that they retain priority over any new Inuit commercial wildlife operations in access to quotas (12.4.20), and that the NG does not "deny or unreasonably restrict" their access to Labrador Inuit Lands (12.10.7). Despite strong condemnation by many Inuit of sports hunting and fishing, the agreement also reflects the provincial government's desire to see Inuit become more involved in the industry through the right to participate in the management, employment, and ownership of outfitting enterprises (12.10).

Inuit concerns when they initiated the land claims process in the 1970s were based on much more than the issue of maintaining priority over various competing interests in fish and wildlife, however; they were focused more generally on the impact of wildlife laws on their ability to make a living, and on their desire for increased control over their resources. Inuit leaders hoped that the land claims process could address these livelihood issues, which were not limited solely to subsistence issues.

The structure of land claims negotiations and associated legal decisions, however, forced the Labrador Inuit to separate these two components. Accordingly, the LIA demonstrated the importance of subsistence harvesting in their land claims campaign, and it succeeded in convincing the other parties of the need to address their concerns. Once dismissed by advocates of modernization, the Inuit subsistence harvest is now understood and accepted by policy makers as vital for cultural continuity, human health, and social well-being (Freeman 1986; Nuttall et al. 2005). These academic and legal efforts highlight the importance of subsistence harvesting as a socially, nutritionally, and economically relevant component of Inuit life.

As a result of these efforts, the final agreement assures Labrador Inuit of more extensive harvesting rights than were previously recognized, and it includes provisions that acknowledge Inuit needs and sharing practices. The removal of most quotas, bag limits, and licences allows Inuit to harvest more cost-effectively for the amount of fish and wildlife needed for extended sharing networks (see Ames 1977; Natcher et al. this volume). The agreement also often allows for the transfer of quotas, when they do exist, so that people can harvest for the needs of others. In addition, the LIA negotiated special privileges for Inuit who live outside the Labrador Inuit Settlement Area to harvest in designated areas outside Nunatsiavut (INAC 2005, 12.13.10).

In contrast to some other land claims agreements, the Labrador Inuit agreement offers limited institutionalized means of support for harvesting. For example, the James Bay and Northern Quebec Final Agreement initiated an income support program for local Cree hunters, and programs have been developed in Nunavik to provide country foods for Inuit communities. In Labrador, the Innu Nation runs an outpost program that allows families to spend long periods of time in the country. These programs help to overcome obstacles to their pursuit of harvesting activities and address the current reality that, given the cost of equipment and fuel, money is an integral part of the harvesting economy (Wenzel et al. 2000; Gombay 2005). Although the Labrador Inuit Land Claims Agreement does recognize Inuit rights to harvesting, and a harvesting support program was discussed at the negotiation table, the agreement does not explicitly outline supportive measures for the harvesting economy in the way that these other jurisdictions have done. Instead, LIA negotiators decided to have the Labrador Inuit agreement provide available funding if the NG chooses to develop harvesting support programs in the future (T. Andersen 2009, pers. comm.). Community freezer programs in Nunatsiavut and in Upper Lake Melville have received NG funding in recent years, and these programs help to distribute country foods such as caribou, salmon, char, and berries to Inuit who do not otherwise have the means to obtain them.

The precise and detailed definition in the final agreement of what exactly constitutes Inuit subsistence highlights some of the cultural politics of land claims negotiations and illustrates the continuation of historical attempts to control Inuit by regulating their harvesting activities. The agreement states that if no harvesting limits are set for conservation purposes, Inuit have "the right to harvest throughout the Labrador Inuit Settlement Area up to their full level of needs for food, social and ceremonial purposes" (INAC 2005, 12.3.2). The sale of wildlife or plants is prohibited except in specific situations (12.3.9), but Inuit "have the right to give, trade, exchange or barter among themselves, and with other aboriginal individuals, any Wildlife or Plants Harvested," subject to certain restrictions (12.3.10). However, Inuit do have the right to sell non-edible wildlife products, as well as tools or artwork made from plants (12.3.12 a and b).

Other Inuit land claims agreements provide similar restrictions, but many are less explicit in distinguishing between monetary and non-monetary disposition of harvested wildlife. The Nunavut Land Claim Agreement (INAC 1993), for instance, gives Inuit the right to harvest up to the "full level of his or her *economic*, social, and cultural needs" (5.6.1, emph. mine). Nunavut Inuit also have the "right to *sell*, barter, exchange and give" harvested wildlife (5.7.30). The Inuvialuit Final Agreement (INAC 1984), although more restrictive, states that "Inuvialuit may *sell*, trade and barter game among Inuvialuit beneficiaries" (section 14.12, emph. mine). Although economic rights are limited (to exchange only among beneficiaries in the Inuvialuit agreement), these other agreements do allow a role for monetary exchange in the sale of harvested wildlife. The Nunatsiavut agreement, on the other hand, strictly limits the disposition of products to non-monetary exchanges.

Most of these limitations on Inuit harvesting centre on the role of subsistence in the definition of what it means to be Aboriginal. According to a LIA negotiator, the federal and provincial governments followed a template for what constituted "Aboriginalness" that was made up of lands, subsistence harvesting, and forestry. "It was just a mindset," he said. "The federal negotiator knew that it held no weight" (T. Andersen 2008, pers. comm.). The LIA engaged this recognition template's criteria to gain subsistence rights, but found them to be constraining in their attempts to achieve all of their harvesting goals. This equivalency of Inuit with subsistence was non-negotiable, despite all LIA attempts to convince the other parties of the importance of a long history of a mixed economy in which subsistence harvesting and commercial activities were intertwined.

Other institutions in Labrador have offered similar opinions about what constitutes "Inuitness." The International Grenfell Association, for instance, a health-care provider in the region during the mid-twentieth century, required that, in order for people to be recognized as Inuit, they demonstrate that they were of "Eskimo [sic] cultural orientation—inclined to lead the traditional Eskimo way of life (economic) and use of Eskimo language" (Brantenberg 1977, 402). However, they would lose "Eskimo" status "if relocated to wage-earning communities and independent means of employment" (ibid.). The requirement that Inuit be confined to a "traditional economic way of life" and not participate in wage labour if they are to be recognized as Inuit (and therefore presumably receive some special benefit) reflects the colonial method of asserting economic control by clothing it in cultural terms.

The recognition of Aboriginal status through the land claims process involved similar assumptions. The "template" that the federal and provincial governments used in this case to determine "Aboriginalness" was based on an image of people who engage in the non-monetary exchange of edible wildlife amongst themselves, and who harvest for their food, social, and ceremonial needs. Recognition was therefore only bestowed if this image remained true, and the rights offered were limited to these practices. Inuit have always engaged, and continue to engage, in the non-monetary exchange of country foods, and the practice is undoubtedly a fundamental aspect of Inuit life. However, limiting authenticity, identity, and associated rights for Inuit to such a simplified understanding of subsistence harvesting ignores the long history of Inuit participation in commercial activities and the ways in which subsistence harvesting has articulated and become embedded in a cash economy (Stern 2006; Searles 2006; Wenzel 2000; Usher 1982; Dahl 2000). It denies Inuit the possibility of social change and adaptation, and it fails to offer any protection for practices that allow them to survive as contemporary communities. This simplification, although perhaps expedient to the land claims recognition process, works to assume control over Inuit social transformation and economic activities (Barcham 2000; Scott 2001; Alfred 2005).

These requirements for recognition also have other controlling political and economic effects. One justification for a restriction on the monetary disposition of country foods is the potential impact that a commercial incentive may have on species conservation (Gombay 2005). Other restrictions in the final agreement may reflect concerns about the need for official food inspection of commercial edible products. However, denying Inuit the right to govern species conservation, harvesting, and processing themselves, either through regulatory or cultural means (such as Inuit customary laws), exposes the underlying desire on the part of other governments to assert control over resources (Sandlos 2007; Kulchyski and Tester 2007). Conservation is a foundation of provincial wildlife policy, but the protection of economic interests in the outfitting industry and the widespread governmental enthusiasm for industrial economic development in Labrador raise doubts about the importance of conservation in overall provincial aims. The structure of land claims agreements and the recognition of Aboriginal rights in Canada thus work to limit Inuit authenticity to insular economic practices, and to deny the legitimacy of Inuit expertise and Inuit rights to have a central and authoritative role in renewable resource management.

The land claims process therefore works to influence the role of harvesting in Inuit communities, but it is much more subtle than earlier efforts to control Inuit livelihoods and society. It does not resort to the sort of direct attempts at guiding Inuit economic activities that the Moravians and early traders used, nor does it use the blatant rhetoric and large-scale programs of the 1950s and 1960s that were concerned with modernization and assimilation. Instead, it encourages Inuit themselves to embrace recognition criteria in order to regain economic and political influence in Labrador. Based in national discussions and legal opinions about Aboriginal rights, these recognition criteria have emerged as a result of ongoing debates between diverse Aboriginal peoples, various governmental interests, legal advisors, and the general public. As a result, many Aboriginal people do see justification behind at least some of the recognition criteria. The ideas about what it means to be Inuit therefore are in many ways more pervasive than earlier definitions and ideas that were summarily dismissed by Inuit as being products of outsider interference. The requirement that Inuit adapt themselves to the criteria of recognition outlined by the federal and provincial governments in the land claims process can, as this chapter has shown, nonetheless result in limited and limiting possibilities for Inuit to control their own livelihoods.

Commercial Rights and Contradictions

When they initiated their land claim in the 1970s, Labrador Inuit had ambitions that encompassed much more than subsistence harvesting rights; their ambitions centred on the ability to determine and sustain their own economic, social, and political futures. The Inuit did succeed in convincing the federal government of the need to acknowledge the role of the commercial fishery in their lives, and they negotiated the right to benefit from this industry. The inclusion of these rights was a first in Inuit land claims agreements, and the LIA heralded this success as a breakthrough (T. Andersen 2008, pers comm.). Subsistence fishing is restricted by many of the same rules as those for wildlife, but commercial fishing is given added consideration. The final agreement provides the NG with the right to specific proportions of commercial fishing and processing licences for any additional allocations of certain species that the Department of Fisheries and Oceans (DFO) may make in the future. In addition, Section 13.12 of the final agreement specifies that the minister of the DFO must take into account the history of Inuit commercial fishing of Arctic char, Atlantic salmon, and scallop when issuing further licences. Priority is also given to Inuit for some opportunities related to aquaculture.

The success of the LIA negotiators in having these commercial fishing rights included in the final agreement illustrates the cracks within the federal and provincial template of "Aboriginalness." If the history of Inuit participation in the commercial char, salmon, and scallop fisheries is recognized, why is the historical Inuit participation in other industries not recognized? These inconsistencies reveal the arbitrary nature of the land claims template for recognition and suggest that it is simply the state's desire for control that underlies the use of such precise definitions in negotiating Inuit rights.

Conclusion

Northern Labrador has endured a long history of outside interests and governments attempting to control Inuit economic activities, either by using ideas of modernization to influence Inuit to cease their harvesting activities, or by using ideas of cultural essentialism to require that Inuit adhere to a simplified and economically restrictive version of themselves. Beginning with the Moravian Mission's efforts to shield Inuit from the effects of full participation in global trading networks, and continuing through years of changing government policy on the ideal role of harvesting in Inuit livelihoods, these ideas have played a major role in shaping the form of interference in Inuit economies. Many of these efforts were certainly made with the best intentions, and in the perceived best interest of the Inuit, but they were forms of interference nonetheless, and most often they occurred without any kind of input from Inuit themselves.

Echoes of modernization and cultural essentialism continue to influence the land claims agreement and recent policy. Throughout the last century, the modernization and economic development ambitions of the federal and provincial governments have driven policies that discourage Inuit harvesting by restricting harvesting, sharing, and the disposition of wildlife products, by giving preferential treatment to sports harvesters, by risking the destruction of habitat from industrial development, and by promoting economic development strategies that do not allow for Inuit participation in harvesting activities. Efforts to restrict Inuit control to mainly subsistence activities similarly allow the provincial and federal governments to control and benefit from any commercial fish and wildlife industries. Such efforts illustrate the underlying motives of the provincial and federal governments to retain control of Nunatsiavut resources and often point to an interest in economic benefit over any interest in either conservation or Inuit needs.

Since the 1970s, Labrador Inuit have managed to question some of the ideas about the role of Inuit harvesting through successful negotiation and advocacy for their rights. They have succeeded in regaining control over their livelihoods through recognized harvesting rights in the land claims agreement, as well as through other economic development and resource governance provisions. Their subsistence harvesting rights acknowledge the fundamental role of country foods in the domestic economy and in cultural vitality and health, and the importance of the commercial fishery was given some consideration in agreement provisions that allow Inuit to benefit from additional quota allocations. Inuit have gained increased involvement in environmental governance, including management over harvesting, land use, and environmental impact assessment, and through negotiated requirements in the Impact and Benefit Agreement for the Voisey's Bay mine.

With these new governance arrangements, the Nunatsiavut government now has the opportunity to influence the future of Inuit harvesting by determining the priority given to Inuit harvesting and to the protection of habitat in its policies and co-management board recommendations. For hundreds of years, Inuit have relied on a combination of commercial and subsistence harvesting for their livelihoods, and these activities' importance remains strong (see Natcher et al., Hanrahan this volume) despite all attempts to restrict, discourage, or guide harvesting practices. The Nunatsiavut government can now determine its own course. Although bound by the restrictions in the final agreement, and thus always affected by outside influences on their harvesting activities, the Labrador Inuit have negotiated a significant increase in authority in resource management, and hopefully also the chance to finally make their own choices about their economic activities and social transformations.

References

Alfred, Taiaiake. 2005. *Wasá'se: Indigenous Pathways of Action and Freedom.* Peterborough: Broadview Press.

Ames, Randy. 1977. *Social, Economic, and Legal Problems of Hunting in Northern Labrador.* Nain: Labrador Inuit Association.

Andersen, William. 1990. "Address at the Opening of Land Claim Negotiations, 22 January 1989." *Northern Perspectives* 18, 2: 4–5.

Barcham, M. 2000. "(De)Constructing the Politics of Indigeneity." In *Political Theory and the Rights of Indigenous Peoples,* edited by D. Ivison, P. Patton, and W. Sanders, 137–151. Cambridge: Cambridge University Press.

Brantenberg, Terje. 1977. "Ethnic Commitments and Local Government in Nain, 1969–76." In *The White Arctic: Anthropological Essays on Tutelage and Ethnicity,* edited by R. Paine, 376–410. St. John's: ISER Books.

Brice-Bennett, Carol, ed. 1977. *Our Footprints Are Everywhere: Inuit Land Use and Occupancy in Labrador.* Nain: Labrador Inuit Association.

_____. 1986. *Renewable Resource Use and Wage Employment in the Economy of Northern Labrador.* St. John's: Royal Commission on Employment and Unemployment, Newfoundland and Labrador.

_____. 1990. "Missionaries as Traders: Moravians and Labrador Inuit, 1771–1860." In *Merchant Credit and Labour Strategies in Historical Perspective,* edited by R. Ommer, 223–46. Fredericton: Acadiensis Press.

Dahl, Jens. 2000. *Saqqaq: An Inuit Hunting Community in the Modern World.* Toronto: University of Toronto Press.

Freeman, Milton. 1986. "Renewable Resources, Economics and Native Communities." In *Native Peoples and Renewable Resource Management,* edited by J. Green and J. Smith, 23–37. Edmonton: Alberta Society of Professional Biologists.

Gombay, Nicole. 2005. "The Commoditization of Country Foods in Nunavik: A Comparative Assessment of its Development, Applications, and Significance." *Arctic* 58, 2: 115–28.

Hefferton, S.J. (Minister of Public Welfare, Government of Newfoundland). 1959. Letter to Minister of Citizenship and Immigration, Ottawa, 26 March 1959. In *The Administration of Northern Labrador Affairs,* Appendix 1. St. John's: Department of Public Welfare, 1964.

Hiller, James. 1971. "Early Patrons of the Labrador Eskimos: The Moravian Mission in Labrador, 1764–1805." In *Patrons and Brokers in the East Arctic,* edited by R. Paine, 89–93. St. John's: ISER.

Hiller, J. 1967. "The Foundation and Early Years of the Moravian Mission in Labrador, 1752-1805." MA thesis. St. John's: Memorial University of Newfoundland.

Hutton, S. 1912. *Among the Eskimos of Labrador: A Record of Five Years' Close Intercourse with the Eskimo Tribes of Labrador.* London: Seeley, Service & Co.

Imai, S. 2008. *Aboriginal Law Handbook*, 3rd edition. Olthius, Kleer, Townshend, corporate authors. Toronto: Thomson Carswell.

INAC (Indian and Northern Affairs Canada). 1984. *Western Arctic Land Claim: The Inuvialuit Final Agreement*. Ottawa: INAC.

_____. 1993. *Agreement between the Inuit of the Nunavut Settlement Area and Her Majesty the Queen in Right of Canada*. Ottawa: INAC and the Tungavik Federation of Nunavut.

_____. 2005. *Labrador Inuit Land Claims Agreement*. Ottawa: INAC.

Jenness, Diamond. 1965. *Eskimo Administration, Vol. III: Labrador*. Technical Paper No. 16. Calgary: Arctic Institute of North America.

Kaplan, Susan. 1983. "Economic and Social Change in Labrador Neo-Eskimo Culture." PhD diss., Bryn Mawr College.

Kennedy, John C. 1977. "Northern Labrador: An Ethnohistorical Account." In *The White Arctic: Anthropological Essays on Tutelage and Ethnicity*, edited by R. Paine, 264–305. St. John's: ISER Books.

Kleivan, Helga. 1966. *The Eskimos of North-East Labrador: A History of Eskimo-White Relations 1771–1955*. Oslo: Norsk Polar-Institut.

Kulchyski, Peter, and Frank Tester. 2007. *Kiumajut (Talking Back): Game Management and Inuit Rights, 1900–1970*. Vancouver: University of British Columbia Press.

LRAC (Labrador Resources Advisory Council). 1976. Meeting of LRAC held in Happy Valley–Goose Bay, 18–20 October 1976.

Natcher, David C. 2009. "Subsistence and the Social Economy of the Aboriginal North." *Northern Review* 30 (Spring): 69–84.

Notzke, Claudia. 1994. *Aboriginal Peoples and Natural Resources in Canada*. Toronto: Captus Press.

Nuttall, Mark, Fikret Berkes, Bruce Forbes, Gary Kofinas, Tatiana Vlassova, and George Wenzel. 2005. "Hunting, Herding, Fishing, and Gathering: Indigenous Peoples and Renewable Resource Use in the Arctic." In *Arctic Climate Impact Assessment*, 649–90. Cambridge: University of Cambridge Press.

Peacock, F.W. 1959. "Some Psychological Aspects of the Impact of the White Man upon the Labrador Eskimo." MA thesis, McGill University.

Rockwood, W.G. 1955. *Memorandum on General Policy in Respect to the Indians and Eskimos of Northern Labrador*. St. John's: Department of Public Welfare.

Royal Commission on Labrador. 1974. St. John's, Newfoundland.

Sandlos, John. 2007. *Hunters at the Margin: Native People and Wildlife Conservation in the Northwest Territories*. Vancouver: University of British Columbia Press.

Scott, Colin, ed. 2001. *Aboriginal Autonomy and Development in Northern Quebec and Labrador*. Vancouver: University of British Columbia Press.

Scott, J.C. 1998. *Seeing Like a State: How Certain Schemes to Improve the Human Condition Have Failed.* New Haven: Yale University Press.

Searles, E. 2006. "Anthropology in an Era of Inuit Empowerment." In *Critical Inuit Studies: An Anthology of Contemporary Arctic Ethnography,* edited by P. Stern and L. Stevenson, 89–101. Lincoln: University of Nebraska Press.

Stern, Pamela. 2006. "From Area Studies to Cultural Studies to a Critical Inuit Studies." In *Critical Inuit Studies: An Anthology of Contemporary Arctic Ethnography,* edited by P. Stern and L. Stevenson, 253–66. Lincoln: University of Nebraska Press.

Tester, Frank, and Peter Kulchyski. 1994. *Tammarniit (Mistakes): Inuit Relocation in the Eastern Arctic.* Vancouver: University of British Columbia Press.

Usher, Peter J. 1982. *Renewable Resources in the Future of Northern Labrador.* Nain: Labrador Inuit Association.

Wenzel, George W. 2000. "Sharing, Money, and Modern Inuit Subsistence: Obligation and Reciprocity at Clyde River, Nunavut." In *The Social Economy of Sharing: Resource Allocation and Modern Hunter-Gatherers,* edited by G. Wenzel, G. Hovelsrud-Broda, and N. Kishigami, 61–85. Senri Ethnological Studies 53. Osaka: National Museum of Ethnology.

Wenzel, George W., G. Hovelsrud-Broda, and N. Kishigami, eds. 2000. *The Social Economy of Sharing: Resource Allocation and Modern Hunter-Gatherers.* Senri Ethnological Studies 53. Osaka: National Museum of Ethnology.

Williamson, Tony. 1997. *Sina to Sikujâluk: Our Footprint. Mapping Inuit Environmental Knowledge in the Nain District of Northern Labrador.* Nain: Labrador Inuit Association.

CHAPTER 9

Adapting to Climate Change in Hopedale, Nunatsiavut

Laura Fleming, Ruth DeSantis, Barry Smit, and Mark Andrachuk

The Arctic is experiencing a period of substantial change (ACIA 2004). Biophysical changes include annual temperature increases, rapid sea ice melt, later winter ice freeze-up, earlier spring sea ice thawing, and earlier and faster snow melt (Stroeve et al. 2007; Rosenzweig et al. 2007). These subtle yet significant changes are affecting communities in the Arctic and subarctic that rely on the natural environment for subsistence needs and well-being. The experiences and observations of Inuit in the Arctic over the past two decades are of particular concern (Nickels et al. 2006; Ford et al. 2006; ACIA 2004). In addition to environmental change, Inuit communities in the Arctic are experiencing socio-economic, political, and cultural change. Wage-based economy, settled communities, and decreased participation in traditional activities on the land and sea, coupled with new forms of government via the settlement of land claims agreements and new Inuit self-governing institutions, have contributed to the transformation that Inuit people in the Canadian Arctic are experiencing. These changes are affecting the ability of Inuit to effectively manage the stresses associated with a changing biophysical environment.

In Hopedale, Nunatsiavut, residents have identified changes that are affecting the livelihoods and well-being of the community. Hopedale residents continue to maintain a traditional connection with the natural environment that extends from leisurely travel to livelihood dependence. This community relies heavily on the freezing and thawing of sea ice, which determines when, where, and what natural resources are accessible and available. The effects of climate change on local transportation networks and access to important hunting areas are of concern to Hopedale residents, yet residents are adapting to these changing circumstances.

Survival in the Arctic is dependent on the ability to adapt. Past conditions and the historic nomadic nature of Inuit in Labrador enabled survival based on an extensive knowledge of the natural environment (Cruikshank 2001). Survival skills were acquired through experience with the natural environment and from peers in the community. Specialized skills and knowledge about the environment continue to be strong in the community today. They serve as a set of resources for Labrador Inuit to draw on in times of change and challenge.

Many livelihoods in the community depend on a combined economy of wage-labour and subsistence activities, commonly referred to as a mixed economic system (AHDR 2004; Berman et al. 2004). In addition to providing food and related resources, harvesting is important for the connections it provides between residents and their culture and traditions. Household participation in harvesting activities depends on the availability of financial resources. In Hopedale, most households rely on input from the wage economy for the financial resources necessary to pursue subsistence activities such as hunting and fishing. However, stresses associated with climate change constrain the ability of community members to pursue subsistence resource gathering and threaten the viability of the subsistence economy. Although Hopedale is experiencing changes within social, economic, political, cultural, and environmental systems, it is a community that is also equipped with the capacity to manage such changes. Through the necessary adjustments and interventions by the community and appropriate levels of governance, the capacity to manage these and anticipated changes can be enhanced within the community of Hopedale and elsewhere in the Nunatsiavut settlement region.

Hopedale, Nunatsiavut

Hopedale is located within the subarctic region of Canada, on the north coast of Labrador adjacent to the Labrador Sea at latitude 55°27' N and longitude 60°13' W. A small community of approximately 550 residents, Hopedale is an Inuit settlement on a large bay that opens to the Labrador Sea (see map in the Introduction). The landscape surrounding Hopedale is characterized by ranges of mountains once covered by glaciers and a lack of vegetation surrounding the immediate community (Roberts, Simon, and Deering 2006).

The climate of Hopedale is influenced by the flow of cold water from the Arctic Oscillation and air mass movements from the interior of Labrador (Environment Canada 2006) and therefore results from interacting Arctic and subarctic forces. For this reason, Hopedale has a tundra climate system that cannot support tree growth, although in the surrounding bays and valleys tree growth is abundant (Hare 1950).

Subsistence provisioning remains an essential component of the economy and of livelihoods in Hopedale, despite the community's immersion in a wage-based economy during the mid 1950s, mainly as a result of intensification of the cod fisheries and employment at American military sites. Residents continue to consume wildfoods harvested from the nearby land and seas and rely on informal community food-sharing networks with friends and family to provide nutrient-rich food resources. Due to this reliance on the land and sea, Hopedale is particularly vulnerable to the risks associated with climate change. Through an analysis of the socio-economic, political, and environmental attributes of the community, this chapter identifies opportunities to enhance adaptive capacity and reduce vulnerabilities in Hopedale.

Assessing the Vulnerability of Hopedale

The community-based vulnerability approach, used widely in the climate change adaptation field, is concerned with the existing socio-economic, political, and environmental attributes of a community and how those shape the community's ability to deal with change or stresses (Ford and Smit 2004; IPCC 2007). Vulnerability is defined in the Intergovernmental Panel on Climate Change (IPCC) as "the degree to which a system is susceptible to, or unable to cope with, adverse effects and climate change, including climate variability and extremes" (IPCC 2007). The vulnerability approach provides a framework for identifying community-specific opportunities to enhance local adaptive capacity to deal with changes associated with climate change. Vulnerability assessments combine community observations and local knowledge with other sources of information (Füssel and Klein, 2006). This approach considers the potential effects of climate change and their interaction with socio-ecological systems. It utilizes multiple methods and research tools to characterize the interrelated vulnerability of social, political, economic, and ecological systems (Smit and Wandel 2006; Adger 2006).

Through a vulnerability approach, community residents analyze underlying attributes of the community in order to provide insight into current and future exposures and potential adaptation measures (Ferguson et al. 1998; Huntington 1998; Usher 2000; Krupnik and Jolly 2002; Ford and Smit 2004).

Vulnerability is associated with the system's coping capacity, which is based on the attributes of that particular system or community. The characterization of vulnerability also includes attributes of a system at multiple levels, from the individual, local, regional, and global scales. Capacity is determined by the existence and effectiveness of existing adaptive strategies at the community level and of potential future adaptations (Yohe and Tol 2002; Smit and Wandel 2006). Capacity captures the human capital, financial, and political aspects that contribute to adaptation.

Analyzing community vulnerability has become an established method of determining the risks and the strategies to manage outcomes associated with climate change. This approach recognizes that communities will experience and manage the effects of climate change differently due to the nature of socio-economic, political, cultural, and ecological variables. Vulnerability may also depend on the nature of values and traditions of a community (Alwang, Siegel, and Jorgensen 2001). This is true for the community of Hopedale, which has strong cultural values attached to the land and the bays that surround the community. Understanding the dynamics of the community is central to a vulnerability approach.

Assessments of Hopedale's vulnerability and ability to manage changes are based on two separate spring and summer field research seasons involving semi-structured interviews, open-ended questionnaires, and participant observations in the community. Secondary sources, such as the Labrador Inuit Land Claims Agreement, were also collected and reviewed. The results of this research detail the climate-change experiences in Hopedale and options for reducing vulnerability to climate and other change in the future.

Hopedale Vulnerabilities

Hopedale is exposed to a range of social, economic, cultural, political, and ecological forces that shape its vulnerability to stresses such as climate change. Climate exposures in Hopedale are occurring not in isolation but rather in addition to a number of other non-climatic stresses. The natures of these stresses are interrelated and significantly shaped by the nature of Hopedale residents' livelihood strategies. Livelihoods in the community of Hopedale depend on a mixture of wage and subsistence activities. Wage-based opportunities in Hopedale are restricted to the limited number of employment opportunities, mainly in government and the services industry. Subsistence activities in Hopedale range from woodcutting and gathering berries to hunting and fishing. These activities are highly valued because they satisfy household needs and also allow individuals and the community to connect with their traditions and culture.

The opportunity to participate in subsistence activities is influenced by access to financial and physical resources as well as the conditions on the land and sea. As a result of the ecosystem-based nature of subsistence activities, suitable conditions on the land and sea are required to ensure safe and reliable travel. Much of the hunting, gathering, and fishing activities takes place in the large bays and inlets along the coast and far inland. Because of the distances to subsistence resource areas, sea ice acts as the community's primary means of transportation. The sea-ice system links the community to traditional areas of hunting, fishing, and trapping and is commonly referred to by community members as their "highway." Poor conditions, in the form of minimal and early melting snowfall, late sea ice freeze-up, and earlier break-up require that Hopedale residents identify alternative means or take extra precautions while travelling and participating in subsistence activities.

Hopedale is also exposed to a number of social, cultural, and political changes. The prevalence of drug and alcohol use in the community is of concern to Hopedale residents, as are the instances of suicide and attempts at suicide among Hopedale residents. Stresses in the community are heightened by and intertwined with changing cultural and political systems and increasing change and uncertainty in environmental conditions.

Sea Ice

The livelihoods of Hopedale residents are sensitive to the conditions of sea ice along the coast. Over the past ten to fifteen years, residents have noticed a significant change in the timing of sea ice freeze-up and break-up. In winter and early spring, sea ice is the community's transportation network. It is the community's winter road infrastructure and is essential for pursuing subsistence activities on the land and in the bays. Changing sea ice impacts livelihoods in a number of ways. The large bays and inlets preferred by Hopedale residents for hunting and fishing are located far from the community and thus are more difficult to access without reliable sea ice. Access to subsistence resources is necessary for community members to connect with who they are as Inuit as well as to contribute to household needs. One participant suggests that the most challenging impact from the changing climate is that sea ice is being compromised: "Ice is the biggest concern because that's our highway. It connects us to every community in the winter and is easier to use" (Hopedale resident, 2007).

Later sea ice freeze has implications for Hopedale residents. For example, most community members use wood resources for energy and heat during the winter. Wood resources supplement other forms of energy the community uses, such as natural gas, and are the preferred method of household heating because of the consistent and more intense warmth wood provides. The later freeze-up, however, creates challenges for community members attempting to access woodcutting areas. Community members informed us that in order to harvest wood before Christmas they must travel over the land, as the ice is not safe. Yet, even travelling over the land restricts accessibility to woodcutting areas, which are often located in bays and are better accessed by sea ice.

Later sea ice freeze also has implications for the fall caribou hunt. Community members find that they cannot access the same areas to hunt caribou. In addition, it is a tradition among many community members to travel to their cabins by boat for the fall hunting season and return to the community before Christmas on snowmobile. In recent years, maintaining this tradition has become somewhat challenging, as explained by the following participant: "Me and my uncle would leave here in late October to go up to the cabin. You wouldn't leave it until the first week of November if you were going to the cabin [sea ice would be frozen]. We would go up there for the fall in boat and come back in freeze up on snowmobile. We could make it back here the 23rd of December on skidoo. Now try it, very rarely can it be done now. If you're coming down now guys are walking" (Hopedale resident, 2007). This individual is referring to the later freeze of ice in December, which contributes to dangerous travel on snowmobile back to the community. This underscores how a change in sea ice freeze can affect the community's ability to access livelihood resources. The effects of climate change, however, are also being experienced at other times of year. In regards to sea ice, an earlier spring melt period has similar implications.

Sea ice has been melting earlier on average and is impacting spring harvesting activities. Community members said that, formerly, the sea would be frozen for six months, but currently they are experiencing a shorter sea ice season by about a month. This impacts spring harvesting activities and has implications for the timing of the natural seasonal migration of fish. Ice is often reported as thinner and slushier in the spring. Many participants have found themselves stuck in slush while out on the sea ice or have returned home earlier from harvesting trips because of unsafe conditions. Some harvesting areas that are typically frozen in the spring are melting earlier, while other areas remain frozen for longer. This influences the community's traditional knowledge about where and when to travel on the land and sea. Many community members identified that sea ice freeze is becoming increasingly unpredictable and that, overall, the sea seems to be freezing later and thawing earlier, as the following statement suggests: "When it freezes at freeze up it seems like it is a bit later every year than years before. It used to be earlier say twenty or thirty years ago now it freezes later and later. We had a later break up this year but last year ice break up was so early. We had the boats out May 24th and the harbour was clear of ice" (Hopedale resident, 2007).

The community's observations of change are supported by scientific documentation of changes in Arctic sea ice. Research has found that Arctic sea ice extent has decreased 5 to 10 percent in the past thirty years (Walsh et al. 2005). In addition, there has been a decrease in the length of sea ice cover due to later freeze and early thaw and an increase in the number of ice-free days, subsequently reducing the period for safe transportation over sea ice (Holloway and Sou 2002). Residents of Hopedale find changes to sea ice duration problematic, as explained by one resident: "The early 90's, we could always go caribou hunting. But now the ice is not good enough at Christmas time to get in the country, cause you can't travel between here and there, it's usually late January. So there's a shift that way" (Hopedale resident, 2007).

Changes in sea ice conditions have implications for Hopedale residents' ability to travel and access resources. These resources are important for household subsistence needs but also to reaffirm Inuit tradition and practices. Sea ice change continues to affect Hopedale residents' ability to pursue these important activities during winter and spring seasons.

Snow

Snowfall also plays an important role in hunting and travelling activities. Transportation along the coast depends significantly on the accumulation of snow pack. Adequate snow cover facilitates a smooth surface for travel over land or sea and also reduces rock exposure, which can lead to expensive damage to skidoos. In recent years, community members have noticed that the timing of snowfall and the amount of snow falling is changing: "I remember that this past winter we were really late in getting our snow, extremely late, so it was hard getting around on the land"(Hopedale resident, 2008)..

Snow and sea ice form the foundation for the winter travel systems in Nunatsiavut. These systems connect the people to the land and to each other; there are no roads or other means of ground transportation between communities along the coast. Any change to these systems has the potential to impact all the coastal communities in Nunatsiavut. This network of winter travel routes allows community members to access key winter hunting and trapping grounds. Changing snowfall, as reported by community members, limits accessibility to these areas: "[It's] harder to get up on the land where you want to go with skidoo when there is no snow, you gotta take chain saws wherever you go to get up on the land I guess.... The boys went caribou hunting last year had to make a path to get into the caribou grounds" (Hopedale resident, 2008).

The impact of changing snowfall patterns and amounts has different meanings for various social groups in Hopedale. For instance, Hopedale residents originally from Hebron continue to travel to Hebron to hunt, fish, and trap. Accessing these areas provides a sense of identity and food security. They feel particularly affected by changing snowfall because of past incidences and situations. For instance, their lack of knowledge of local resources and claims over certain bays and local harvesting areas made by original residents of Hopedale influenced their decision to continue to travel to Hebron. Travelling to Hebron allowed them to maintain household livelihoods until they became integrated into the community and gained experience in their new surroundings, a fact expressed by a community member: "My father, my brother, my uncle they weren't suppose to go hunting in certain areas, they had to go somewhere else to go hunting. They weren't supposed to shoot in some places or they would scare the animals away. That is not fair to us. So my father, my brother, my uncle they all have to go somewhere else to go hunting. They had to go up past Nain because they had no choice (Hopedale resident, 2007).

The impacts of climate change experienced and observed by the community of Hopedale pose risks for the community. Community members are experiencing a notable change in the time of sea ice freeze and melt as well as decreased duration in snow pack. Hopedale residents are particularly vulnerable to these types of change because of their livelihood connections to the surrounding environment. The implications of the changing biophysical environment on subsistence activities are compounded by other socio-economic stresses that further influence Hopedale residents' ability to participate in important subsistence harvesting.

Non-climatic Influences on Subsistence Activities

The ability of Hopedale residents to participate in traditional hunting and harvesting activities is also related to the acquisition of necessary physical and financial resources. Access to a boat or skidoo is an example of the type of resource needed to access the ideal areas for hunting and fishing. Public transportation is unavailable in the community, with the exception of two airlines that service the northern coast from Goose Bay: Innu Mikun and Air Labrador. Having one's own means to travel within town and out on the land is beneficial and highly valued in the community.

Community members who do not own a boat or skidoo often access these resources through immediate and extended family members. Another option is to informally "rent" access to a boat by contributing funds toward gas and joining a group going out by boat. Both options, however, require financial resources to buy the gas and supplies needed. Without access to either a boat or skidoo, hunting and harvesting opportunities are limited to resources in and around town. The contamination of nearby harvesting locations by the American military base limits local accessibility to safe wildfoods such as berries, ptarmigan, and Arctic hare. Community members find that it is better to travel to the surrounding islands, where these resources are free from contamination; however, this requires access to either a skidoo or a boat, depending on the season and conditions. "Rodding" in local ponds is often undertaken to supplement off-shore fishing in boats. However, locations accessible by foot are viewed as less favourable for fishing. A stigma is associated with fishing in nearby trout ponds, which are viewed as poorer locations for obtaining fish.

The ability of Hopedale residents to access resources and regularly participate in subsistence activities is further undermined by the challenges associated with securing employment, the high costs of living, and new changes within social and cultural systems. These challenges also influence the capacity of Hopedale residents to manage and adapt to the stresses of environmental changes.

Limited Employment Opportunities, High Costs of Living

Households in Hopedale experience the stress of scarce employment and income-generating opportunities at the same time that they are trying to deal with a high cost of living. Although Labrador overall has experienced increasing employment opportunities in recent years, there continues to be an under-representation of particular groups in Labrador, including Labrador Inuit (Government of Newfoundland and Labrador 2007). A lack of adequate infrastructure, financial resources, and marketable natural resources disables the community's ability to develop industries locally. This situation, combined with the community's reliance on diesel energy supply and on air transportation for most of the year, as well as rising fuel costs, inhibits the development of cost-effective economic activities (Government of Newfoundland and Labrador 2007).

Employment opportunities exist outside the community, but these are often seasonal, and they also remove residents from the community either temporarily or permanently. For example, many residents seek seasonal employment at fish processing plants in Makkovik and Nain, but employment is dependent on fish catches and market demand. These plants have also recently been forced to reduce their operations, with Makkovik non-operational and Nain operational for only three weeks in 2008. Other opportunities are available through the Voisey's Bay nickel mine, now owned by Vale Inco, but

Hopedale residents compete with other Nunatsiavut residents, as well as with many other applicants from outside the coastal area. Access to these positions is also restricted to those with the required level of education. With low rates of high-school and post-secondary education completion in Hopedale, such positions are out of reach for many residents. The current employment situation leaves residents concerned about Hopedale's lack of economic opportunities and future opportunities for the next generation: "It's hard for people here to get jobs; they'd have to actually leave the community to try to find something—there's not much employment here, and what's already there, it's already been taken up by other people.... If they pick something that's not here, they've got to stay outside and make their money, they pick something that's here, it's already taken, so basically we're losing our young people" (Hopedale resident, 2008).

Community members express concern regarding employment and income opportunities due in part to the financial resources required to engage in subsistence activities and to purchase store food items. "Store items" cost significantly more in Hopedale than in the closest town of Happy Valley–Goose Bay. This is mainly a result of the high cost of transportation associated with shipping items up the coast. In the winter, for example, access is limited to air transportation. Networks of sea ice and snow trails do connect the community to Happy Valley–Goose Bay, but it is not feasible to transport store items regularly using this network, which has a travel time of roughly eight hours by snowmobile. In the summer after the ice has cleared, the community has regular ferry service and large supplies of market food items are transported that way. Yet, despite this service, residents report that the cost of market food items does not decrease in the summer months. Households thus engage in both the subsistence and market economies to maintain their livelihoods.

Not all residents in Hopedale are exposed to the same challenges. A number of community members have the necessary financial capital to own their own boat, skidoo, and truck, which are used throughout the changing seasons. Others own only a skidoo and share access to a boat through family members, while still others are without access to any type of transportation or vehicle and are significantly disadvantaged to access preferred harvesting areas.

Social and Cultural Change

Over the past century, the social structure of Hopedale has changed significantly. As explained in earlier chapters, the arrival of European settlers, the Moravian Mission, and community settlement and relocation were events that influenced the social structure and culture of Inuit along the Labrador coast. Further, recent stresses associated with environmental change are transforming the social dynamics in Hopedale. Kinship sharing networks have been compromised by decreases in harvest levels and hunting excursions. They are less reliable as a source of wildfoods for some members of the community, as the following comment suggests: "Some people can't go they don't have a machine [snowmobile] or they are not healthy then you got to share out your meat. It's kind of hard now days got to be tight with it before you gave them what they wanted seals and that" (Hopedale resident, 2007).

Integration into a wage-based economy and greater exposure to the south have played a role in shaping social change in Hopedale. Some community members have taken advantage of the opportunities associated with a changing social structure. They have found wage employment while maintaining connections to their culture and identity as Inuit. For others, however, the transition has been quite difficult. Drug and alcohol use in the community has increased. Community members are concerned about the amount of drugs and alcohol consumed, particularly by youth. Some attribute this increase to the scarce opportunities for youth, as the following quote from a Hopedale resident suggests: "There are not enough opportunities for youth and if they don't want to leave then they're into that cycle of not going anywhere. The cycle of drugs and alcohol" (Hopedale resident, 2007).

The community is caught between the desire to maintain traditional connections to the land and culture and the need to exploit economic activities for the future of its youth. For instance, recent uranium exploration near Postville, south of Hopedale, is generating discussions about the topic of future mining development in Nunatsiavut. Some participants feel that they are not well informed about the potential consequences of uranium mining and its impact on subsistence activities, as one participant's question indicates: "What is it going to do to the communities along the coast near the sites?" (Hopedale resident, 2008).

Many residents of Hopedale have cabins located in the bays along the Nunatsiavut coast. Participants indicated that most hunting, fishing, and trapping occurs in these areas. The bays contribute to Hopedale's subsistence needs and have been relied on by Labrador Inuit for decades. They have historical and cultural significance for many of the families that live in the community. Residents are concerned that uranium mining will affect these activities, as the following comment suggests: "Mining companies are coming in and doing test on the lands where we hunt, fish, and trap. If they take this terrible stuff out of the ground, what is going to happen to the lands that we use?" (Hopedale resident, 2007).

The community feels that the possibility for employment through a uranium mining development does not outweigh the potential negative impact of that mining on the environment. Harvesting activities not only contribute to livelihoods but also enable community members to be active and to contribute to the well-being of the community. Hopedale residents rely on the natural environment both to supplement their incomes and to connect to and reaffirm their identity as Inuit. On the other hand, despite the importance of subsistence activities, finding employment in Nunatsiavut is a necessity. The young population will be dealing with this challenge in the future if opportunities for employment are not developed. Similarly, the preservation of traditional knowledge and culture will be compromised if youth are not engaged.

Over time, Hopedale residents have inherited a valuable knowledge system that they rely on to transmit information about the land and sea. This knowledge system contains information about where, when, what, and how to harvest the natural resources that surround the community, and it involves principles of sustainability, preservation, and respect for resources. These principles have helped to ensure longevity and abundance of Labrador's resources for centuries. Information passed from elders to younger generations through storytelling and hands-on illustration gives younger generations the tools and values needed to maintain their traditional harvesting activities and reinforce cultural practices. Interruptions in culture and social structure in Hopedale, along with abnormal environmental conditions in recent decades, are compromising the existence of this knowledge system. As youth are less engaged in harvesting activities, there are fewer opportunities to transfer information about the land and sea.

This knowledge system is understood by Hopedale residents as an effective resource for preparing hunters and others travelling on the land and sea. One hunter explained how the knowledge given to him by an elder about survival on the land in a snowstorm saved his life. He learned from the elder to dig himself a protective space in the snowbank to stay warm and wait out the storm. When youth and inexperienced hunters and fishers do take to the land and sea, this knowledge can be highly useful and can better prepare them with survival and hunting skills.

Managing Change in Hopedale

Residents have long used a range of adaptive strategies to manage exposures in Hopedale and to continue to meet their livelihood needs. These strategies range from adjusting hunting and travelling timing to sharing and pooling resources within the community. Although many of these strategies are currently effective, the reality of persistent vulnerabilities in Hopedale suggests that additional interventions from beyond the community level are necessary. Insights into existing adaptive strategies undertaken in Hopedale demonstrate the ingenuity, adaptability, and perseverance of Inuit of Hopedale, but these insights also reveal the limitations of current capacities, as well as the presence of challenges beyond the control of individuals and households. By addressing the limitations of existing adaptation strategies through formal capacity-enhancing strategies and programs by the government and other related institutions and departments beyond the community, Hopedale residents will be better equipped to manage further climate-related changes in the future.

Existing Adaptive Strategies

Hopedale residents implement many adaptations to manage the immediate concerns of changing sea ice and snow conditions. In the fall, hunters usually travel by snowmobile on the sea ice and over the land to access caribou hunting areas. Later freeze-up and poor snow pack limit accessibility to these areas and shorten the hunting season. Community members are adapting by hunting later, harvesting more, using the "buddy system," diversifying harvested resources, using boats instead of snowmobiles, and relying more on sharing networks to obtain caribou meat. People are also more dependent on store-bought food when caribou are not accessible.

Using the buddy system, residents with limited access to a boat join friends or family on hunting trips to reduce costs. The ability to participate in this strategy depends on access to financial capital, since the cost of the hunting trip is divided among those participating; individuals involved in the harvesting group share the cost of food and gas for the trip. The buddy system used in Hopedale is a response to the high cost associated with hunting and fishing, but it also serves as a safety measure. Although most community members employ this adaptation, it increases pressure on the group to return with adequate harvests to compensate for the cost of the trip. If the group is unsuccessful during a hunting trip, tension increases among individuals. The buddy system also influences the amount of wildfoods available to households, since harvested wildlife is divided equally among the hunting group. Therefore, more hunting trips are required to harvest enough food, as the following comment implies: "If you are hunting for four people versus two you are going to go further cause you have to get more and then you spend more money on gas". (Hopedale resident, 2007).

This adaptation has its limitations, as less wildfood is available to share within community kinship networks. Some people in the community are now going without wildfoods periodically. Community members express increased concern about the recent availability of wildfoods in the community, stating that now people are tighter with their wildfoods and there is less willingness to share. Residents explained that it is possible to phone another community member to ask about available wildfoods to share, but some residents are reluctant to do so. Although sharing continues to be prevalent in the community, these signs indicate that sharing networks have become strained and are less reliable. In particular, residents lacking both the physical and financial resources required to participate in subsistence activities are increasingly experiencing this strain.

Fewer adaptive strategies are available, however, to overcome the challenges associated with operating a snowmobile with a deceasing snowfall and snow pack. The chance of costly damages to snowmobiles is increasing with a smaller snowfall. A household's livelihood is compromised without access to an operable snowmobile. Current strategies to prevent damage to snowmobiles include, for example, waiting until there is sufficient snow cover for travel and travelling at different times. Nonetheless, most community members continue to use snowmobiles regardless of snow conditions. The need to travel outside the community during the critical spring season to obtain resources such as wood and wildfoods often outweighs the risk of damages. If residents are not able to maximize the ideal spring conditions of warmer temperatures and fewer storms, they risk not securing sufficient firewood for the summer and fall months. Although wood can be purchased in town, it being the only saleable resource in Nunatsiavut, residents find it cost effective to load up on wood supplies while out on the land pursuing other activities such as hunting or spending time at their cabins. The shortened season, however, is causing some residents to make tradeoffs in their activities, often focusing on wood gathering and forgoing hunting activities to maximize ideal conditions.

Harvesting wood in Hopedale provides households with an alternative to using oil or electricity to heat their homes and maintains energy costs at a manageable level. The cost of purchasing a box of wood to heat a home for four to five days in Hopedale is fifty dollars. Most residents also prefer the warmth of wood to that of other sources of energy. This provides financial incentive for community members who gather the wood to continue to do so. Selling the wood also sustains the use of an alternative form of energy by residents. However, as conditions during the spring continue to worsen with a changing climate, it will be a challenge for snowmobile owners to find strategies to deal with reduced snow cover and faster melt.

Snowmobile owners must also deal with decreasing snowfall that leaves rocks bare and able to damage snowmobiles. Many residents report more snowmobile damage from travelling on the land. This creates more challenges and frustration, as it is difficult to find snowmobile parts in Hopedale in order to repair the machines. Local stores do not always stock the necessary item. Instead, community members order parts from Happy Valley–Goose Bay and have them shipped in via air transport. This increases the costs of operating a snowmobile, since the individual or household must also pay for the costs associated with shipping the item. In addition, the household may not have access to a snowmobile during the time required to ship the part and then repair the snowmobile. Without access to a snowmobile during ideal conditions, a household could potentially miss the opportunity to gather important natural resources such as wood.

Decreasing snowfall has other implications for snowmobile operation. Most of the community operates newer snowmobile models that use a snow-dependent coolant system to cool the engine. The effectiveness of this system in cooling the snowmobile is dependent on a substantial amount of snowfall. Less snowfall causes snowmobile engines to overheat and become inoperable. Some community members are adapting to this by cutting ice blocks and placing them under the snowmobile's engine to cool it before it overheats. Individuals are also adapting by travelling more on the winter trail system. The winter trail system is a well-maintained connection of trails that rely on sea ice trails in the Hopedale area and connect with land trails in southern Nunatsiavut. Managed by the Labrador Inuit Development Corporations in each of the coastal communities, this system is continually groomed and marked for snowmobile riders along the coast. This trail, however, is not immune to the changes in conditions and has recently been re-marked and adjusted to accommodate poorer ice and snow conditions. Furthermore, this trail system does not link directly with the remote areas Hopedale residents travel to for desirable "burn wood." For these reasons, obtaining firewood may continue to challenge Hopedale residents in the future. Investments on the part of local government into alternative energy resources such as windmills might decrease dependency on wood resources and better enhance residents' capacity to manage changes in snowfall in the future. Hopedale residents are also relying more on technology in response to changes in environmental conditions. The Internet is used to obtain updates on weather and sea ice conditions as well as to track caribou migration patterns. The integration of technology into hunting activities is evident in the following statement: "You also see people choosing a time to go. For example, if you wanted to go you would go now and you just can't do that anymore. You have to wait for the weather to be good and watch the forecast" (Hopedale resident, 2007).

Hunters also use satellite phones as a safety precaution when travelling in potentially unsafe conditions. However, the cost of satellite phones is high and some do not offer adequate service in the Hopedale area. Furthermore, the weather services and infrastructure along the coast are basic, and weather information reported on the Internet can often be inaccurate. Information regarding sea ice conditions or future environmental conditions at the local scale is not available currently.

Future Adaptive Capacity and the Role of Government

Despite the success of a number of adaptive strategies employed in the community by Hopedale residents, there is also a role for government intervention at regional as well as provincial levels to further enhance the community's capacity to manage climate change. Investments from the local or regional Nunatsiavut government into public resources such as skidoos, boats, or a community freezer, for example, could improve the capacity of individuals and households to access subsistence resources in Hopedale. Access to a means of transportation to harvest wildfoods would enable residents to maintain participation in traditional harvesting activities and would increase the supply of wildfood in the community. Participation in traditional harvesting activities would ultimately contribute to maintaining Inuit identity in the community as well. The viability of community sharing networks could also remain intact. The participation of more residents in the hunt could reduce existing strains on sharing networks. Those unable to operate a boat or snow machine could access pooled wildfoods from a community freezer. Other communities in Nunatsiavut currently implement community freezer programs that operate on donations from community members with extra harvests (Furgal and Seguin 2006). This program is intended to supplement other sources of income and food sources available to households. Although Hopedale had a food bank freezer program at one time, it was eventually shut down due to improper use of its services. Implementation of this type of program could be useful to respond to the stresses of a changing climate, but it would require better management to avoid similar problems in the future.

Labrador Inuit knowledge is another resource within the community that could further enhance adaptive strategies through the involvement of the Nunatsiavut government. The information and knowledge transmitted throughout generations and held by elders and active hunters provide insights into hunting strategies and safety precautions while travelling on the land or sea. One resident illustrates how this knowledge improves his ability to read the conditions of the ice: "If you're going off on skidoo you tend to try the ice more, to test the thickness using an axe by cutting down four or five chops" (Hopedale resident, 2007). As this resident indicates, testing ice conditions by a certain number of chops informs the individual whether it is safe or not to rely on the ice. In the context of Hopedale's livelihoods, knowledge of the land and sea and wildlife behaviour is central to safe participation in subsistence activities. The transmission of Inuit knowledge between elders and youth in Hopedale, however, has been limited. In addition, the underlying values and principles of sustainability, preservation, and respect for the land and sea that Inuit elders maintain is of equal importance for improving adaptation to climate change. Taboos against wastage and over-harvesting in the community are evidence of such principles. However, responses to recent environmental changes are in some circumstances leading individuals to over-harvest as a precaution. The Nunatsiavut government could provide greater support for the promotion of Labrador Inuit knowledge transmission in the community through school programs or community meetings. One example of this currently taking place in Hopedale is a land skills course offered to grade nine students at Amos Comenius School. This course, taught by an experienced hunter and fisher, takes place in the classroom and out on the land, where youth are taught to use both traditional and modern hunting tools and equipment, including rifles and GPS units. Additional opportunities for youth and elders to engage in sharing these important tools and information beyond this one course could enhance the capacity of the next generations to manage changes associated with climate change.

Improvements in local weather technologies and services from provincial and federal levels could also enhance the capacity of the community. With more accurate weather forecasts and sea ice conditions at the community scale, Hopedale residents could make more informed decisions about the safety of travelling over sea ice and snow on the land. Providing a publicly accessible location in the community where this information could be posted would avoid privileging this information to only those with access to a computer and Internet connection. Additionally, the bilingual local radio station could further disseminate this information in Inuktitut and English to those unable to read English or those fluent in Inuktitut. With the assistance of regional and federal climate services and departments, for example, the community would be better equipped and knowledgeable about potential local impacts of climate change.

Although the future may continue to bring significant change to Hopedale, the legacy of adaptability and resilience of Labrador Inuit will likely shape the future of the region as well. Hopedale residents are equipped with tools, strategies, and values that help them adapt and manage change. Complementary strategies and formal interventions by appropriate levels of government or management can further enhance the capacity of the community to manage changes associated with climate change.

Conclusion

The community of Hopedale is undergoing a period of change. The community's observations of environmental change are largely consistent with the scientific data from across the Arctic. Their observations confirm that the risks posed by climate change are impacting community livelihoods and well-being. These factors influence sea ice conditions, snowfall, and freshwater freeze, all of which are impeding access to harvesting areas. Reduced access to harvesting areas is a concern for the community, as subsistence resources contribute to livelihoods. Sea ice is a prominent concern in the community. It is the primary transportation infrastructure and connects the community to harvesting areas. This transportation network also supports the community's continuation of relationships with family and friends in other Nunatsiavut communities. Recent environmental change compromises the use of sea ice and affects access to harvesting areas. Limited access to harvesting areas increases food and fuel expenses, as the community will tend to rely more on market food items and other forms of energy instead of wood. Hopedale residents are coping with these changes through initiating adaptations.

Adaptations depend on factors that are sometimes beyond individual and community control. The availability of fish and wildlife is identified as problematic for the household economy in Hopedale. The community is adapting through many different methods. Some community members purchase more store foods or harvest extra fish and wildlife when available and save these resources. However, the consequence of a diet more reliant on store-bought foods may result in decreasing nutrition, and excessive harvesting can lead to reductions in species abundance. Research has shown that as Arctic indigenous diets transition to diets more reliant on market food items, there is an increase in cardiovascular diseases, diabetes, dental cavities, and obesity (Van Oostdam et al. 2003; Hanrahan this volume).

The cost of living in Hopedale also puts additional pressure on households to be involved in both the wage and subsistence economy. In addition, in order to compensate for times of unemployment and inaccessibility to harvesting areas, households store more harvested resources. This is contingent, however, on access to a freezer, sufficient and opportune time, and the financial circumstances of the household. Furthermore, environmental change is increasing community exposure to other problematic conditions, such as a lack of employment opportunities, higher living costs, increased drug and alcohol abuse, and future developments in Nunatsiavut. Residents express concern about drug and alcohol abuse and the future impact of development on their community. They worry about the future of their youth. Residents identify that as youth become more involved in activities concerning drugs and alcohol, they are less interested in learning land skills. Skills and knowledge about subsistence activities are essential to ensuring safety on the land and sea. These skills are particularly important in the context of increasing environmental change.

Many Hopedale residents maintain the attitude that they will be able to sustain their livelihoods in spite of environmental and other problematic conditions. In fact, for some residents who have the necessary financial and physical resources, environmental change does not appear to be an issue, for the time being. These individuals can still access harvesting areas by implementing a combination of adaptations. The community also feels that they cannot reduce the impact of climate change, since they cannot control the environment. Many are confident that, given their ancestors' ability to deal with change, they too will find the approaches to manage change in the future. Although this may be true, the exacerbated nature of change expected within the Arctic from global environmental change calls for new interventions and strategies beyond the level of the community, and for more involvement of government and management institutions to ensure livelihood sustainability for Hopedale's future generations.

Acknowledgements

The authors would like to acknowledge the generous support made available from ArcticNet, the International Polar Year Canada, Social Sciences and Humanities Research, Northern Scientific and Training Program, Canada Research Chairs Program and the University of Guelph that made this research possible. This research would not have been possible without the involvement of the community of Hopedale and in particular the research assistance from Tiffany Flowers, Krista Lane, Selma Boase and Augusta Irvine.

References

ACIA. 2004. *Impacts of a Warming Climate: Arctic Climate Impact Assessment*. Cambridge: Cambridge University Press.

Adger, W.N. 2006. "Vulnerability." *Global Environmental Change* 16, 3: 268–81.

AHDR (Arctic Human Development Report). 2004. Akureyri: Stefansson Arctic Institute.

Alwang, Jeffrey, Paul B. Siegel and Steen Jorgensen. 2001. "Vulnerability Measurement." *World Bank Spectrum*, Sector Strategy Launch Issue (Winter 2001): 36–38.

Berman, M., C. Nicholson, G. Kofinas, J. Tetlichi, and S. Martin. 2004. "Adaptation and Sustainability in a Small Arctic Community: Results of an Agent-based Simulation Model." *Arctic* 57, 4: 401–14.

Cruikshank, J. 2001. "Glaciers and Climate Change: Perspectives from Oral Tradition." *Arctic* 54, 4: 377–93.

Environment Canada. 2006. *The Climate of Labrador*. http://atlantic-web1.ns.ec.gc.ca/climatecentre/default.asp?lang=En&n=02ECF58A-1

Ferguson, M.A.D., R.G. Williamson, and F. Messier. 1998. "Inuit Knowledge of Long-term Changes in a Population of Arctic Tundra Caribou." *Arctic* 51, 3: 201–19.

Ford, James D., J. MacDonald, B. Smit, and J. Wandel. 2006. "Vulnerability to climate change in Igloolik, Nunavut: What we can learn from the past and present." *Polar Record* 42, 221: 127–138.

Ford, James D., and Barry Smit. 2004. "A Framework for Assessing the Vulnerability of Communities in the Canadian Arctic to Risks Associated with Climate Change." *Arctic* 57, 4: 389–400.

Furgal, C., and J. Seguin. 2006. "Climate Change, Health and Vulnerability in Canadian Northern Aboriginal Communities." *Environmental Health Perspectives* 114, 12: 1964–70.

Füssel, H.M., and R.J.T. Klein. 2006. "Climate Change Vulnerability Assessments: An Evolution of Conceptual Thinking." *Climatic Change* 75, 3: 301–29.

Government of Newfoundland and Labrador. 2007. *A Northern Strategic Plan for Labrador*. St. John's: Department of Labrador and Aboriginal Affairs.

Hare, F.K. 1950. "The Climate of the Eastern Canadian Arctic and Subarctic." Ph.D. diss., University of Montreal.

Holloway, G., and T. Sou. 2002. "Has Arctic Sea Ice Rapidly Thinned?" *Journal of Climate* 15: 1691–1701.

Huntington, H.P. 1998. "Observations on the Utility of the Semi-directive Interview for Documenting Traditional Ecological Knowledge." *Arctic* 51, 3: 237–42.

IPCC (Intergovernmental Panel on Climate Change). 2007. *Climate Change 2007: Impacts, Adaptation and Vulnerability: Contribution of Working*

Group II to the Fourth Assessment Report of the Intergovernmental Panel on Climate Change, edited by M.L. Parry, O.F. Canziani, J.P Palutikof, P.J. van der Linden, and C.E. Hanson. Cambridge: Cambridge University Press.

Krupnik, I., and D. Jolly. 2002. *The Earth is Faster Now: Indigenous Observations of Arctic Environmental Change*. Fairbanks, AK: Arctic Research Consortium of the United States.

Nickels, S., C. Fugal, M. Buell, and H. Moquin. 2006. *Unikkaaqatigiit—Putting the Human Face on Climate Change, Perspectives from Inuit in Canada*. Ottawa: Inuit Tapiriit Kanatami, Nusivvik Centre for Inuit Health, and Changing Environments at Université Laval and the Ajunnginiq Centre at the National Aboriginal Health Organization.

Roberts, B.A., N.P.P. Simon, and K.W. Deering. 2006. "The Forests and Woodlands of Labrador, Canada: Ecology, Distribution and Future Management." *Ecological Research* 21, 6: 868–80.

Rosenzweig, C., G. Casassa, D.J. Karoly, A. Imeson, C. Liu, A. Menzel, S. Rawlins, T.L. Root, B. Seguin, and P. Tryjanowski. 2007. "Assessment of Observed Changes and Responses in Natural and Managed Systems." In *Climate Change 2007: Impacts, Adaptation and Vulnerability: Contribution of Working Group II to the Fourth Assessment Report of the Intergovernmental Panel on Climate Change*, edited by M.L. Parry, O.F. Canziani, J.P Palutikof, P.J. van der Linden, and C.E. Hanson, 79–131. Cambridge: Cambridge University Press.

Smit, Barry, and J. Wandel. 2006. "Adaptation, Adaptive Capacity and Vulnerability." *Global Environmental Change* 16, 3: 282–92.

Stroeve, J., M.M. Holland, W. Meier, T. Scambos, and M. Serreze. 2007. "Arctic Sea Ice Decline: Faster than Forecasted." *Geophysical Research Letters* 34: 1–5.

Usher, Peter J. 2000. "Traditional Ecological Knowledge in Environmental Assessment and Management." *Arctic* 53, 2: 183–93.

Van Oostdam, J., S. Donaldson, M. Feeley, and N. Tremblay. 2003. *Toxic Substances in the Arctic and Associated Effects: Human Health*. Canadian Arctic Contaminants Assessment Report Phase II. Ottawa: Department of Indian Affairs and Northern Development, Minister of Public Works and Government Services Canada.

Walsh, J.E., O. Anisimov, J.O.M. Hagen, T. Jakobsson, J. Oerlemans, T.D. Prowse, V. Romanovsky, N. Savelieva, M. Serreze, I. Shiklomanov, and S. Solomon. 2005. "Cryosphere and Hydrology." In *Arctic Climate Impacts Assessment, ACIA*. edited by L. Arris Symon and B. Heal, 183–242. Cambridge, Cambridge University Press.

Yohe, G., and R.S.J. Tol. 2002. "Indicators for Social and Economic Coping Capacity—Moving toward a Working Definition of Adaptive Capacity." *Global Environmental Change* 12, 1: 25–40.

CHAPTER 10

Our Beautiful Land: Current Debates in Land Use Planning in Nunatsiavut

Andrea Procter and Keith Chaulk

For years, the Labrador Inuit have struggled to regain control of the management of their lands and resources. After more than thirty years of negotiations with the federal and provincial governments, some measure of control was achieved with the final ratification of the Labrador Inuit Land Claims Agreement (INAC 2005), the last Inuit land claim to be negotiated in Canada.

On 1 December 2005 the Labrador Inuit assumed responsibility for the governance of Nunatsiavut ("our beautiful land"), a vast region in northern Labrador (Figure 1). In some areas of Nunatsiavut, the Inuit own the land,[1] while in other areas they share control of land, water, and resources with the provincial and federal governments, and/or have special overlap agreements with Inuit of northern Quebec and the Innu of Labrador.

Chapter 10 of the final agreement requires that the Nunatsiavut government (NG) and the provincial government of Newfoundland and Labrador jointly develop and approve a land use plan for the Labrador Inuit Settlement Area (LISA), not including federal lands and waters (INAC 2005). The

---

1 Inuit own Labrador Inuit Lands, but not the subsurface resources of these lands (although they will share in the royalties if these resources are developed) (INAC 2005, 4.4.1).

Regional Planning Authority (RPA), consisting of two NG-appointed representatives and two provincially appointed representatives, is tasked with overseeing the development of a land use plan over a three-year period. The RPA has secured the services of a certified planner to assist in the drafting of the plan.

This chapter explores the historical and political context of land use planning in northern Labrador and the possibilities for the Nunatsiavut land use planning process to address Inuit interests and perspectives. The first section outlines the context of land use planning in Nunatsiavut. The subsequent sections examine a number of challenges faced by participants in the planning process as they attempt to adapt the techniques of planning to the realities of Nunatsiavut.

Background

The original idea of co-managed land use planning emerged in land claims talks as a solution to an impasse about land quantum between the Labrador Inuit Association and the provincial government. During the negotiations in the 1990s, Inuit leaders had pressured the Newfoundland and Labrador government to grant them ownership of large areas of land in northern Labrador. The provincial government refused, and the talks stalled. But then a compromise was reached: in return for a reduced land quantum of Inuit-owned lands, the Inuit and the province would co-manage land use planning for the entire region (Toby Andersen, NG, personal communication, 2008; B. Warren, personal communication, 2008). The Inuit would therefore be able to influence the type and extent of human activities permitted in most of Nunatsiavut, but the province would retain ownership of the majority of the co-managed region. This compromise was difficult for both the provincial government and the Labrador Inuit Association to sell internally. Land use planning lacked support from provincial government officials at the administrative level because politicians wished to maintain their discretionary control over land issues (B. Warren, pers. comm. 2008). Many Inuit were very unhappy with the small amount of land offered as Inuit-owned lands, and the Labrador Inuit Association had to convince its members that the compromise was worthwhile. With the final ratification of the land claims agreement, the process of sharing decision-making power over land use in Nunatsiavut commenced. Since 2008 Inuit and the provincial government have been working together to develop a plan that will determine future land use possibilities for the region.

Land Use Planning in Nunatsiavut

The land use plan for LISA, as the provincial government officially calls Nunatsiavut,[2] will "guide the future conservation, development, and utilization of the land, waters, and other resources within LISA" for a ten-year planning period (2011–2021), with a review of the plan every five years (RPA Dec. 2009, 7). The emphasis of this plan is "the protection of the ecosystem and the rights and health of Inuit including their culture and history while providing for the use of natural resources and the economic vitality of the area" (RPA Dec 2009, 5). Traditional subsistence land uses, such as hunting, fishing, and gathering, are not governed by the plan, as the land claims agreement protects the Inuit right to harvest throughout Nunatsiavut; instead, the plan applies to all land uses that require a permit, licence, or agreement.

The RPA envisions that the plan will respond to Inuit environmental, social, cultural, and economic interests in LISA. The plan incorporates sections from the Labrador Inuit constitution that relate to the Inuit relationship with the region and to the need to develop culturally relevant policies, and it identifies three interrelated goals that the plan will attempt to balance: 1) environmental protection; 2) social, cultural, and quality of life protection; and 3) economic development (RPA January 2010, 28–30). The RPA intends to create a plan that will help to guide future land use decisions by establishing broad principles and values about the relative importance of these three goals. The plan will also include detailed designations about permitted land uses on specific lands.

This vision of a coherent plan for the entire region is ambitious, given the lack of coherency in land jurisdiction. The land claim agreement divided the jurisdiction of lands and resources of Nunatsiavut among four different government bodies. In general terms, the Nunatsiavut government owns the surface rights of Labrador Inuit Lands (LIL) (15,799 km²), and the provincial government owns Labrador Inuit Settlement Area lands outside LIL (43,071 km²). In addition, the federal government has jurisdiction over Torngat Mountains National Park (where land use planning is controlled by a separate park co-management board), as well as all tidal waters, a region referred to in the final agreement as the Marine Zone (Figure 1). Finally, the Inuit Community Governments (ICGs) control land use planning for the Inuit Community Lands (see Table 1 for more information). Subsurface rights and royalty regimes vary with each land category.

---

2 The provincial government recognizes the "Nunatsiavut government" but does not officially recognize the region as "Nunatsiavut" (RPA notes September 2009).

Table 1. *Major land and water categories in Nunatsiavut.*

Land or water category	Jurisdiction	Area
Labrador Inuit Lands (LIL)	Nunatsiavut Government	15,799 km^2
Torngat Mountains National Park	Federal Government	9,700 km^2
Specified Material Lands (all are within LIL)	Nunatsiavut Government	3,950 km^2
Inuit Communities	Inuit Community Governments (with NG on LIL)	Includes 4.58 km^2 of LIL
LISA Outside of the Above	Provincial Government	43,071 km^2
Total Area of Land in LISA		72,520 km^2
Tidal Waters (the "Zone")	Federal Government	48,690 km^2

The Regional Land Use Plan has jurisdiction only on lands that are controlled by the Nunatsiavut and provincial governments (LIL, and LISA outside LIL), and therefore the official drafting process involves only these two governments. However, the complexity of land jurisdictions results, in reality, in the participation of the federal government and ICGs in discussions about land use management in areas of adjacent jurisdictions.

Once the plan has been finalized and approved, it is legally binding to both the Nunatsiavut and provincial governments, so it is crucial that all parties work to create a plan that is acceptable to everyone involved. During the drafting process, community residents and the Nunatsiavut and the provincial governments will review and comment on the plan. During this review, both governments have the authority to suggest changes to sections of the plan that pertain to lands under their own jurisdiction. The success and strength of the co-management process will therefore depend on the ability of the RPA and the planner to incorporate values and interests into the plan in a way that allows all parties to reach an acceptable level of consensus about land use, and to persuade both governments to honour their commitment to the co-management process. Because each government has final authority over its respective jurisdiction, this type of co-management runs the risk of developing a plan that may be partially overruled during the review process, but this is a risk that most co-management boards face. A fundamental aspect in this case is that both governments hold some degree of ultimate authority over their own jurisdictions, and once the plan has been approved, all land use decisions and developments must comply with its principles. Many other boards, by way of contrast, including some developed

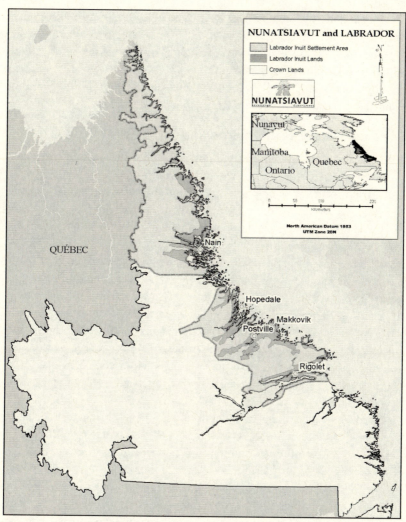

Figure 1: Map of Nunatsiavut *(courtesy of Bryn Wood, Nunatsiavut government, Department of Lands and Resources).*

under the Labrador Inuit Land Claims Agreement (i.e., the Torngat Wildlife and Plants Co-Management Board), serve, in some cases, only an advisory role to a provincial or federal minister.

The risk that the provincial government, especially, might choose to overrule decisions during the review process has been discussed in RPA meetings. The mandates of various departments within both governments often conflict with one another, and the RPA anticipates that some departments in the provincial government that strongly promote resource development may oppose parts of a plan that prevent development in certain areas (RPA notes May 2009). Such intra-governmental politics may well become an issue in the final stages of consultation and governmental approval, and although the RPA members remain cognizant of this possibility, the RPA is attempting to develop a plan that prioritizes Inuit interests and is not guided by jurisdictional distinctions or interests (RPA notes September 2009).

Designations and Territorialization

The plan is designed around its guiding principles and goals, and it incorporates land use designations that establish permitted activities in specific areas. Early in the drafting process, the RPA created designations to relate to three main issues: the Inuit desire to have a sustainable supply of country food (and therefore to protect important habitat), the potential for tourism, and the potential for mineral development (RPA May 2009). The choice of these three issues originated with early consultations with Inuit communities and officials, RPA discussions, and the planner's literature review of material related to social and economic issues in Nunatsiavut. The proposed designations therefore allow different combinations of land uses, with the focus on development and its impact on traditional harvesting activities and ecological integrity. The seven proposed designations (as of January 2010) are: Environmentally Sensitive Area, Torngat Mountains National Park, Heritage Area, Traditional Use, Community Designation, General Use, and Resource Development.[3]

The use of designations simplifies the process of making further decisions about land use, the central aspect of which, in Nunatsiavut today, is industrial development—or "mining or no mining," as one RPA member commented (RPA notes May 2009). Designations serve to outline areas in which development may occur and areas in which it may not. In one sense, therefore, the use of designations facilitates development by allocating specific lands for this purpose. A land use plan removes any uncertainty about access to resources and allows both governments to promote confidence among potential investors (among which Inuit organizations and the Nunatsiavut government itself may be counted).

---

3 The Torngat Mountains National Park Designation and the Community Designation are under the jurisdiction of the federal government and Inuit Community Governments respectively, and so these designations are not discussed in this chapter. Although not directly under the jurisdiction of the plan itself, these two land categories are included in the plan in order to encompass all land in LISA.

In one respect, removing uncertainty about access to resources could be seen as simply continuing the process initiated by the land claims agreement of advancing the economic development goals of the state by opening up lands for development. Potential industrial development has always been the major incentive for federal, provincial, and territorial governments with respect to comprehensive land claims in northern Canada, and in Nunatsiavut this incentive was provided by the proposal of a nickel mine at Voisey's Bay, South of Nain in the 1990s. Unresolved Inuit claims to land and resources in the region impeded the proposed mine, and the provincial government was pressured to finally settle the issue of Inuit land rights. The ensuing land claim agreement removed the uncertainty caused by the existence of potentially extensive Inuit rights to the entire area by limiting and defining these rights to smaller and more specific regions and jurisdictions.[4] The land use plan could be seen as furthering the process by identifying areas where developments may now occur.

This process is not unique to Labrador. The tools of land use planning have been employed by state governments worldwide to further goals of economic development and social transformation, often under the aegis of colonialization and modernization. States have demarcated territories and categorized people and lands in the attempt to subject ethnic minorities to dominant norms and institutions (Escobar 1992). These planning methods have had a particularly insidious effect on indigenous peoples, as states have appropriated traditional lands through the techniques of surveying, (re)naming, classifying land by its potential economic uses, and facilitating state-led social and economic development. In the process, they have often rendered indigenous philosophies and relationships with the land invisible and unimportant (Porter 2007; Howitt 2001).

However, with the ratification of the land claims agreement, Labrador Inuit have themselves taken on many of the state's roles. As a result, they now have much greater authority to decide on the extent and pace of development than they did in the recent past. In the hands of Inuit, the tools of land use planning have equal power to determine possibilities for development, human activity, and ecosystem protection. It is this power that was

---

4 During this time, the provincial government also removed the Voisey's Bay area completely from the land selection process in the land claims negotiations. In exchange for Inuit rights and benefits as outlined in Chapter 8 of the final agreement, the Voisey's Bay area was excluded from both LISA and LIL (see the excluded area south of Nain on the map of Nunatsiavut in Figure 1) (B. Warren, pers. comm. 2009).

so threatening, during the negotiations, to officials in the Newfoundland and Labrador government, who had long been accustomed to unrestricted control over provincial resources. Nunatsiavut land use planning, therefore, offers Inuit the opportunity to employ techniques of state control to pursue their own goals and to control their own social and economic development.

This situation does have its limitations for the Inuit, however, because planning structures and procedures sometimes conflict with the realities of Nunatsiavut, and because much of the settlement area remains as Crown land, controlled and managed by the provincial government. Much will depend on the characteristics of the plan itself and on the success of the co-management process. However, many Inuit are embracing the potential of land use planning for a number of reasons that become clear in the context of Inuit experience with land use governance, as the next section explores.

Historical Experiences with Land Governance and Territorialization

Historically, uncertainty about Aboriginal rights has not been much of an obstacle for potential developers. Inuit have experienced many years of outside interests laying claim to their lands and resources, often at the encouragement of the provincial government. In the late 1700s, the Newfoundland government supported Moravian missionaries in their efforts to contain Inuit on mission lands in northern Labrador because Inuit were threatening British commercial fishing interests to the south. The Crown agreed to give 100,000-acre land grants to the Moravians around their missions in northern Labrador. These grants provided the Moravians with almost complete control of trade and other economic and social aspects of the north coast, a situation that lasted until the early 1900s.

In the twentieth century, however, provincial economic priorities gradually changed as the government became increasingly interested in Labrador's resource potential. A conflict with Quebec over rights to the region's resources in the early 1900s resulted in the establishment of the Labrador boundary in 1927, a dividing line that effectively separated Labrador Inuit from their relatives in Ungava, to the west. Since mid-century, the Newfoundland government has consistently tried to maintain a policy of treating all regions and citizens as equal and identical, in the interest of treating all land and resources as public property available for development. Exclusive Moravian Inuit territory in northern Labrador inferred an uncertain degree of non-public land and resource ownership, and was therefore politically and economically unpalatable to the province. The government attempted instead to treat Inuit in the same manner as it did other citizens, and to underplay any cultural difference while promoting assimilation: "Eskimos and Indians can't continue to exist as isolated minorities," provincial officials wrote in 1956. "[They] must be integrated into the general body of our Society" (Kennedy 1977, 284). The Moravian goal of containment had, over the years, created a northern Inuit homeland, but this de facto Inuit land ownership did not agree with the provincial goals of developing mineral, hydroelectric, and timber resources in Labrador (Brice-Bennett 1986; Hillier 1971).

In order for the province to facilitate these potential resource developments, the government emphasized the fact that all lands were to remain open and available for resource exploration. In Nunatsiavut, residents felt the direct impact of this open access policy, especially during the 1970s uranium exploration work near Makkovik and Postville and the 1990s exploration rush in northern Labrador after the Voisey's Bay nickel, cobalt, and copper discovery. Local people were startled by the ability of exploration companies to draw boundaries around land that families had used for generations, and to control access and activities on this land. In the late 1990s a story circulated along the coast about a Nain elder who had his rifle confiscated by workers at an exploration site while he was hunting and collecting firewood. Another story circulated about the posting of a "No Trespassing" sign by an exploration company. These incidents upset and offended residents and served to highlight the power the provincial government had in granting mineral rights to industry in spite of a long history of local use and perceived Inuit ownership of the land (Williamson 1996). Many Inuit also identified strongly with the church and saw Moravian lands as belonging to them: "What is church land? The Moravian Mission has never given up its lands. The people are the church. We would like to ensure LIA has control over the land" (Makkovik resident in Williamson 1996, 44). This sense of apprehension is also apparent in a LIA pamphlet on "Mineral Development in Northern Labrador" published in 1996 during the midst of the staking claim rush: "Today, as in the past, we live in a world where resource industries, governments and other interest groups work to have their beliefs become our rules, their values our way of life, and our resources their wealth. But unlike in the past, we may not be able to adopt what we find good and reject what is a threat because now it is our land that is being devoured" (LIA 1996). Inuit frustration with their obvious lack of power to influence decisions about land and resources underscored provincial political inequalities and fuelled their sense of urgency to finalize a land claims settlement and establish Inuit rights to management, use, and ownership (Andersen and Rowell 1993).

Since the land claims agreement was signed in 2005, exploration companies have revived their interest in the uranium deposits near Makkovik and Postville. This new activity is reminiscent of previous exploration work in the region, but with the key difference that Inuit are now empowered, through the land claim agreement, to influence the outcome. The intense debate that currently rages is no longer focused on indignation about the actions of outside interests, but on the suitability of a uranium mine in the region. The Nunatsiavut government established a moratorium on uranium development on Labrador Inuit Lands for three years in 2008 and has since been studying the potential effects of uranium mining in other localities. The provincial government, on the other hand, has made it clear that it remains open to uranium development (GNL 2008). Many Inuit see the land use plan as being fundamental to determining how this question will play itself out.

Co-managed land use planning may also prove to be a useful tool in protecting the habitat of species that are of fundamental importance to Labrador Inuit, such as caribou. As LIA negotiators explained in 1993, the Inuit wanted a land claim agreement that allowed them "to maintain a way of life that respects the importance of hunting, trapping, fishing, and gathering in the modern world" (Andersen and Rowell 1993). They succeeded in bargaining for co-managed control over land use activities for the entire region in a way that allows them to address the issue of habitat protection more extensively than if they had ownership over only portions of land. Migratory species such as caribou have wide ranges, and Inuit-owned land holdings, even if they were much larger than the current LIL, would not be extensive enough to ensure that Inuit could control adequate habitat protection. Land ownership under Canadian law also does not by itself provide protection against incursions by the state or by mining companies, who are guaranteed free entry for exploration under provincial mining laws. Co-managed land use planning, on the other hand, offers Inuit much greater influence over habitat protection and other aspects of land management related to harvesting concerns (Andersen and Rowell 1993; Usher 1982). The combination of land ownership and land use planning co-management in the final land claims agreement therefore provides the Nunatsiavut government with multiple means to achieve their goals.[5]

---

5 Other instruments under the final agreement that influence land governance include conditions established for Specified Material Lands (see INAC 2005, Ch. 4), Nuclear Substances (Ch. 4), NG Exploration Standards requirements for LIL, NG environmental assessment legislation (Ch. 11), water and ocean management (Chs. 5 and 6), wildlife and plant management (Ch. 12), fisheries management (Ch. 13), access to LIL (Ch. 4), archaeology (Ch. 15), and self-government provisions (Ch. 17), as well as the land use planning regime in Ch. 10.

Both the final agreement and the land use plan counteract the ambitions of the provincial government in maintaining an open access policy for province-wide undifferentiated public lands. The division of Nunatsiavut into multiple land jurisdictions, including LIL and LISA outside LIL, and new co-management regimes offer the Labrador Inuit a substantial role in land governance. This territorialization may, in the end, serve to facilitate provincial goals of economic development, but it offers the Nunatsiavut government economic benefits, a degree of land ownership, and the authority to guide this development. Given the long history of failed Inuit attempts to assert control over lands and resources, many Inuit see these new governance arrangements as acceptable compromises.

Challenges of Land Use Planning in Nunatsiavut

Sea ice

Despite its potential strengths in providing Inuit with increased control, the governance technique of dividing land and resources into jurisdictions fails to reflect Inuit perspectives and values when it comes to sea ice. Like elsewhere in Canada, the ocean and its resources are under the jurisdiction of the federal Department of Fisheries and Oceans, while land usually falls under provincial jurisdiction. However, this conceptual division of the environment is not a model shared by Labrador Inuit, who consider the sea ice to be an extension of the land. From late autumn to early summer, land-fast sea ice forms along the Labrador coast and provides many important travelling routes and harvesting opportunities. Sea ice was specifically included in the original land claim proposal as an area of importance to the Inuit, but the other governments failed to recognize this interest during the land claims negotiations.

Labrador Inuit call themselves *Sikumiut*, or "people of the sea ice." They have always used the sea ice as a crucial transportation area because it offers a relatively flat and open route in comparison to inland terrain. Inuit use the ice to travel between communities, to harvesting areas, to islands, and to cabins and *aullâsimavet* (seasonal camping sites). Inuit also use the sea ice and the floe edge (the *sina*), for harvesting seals, polar bears, walrus, whales, migratory birds, and white fox (Williamson 1997; Brice-Bennett 1977). Inuit consider the "outside" to be a free access region where anyone can hunt or trap, in much the same way as anyone can hunt caribou in the interior hinterlands, wherever the caribou migrate (Brody 1977). The animals most commonly pursued in this region—fox, seals, polar bear, and walrus—are wide ranging and vary in their movements and availability from year to year, and as a result they are not well suited to management based on defined areas.

Jurisdictional boundaries that do not consider these kinds of relationships but are instead based on a southern understanding of the environment have caused much frustration among Inuit in Labrador, as well as across the Canadian Arctic (Mulrennan and Scott 2001). In the late 1990s, during the Voisey's Bay environmental assessment process, the Labrador Inuit raised concerns about the impact of winter shipping to and from the mine site. They fought strenuously to highlight the importance of the sea ice in their lives; in order to do so, they had to first convey to the assessment officials the Inuit perspective about the continuity of the land and sea ice, and then to convince the officials of the artificiality of existing jurisdictional boundaries (RPA notes October 2008; Reschny 2007). The Inuit finally succeeded in forcing the proponent to agree to explore mitigation measures related to the ice-breaking activities that threatened to disrupt their traditional ice travel routes.

In the Labrador Inuit Land Claims Agreement, these jurisdictional issues resulted in recognition of Inuit rights to travel and harvest on the sea ice, but the federal government refused to concede any rights to ownership or governance beyond an advisory role.[6] The land use plan, as a creation of the final agreement, is required to follow these jurisdictions, and it has no power to control activities on sea ice. The plan therefore officially includes coastal regions and islands, but, incongruously, not the water or sea ice that surround them. RPA discussions have led to the inclusion of references in the plan about the importance of traditional land uses on sea ice and the need to consider these uses when considering potential developments and transportation links, but the plan has no real authority to control sea ice issues. Inuit will be able to influence activities on the sea ice only in ways disjointed from the regional planning process, and on a rather piecemeal basis. These ways include: 1) in as far as the land use plan indirectly affects the sea and sea ice; 2) through the provisions in the final agreement for consultation with the federal government about ocean and fisheries management; 3) for the negotiations of impact and benefit agreements with developers; and 4) through an environmental assessment or similar processes concerning case-by-case

---

6 The Labrador Inuit agreement is similar in this respect to other land claims agreements, with one significant difference: although the federal government did not recognize Inuit ownership rights, it did agree to define Inuit rights to commercial marine harvesting (see Procter, this volume; Mulrennan and Scott 2001).

development issues. Considering the fundamental importance of the sea ice to Inuit, this piecemeal approach to management and to jurisdictions will likely remain a point of contestation.

Economic Perspectives and Cultural Concerns

Economic factors and goals are a major incentive for the planning process, and they play a major role in both Nunatsiavut and provincial government decision making. The Labrador Inuit Land Claims Agreement specifies eleven factors that the land use plan must consider.[7] Economic needs and opportunities are explicitly identified in only one of these factors, but economic issues arguably play a fundamental part in determining the framing of the other factors within the planning process (INAC 2005). Similarly, the RPA envisions planning for Nunatsiavut to be specific to Inuit goals and concerns, which encompass more than simply economic issues, but many RPA discussions illustrate how the planning perspective can use an economic lens on other factors. At a meeting in October 2008, for instance, RPA members were discussing how the issue of traplines would come up in community meetings, despite the fact that very few trappers are still active. Someone suggested that this information would at least be useful, because the existence of traplines would suggest that wildlife was also there, and so traplines could be "tied to productivity." Another member suggested that, alternatively, some traplines had been inherited and are used because they are people's connection to the land, not necessarily because there are high numbers of animals there (RPA notes October 2008). The centrality of "productivity"—an economic validation—from a planning perspective was juxtaposed with the cultural and social importance of the trapline. However, despite the tendency towards economic interpretations of non-economic issues, these discussions and the evolution of the draft plan also illustrate how RPA members have modified their perspectives through dialogue about Inuit-specific planning and the relative importance of economic, cultural, intrinsic, aesthetic, and spiritual values.

---

7 The eleven issues that must be considered in the land use plan are: a) natural resources; b) health and quality of life of residents; c) economic needs and opportunities; d) environmental considerations; e) protected areas; f) cultural priorities and sites; g) local and regional considerations; h) considerations respecting coastal and marine ecosystems; i) rights of Inuit; j) mandatory requirements for plans under provincial planning legislation; and k) any other relevant factors (paraphrased from INAC 2005, 10.4.3).

Nonetheless, planning's economic framework and basis for decision making remain prominent. In order to guide regional development, the land use plan and its designation system focus on potential economic uses of land and the kind of economic activities that will be allowed or prohibited. Designations developed for the draft plan identify either purely economic uses, such as the Resource Development designation, or various combinations of land uses that prohibit destructive economic activities, such as the Environmentally Sensitive Area designation, which permits only traditional uses (hunting, fishing, gathering, travelling by winter trails, and cabin and *aullâsimavet* use), and then only if minimal physical alteration is made to the land. Economic factors are central, both in the sanction or the prohibition of economic activities. As one RPA member has argued, the plan must justify why it removes certain land from development; in other words, development is the norm, and exceptions to this norm must be validated (RPA notes April 2008 and May 2009).

Most of the justifications for removing lands from development in the draft plan are based on economic values, although the RPA and the planner have attempted to adapt the limitations of this economic perspective to include cultural concerns. Such attempts most often put an economic slant onto cultural values, in order to validate non-economic factors through economic means. The Traditional Use designation is one example of an attempt to address cultural concerns on economic grounds. Following the plan's rationale, a major reason given for protecting habitat is not its intrinsic ecological value but its value in maintaining a sustainable supply of country food—an economic facet of a cultural issue. The Traditional Use designation, which allows only relatively non-destructive land uses, is described in the draft plan as the primary area where "Inuit continue to live, gather, hunt and trap for country food" (RPA December 2009, 12). The proposed areas for this designation include a linear strip along the coast as well as coastal islands, caribou habitat, and waterfowl staging areas. Under the land claims agreement, Inuit have the right to pursue their traditional land use activities throughout Nunatsiavut. Through this designation, the land use plan works to support traditional activities by explicitly acknowledging their cultural importance: "Inuit have a strong desire to retain Inuktitut, traditional knowledge, cultural, spiritual, and historical ties to the land. To accomplish this, they require a sustainable supply of country food which in turn requires protection of *land* in the all-inclusive Inuit understanding of the word." The rationale for the designation continues by arguing that "the traditional use of the land is based on Inuit hunting, fishing, and gathering," and that most of these activities take place in coastal areas, rivers, lakes, and inland regions.

"To maintain this way of life these areas need to be protected so wildlife habitat will not be adversely affected by development thus providing a sustainable level of country food" (RPA December 2009, 12).

The structure of land use planning encourages the incorporation of aspects that can be framed in economic or productivity terms (a sustainable level of country food and the activities of hunting, fishing, and gathering) in response to Inuit aspirations. The land use plan has limited structural abilities to incorporate these non-economic goals, but in recognizing the need to protect and support the economic features of cultural concerns, the planning process is partially able to address such interests. Although harvesting activities are often the focus of policies, advocacy, and research, they are only one economic facet of a broader cultural framework that includes sharing, kinship, spirituality, intergenerational learning, shared values, and a relationship with the land. Participation in hunting, fishing, and gathering, and in the subsequent processing, sharing, and eating of country foods, help to perpetuate cultural vitality (Usher et al. 1995; Nuttall et al. 2005). As one RPA member says, "I want a plan that recognizes the significance of resources and the Inuit reliance on the land to maintain our culture. I want to develop a plan that allows Inuit to live as Inuit" (RPA notes April 2008). The Traditional Use designation explicitly recognizes the importance of hunting, fishing, and gathering, and although the planning process favours an economic perspective on cultural concerns, it manages to acknowledge some Inuit interests that have formerly been overlooked and undermined by government authorities (see Procter, this volume).

The primacy of economic justification is further illustrated in some of the other reasons provided in early drafts of the plan for protecting the proposed Traditional Use lands from development:

- A limitation of uses to traditional ones maintains a visual pristine appearance along the coastal area to help promote geotourism as seen by those traveling the coast by ship;

- If mining activities are situated inland then they are visually hidden and therefore are not visible to tourists and the historic and traditional appearance of the coastline area is maintained (RPA May 2009, 22).

Aesthetic values can be translated into potential economic benefits from tourism, and aesthetic vistas can be used to hide other economic activities. RPA members have suggested on occasion that the plan should include a special designation for spiritual, burial, and archaeological sites, as well as for travel routes, but this has not been pursued because it is felt that the

Traditional Use designation encompasses the majority of these sites. The Environmentally Sensitive Area designation aims to protect ecologically sensitive regions and does not involve cultural sites. Instead, the coastal strip that is under the Traditional Use designation was given that designation in part because the coast contains most of these cultural sites. RPA discussions have also helped to identify important travel routes, which were then included under the designation (RPA notes May 2009). The draft plan therefore attempts to address cultural concerns by incorporating their economic aspects, by using economic justifications for their protection, and by having broad designations indirectly encompass them.

Flexibility and Certainty

Both the provincial and the Nunatsiavut governments want to have a degree of certainty about future land uses in Nunatsiavut. The land use planning process strives to provide this certainty, but it faces a number of obstacles in doing so that relate to the inconsistency between the structure of land use planning and existing circumstances in Nunatsiavut. These obstacles illustrate the often-conflicting need for both flexibility and certainty.

One of the most commonly discussed obstacles to this planning process has been the lack of documented information about ecological and social aspects of the region. Given the time and resource limitations of the plan drafting process, the planner was not able to initiate new information-gathering research but instead has to rely on previous research and maps made of the area. For the requirements of planning, this collection of information for the entire region of LISA is incomplete, and the planner often finds it challenging to produce physical boundaries on maps around uncertain factors. In some cases, the planner was compelled to draw boundaries as straight lines or geometric shapes, which obviously do not correspond with the geographical reality.

On more than one occasion, RPA members have discussed how the planning process could include new information, and it was suggested at one meeting that the degree of flexibility in the plan could be enhanced by allowing some boundaries to change without going through an amendment process or plan review when additional research information is added to a central database (RPA notes May 2009). However, this suggestion was not pursued because the RPA members agreed that changing boundaries based on new information was a process that must comply with the larger principles of the plan. Designating bounded areas for allowable activities is a political act, they agreed, and not something that should be done without public discussion. The land designations on the map, however arbitrary, must therefore remain as they are once they are agreed upon. Authority members hoped, however, that when the communities were consulted about the draft plan during the review process, residents and other experts would provide information that would improve the accuracy of the maps (RPA notes May 2009).

This discussion illustrates the limitations of the planning process in allowing for flexibility in the face of uncertainty. Political decisions about designating areas for specific uses create certainty in the plan, but this certainty results in a degree of inflexibility that limits the ability to correct potentially erroneous assumptions or statements in the plan. The potential for inaccuracy is a result of limited ecological and social information about existing circumstances and uncertainty about future change—for instance, market price of various resources, or community growth and relocation. The planning process attempts to overcome this problem by acquiring more and better information. This appetite for more and more information can be seen as a continuation of the colonial process of rendering everything "legible" to the state so that it can be controlled (following Scott 1998), although in this case, the Inuit have assumed many state roles. The control gained by Inuit through land claims negotiations and the resulting participation in the planning process is tied to the requirement that both governments work to acquire this information; the Nunatsiavut government is compelled to join the bureaucratic pursuit of data about its territory and its residents in order to protect its own best interest. The level of community participation will therefore help to determine both the amount of information available and the level of political support for the process among Nunatsiavut beneficiaries.

In order to deal with these obstacles to the planning process, the RPA is attempting to incorporate flexibility by using temporary and seasonal restrictions on land uses if harmful or conflicting uses only occur in specific situations. Activities that might disturb caribou during the calving and wintering periods, for example, or activities that might disrupt certain bird species during their nesting period, will not be permitted during the critical time periods.

The RPA is also attempting to incorporate flexibility by leaving all decisions about designating areas for resource development to future plan amendments (as of the January 2010 draft plan). Because activities such as mining and other large-scale developments are allowed only within the Resource Development designation (in this draft of the plan), the decision to limit the extent of this designation means that any future development of this kind will only be considered if project proponents first apply to have the plan amended. The draft plan also specifies that, for the first ten years of the plan, only areas designated General Use may be changed into the Resource Development designation. This strategy puts the onus—and some of the expense—on companies to prove the appropriateness of each proposal for mineral development before the plan is amended to change land designations. The amendment process will be done in conjunction with an environmental assessment and will involve public consultation and government approval in each case (RPA December 2009). Given the public's eagerness for final answers to the uranium mining issue, the reaction to this tactic remains to be seen, but this approach seems to follow the Nunatsiavut government's own attitude towards uranium development, as the acting president described in March 2008 during a debate about the issue: "We are the decision body, we will make the rules that apply to our land. It is our land and we will continue to protect it and we have newfound powers that we will use to ensure that development that takes place will be done so on our terms.... Let [the mining companies] go do their work now. Let them find the techniques that will give us the confidence that perhaps, someday, uranium mining could be accepted in Labrador Inuit Lands" (Andersen 2008). "The Nunatsiavut government will not operate on somebody else's timeline," the minister for Lands and Resources at the time stated. "First and foremost, we won't be rushed. We will make our decision on the most recent information available" (Barbour 2008).

Land use planning endeavours to achieve certainty in terms of political decisions about land use and in the justification of these decisions, based on extensive data. This political requirement for certainty in Nunatsiavut is hampered by the limited information available to the planner and often results in unavoidably rigid generalizations. Given these restrictions, the RPA and the planner aim to create flexibility within the planning process by using temporal or seasonal prohibitions in land use designations, and by relying heavily on the amendment procedures and on the five-year review process. Many present and future circumstances are unknown, and as a result the RPA sees this approach as allowing the plan to adapt to changes in information, policies, or opportunities while encouraging decisions to be made and evaluated against the guiding principles (RPA notes Sept 2009).

Conclusion

The land use planning process for Nunatsiavut is the result of negotiated compromises between Labrador Inuit and the provincial government. In return for a smaller amount of Inuit-owned lands, the Nunatsiavut government gained co-management influence over all lands of LISA. The planning process offers an opportunity for Nunatsiavut beneficiaries to advance and protect their interests and perspectives, and the RPA and the planner are attempting to instil these perspectives into the plan. As a creation of the final agreement, however, the planning process is tied to the territorial and jurisdictional boundaries, timelines, and political arrangements outlined in the final agreement and the associated implementation plan. Although the provincial and Nunatsiavut governments will approve parts of the plan in separate processes, participants in the planning process must attempt to organize this jumble of jurisdictions into a coherent vision for the entire region.

By agreeing to the negotiated governance arrangements in the land claims agreement, the Nunatsiavut government is now also faced with participation in bureaucratic methods that have the potential to facilitate development but overlook cultural considerations. However, by being players at the table with legally recognized and legislated authority, Inuit hope to avoid situations like those that occurred in the past, where Inuit concerns were entirely overlooked. The Regional Planning Authority and the land use planner are working to both offset and capitalize on the tendency within the planning process to consider all aspects through an economic lens, and are attempting to incorporate other interests that Inuit wish to promote in Nunatsiavut. The RPA is also attempting to negotiate the tension between the dual need for certainty and for flexibility, and to ensure that land use planning in Nunatsiavut addresses complex issues with adequate information, time, and resources.

The ultimate success of the planning process will depend heavily on the strength of the co-management between the two governments, and on the respect and commitment shown by both governments towards shared decision making. The draft plan will undergo many more revisions through RPA meetings, community consultations, and government reviews before it is finalized, and even then, it will be only the first such plan in the Nunatsiavut planning process. Many unknowns currently exist. Will many community residents contribute their expertise and their energy towards developing the plan? Has the RPA been allocated enough resources and time to succeed? Will this process develop enough capacity within the Nunatsiavut government to meet future planning needs?

In its first two years, this co-management process has offered a forum that allows for dialogue, mutual learning, flexibility, and creativity in developing Nunatsiavut-specific planning. Hopes are high that it will continue to foster an approach to land governance that can adapt planning techniques to Inuit priorities and bring provincial and Nunatsiavut governments together under shared visions of the future.

References

Andersen, Toby, and Judy Rowell. "Environmental Implications for the Labrador Inuit of Canada's and Newfoundland's Land Claims Policies." In *Common Ground: Northern People and the Environment*, edited by John Jacobs and William Montevecchi, 29–41. St. John's: ISER Books.

Andersen, Tony. 2008. Speech to Nunatsiavut Assembly, 5 March 2008. Nunatsiavut Hansard. http://www.nunatsiavut.com/pdfs/March_3_Hansard_Revised_08.pdf

Barbour, W. 2008. "Labrador Inuit Prepare to Debate Suspending Uranium Mining and Milling." Interview, CBC, 6 April 2008.

Brice-Bennett, Carol. 1977. "Land Use in the Nain and Hopedale Regions." In *Our Footprints Are Everywhere: Inuit Land Use and Occupancy in Labrador*, edited by Carol Brice-Bennett. Nain: Labrador Inuit Association.

_____. 1986. *Renewable Resource Use and Wage Employment in the Economy of Northern Labrador*. Newfoundland and Labrador: Royal Commission on Employment and Unemployment, 1986.

Brody, H. 1977. "Permanence and Change among the Inuit and Settlers of Labrador." In *Our Footprints Are Everywhere: Inuit Land Use and Occupancy in Labrador*, edited by Carol Brice-Bennett. Nain: Labrador Inuit Association.

Escobar, A. 1992. "Planning." In *The Development Dictionary: A Guide to Knowledge as Power*, edited by W. Sachs. London: Zed Books.

GNL (Government of Newfoundland and Labrador). 2008. "Province Promotes Uranium Development within Its Jurisdiction." Press release, 14 April 2008. http://www.releases.gov.nl.ca/releases/2008/nr/0414n05.htm

Hillier, James. 1971. "Early Patrons of the Labrador Eskimos: The Moravian Mission in Labrador, 1764–1805." In *Patrons and Brokers in the East Arctic*, edited by R. Paine, 89–93. St. John's: ISER Books.

Howitt, R. 2001. *Rethinking Resource Management: Justice, Sustainability, and Indigenous Peoples*. New York: Routledge Press.

INAC (Indian and Northern Affairs Canada). 2005. *Labrador Inuit Land Claims Agreement*. Ottawa: INAC.

Kennedy, John C. 1977. "Northern Labrador: An Ethnohistorical Account." In *The White Arctic: Anthropological Essays on Tutelage and Ethnicity*, edited by R. Paine, 264–305. St. John's: ISER Books.

LIA (Labrador Inuit Association). 1996. *Mineral Development in Northern Labrador*. Pamphlet. Nain: LIA.

Mulrennan, M., and C. Scott. 2001. "Aboriginal Rights and Interests in Canadian Northern Seas." In *Aboriginal Autonomy and Development in Northern Quebec and Labrador*, edited by C. Scott, 78–97. Vancouver: University of British Columbia Press.

Nuttall, M., F. Berkes, B. Forbes, G. Kofinas, T. Vlassova, and G. Wenzel. 2005. "Hunting, Herding, Fishing, and Gathering: Indigenous Peoples and Renewable Resource Use in the Arctic." In *Arctic Climate Impact Assessment,* 649–90. Cambridge: University of Cambridge Press.

Porter, L. 2007. "Producing Forests: A Colonial Genealogy of Environmental Planning in Victoria, Australia." *Journal of Planning Education and Research* 26: 466–77.

RPA (Regional Planning Authority). May 2009. Draft Regional Land Use Plan for the Labrador Inuit Settlement Area. St. John's and Happy Valley–Goose Bay: RPA.

———. December 2009. Draft Regional Land Use Plan for the Labrador Inuit Settlement Area. St. John's and Happy Valley–Goose Bay: RPA.

———. January 2010. Draft Regional Land Use Plan for the Labrador Inuit Settlement Area. St. John's and Happy Valley–Goose Bay: RPA.

RPA (Regional Planning Authority) notes. April 2008. A. Procter, meeting observer.

———. October 2008. A. Procter, meeting observer.

———. May 2009. A. Procter, meeting observer.

———. September 2009. A. Procter, meeting observer.

Reschny, J. 2007. "Mining, Inuit Traditional Activities and Sustainable Development: A Study of the Effects of Winter Shipping at the Voisey's Bay Nickel Mine." Master's thesis, Memorial University of Newfoundland.

Scott, J.C. 1998. *Seeing Like a State: How Certain Schemes to Improve the Human Condition Have Failed.* New Haven: Yale University Press.

Usher, Peter J. 1982. *Renewable Resources in the Future of Northern Labrador.* Nain, Labrador Inuit Association.

Usher, Peter J., M. Baikie, D. Demmer, D. Nakashima, M. Stevenson, and M. Stiles. 1995. *Communicating about Contaminants in Country Food: The Experience in Aboriginal Communities.* Ottawa: Inuit Tapirisat Kanatami.

Williamson, T. 1996. *Seeing the Land is Seeing Ourselves: Labrador Inuit Association Issues Scoping Report.* Nain, Labrador Inuit Association.

———. 1997. *Sina to Sikujâluk: Our Footprint. Mapping Inuit Environmental Knowledge in the Nain District of Northern Labrador.* Nain, Labrador Inuit Association.

Going Forward: Challenges and Opportunities for Nunatsiavut Self-governance

Lawrence Felt, David C. Natcher, and Andrea Procter

As a new government, Nunatsiavut faces important opportunities and challenges in the future. While the land claims agreement and the lengthy negotiating process underlying it will continue to be important benchmarks for understanding how the events of the past have led to political change, it is also important to consider how the past will inform future political decision making. In particular it remains to be seen: 1) how the Labrador Inuit Land Claims Agreement (LILCA) will serve to empower and/or constrain government-to-government relationships while advancing Inuit values and institutions; 2) how the ethnic basis of membership and political representation can be accommodated within Nunatsiavut governance; and 3) how effective Inuit participation in and relationships with other levels of government at regional, provincial, national, and pan-ethnic levels can be best assured.

Before exploring these questions, it is important to differentiate between government and governance. *Government* refers to the specific institutions and structures through which people govern. Institutions of government include legislatures, state bureaucracies, judicial organizations, and executive offices. *Governance* is a broader term that encompasses wider processes and organizations. These include citizen involvement, business organizations, non-governmental organizations, the media, and other associations that increasingly play an important role in how societies and their governments operate (Felt and Natcher 2008; Bowles and Gintis 2002; Graham, Amos, and Plumtre 2003).

The process of governance is well captured by David Freshwater and Stephen Tomblin (2009) as the system of rules, understandings, norms, and protocols through which relations among organizations and groups—governmental, private, and citizen—interact and are managed in the process of decision making. It is through effective governance that a people establish priorities, mediate conflict, and build a common future. In recent years, several essential principles of governance have dramatically changed. Collectively, these changes emphasize the rejection of more aloof, impersonal decision making (constrained governance) in favour of more participatory, devolved governing processes in which hierarchical state structures are seen as outmoded and localized non-governmental organizations play an increasingly important (though informal) role in making important decisions for a people (inclusive governance). The term *civil society* (O'Connell 1999; Putnam 2000) is frequently offered to describe this more horizontal, informal, and participatory process of collective decision making that governments increasingly follow.

The process of governance operates at a number of levels, each of which has varying degrees of linkage to those above and below. These levels include global, national, institutional, and community. While all levels are not necessarily seamlessly integrated, one can more easily appreciate governance patterns at one level if one knows something of adjacent levels. J. Graham, B. Amos, and T. Plumtre (2003, 2) make this point convincingly: "Governance is not only about where to go but also about who should be involved in deciding, and in what capacity." They identify global space, national space, organizational space (including within governments), and community space as four zones where this concept is particularly useful.

The utilization of this wider process of governance therefore expands the arena of intellectual and analytical focus. It allows us to understand "end of line" government decisions within a much broader array of players and reinforces the perspective that government decision making is the final step in a complex and increasingly inclusive process of interaction, lobbying, and negotiation. Thus to best understand the future of Nunatsiavut governance, one needs to understand its complex relationship with regional, provincial, and national levels of government as well as its relationships with its own citizenry.

Empowerment and Constraint in the LILCA

The signing of the land claims agreement and the resulting establishment of Nunatsiavut were simultaneously acts of empowerment and constraint for the Labrador Inuit. The agreement has bestowed upon the Nunatsiavut government considerable power over a wide range of areas, including education, health, renewable resources, culture, land planning, and economic development. While most of these powers are to be shared with other levels of government, there is considerable room for Nunatsiavut to assume larger roles as it wishes in the future. Conversely, the terms of the agreement also impose constraints, perhaps the most obvious one being the organizational structure of the Nunatsiavut government itself. Although ethnically Inuit, with a mandate to protect and extend Inuit cultural values and social institutions, the structure of the new Nunatsiavut government in many ways mirrors those structures found in federal and provincial bureaucracies. The offered rationale for such a close resemblance is that it expedites "government-to-government" communication and co-operation, leading to more effective and timely decision making. Although it is yet to be seen if this form of government is best to advance Nunatsiavut objectives, one hopes that it can empower Nunatsiavut in its future dealings with public and private entities.

Despite its more or less Western organization structure, the Nunatsiavut government has a critical role in preserving traditional culture, including its linguistic foundation and the social relationships upon which it is ultimately based. The Labrador Inuit Constitution, ratified in 2002, outlines the values on which the Nunatsiavut government and its actions should be based. It reflects the balance between maintaining traditional practices and adapting to changing circumstances that has long been a part of Inuit life, and that the new government is now working to find. The importance of Inuit culture is paramount: "Labrador Inuit political, social, cultural and economic institutions exist to consider and provide for Labrador Inuit culture, Labrador Inuit distinctiveness and the aspirations of Labrador Inuit by making policies and laws that meet Labrador Inuit needs, reflect Labrador Inuit culture, customs, traditions, observances, practices and beliefs" (LIA 2002, 1.1.3[r]). The ability to change and adapt is also fundamental, and the constitution states that Nunatsiavut government institutions "must have the freedom to evolve in their own way" and "address innovation and the adaptation of new ideas and technologies in ways that are appropriate to Labrador Inuit needs, values and aspirations" (1.1.3 [t] and [x]). "The Inuit of Labrador have experienced change, new ideas and new technologies which we have integrated into our culture and way of life," the constitution states, and the Nunatsiavut government and its institutions should therefore strive to emulate this adaptive strategy.

Since its establishment in 2005, the Nunatsiavut government has endeavoured to reflect the values of its constitution, despite constant pressure to conform to existing structures and the programs of other governments. For example, during the transition to the Nunatsiavut government in 2005–2006, one minister from the Nunatsiavut government oversaw the Department of Health, Education, and Social and Economic Development, a department that dealt with a range of concerns covered by at least nine corresponding provincial departments (Nunatsiavut Government, 2006a). According to the Nunatsiavut government, this amalgamation "reflects a holistic approach to health, social policy and education, showing how, for the Labrador Inuit, these facets of government are naturally interrelated" (Nunatsiavut Government 2006c). Despite the holistic nature and interrelated focus of the department, it was soon divided into two distinct departments: the Department of Health and Social Development and the Department of Education and Economic Development. The decision to create two departments was based on the administrative need to be more closely aligned with their federal and provincial counterparts (Nunatsiavut Government 2006b: 4; Nunatsiavut Government 2006d, 62). While these two departments maintain broader responsibility than the provincial departments formally hold, and they can arguably better relate to a more holistic manner of approaching governance, the entrenched nature of the federal and provincial government model (and the ideologies that support them) forced the Nunatsiavut government to realign its own departments. Thus in order to promote "efficient" government-to-government relations, the organizational structure of the Nunatsiavut government was reorganized in large part to parallel federal and provincial bureaucracies. Today, each Nunatsiavut government department has a minister, deputy ministers, directors, and staff. Yet filling these positions, and retaining staff, remains an ongoing challenge for a government faced with limited resources and personnel. Continuous changes in personnel can lead to an inability to build an institutional memory, causing delays, inconsistency, and public frustration. Already challenged by a general lack of financial and human resources, Nunatsiavut government bureaucrats may find themselves simply administering existing government programs that they themselves have criticized for being out of step with the priorities and needs of their citizenry. In this sense, the Nunatsiavut government may become complicit in the perpetuation of federal and provincial policies and programs.

A related challenge lies in finding a suitable role for Inuit elders and elder councils (*TungavittalauKit Inutukavut*) in the wider process of governance. Historically, elders performed many of the roles of government, whether in dispute resolution or in responding to social crises. With Moravian pressures for more permanent settlement, elder councils became more formally institutionalized as the most important consultative and governing institution for Inuit residing in communities such as Nain and Hopedale (Brantenberg, 1985a; 1985b). While elders are still held in high respect in Inuit society and culture, there is no formal role for them in the new government. This has left the future role of elders in Nunatsiavut and community governance ill defined (Frederick Andersen, personal communication 2009).

A final challenge involves the role of Inuit Community Governments (ICGs). The general approach contained in the LILCA is one of devolved and decentralized governance (INAC 2005, 17.38–17.43). With this, certain powers, for example in areas of local economic development, have been specifically assigned to ICGs under the constitution. While these powers may enable community leaders to be more than "service providers," those leaders' input into Nunatsiavut government decisions largely occurs through their representation in the Nunatsiavut Assembly. It will be important for the Nunatsiavut government to resist appropriating more powers for itself at the expense of ICGs. At the same time, ICGs must ensure that such decentralization does not promote extensive divisions and a lack of consensus on critical issues, which might undermine Nunatsiavut's dealings with other levels of government.

Ethnic Membership Criteria and Political Representation

As discussed in our introduction, a unique feature of Nunatsiavut is its explicit linkage of ethnicity and political representation in which only those meeting the definition of Inuit under the agreement are permitted to vote and avail of certain services. The current territorial boundaries of Nunatsiavut do not reflect current configurations of Inuit residence, given that nearly half of those listed as beneficiaries by the agreement live outside the land claims settlement area (Nunatsiavut Government 2009b). Given demographic and migration trends, this disjuncture may grow considerably in the future. This situation may in turn put a strain on the relationship between those who live inside and those outside the territory, as the latter are often forced to struggle for access to limited resources and for political influence. The distribution of Nunatsiavut Assembly positions illustrates this potential challenge.

Most members of the Nunatsiavut Assembly represent the coastal communities, whether they are elected members for their community or

AngajukKâk (mayors). The only exception is the president of Nunatsiavut, who is regionally elected by all eligible beneficiaries. The issue of proportional representation is a second priority, so that a community is represented by one member per 1000 beneficiaries. This reliance on community representation means that those named under the agreement but not living in a Nunatsiavut community are, despite their numerical strength, represented by proportionally fewer members. For instance, Nain (population 1,180) has two members and one AngajukKâk, and Rigolet (population 299) has one member and one AngajukKâk. Outside the settlement area, the Upper Lake Melville area, consisting of Happy Valley–Goose Bay/Mud Lake (2,020 beneficiaries in 2009) and North West River (303 beneficiaries in 2009) are represented by two elected members, the chairperson of the NunaKatiget Inuit Community Corporation, and the chairperson of the Sivunivut Community Corporation. Beneficiaries who live outside of Upper Lake Melville and Nunatsiavut in what is called the Canadian Constituency (approximately 2,095 beneficiaries) were represented by only one member of the assembly, although this was increased to two members in the May 2010 elections (Nunatsiavut Government 2009a, 2009b). This emphasis on the interests of communities within Nunatsiavut may translate into decision making that favours keeping Nunatsiavut resources within the settlement area, despite the high concentration of beneficiaries outside the area.

While using ethnic status to define membership offers the advantage of a clear focus and rationale for protecting culture and traditional lifestyle, Thierry Rodon and Minnie Grey (2009) speak to some potential negative consequences as well. In their view, the most important is the creation of a new distinction between beneficiaries and non-beneficiaries who live within the settlement area. Under the terms of the agreement, only beneficiaries can receive a range of important government services in health and education, among other areas. As they indicate, the distinction may be particularly poignant in small communities where beneficiaries and non-beneficiaries alike share the same lifestyle. This issue has been recognized but responses have largely been at the ICG level, where eligibility for voting has been modified, rather than at the larger government level. There is also the bigger, perhaps more speculative, issue concerning the consequences of beneficiary versus citizen status. According to Rodon and Grey (2009, 337), "Beneficiaries have rights, while citizens have not only rights but also a duty to their community." If the number of beneficiaries outside the settlement area continues to grow, and programs to develop a strong sense of identity with and participation in Nunatsiavut are not successfully promoted, challenges of governance could easily arise.

Participation in Wider Levels of Governance

As indicated above, a useful way to think of systems of governance is in terms of scale. To use the Nunatsiavut example, there is a system of governance largely within the land claims society itself articulating who legitimate participants are, their roles, and the general arena in which they operate. One might think of this as the broader social fabric of organizations and sentiment necessary for expansive participation. Above this is yet another system of governance in which Nunatsiavut participates by virtue of its legitimate place as an Aboriginal government in Canada. In between these levels is a system of governance at the Labrador regional level that is composed of town governments, other Aboriginal organizations, numerous non-governmental associations and organizations, numerous private sector organizations, and media outlets. This level of government is affected negatively by government cutbacks and positively by an emergent participatory ideology expressing itself in activities such as local management of state programs, alternative types of service delivery, and a view that "ground up," place-based solutions are far preferable to more typical "top down" solutions. The net result is an expanded arena in which decisions are made and a greater reliance on local delivery of services and programs, which are hopefully more sensitive to local requirements. A largely decentralized and distributive pattern of governance is therefore being created in Labrador at a time when resource development and other economic initiatives pose greater challenges and opportunities than ever before. To prosper, the Inuit and their government, along with all other Labradorians, will need to be part of this larger system of regional governance. Effective engagement within and between these layers of governance is required for the creation of development and a larger society that is most attuned to local needs and desires.

As governance in Labrador becomes increasingly decentralized and more inclusive, local governments, Aboriginal and non-Aboriginal alike, must acquire not only the right to govern but also the capacity to do so. Capacity means, above all, some flexibility with regard to financial autonomy. While the decentralization associated with governance requires a genuine transference of administrative responsibility, a reliable source of funding is equally critical (Natcher and Davis 2007). This will no doubt prove true in Labrador as Aboriginal and non-Aboriginal governments face many new and demanding challenges in the years to come, particularly the challenge of securing financial resources sufficient for implementing programs and services that require extensive activities of governance. Larger governments seem only too willing to "down size" and re-allocate services to lower levels of government without accompanying financial transfers. The result can be intergovernmental tension, with local governments finding themselves in financial vices. Even where sizeable funds are transferred, there are typically extensive limitations attached to their use, which all too often turn local governments into mere dispensers and administrators of programs that they had minimal influence in establishing. This can severely limit the ability of local governments to implement alternative programs and can further alienate local governance participants from the decision-making process.

The Nunatsiavut government is well aware that change, though it has begun, will take many years to craft a government that is fully grounded in the Labrador Inuit experience. Because many elements of Inuit governance have for centuries been undermined by a colonial presence in the name of religious conversion, commerce, and other justifications, many aspects unique to Inuit culture have been weakened and in some cases completely lost. As a result, one cannot realistically expect traditional Inuit institutions of governance to resurface automatically in the wake of the land claims settlement. Rather, success will depend on the rebuilding of trust in Inuit authority and on generating and sustaining effective forms of inter-governmental relations. It is important to emphasize that effective governance is neither automatic nor problem-free. Rather, it is shaped by the traditions, cultures, and social locations of different parties. Where differing political cultures co-exist and participatory traditions of local government are nascent, as they are in Labrador, even those sharing the same general geographical boundaries may have to pursue different paths to governance that is successful for themselves as well as for the region. For the Nunatsiavut government to be successful in the longer term, federal and provincial authorities will need to demonstrate a renewed commitment to the initiatives and self-governing efforts of Nunatsiavut. This includes providing the necessary financial resources to make self-government a reality. Failing to honour these commitments will surely bring about renewed criticism for indifference to the needs of Nunatsiavut and for fostering conditions of continued political dependency. For its part, the Nunatsiavut government will need to reach out to other levels of government to identify and implement effective mechanisms for intergovernmental relations and legislative coordination. As this is done, other players will become relevant, and new, extended systems of governance may evolve. Over time, these changes in government relations will prove critical to the future of Labrador. Success, by any relevant indicator, will be measured over the long term. By virtue of their prominence and recent success, the Labrador Inuit will be an important part of Labrador's social and political fabric. While many of the challenges noted above are not Nunatsiavut's alone, the Nunatsiavut government's responses will have significant implications for the future of Labrador.

This volume has explored the path Labrador's Inuit have followed over several hundred years and shown how that path has led to the land claims agreement and the subsequent formation of Nunatsiavut. Our intent has been to provide a glimpse of the complex history that has brought the Labrador Inuit to this point in time, and to offer some points of reflection on what may await the Labrador Inuit in the future. Having faced even more daunting challenges in the past, the Nunatsiavummiut will no doubt again adapt and thrive through a shared sense of responsibility for the future of Nunatsiavut and for all those who call Labrador home.

References

Bowles, S. and Gintis, H., 2002. Social Capital and Community Governance, *Working Paper 01-01-003*, Santa Fe Institute, www.santafe.edu/sfi/publications/wplist/2001

Brantenberg, Terje. 1985a. "Ethnic Commitments and Local Government in Nain, 1969–1976." In *The White Arctic: Anthropological Essays on Tutelage and Ethnicity: Part Two, Labrador,* edited by R. Paine, 376–410 . St. John's: ISER Books.

_____. 1985b. "Ethnic Values and Ethnic Recruitment in Nain." In *The White Arctic: Anthropological Essays on Tutelage and Ethnicity: Part Two, Labrador,* edited by R. Paine, 326–43. St. John's: ISER Books.

Felt, Lawrence. 2009. "A Tale of Two Towns: Municipal Agency and Economic Development in Akyretri, Iceland and Corner Brook, Newfoundland and Labrador." In *Remote Control: Governance Lessons for and from Small, Insular and Remote Regions,* edited by Godfrey Baldacchino, Rob Greenwood, and Lawrence Felt, 148–69. St. John's: ISER Books.

Felt, Lawrence, and David Natcher. 2008. "Effective Governance in the Changing Political Landscape of Labrador." *Newfoundland Quarterly* 101, 1 (2008): 32–35.

Freshwater, David, and S. Tomblin. "Making Sense of Changing Realities in the "Uncharted Fringe." In *Remote Control: Governance Lessons for and from Small, Insular and Remote Regions,* edited by Godfrey Baldacchino, R. Greenwood, and Lawrence Felt, 19–46. St. John's: ISER Books, 2009.

Graham, J., B. Amos, and T. Plumptre. 2003. "Principles for Good Governance in the 21st Century." Policy Brief No. 15, August 2003. Ottawa: Institute of Governance, University of Ottawa.

INAC (Indian and Northern Affairs Canada). 2005. *Labrador Inuit Land Claims Agreement.* Ottawa: INAC.

LIA (Labrador Inuit Association). 2002. Labrador Inuit Constitution. Nain: LIA.

Natcher, David C., and Susan Davis. 2007. "Rethinking Devolution: Challenges for Aboriginal Resource Management in the Yukon Territory." *Society and Natural Resources* 20, 3: 271–79.

Nunatsiavut Government. 2006a. News Bulletin, February 2006. http://www.nunatsiavut.com/pdfs/newsletters/nunatsiavutgovt_newsletter_02_06_eng.pdf

_____. 2006b. News Bulletin, June 2006. http://www.nunatsiavut.com/pdfs/newsletters/nunatsiavutgovt_newsletter_07_06_eng.pdf

_____. 2006c. Nunatsiavut Government Operations. http://www.nunatsiavut.com/pdfs/Operations_Backgrounder.pdf

_____. 2006d. Hansard of Assembly Meeting, 12–14 October 2006. http://www.nunatsiavut.com/pdfs/October_Hansard_06.pdf

_____. 2009a. "Nunatsiavut Assembly Act Amended to Allow for Additional Elected Member for Canadian Constituency." Press release, 14 December 2009. http://www.nunatsiavut.com/pdfs/Additional_Member_Dec_09.pdf

_____. 2009b. Membership data provided by Beneficiary Office, Nunatsiavut government.

O'Connell, Brian. 1999. *Civil Society: The Underpinnings of American Democracy.* Medford, MA: Tufts University Press.

Putnam, Robert. 2000. *Bowling Alone: The Collapse and Revival of American Community.* New York: Simon and Schuster.

Rodon, Thierry, and Minnie Grey. 2009. "The Long and Winding Road to Self-Government: The Nunavik and Nunatsiavut Experiences." In *Northern Exposure: Peoples, Powers and Prospects in Canada's North,* edited by Frances Abele, Thomas Courchene, Leslie Seidle, and France St-Hilaire, 317–43. Montreal: Institute for Research on Public Policy.

BIBLIOGRAPHY

Archives

Provincial Archives of Newfoundland and Labrador. The Rooms, St. John's.
Library and Archives Canada, Ottawa.
Centre for Newfoundland Studies, Memorial University Archives, St. John's.
Moravian Archives, Muswell Hill, London.

Decisions

Delgamuukw v. British Columbia. 1997. Supreme Court of Canada. www.canlii.
org/en/ca/scc/doc/1997/1997canlii302/1997canlii302.html.

Haida Nation v. British Columbia (Minister of Forests). 2004. Supreme Court of
Canada. www.canlii.org/en/ca/scc/doc/2004/2004scc73/2004scc73.html.

Sources

ACIA. *Impacts of a Warming Climate: Arctic Climate Impact Assessment.*
Cambridge: Cambridge University Press, 2004.

Adger, W.N. "Vulnerability." *Global Environmental Change* 16, 3 (2006): 268–81.

AHDR (Arctic Human Development Report). Akureyri: Stefansson Arctic
Institute, 2004.

Alcantara, C. "Explaining Aboriginal Treaty Negotiation Outcomes in Canada:
The Cases of the Inuit and Innu in Labrador." *Canadian Journal of Political
Science* 40, 1 (2007): 185–207.

Alfred, Taiaiake. *Wasa'se: Indigenous Pathways of Action and Freedom.*
Peterborough: Broadview Press, 2005.

Alix, Claire. "Deciphering the Impact of Change on the Driftwood Cycle.
Contribution to the Study of Human Use of Wood in the Arctic." *Global
and Planetary Change* 47 (2005): 83–98.

Alwang, J., P.B. Siegel, and S.L. Jorgensen. 2001. "Vulnerability." *Spectrum* Sector
Launch Issue, Fall 2001. Washington, DC: Social Protection Unit, Human
Development Network, World Bank.

Ames, Randy. *Social, Economic, and Legal Problems of Hunting in Northern Labrador.* Nain: Labrador Inuit Association, 1977.

Andersen, Toby, and Judy Rowell. "Environmental Implications for the Labrador Inuit of Canada's and Newfoundland's Land Claims Policies." In *Common Ground: Northern People and the Environment,* edited by John Jacobs and William Montevecchi, 29–41. St. John's: ISER Books, 1993.

Andersen, William. "Address at the Opening of Land Claim Negotiations, 22 January 1989." *Northern Perspectives* 18, 2 (1990): 4–5.

_____. President's Message. *Nunatsiavut* 10, 1 (2005): 3. Nain: Labrador Inuit Association.

Anderson, David. "The Development of Settlement in Southern Coastal Labrador with Particular Reference to Sandwich Bay." *Bulletin of Canadian Studies* 8, 1 (1984): 23–49.

Appleton, V.B. "Observations of Deficiency Diseases in Labrador." *American Journal of Public Health* 11 (1921): 617–21.

Arnold, Charles D. "In Search of the Thule Pioneers." In *Thule Pioneers,* edited by E. Bielawski, C. Kobelka, and R. Janes, 1–93. Occasional Paper No. 2. Yellowknife: Prince of Wales Northern Heritage Centre, 1986.

Auger, Reginald. *Labrador Inuit and Europeans in the Strait of Belle Isle: From the Written Sources to the Archaeological Evidence.* Nordicana 55. Quebec City: Centre d'Études Nordiques, Université Laval, 1991.

Aykroyd, W.R. "Vitamin A Deficiency in Newfoundland." *Irish Journal of Medical Sciences* 28 (1928): 161–65.

_____. "Beriberi and Other Food–Deficiency Diseases in Newfoundland and Labrador." *Journal of Hygiene* 30 (1930): 357–86.

Baikie, Maureen. "Perspectives on the Health of the Labrador Inuit." *Northern Perspectives* 18, 2 (1990): www.carc.org/pubs/v18no2/index.html.

Bain, Allison. "Uivak Archaeoentomological Analysis 2." Report on file in the office of Susan A. Kaplan, Bowdoin College, 2000.

Banfield, A.W.F. *The Mammals of Canada.* Toronto: University of Toronto Press, 1974.

Barbour, W. "Labrador Inuit Prepare to Debate Suspending Uranium Mining and Milling." Interview, CBC, 6 April 2008.

Barcham, M. "(De)Constructing the Politics of Indigeneity." In *Political Theory and the Rights of Indigenous Peoples,* edited by D. Ivison, P. Patton, and W. Sanders. Cambridge: Cambridge University Press, 2000.

Barkham, Selma. "Guipuzcoan Shipping in 1571 with Particular Reference to the Decline of the Transatlantic Fishing Industry." In *Anglo-American Contributions to Basque Studies: Essays in Honor of Jon Bilbao,* edited by William A. Douglass, Richard W. Etulain, and William H. Jacobsen Jr., 73–81. Publications on the Social Sciences No. 13. Reno: Desert Research Institute, 1977.

_____. "The Basques: Filling a Gap in our History between Jacques Cartier and Champlain." *Canadian Geographical Journal* 49, 1 (1978): 8–19.

_____. "A Note on the Strait of Belle Isle during the Period of Basque Contact with Indians and Inuit." *Études/Inuit/Studies* 4, 1–2 (1980): 51–58.

Beaudoin, Matthew. "Sweeping the Floor: An Archaeological Examination of a Multi-ethnic Sod House in Labrador (FkBg-24)." Master's thesis, Memorial University of Newfoundland, 2008.

Beazley, Kim. "Interrogating Notions of the Powerless Oustee." *Development and Change* 40, 2 (2009): 219–48.

Ben-Dor, Shmuel. *Makkovik: Eskimos and Settlers in a Labrador Community.* St. John's: ISER Books: 1966.

Berman, M., C. Nicholson, G. Kofinas, J. Tetlichi, and S. Martin. "Adaptation and Sustainability in a Small Arctic Community: Results of an Agent-based Simulation Model." *Arctic* 57, 4 (2004): 401–14.

Berry, J.W. "Acculturation and Adaptation: Health Consequences of Culture Contact among Circumpolar Peoples." *Arctic Medical Research* 49 (1990): 142–50.

Bird, Junius B. *Archaeology of the Hopedale Area, Labrador.* Anthropological Papers of the American Museum of Natural History 39, 2. New York: American Museum of Natural History, 1945.

Bjerregaard, Peter, and T. Kue Young. *The Circumpolar Inuit: Health of a Population in Transition.* Copenhagen: Munksgaard, 1998.

Bodenhorn, Barbara. "'I'm Not a Great Hunter, My Wife Is: Iñupiat and Anthropological Models of Gender." *Études/Inuit/Studies* 14, 1–2 (1990): 55–74.

Boles, Bruce. *Offshore Labrador Biological Studies, 1979: Seals.* St John's: Atlantic Biological Services, 1980.

Bovaird, T., and E. Loffler. "Emerging Trends in Public Management and Governance." *BBS Teaching and Research Review*, 5. 2001. http://www.uwe. ac.uk/bbs/trr/Issue5/Is5intro.pdf.

Bowles, S., and H. Gintis. 2002. Social Capital and Community Governance, *Working Paper 01-01-003*, Santa Fe Institute. http://www.santafe.edu/sfi/ publications/wplist/2001.

Brewster, Natalie. *The Inuit in Southern Labrador: The View from Snack Cove.* Occasional Papers in Northeastern Archaeology No. 15. St. John's: Copetown Press, 2006.

_____. "The Archaeology of Snack Cove 1 and Snack Cove 3." *North Atlantic Archaeology* 1 (2008): 25–42.

Brice-Bennett, Carol, ed. *Our Footprints Are Everywhere: Inuit Land Use and Occupancy in Labrador.* Nain: Labrador Inuit Association, 1977.

_____. "Two Opinions: Inuit and Moravian Missionaries in Labrador 1804–1860." MA thesis, Memorial University of Newfoundland, 1981.

_____. *Renewable Resource Use and Wage Employment in the Economy of Northern Labrador.* St. John's: Royal Commission on Employment and Unemployment, Newfoundland and Labrador, 1986.

_____. "Missionaries as Traders: Moravians and Labrador Inuit, 1771–1860." In *Merchant Credit and Labour Strategies in Historical Perspective*, edited by R. Ommer, 223–46. Fredericton: Acadiensis Press, 1990.

_____. *Dispossessed: The Eviction of Inuit from Hebron, Labrador*. Happy Valley: Labrador Institute of Northern Studies, 1994.

_____. "The Redistribution of the Northern Labrador Inuit Population: A Strategy for Integration and Formula for Conflict." *Zeitschrift für Kanada-Studien* 14, 2 (1994): 95–106.

Briggs, Jean. *Never in Anger: Portrait of an Eskimo Family*. Cambridge: Harvard University Press, 1970.

Broughton, Jack M., and James F. O'Connell. "On Evolutionary Ecology, Selectionist Archaeology, and Behavioral Archaeology." *American Antiquity* 64, 1 (1999): 153–65.

Burch, Ernest S. "The Nonempirical Environment of the Arctic Alaskan Eskimos." *Southwestern Journal of Anthropology* 27, 2 (1971): 148–65.

Burke, Charles. "Nineteenth Century Ceramic Artifacts from a Seasonally Occupied Fishing Station on Saddle Island, Red Bay, Labrador." Master's thesis, Memorial University of Newfoundland, 1991.

Cabak, Melanie. "Inuit Women as Catalysts of Change: An Archaeological Study of 19th Century Northern Labrador." PhD diss., University of South Carolina, 1991.

Collings, Peter, George Wenzel, and Richard G. Condon. "Modern Food Sharing Networks and Community Integration in the Central Canadian Arctic." *Arctic* 51, 4 (1998): 301–14.

Couglan, D., and T. Brannick. *Doing Action Research in Your Own Organization*. Thousand Oaks, CA: Sage Publications, 2007.

Cox, Steven. "Prehistoric Settlement and Culture Change at Okak, Labrador." PhD diss., Harvard University, 1977.

Cruikshank, J. "Glaciers and Climate Change: Perspectives from Oral Tradition." *Arctic* 54, 4 (2001): 377–93.

Curtis, Roger. "Particulars of the Country of Labradore, Extracted from the Papers of the Lieutenant Roger Curtis, of his Majesty's Sloop the Otter, with a Plane-Chart of the Coast." *Philosophical Transactions of the Royal Society* 64 (1774): 372–88.

Dahl, Jens. *Saqqaq: A Inuit Hunting Community in the Modern World*. Toronto: University of Toronto Press, 2000.

Damas, David. *Arctic Villagers, Arctic Migrants*. Montreal and Kingston: McGill-Queen's University Press, 2002.

D'Arrigo, Rosanne, Brendan Buckley, Susan A. Kaplan, and Jim Woollett. "Interannual to Multidecadal Modes of Labrador Climate Variability Inferred from Tree Rings." *Climate Dynamics* 20 (2003): 219–28.

Delanglez, Jean. *The Life and Voyages of Louis Jolliet (1645–1700)*. Chicago: Institute of Jesuit History, 1948.

Department of Indian and Northern Affairs. *Royal Commission on Aboriginal Peoples*. Ottawa: Government of Canada, 1996.

Escobar, A. "Planning." In *The Development Dictionary: A Guide to Knowledge as Power*, edited by W. Sachs. London: Zed Books, 1992.

Fall, James A. "The Division of Subsistence of the Alaska Department of Fish and Game: An Overview of its Research Program and Findings." *Arctic Anthropology* 27, 2 (1990): 68–92.

Feild, E. (Bishop). *Visitation to Sandwich Bay, Autumn 1848*. Report on file with Hans Rollmann. St. John's: Memorial University of Newfoundland, 1848.

Felt, Lawrence. "A Tale of Two Towns: Municipal Agency and Economic Development in Akyretri, Iceland and Corner Brook, Newfoundland and Labrador." In *Remote Control: Governance Lessons for and from Small, Insular and Remote Regions*, edited by Godfrey Baldacchino, Rob Greenwood, and Lawrence Felt, 148–69. St. John's: ISER Books, 2009.

Felt, Lawrence, and David C. Natcher. 2008. "Effective Governance in the Changing Political Landscape of Labrador." *Newfoundland Quarterly* 101, 1 (2008): 32–35.

Ferguson, M.A.D., R.G. Williamson, and F. Messier. "Inuit Knowledge of Long-term Changes in a Population of Arctic Tundra Caribou." *Arctic* 51, 3 (1998): 201–19.

Fitzhugh, William. "Winter Cove 4 and the Point Revenge Occupation of the Central Labrador Coast." *Arctic Anthropology* 15, 2 (1978): 146–74.

_____. "Preliminary Results of the Torngat Archaeological Project." *Arctic* 33 (1980): 585–606.

_____. "Hamilton Inlet and Cartwright Reconnaissance." In *Archaeology in Newfoundland and Labrador 1986: Annual Report #7*, edited by J. Callum Thomson and Jane Sproull Thomson, 164–81. Historic Resources Division, Newfoundland Museum. St. John's: Department of Municipal and Provincial Affairs, 1989.

_____. "Staffe Island 1 and the Northern Labrador Dorset-Thule Succession." In *Threads of Arctic Prehistory: Papers in Honour of William E. Taylor, Jr.*, edited by David Morrison and Jean-Luc Pilon, 239–69. Hull: Canadian Museum of Civilization, 1994.

_____. "Biogeographical Archaeology in the Eastern North American Arctic." *Human Ecology* 25, 3 (1997): 385–418.

Fitzhugh, William, Richard H. Jordan, and Steven Cox. "1977 Field Season Summary Report." Report on file with the Provincial Archaeology Branch, St. John's, Newfoundland and Labrador, 1977.

Fitzhugh, William, Richard H. Jordan, Steven L. Cox, Christopher Nagle, and Susan A. Kaplan. "Report to the Newfoundland Museum on the Torngat Archaeological Project 1978 Field Season." Report on file with the Provincial Archaeology Branch, St. John's, Newfoundland and Labrador, 1978.

Flanagan, P. "Schooling, Souls, and Social Class: The Labrador Inuit." MA thesis, University of New Brunswick, Fredericton, 1984.

Ford, James D., and Barry Smit. "A Framework for Assessing the Vulnerability of Communities in the Canadian Arctic to Risks Associated with Climate Change." *Arctic* 57, 4 (2004): 389–400.

Ford, James D., Barry Smit, Johanna Wandel, Mishak Allurut, Kik Shappa, Harry Ittusarjuat, and Kevin Qrunnut. "Climate Change in the Arctic: Current and Future Vulnerability in Two Inuit Communities in Canada." *The Geographical Journal* 174, 1 (2008): 45–62.

Fortescue, Michael. *Eskimo Orientation Systems.* Man and Society 11. Copenhagen: Meddelelser om Grønland, 1988.

Freeman, Milton. "Renewable Resources, Economics and Native Communities." In *Native Peoples and Renewable Resource Management,* edited by J. Green and J. Smith, 23–37: Edmonton: Alberta Society of Professional Biologists: 1986.

Freshwater, David, and S. Tomblin. "Making Sense of Changing Realities in the "Uncharted Fringe." In *Remote Control: Governance Lessons for and from Small, Insular and Remote Regions,* edited by Godfrey Baldacchino, R. Greenwood, and Lawrence Felt, 19–46. St. John's: ISER Books, 2009.

Furgal, C., and J. Seguin. "Climate Change, Health and Vulnerability in Canadian Northern Aboriginal Communities." *Environmental Health Perspectives* 114, 12 (2006): 1964–70.

Füssel, H.M., and R.J.T. Klein. "Climate Change Vulnerability Assessments: An Evolution of Conceptual Thinking." *Climatic Change* 75, 3 (2006): 301–29.

Giddings, J. Louis, and Douglas D. Anderson. *Beach Ridge Archeology of Cape Krusenstern.* Publications in Archaeology 20. Washington, DC: National Park Service, U.S. Department of the Interior, 1986.

Gombay, N. "The Commoditization of Country Foods in Nunavik: A Comparative Assessment of its Development, Applications, and Significance." *Arctic* 58, 2 (2005): 115–28.

Gosling, W.G. *Labrador: Its Discovery, Exploration and Development.* Facsimile edition. Alston Rivers, London: Elibron Classics, 1910.

Goudie, Elizabeth. *Woman of Labrador.* Agincourt, ON: Book Society of Canada, 1983.

Government of Canada. *Agreement between the Inuit of the Nunavut Settlement Area and Her Majesty in Right of Canada.* Ottawa: Indian and Northern Affairs Canada and Tungavik Federation of Nunavut, 1993.

_____. *Agreement between the Inuit of Labrador and Her Majesty in Right of Canada (Labrador Inuit Land Claims Agreement).* Ottawa: Indian and Northern Affairs Canada, Government of Newfoundland and Labrador and Labrador Inuit Association. Queen's Printer: Ottawa and Labrador Inuit Association, Nain, Labrador. 2005.

_____. *Agreement between Nunavik Inuit and Her Majesty the Queen Concerning Nunavik Land Claims.* Ottawa: Indian and Northern Affairs Canada, 2006.

Government of Newfoundland. *Labrador Conference* (Proceedings). Ottawa: Queens Printer, 1956.

_____. *Report of the Royal Commission of Labrador.* Vol. 6. St. John's: Dollco Printing, 1974.

_____. *A Northern Strategic Plan for Labrador.* St. John's: Department of Labrador and Aboriginal Affairs, 2007.

Grenier, Robert, Marc-André Bernier, and Willis Stevens, eds. *The Underwater Archaeology of Red Bay: Basque Shipbuilding and Whaling in the 16th Century.* Ottawa: Parks Canada Publishing and Depository Services, 2007.

Grønnow, Bjarne. "Blessings and Horrors of the Interior: Ethno-historical Studies of Inuit Perceptions Concerning the Inland Region of West Greenland." *Arctic Anthropology* 46, 1–2, 2010.

Hamilakis, Y., M. Pluciennik, and S. Tarlow. *Thinking through the Body: Archaeologies of Corporeality.* New York: Kluwer Academic/Plenum Publishers, 2002.

Hamilton, Sue, and Ruth Whitehouse. "Phenomenology in Practice: Towards a Methodology for a 'Subjective' Approach." *European Journal of Archaeology* 9, 1 (2006): 31–71.

Handcock, Gordon. "A Cartographic and Toponymic Analysis of the Jens Haven Maps of Coastal Labrador, 1765." In *The 1765 Map of Jens Haven: Linguistic, Toponymic, and Geographical Studies,* edited by Hans Rollmann, 1–23. Report on file. Goose Bay: Labrador Métis Nation, 2007.

Hanrahan, Maura. *Brooks, Buckets, and Komatiks: The Problem of Water Access in Black Tickle.* St. John's: Faculty of Medicine, Memorial University of Newfoundland, 2000.

_____. "Industrialization and the Politicization of Health in Labrador Métis Society." *Canadian Journal of Native Studies* 20, 2 (2002): 231–50.

_____. *The Lasting Breach: The Omission of Aboriginal People from the Terms of Union between Newfoundland and Canada and its Ongoing Impacts.* Report for the Royal Commission on Renewing and Strengthening our Place in Canada. Ottawa: Indian and Northern Affairs Canada, 2003.

Hanrahan, Maura, and Marg Ewtushik, eds. *A Veritable Scoff: Sources on Foodways and Nutrition in Newfoundland and Labrador.* St. John's: Flanker Press, 2001.

Hare, F.K. "The Climate of the Eastern Canadian Arctic and Subarctic." PhD diss., University of Montreal, 1950.

Hart, Keith. "Bureaucratic Form and the Informal Economy." In *Linking the Formal and Informal Economy—Concepts and Policies,* edited by Basudeb Guha-Khasnobis, Ravi Kanbur, and Elinor Ostrom, 21–35. Oxford: Oxford University Press, 2006.

Haven, Jens. "A Brief Account of the Dwelling Places of the Eskimaux to the North of Nagvack to Hudson Straits, Their Situation and Subsistence." Unpublished translation by James Hiller on file at the Centre for Newfoundland Studies, Memorial University of Newfoundland, St. John's, 1773.

_____. "Extract of the Voyage of the Sloop George from Nain to Reconnoitre the Northern Parts of Labradore in the Months of August and September, 1773." Copy of manuscript on file at the Centre for Newfoundland Studies, Memorial University of Newfoundland, St. John's, 1773.

Hawkes, E.W. *The Labrador Eskimo*. Canadian Department of Mines, Geological Survey Memoir 91, Anthropological Series No. 14. 1916. Ottawa: Government Printing Bureau, 1970.

Haysom, Veryan. "The Struggle for Recognition: Labrador Inuit Negotiations for Land Rights and Self-government." *Études/Inuit/Studies* 16, 1–2 (1992): 179–97.

Hiller, James. "Early Patrons of the Labrador Eskimos: The Moravian Mission in Labrador, 1764–1805." In *Patrons and Brokers in the East Arctic*, edited by R. Paine, 89–93. St. John's: ISER Books, 1971.

Holland, Robert. "Newfoundland and the Pattern of British Decolonization." In "Confederation," special issue, *Newfoundland and Labrador Studies* 14, 2 (1998): 141–53.

Holloway, G., and T. Sou. "Has Arctic Sea Ice Rapidly Thinned?" *Journal of Climate* 15 (2002): 1691–1701.

Holmes, W.H. *Handbook of Aboriginal American Antiquities*. Washington, DC: Government Printing Office, 1919.

Hood, Bryan. "Pre-Dorset/Maritime Archaic Social Boundaries in Labrador." In *Identities and Culture Contacts in the Arctic*, edited by Martin Appelt, Joel Berglund, and Hans Christian Gullov, 120–28. Copenhagen: Danish National Museum and Danish Polar Center, 2000.

Horwood, Harold. "Policy in Labrador Part I." Political Notebook, *St. John's Evening Telegram*, 1952.

_____. "Policy in Labrador Part II." Political Notebook, *St. John's Evening Telegram*, 1952.

Howitt, R. *Rethinking Resource Management: Justice, Sustainability, and Indigenous Peoples*. New York: Routledge Press, 2001.

Hund, A. "From Subsistence to the Cash-Based Economy: Alterations in the Inuit Family Structure, Values, and Expectations." Paper presented at the annual meeting of the American Sociological Association, San Francisco, CA, 2004. http://www.allacademic.com/meta/p108826_index.html

Huntington, H.P. "Observations on the Utility of the Semi-directive Interview for Documenting Traditional Ecological Knowledge." *Arctic* 51, 3 (1998): 237–42.

Hutton, Samuel K. *A Thesis on the Health and Diseases of the Eskimos*. Derby: James Harwood, 1909.

Imai, S. *Aboriginal Law Handbook*, 3rd edition. Olthius, Kleer, Townshend, corporate authors. Toronto: Thomson Carswell, 2008.

INAC (Indian and Northern Affairs Canada). *Western Arctic Land Claim: The Inuvialuit Final Agreement*. Ottawa: INAC, 1984.

_____. *Agreement between the Inuit of the Nunavut Settlement Area and Her Majesty the Queen in Right of Canada.* Ottawa: INAC and the Tungavik Federation of Nunavut, 1993.

_____. *Labrador Inuit Land Claims Agreement.* Ottawa: INAC, 2005.

IPCC (Intergovernmental Panel on Climate Change). *Climate Change 2007: Impacts, Adaptation and Vulnerability: Contribution of Working Group II to the Fourth Assessment Report of the Intergovernmental Panel on Climate Change*, edited by M.L. Parry, O.F. Canziani, J.P Palutikof, P.J. van der Linden, and C.E. Hanson. Cambridge: Cambridge University Press, 2007.

Jackson, Lawrence. *Bounty of a Barren Coast: Resource Harvest and Settlement in Southern Labrador, Phase One.* Calgary: PetroCanada Explorations, 1982.

Jahn, R.G., P. Devereux, and M. Ibison. "Acoustical Resonances of Assorted Ancient Structures." *Journal of the Acoustical Society of America* 99, 2 (1996): 649–58.

Jenness, Diamond. *Eskimo Administration, Vol. III: Labrador.* Technical Paper No. 16. Calgary: Arctic Institute of North America, 1965.

Johnson, G. "Nutritional Deficiency Diseases in Newfoundland and Labrador: Their Recognition and Elimination." Unpublished paper, n.d., c. 1980.

Jordan, Richard H. "Archaeological Investigations of the Hamilton Inlet Labrador Eskimo: Social and Economic Responses to European Contact." *Arctic Anthropology* 15, 2 (1978): 175–85.

Jordan, Richard H., and Susan A. Kaplan. "An Archaeological View of the Inuit/ European Contact Period in Central Labrador." *Études/Inuit/Studies* 4, 1–2 (1980): 35–45.

Jorgenson, Joseph G. *Effects of Renewable Resource Harvest Disruptions on Socioeconomic and Sociocultural Systems: Norton Sound.* Social and Economic Studies Program Technical Report No. 90. Anchorage: United States Department of Interior, Minerals Management Service Alaska, OCS Region, 1984.

Jurakic, Irena. "Up North: European Ceramics and Tobacco Pipes at the Nineteenth-century Contact Period Inuit Winter Village Site of Kongu (IgCv-7), Nachvak Fiord, Northern Labrador." MA thesis, Memorial University of Newfoundland, 2007.

Kaplan, Susan. "Neo-Eskimo Occupations of the Northern Labrador Coast." *Arctic* 33, 3 (1980): 646–58.

_____. "Economic and Social Change in Labrador Neo-Eskimo Culture." PhD diss., Bryn Mawr College, 1983.

_____. "European Goods and Socio-economic Change in Early Labrador Inuit Society." In *Cultures in Contact: The European Impact on Native Cultural Institutions in Eastern North America, A.D. 1000–1800*, edited by W.W. Fitzhugh, 45–70. Washington, DC: Smithsonian Institution Press, 1985.

_____. "From Forested Bays to Tundra Covered Passes: Transformation of the Labrador Landscape." In *On Track of the Thule Culture from Bering*

Strait to East Greenland, edited by Bjarne Grønnow, 119–28. Studies in Archaeology and History, Vol. 15. Copenhagen: National Museum, 2009.

Kaplan, Susan A., and James M. Woollett. "Challenges and Choices: Exploring the Interplay between Climate, History, and Culture on Canada's Labrador Coast." *Arctic, Antarctic, and Alpine Research* 32, 3 (2000): 351–59.

Keenleyside, A. "Euro-American Whaling in the Canadian Arctic: Its Effects on Eskimo Health." *Arctic Anthropology* 27, 1 (1990): 1–19.

Kemmis, S., and R. McTaggart. "Participatory Action Research." In *Handbook of Qualitative Research*, 2nd ed., edited by N.K. Denzin and Y. S. Lincoln, 567–605. Thousand Oaks, CA: Sage Publications, 2000.

Kennedy, John C. *Brief to the Royal Commission*. St. John's: ISER, 1973.

_____. *Holding the Line: Ethnic Boundaries in a Northern Labrador Community*. St. John's: ISER, 1982.

_____. *People of the Bays and Headlands: Anthropological History and the Fate of Communities in the Unknown Labrador*. Toronto: University of Toronto Press, 1995.

_____. "New Foods, Lost Foods: Local Knowledge about Changing Resources in Coastal Labrador." In *Resetting the Kitchen Table: Food Security, Culture, Health and Resilience in Coastal Communities*, edited by Christopher Parrish et. al., 87–98. New York: Nova Science Publishers, 2007.

_____. "Two Worlds of Eighteenth-Century Labrador Inuit." In *Moravian Beginnings in Labrador: Papers from a Symposium Held in Makkovik and Hopedale*, edited by H. Rollman, 23–36. St. John's: Newfoundland and Labrador Studies, 2009.

King, Judith E. *Seals of the World*. 2nd edition. Oxford: Oxford University Press, 1983.

Kleivan, Helga. *The Eskimos of North-East Labrador: A History of Eskimo-White Relations 1771–1955*. Oslo: Norsk Polar-Institut, 1966.

Kohlmeister, Benjamin and George Kmoch. *Journal of a Voyage from Okkak, on the Coast of Labrador, to Ungava Bay, Westward of Cape Chudleigh Undertaken to explore the Coast, and visit the Esquimaux in that unknown Region*. London: W. McDowell, 1814.

Krupnik, I., and D. Jolly. *The Earth is Faster Now: Indigenous Observations of Arctic Environmental Change*. Fairbanks, AK: Arctic Research Consortium of the United States, 2002.

Kruse, Jack. "Alaska Inupiat Subsistence and Wage Employment Patterns: Understanding Individual Choice." *Human Organization* 50, 4 (1991): 317–626.

Kulchyski, P., and F. Tester. *Kiumajut (Talking Back): Game Management and Inuit Rights, 1900–1970*. Vancouver: University of British Columbia Press, 2007.

Kuhnlein, Harriet V., and Nancy J. Turner. *Traditional Plant Foods of Canadian Indigenous Peoples: Nutrition, Botany and Use*. Vol. 8, Food and Nutrition

Bibliography 273

in History and Anthropology. Philadelphia: Gordon and Breach Science Publishers, 1991.

Laeyendecker, Dosia. "Analysis of Wood and Charcoal Samples from Inuit Sites in Frobisher Bay." In *The Meta Incognita Project,* edited by S. Alsford, 199–210. Contributions to Field Studies, Vol. 6. Gatineau, QC: Canadian Museum of Civilization, 1993.

Laugrand, Frédéric, and Jarich Oosten. "*Qupirruit*: Insects and Worms in Inuit Traditions." *Arctic Anthropology* 47, 1 (2010).

Laugrand, Frédéric, Jarich Oosten, and François Trudel. "Hunters, Owners, and Givers of Light: The Tuurngait of South Baffin Island." *Arctic Anthropology* 39, 1–2 (2002): 27–50.

Lazenby, M.E. Colleen. "Prehistoric Sources of Chert in Northern Labrador: Field Work and Preliminary Analysis." *Arctic* 33, 3 (1980): 628–45.

LIA (Labrador Inuit Association). *Mineral Development in Northern Labrador.* Pamphlet. Nain: LIA, 1996.

_____. *Labrador Inuit Constitution.* Nain: LIA, 2002.

Little, J.M. "An Eskimo 'Deficiency Disease.'" *Boston Medical and Surgical Journal* 176, 18 (1917): 642–43.

Loder, Millicent Blake. *Daughter of Labrador.* St. John's: Harry Cuff Publications, 1989.

Logan, Judith A., and James A. Tuck. "A Sixteenth Century Basque Whaling Port in Southern Labrador." *Association for Preservation Technology International,* Bulletin 22, 3 (1990): 65–72.

Lonner, Thomas D. 1980. *Subsistence as an Economic System in Alaska: Theoretical and Policy Implications.* Technical Paper No. 67. Anchorage: Alaska Department of Fish and Game, Division of Subsistence.

Loren, Diana DiPaolo. "Beyond the Visual: Considering the Archaeology of Colonial Sounds." *International Journal of Historical Archaeology* 12 (2008): 360–69.

Loring, Stephen. "Princes and Princesses of Ragged Fame: Innu (Naskapi) Archaeology and Ethnohistory in Labrador." PhD diss., University of Massachusetts, 1992.

_____. "'And they took away the stones from Ramah: Lithic Raw Material Sourcing and Eastern Arctic Archaeology." In *Honoring Our Elders: A History of Eastern Arctic Archaeology*, edited by William Fitzhugh, Stephen Loring, and Daniel Odess, 163–85. Washington, DC: Arctic Studies Center, Smithsonian Institution, 2002.

Loring, Stephen, and Beatrix Arendt. "'…they gave Hebron, the city of refuge…' (Joshua 21:13): An Archaeological Reconnaissance at Hebron, Labrador." *Journal of the North Atlantic* Special Volume 1(2009): 33–56.

Loring, Stephen, and Melanie Cabak. "A Set of Very Fair Cups and Saucers: Stamped Ceramics as an Example of Inuit Incorporation." *International Journal of Historical Archaeology* 4, 1 (2000): 34–52.

Loring, Stephen, and Leah Rosenmeier, eds. *Angutiup Ânguanga*/Anguti's Amulet. Central Coast of Labrador Archaeology Partnership. Truro, NS: Eastern Woodland Publishing, Millbrook First Nation, 2005.

LRAC (Labrador Resources Advisory Council). 1976. Meeting of LRAC held in Happy Valley–Goose Bay, 18–20 October 1976.

McCartney, Allen P. "The Nature of Thule Eskimo Whale Use." *Arctic* 33, 3 (1980): 517–41.

McGhee, Robert. "Radiocarbon Dating and the Timing of the Thule Migration." In *Identities and Cultural Contacts in the Arctic*, edited by Martin Appelt, Joel Berglund, and Hans Christian Gulløv, 181–91. Copenhagen: Danish National Museum and Danish Polar Centre, 2000.

Mackey, Mary G. Alton. *Country Food Use in Selected Labrador Coast Communities, Comparative Report, June–July 1980 and June–July 1981*. St. John's: Faculty of Medicine, Memorial University of Newfoundland, 1984.

———. *An Evaluation of Household Country Food Use, Black Tickle, Labrador, July 1980–June 1981*. St. John's: Faculty of Medicine, Memorial University of Newfoundland, 1984.

———. *An Evaluation of Household Country Food Use, Makkovik, Labrador, July 1980–June 1981*. St. John's: Faculty of Medicine, Memorial University of Newfoundland, 1984.

———. *An Evaluation of Household Country Food Use, Nain, Labrador, July 1980–June 1981*. St. John's: Faculty of Medicine, Memorial University of Newfoundland, 1984.

———. *An Evaluation of Household Country Food Use, St. Lewis, Labrador, July 1980–June 1981*. St. John's: Faculty of Medicine, Memorial University of Newfoundland, 1984.

———. "The Impact of Imported Foods on the Traditional Inuit Diet." *Arctic Medical Research* 47 (Supp. 1, 1988): 128–33.

Mackey, Mary G. Alton, and K.M. Boles. *The Birthing of Nutrition Education in Labrador: A Summary Report*. Goose Bay: Labrador Institute of Northern Studies, Memorial University of Newfoundland, n.d., c. 1984.

Mackey, Mary G. Alton, and Robin D. Orr. "Infant Feeding Practices in Metropolitan, Urban and Small Communities in Newfoundland." *Journal of Canadian Dietetic Association* 39 (1978): 236.

———. "Country Food Use in Makkovik, Labrador, July 1980 to June 1981." *Proceedings of the Sixth International Symposium on Circumpolar Health*, edited by R. Fortune, special issue of *Circumpolar Health* 84 (1985).

———. "The Seasonal Nutrient Density of Country Food Harvested in Makkovik, Labrador." *Arctic* 41, 2 (1988): 105–09.

McKim, E.M. Laryea, S. Banoub-Baddour, K. Matthews, and K. Webber. "Infant–feeding Practices in Coastal Labrador." *Journal of the Canadian Dietetic Association* 59, 1 (1998): 41.

McLaren, Ian A. *The Biology of the Ringed Seal* (Phoca hispida schreber) *in the Eastern Canadian Arctic.* Bulletin 118. Ottawa: Fisheries Research Board of Canada, 1958.

Magdanz, James S., Charles J. Utermohle, and Robert J. Wolfe. *The Production and Distribution of Wild Food in Wales and Deering, Alaska.* Technical Paper No. 259. Juneau: Alaska Department of Fish and Game, Division of Subsistence, 2002.

Maggo, Paulus. *Remembering the Years of My Life: Journeys of an Inuit Hunter,* edited by Carol Brice-Bennett. St. John's: ISER Books, 1999.

Marcus, Alan Rudolph. *Relocating Eden: The Image and Politics of Inuit Exile in the Canadian Arctic.* Hanover and London: Dartmouth College, University Press of New England, 1995.

Marks, Stuart S. "Hunting Behavior and Strategies of the Valley Bisa in Zambia." *Human Ecology* 5, 1 (1977): 1–36.

Martin, Joanne. "We Knew Hard Work, Them Days." *Stories of Early Labrador* 2, 1 (1976): 41–45.

Meyers, Heather, Stephanie Powell, and Gerard Duhaime. "Food Production and Sharing in Nunavut: Not Only Discourse, But Reality." In *Arctic Food Security,* edited by Gerard Duhaime and Nick Bernard, 121–38. Edmonton: Canadian Circumpolar Institute Press, 2008.

Montevecchi, W.A., H. Chaffey, and C. Burke. "Hunting for Security: Changes in the Exploitation of Marine Birds in Newfoundland and Labrador." In *Resetting the Kitchen Table: Food Security, Culture, Health and Resilience in Coastal Communities,* edited by Christopher Parrish et. al., 99–114. New York: Nova Science Publishers, 2007.

Mulrennan, M., and C. Scott. "Aboriginal Rights and Interests in Canadian Northern Seas." In *Aboriginal Autonomy and Development in Northern Quebec and Labrador,* edited by C. Scott, 78–97. Vancouver: University of British Columbia Press, 2001.

Nagle, Christopher L. "Lithic Raw Materials Procurement and Exchange in Dorset Culture Along the Labrador Coast." PhD diss., Brandeis University, 1984.

Natcher, David C. "Subsistence and the Social Economy of the Aboriginal North." *Northern Review* 30 (Spring 2009): 69–84.

Natcher, David C, and Susan Davis. "Rethinking Devolution: Challenges for Aboriginal Resource Management in the Yukon Territory." *Society and Natural Resources* 20, 3 (2007): 271–79.

Natcher, David C., Lawrence Felt, Andrea Procter, and the Nunatsiavut Government. "Monitoring Food Security in Nunatsiavut, Labrador." Special issue, *Plan Canada* 49, 2 (2009): 52–55.

Naves, Liliana C. *Alaska Migratory Bird Subsistence Harvest Estimates, 2004–2007.* Technical Paper 349. Anchorage: Alaska Department of Fish and Game, Subsistence Division, 2009.

Neale, Walter C. "Monetization, Commercialization, Market Orientation, and Market Dependence." In *Studies in Economic Anthropology*, edited by G. Dalton, 25–29. Washington, DC: American Anthropological Association, 1971.

Neis, Barbara, and Lawrence Felt. *Finding Our Sea Legs: Linking Fishery People and Their Knowledge with Science and Management.* St. John's: ISER Books, 2000.

Nelson, Mark, David C. Natcher, and Clifford G. Hickey. "The Role of Natural Resources in Community Sustainability." In *Seeing Beyond the Trees: The Social Dimensions of Aboriginal Forest Management*, edited by David C. Natcher, 38–49.Concord, ON: Captus Press, 2008.

Nickels, S., C. Fugal, M. Buell, and H. Moquin. *Unikkaaqatigiit—Putting the Human Face on Climate Change, Perspectives from Inuit in Canada.* Ottawa: Inuit Tapiriit Kanatami, Nusivvik Centre for Inuit Health, and Changing Environments at Université Laval and the Ajunnginiq Centre at the National Aboriginal Health Organization, 2006.

Northland Associates. 1986. *Native Waterfowl Harvest in Coastal Labrador.* Prepared under Supply and Services Canada Tender: KL 103-0-0398.

Nunavut Wildlife Management Board (NWMB). 2004. Nunavut Wildlife Harvest Study. Available from NWMB: Nunavut, Canada. http://www.nwmb.com/english/resources/harvest_study/NWHS 2004 Report.pdf.

Nuttall, Mark, Fikret Berkes, Bruce Forbes, Gary Kofinas, Tatiana Vlassova, and George Wenzel. "Hunting, Herding, Fishing and Gathering: Indigenous Peoples and Renewable Resource Use in the Arctic." In *Arctic Climate Impact Assessment*, 649–90. Cambridge: University of Cambridge Press, 2005.

O'Connell, Brian. *Civil Society: The Underpinnings of American Democracy.* Medford, MA: Tufts University Press, 1999.

Oswalt, W.H. *Bashful No Longer: An Alaskan Eskimo Ethnohistory, 1778-1988.* Norman: University of Oklahoma Press, 1990.

Otto, John Solomon. "Artifacts and Status Differences: A Comparison of Ceramics from Planter, Overseer and Slave Sites on an Antebellum Plantation." In *Research Strategies in Historical Archaeology*, edited by Stanley South, 91–118. New York: Academic Press, 1977.

Packard, A.S. "Notes on the Labrador Eskimo and their Former Range Southward." *American Naturalist* 19 (1885): 471–81, 533–560.

Paine, R., ed. *The White Arctic: Anthropological Essays on Tutelage and Ethnicity: Part Two, Labrador.* St John's: ISER Books.

Park, Robert W. "The Dorset-Thule Succession Revisited." In *Identities and Cultural Contacts in the Arctic*, edited by Martin Appelt, Joel Berglund, and Hans Christian Gulløv, 192–205. Copenhagen: Danish National Museum and Danish Polar Centre, 2000.

Parrish, Christopher C., N.J. Turner, and S.M. Solberg. *Resetting the Kitchen Table: Food Security, Culture, Health and Resilience in Coastal Communities*. New York: Nova Science Publishers, 2007.

Payette, S., L. Filon, L. Gauthier, and Y. Boutin. "Secular Climate Change in Old-growth Tree-line Vegetation of Northern Quebec." *Nature* 315 (1985): 135–38.

Peacock, F.W. "Some Psychological Aspects of the Impact of the White Man upon the Labrador Eskimo." Master's thesis, McGill University, 1959.

Peterson, Randolph, L. *The Mammals of Eastern Canada*. Oxford: Oxford University Press, 1966.

Petrone, Penny, ed. *Northern Voices: Inuit Writing in English*. Toronto: University of Toronto Press, 1988.

Pinhorn, A.T. *Living Marine Resources of Newfoundland-Labrador: Status and Potential*. Fisheries Research Board of Canada Bulletin 194. Ottawa: Department of the Environment, Fisheries and Marine Service, 1976.

Porter, L. "Producing Forests: A Colonial Genealogy of Environmental Planning in Victoria, Australia." *Journal of Planning Education and Research* 26 (2007): 466–77.

Putnam, Robert. *Bowling Alone: The Collapse and Revival of American Community*. New York: Simon and Schuster, 2000.

Rankin, Lisa. *The Porcupine Strand Archaeology Project: Interim Report on the 2001 Field Season*. On File, Provincial Archaeology Office. St. John's: Department of Tourism, Culture and Recreation, 2002.

———. *The Porcupine Strand Archaeology Project: Interim Report on the 2002 Field Season*. On File, Provincial Archaeology Office. St. John's: Department of Tourism, Culture and Recreation, 2003.

———. *The Porcupine Strand Archaeology Project: Interim Report on the 2003 Field Season*. On File, Provincial Archaeology Office. St. John's: Department of Tourism, Culture and Recreation, 2004.

———. *The Porcupine Strand Archaeology Project: Interim Report on the 2004 Field Season*. On File, Provincial Archaeology Office. St. John's: Department of Tourism, Culture and Recreation, 2006.

———. *An Archaeological View of the Thule/Inuit Occupation of Labrador*. Goose Bay: Report on File with the Labrador Métis Nation, 2009.

———. *The Porcupine Strand Archaeology Project: Interim Report on the 2006 Field Season*. On File, Provincial Archaeology Office. St. John's: Department of Tourism, Culture and Recreation, 2009.

Reason, P., and H. Bradbury, eds. *Handbook of Action Research: Participative Inquiry and Practice*. Thousand Oaks, CA: Sage Publications, 2001.

Reschny, J. "Mining, Inuit Traditional Activities and Sustainable Development: A Study of the Effects of Winter Shipping at the Voisey's Bay Nickel Mine." Master's thesis, Memorial University of Newfoundland, 2007.

Richling, B. "Hard Times, Them Times: An Interpretative Ethnohistory of Inuit and Settlers in the Hopedale District of Northern Labrador." PhD diss., McGill University, 1978.

Robbins, L., and F.L. Little. "Subsistence Hunting and Natural Resource Extraction: St. Lawrence Island." *Society and Natural Resources* 1 (1988): 17–29.

Roberts, B.A., N.P.P. Simon, and K.W. Deering. "The Forests and Woodlands of Labrador, Canada: Ecology, Distribution and Future Management." *Ecological Research* 21, 6 (2006): 868–80.

Rockman, Marcy. "Knowledge and Learning in the Archaeology of Colonization." In *Colonization of Unfamiliar Landscapes: The Archaeology of Adaptation*, edited by Marcy Rockman and James Steele, 3–24. New York: Routledge, 2003.

Rockwood, W.G. *Memorandum on General Policy in Respect to the Indians and Eskimos of Northern Labrador.* St. John's: Department of Public Welfare, 1955.

Rodon, Thierry, and Minnie Grey. "The Long and Winding Road to Self-government: The Nunavik and Nunatsiavut Experiences." In *Northern Exposure: Peoples, Powers and Prospects in Canada's North*, edited by Frances Abele, Thomas Courchene, Leslie Seidle, and France St-Hilaire, 317–43. Montreal: Institute for Research on Public Policy, 2009.

Rollmann, Hans. "Religion, Society, and Culture in Newfoundland and Labrador." N.d. http://www.ucs.mun.ca/~hrollman/.

Romero, Aldemaro, and Shelly Kannada. "Comment on 'genetic analysis of 16th-century whale bones prompts a revision of the impact of Basque whaling on right and bowhead whales in the western north Atlantic.'" *Canadian Journal of Zoology* 84 (2006): 1059–65.

Rosenzweig, C., G. Casassa, D.J. Karoly, A. Imeson, C. Liu, A. Menzel, S. Rawlins, T.L. Root, B. Seguin, and P. Tryjanowski. "Assessment of Observed Changes and Responses in Natural and Managed Systems." In *Climate Change 2007: Impacts, Adaptation and Vulnerability: Contribution of Working Group II to the Fourth Assessment Report of the Intergovernmental Panel on Climate Change*, edited by M.L. Parry, O.F. Canziani, J.P Palutikof, P.J. van der Linden, and C.E. Hanson. Cambridge: Cambridge University Press, 2007.

RPA (Regional Planning Authority). Draft Regional Land Use Plan for the Labrador Inuit Settlement Area, May 2009. St. John's and Happy Valley–Goose Bay: RPA.

———. Draft Regional Land Use Plan for the Labrador Inuit Settlement Area, December 2009. St. John's and Happy Valley–Goose Bay: RPA.

Sahlins, Marshall. "The Intensity of Domestic Production in Primitive Societies: Social Inflections of the Chayanov Slope." In *Studies in Economic Anthropology*, edited by G. Dalton, 30–51. Washington, DC: American Anthropological Association, 1971.

Saladin D'Anglure, Bernard. «Du foetus au chamane: la construction d'un "troisième sexe" inuit, *Études/Inuit/Studies* 10, 1–2 (1986): 25–114.

Sandlos, John. *Hunters at the Margin: Native People and Wildlife Conservation in the Northwest Territories.* Vancouver: University of British Columbia Press, 2007.

Savelle, James M., and Junko Habu. "A Processual Investigation of a Thule Whale Bone House: Somerset Island, Arctic Canada." *Arctic Anthropology* 41, 2 (2004): 204–21.

Savelle James M., and Allen P. McCartney. "Thule Inuit Bowhead Whaling: A Biometrical Analysis." In *Threads of Arctic Prehistory: Papers in Honour of William E Taylor Jr.*, edited by D. Morrison and J-L Pilon, 281–310. Archaeological Survey of Canada Mercury Series Paper 149. Hull: Canadian Museum of Civilization, 1994.

Scarre, Chris, and Graeme Lawson, eds. *Archaeoacoustics.* Cambridge: McDonald Institute for Archaeological Research, 2006.

Schaefer, Otto. "Changing Dietary Patterns in the Canadian North: Health, Social and Economic Consequences." *Canadian Dietetic Association Journal* 38, 1 (1977): 17–25.

Schledermann, Peter. "The Thule Tradition in Northern Labrador." MA thesis, Memorial University of Newfoundland, 1971.

Scott, Colin, ed. *Aboriginal Autonomy and Development in Northern Quebec and Labrador.* Vancouver: University of British Columbia Press, 2001.

Scott, J.C. *Seeing Like a State: How Certain Schemes to Improve the Human Condition Have Failed.* New Haven: Yale University Press, 1998.

Searles, E. "Anthropology in an Era of Inuit Empowerment." In *Critical Inuit Studies: An Anthology of Contemporary Arctic Ethnography,* edited by P. Stern and L. Stevenson, 89–101. Lincoln: University of Nebraska Press, 2006.

Sheppard, W.L. "Population Movements, Interaction, and Legendary Geography." *Arctic Anthropology* 35, 2 (1998): 147–65.

Skeates, Robin. "Making Sense of the Maltese Temple Period: An Archaeology of Sensory Experience and Perception." *Time and Mind* 1, 2 (2008): 207–38.

Smit, Barry, and J. Wandel. "Adaptation, Adaptive Capacity and Vulnerability." *Global Environmental Change* 16, 3 (2006): 282–92.

Smith, E.A. *Inujjuamiut Foraging Strategies: Evolutionary Ecology of an Arctic Hunting Economy.* New York: Aldine De Gruyter, 1991.

Spiess, Arthur. "Caribou, Walrus and Seals: Maritime Archaic Subsistence in Labrador and Newfoundland." In *Archaeology of Eastern North America: Papers in Honour of Stephen Williams,* edited by James B. Stoltman, 73–100. Archaeological Report No. 25. Jackson, MS: Department of Archives and History, 1993.

Stanek, Ronald T., Davin L. Holen, and Crystal Wassillie. *Harvest and Uses of Wild Resources in Tyonek and Beluga, Alaska, 2005–2006.* Technical Paper No. 321. Anchorage: Alaska Department of Fish and Game, Division of Subsistence, 2007.

Stern, P. "From Area Studies to Cultural Studies to a Critical Inuit Studies." In *Critical Inuit Studies: An Anthology of Contemporary Arctic Ethnography,* edited by P. Stern and L. Stevenson, 253–66. Lincoln: University of Nebraska Press, 2006.

Steward, Julian H. *The Theory of Culture Change.* Urbana: University of Illinois Press, 1955.

_____. "Eighteenth Century Labrador Inuit in England." *Arctic* 62, 1 (2009): 45–64.

Stopp, Marianne P. "Reconsidering Inuit Presence in Southern Labrador." *Études/Inuit/Studies* 26, 2 (2002): 71–108.

Stroeve, J., M.M. Holland, W. Meier, T. Scambos, and M. Serreze. "Arctic Sea Ice Decline: Faster than Forecasted." *Geophysical Research Letters* 34 (2007): 1–5.

Sturtevant, W.C. "The First Inuit Depiction by Europeans." *Études/Inuit/Studies* 4 (1980): 47–49.

Tanner, Adrian. "The Aboriginal Peoples of Newfoundland and Labrador and Confederation." In "Confederation," special issue, *Newfoundland and Labrador Studies* 14, 2 (1998): 238–52.

Tanner, Adrian, John C. Kennedy, Susan McCorquodale, and Gordon Inglis. *Aboriginal Peoples and Governance in Newfoundland and Labrador.* St. John's: Royal Commission on Aboriginal Peoples, 1994.

Taylor, J. Garth. *Labrador Eskimo Settlements of the Early Contact Period.* National Museums of Canada Publications in Ethnology, 9. Ottawa: National Museums of Canada, 1974.

_____. "The Inuit of Southern Quebec-Labrador: Reviewing the Evidence." *Études/Inuit/Studies* 4, 1–2 (1980): 185–93.

_____. "Labrador Inuit Whale Use during the Early Contact Period." *Arctic Anthropology* 25, 1 (1988): 120–30.

_____. "Deconstructing Deities: *Tuurngatsuak* and *Tuurngaatsuk* in Labrador Inuit Religion." *Études/Inuit/Studies* 21, 1–2 (1997): 141–53.

Temple, Blair. "'Their House is the Best I've Seen on the Labrador': A Nineteenth-century Jersey Dwelling at L'Anse au Cotard." In "From Arctic to Avalon: Papers in Honour of Jim Tuck," edited by Lisa Rankin and Peter Ramsden, special issue, *Canadian Journal of Archaeology* 31, 2 (2006): 43–52.

Tester, Frank, and Peter Kulchyski. *Tammarniit (Mistakes): Inuit Relocation in the Eastern Arctic.* Vancouver: University of British Columbia Press, 1994.

Thornton, P.A. "The Demographic and Mercantile Bases of Initial Permanent Settlement in the Strait of Belle Isle." In *The Peopling of Newfoundland,* edited by J.J. Mannion, 152–83. Newfoundland Social and Economic Papers No.8. St. John's: ISER Books, 1977.

Tilley, Christopher. *A Phenomenology of Landscape: Places, Paths, and Monuments*. Oxford: Berg, 1994.

Todd, W.E. Clyde. *Birds of the Labrador Peninsula and Adjacent Areas*. Toronto: University of Toronto Press, 1963.

Trudel, François. "The Inuit of Southern Labrador and the Development of French Sedentary Fisheries (1700–1760)." In *Canadian Ethnology Society, Papers from the Fourth Annual Congress, 1977*, edited by Richard J. Preston, 99–120. Mercury Series, Canadian Ethnology Service, Paper No. 40. Ottawa: National Museum of Man, 1978.

_____. "Les relations entre les Français et les Inuit au Labrador Méridional, 1660–1760." *Études/Inuit/Studies* 4, 1–2 (1980): 135–45.

Tuck, James A. *Prehistory of Saglek Bay, Labrador: Archaic and Palaeo-Eskimo Occupations*. Mercury Series, Archaeological Survey of Canada No. 32. Ottawa: National Museum of Man, 1975.

Tuck, James A., and R. Grenier. "A Sixteenth-century Basque Whaling Station in Labrador." *Scientific American* 245 (1981): 125–36.

Turner, Lucien M. *Ethnology of the Ungava District, Hudson Bay Territory*. Eleventh Annual Report of the Bureau of Ethnology. 1894. Reissued as part of Classics of Smithsonian Anthropology Series. Washington, DC: Smithsonian Institution, 2001.

Usher, Peter J. *Renewable Resources in the Future of Northern Labrador*. Nain, Labrador Inuit Association, 1982.

_____. "Traditional Ecological Knowledge in Environmental Assessment and Management." *Arctic* 53, 2 (2000): 183–93.

Usher, Peter J., and George Wenzel. "Native Harvest Surveys and Statistics: A Critique of Their Construction and Use." *Arctic* 40, 2 (1987): 145–60.

Usher, Peter J., M. Baikie, D. Demmer, D. Nakashima, M. Stevenson, and M. Stiles. *Communicating about Contaminants in Country Food: The Experience in Aboriginal Communities*. Ottawa: Inuit Tapirisat Kanatami, 1995.

Van Oostdam, J., S. Donaldson, M. Feeley, and N. Tremblay. *Toxic Substances in the Arctic and Associated Effects: Human Health*. Canadian Arctic Contaminants Assessment Report Phase II. Ottawa: Department of Indian Affairs and Northern Development, Minister of Public Works and Government Services Canada, 2003.

Wahdan, M.H. "The Epidemiologic Transition." *Eastern Mediterranean Journal* 2, 1 (1996): 8–20.

Walsh, J.E., O. Anisimov, J.O.M. Hagen, T. Jakobsson, J. Oerlemans, T.D. Prowse, V. Romanovsky, N. Savelieva, M. Serreze, I. Shiklomanov, and S. Solomon. "Cryosphere and Hydrology." In *Arctic Climate Impacts Assessment, ACIA*, edited by L. Arris Symon and B. Heal, 183–242. Cambridge: Cambridge University Press, 2005.

Waugh, L.M. "Nutrition and Health of the Labrador Eskimo with Special Reference to the Mouth and Teeth." *Journal of Dental Health* 8 (1928): 428–29.

Weiss, K.M. R.E. Ferrell, and C.L. Harris. "A New World Syndrome of Metabolic Diseases with a Genetic and Evolutionary Basis." *Yearbook of Physical Anthropology* 27 (1984): 153–78.

Wenzel, George W., G. Hovelsrud-Broda, and N. Kishigami, eds. 2000. *The Social Economy of Sharing: Resource Allocation and Modern Hunter-Gatherers*. Senri Ethnological Studies 53. Osaka: National Museum of Ethnology, 2000.

Wheeler, E.P. *List of Labrador Eskimo Place Names*. Bulletin No. 131, Anthropological Series No. 34. Ottawa: National Museum of Canada, 1953.

Wheelersburg, Robert P. "The Need to Conduct Studies of Swedish Saami Reindeer-Herder Subsistence Behaviours: A Case of Indigenous Resource-Use Rights." *The Northern Review* 28 (2008): 161–80.

Whiteley, W.H. "The Establishment of the Moravian Mission in Labrador and British Policy 1763–83." *Canadian Historical Review* 45, 1 (1964): 29–50.

Whitridge, Peter. "The Construction of Social Difference in a Prehistoric Inuit Whaling Community." PhD diss., Arizona State University, 1999.

_____. "The Prehistory of Inuit and Yupik Whale Use." *Revista de Arqueología Americana* 16 (1999): 99–154.

_____. "Gender, Households, and the Material Construction of Social Difference: Metal Consumption at a Classic Thule Whaling Village." In *Many Faces of Gender: Roles and Relationships Through Time in Indigenous Northern Communities*, edited by L. Frink, R. Shepard, and G. Reinhardt, 165–92. Boulder: University Press of Colorado, 2002.

_____. "Landscapes, Houses, Bodies, Things: 'Place' and the Archaeology of Inuit Imaginaries." *Journal of Archaeological Method and Theory* 11, 2 (2004): 213–20.

_____. "Reimagining the Iglu: Modernity and the Challenge of the Eighteenth Century Labrador Inuit Winter House. *Archaeologies* 4, 2 (2008): 288–309.

Wilkinson, Richard G. "The Epidemiologic Transition: From Material Scarcity to Social Disadvantage?" In *Population and Society: Essential Readings*, edited by Frank Trovato, 107–16. Don Mills, ON: Oxford University Press, 2002.

Williamson, H. Anthony. "The Moravian Mission and its Impact on the Labrador Eskimos." *Arctic Anthropology* 2, 2 (1964): 32–36.

_____. "Population Movement and the Food Gathering Economy of Northern Labrador." Master's thesis, McGill University, 1964.

Williamson, T. *Seeing the Land is Seeing Ourselves: Labrador Inuit Association Issues Scoping Report*. Nain, Labrador Inuit Association, 1996.

_____. *Sina to Sikujâluk: Our Footprint. Mapping Inuit Environmental Knowledge in the Nain District of Northern Labrador*. Nain, Labrador Inuit Association, 1997.

Witmore, C.L. "Four Archaeological Engagements with Place: Mediating Bodily Experience through Peripatetic Video." *Visual Anthropology Review* 20, 2 (2004): 57–71.

Wolfe, Robert W. "The Super-Household: Specialization in Subsistence Economies." Paper presented at the 14th Annual Meeting of the Alaska Anthropological Association, Anchorage, Alaska, 22–25 March 1987.

Woollett, James M. "An Historical Ecology of Labrador Inuit Culture Change." PhD diss., City University of New York, 2003.

_____. "Labrador Inuit Subsistence in the Context of Environmental Change: An Initial Landscape History Perspective." *American Anthropologist* 109, 1 (2007): 69–84.

Yohe, G., and R.S.J. Tol. "Indicators for Social and Economic Coping Capacity—Moving toward a Working Definition of Adaptive Capacity." *Global Environmental Change* 12, 1 (2002): 25–40.

Zimmerly, David William. *Cain's Land Revisited: Culture Change in Central Labrador, 1775–1972*. St. John's: ISER Books, 1975.

Zutter, Cynthia. "Archaeobotanical Investigations of the Uivak Archaeological Site, Labrador, Canada." Report on file in the office of Susan A. Kaplan, Bowdoin College, 2000.

_____. "Paleoethnobotanical Contributions to 18th-century Inuit Economy: An Example from Uivak, Labrador." *Journal of the North Atlantic* Special Volume 1 (2009): 23–32.

CONTRIBUTORS

Sheldon Andersen
Nunatsiavut Government

Mark Andrachuk
Department of Geography
University of Guelph

Matthew Beaudoin
Department of Anthropology
University of Western Ontario

Natalie Brewster
PhD candidate,
Department of Anthropology
McMaster University

Keith Chaulk
Director, Labrador Institute
Memorial University of Newfoundland

Ruth DeSantis
Department of Geography
University of Guelph

Peter Evans
Scott Polar Research Institute
Cambridge, UK

Lawrence Felt
Department of Sociology
Memorial University of
Newfoundland

Laura Fleming
Department of Geography
University of Guelph

Holly Flowers
Nunatsiavut Government

Rose Ford
Nunatsiavut Government

Tristan Gear
Nunatsiavut Government

Maura Hanrahan
Economics and Policy
London School of Economics

Susan A. Kaplan
Director, Peary-MacMillan Arctic
Museum and Arctic Studies Center
Bowdoin College, Maine

Roland Kemuksigak
Nunatsiavut Government

Jill McDonald
Indigenous Land Management Institute
University of Saskatchewan

David C. Natcher
College of Agriculture and Bioresources
University of Saskatchewan

Susan Nochasak
Nunatsiavut Government

Andrea Procter
Department of Anthropology
Memorial University of Newfoundland

Lisa Rankin
Department of Anthropology and
Archaeology
Memorial University of Newfoundland

Susan Rich
Nunatsiavut Government

Nancy Sillitt
Nunatsiavut Government

Barry Smit
Department of Geography
University of Guelph

Peter Whitridge
Department of Anthropology and
Archaeology
Memorial University of Newfoundland

Darren Winters
Nunatsiavut Government

Katie Winters
Nunatsiavut Government